500

Low-Fat and
Fat-Free
Appetizers,
Snacks, and
Hors d'Oeuvres

500
LOW-FAT AND FAT-FREE APPETIZERS, SNACKS, AND HORS D'OEUVRES

SARAH SCHLESINGER

Villard · New York

All rights reserved under International and Pan-American Copyright
Conventions. Published in the United States by Villard Books, a division
of Random House, Inc., New York, and simultaneously in Canada by
Random House of Canada Limited, Toronto.

Villard Books is a registered trademark of Random House, Inc.

Library of Congress Cataloging-in-Publication Data
500 low-fat and fat-free appetizers, snacks, and hors d'oeuvres /
Sarah Schlesinger.
p.   cm.
Includes index.
ISBN 0-679-43278-7 (acid-free paper)
1. Low-fat diet—Recipes.   2. Appetizers.
RM237.7.A18   1996
641.5'638—dc20   95-246

Manufactured in the United States of America on acid-free paper
2 4 6 8 9 7 5 3
First Edition

To Sam, whose good heart is the source and center of my happiness

To Steve and Barbara Crane,
in gratitude for their support and friendship

Special thanks to Robert Cornfield, Diane Reverand, David Rosenthal, Ruth Fecych, Gail Bradney, and all the enthusiastic cooks and tasters who shared in the process of creating this book.

CONTENTS

⠿

APPETIZER COOKING   3

500 LOW-FAT AND FAT-FREE APPETIZER RECIPES

500

Low-Fat and Fat-Free Appetizers, Snacks, and Hors d'Oeuvres

APPETIZER COOKING

∷

While the concept of appetizers once prompted visions of a hostess with either endless time on her hands or a caterer on her payroll, these bite-size delights have reemerged as a vibrant and vital survival strategy for contemporary cooks.

Although our schedules are becoming more and more frenetic, our desire to entertain and to share meaningful time with family and friends remains constant. Faced with dramatically fewer hours to spend in the kitchen and with the tidal wave of interest in eating light, we are more frequently turning to entertaining with appetizers as a way of life. Now, instead of being the prelude to a complex home-cooked meal, appetizers are often the main event or the only course served at home prior to an evening out.

Serving appetizers affords us a chance to welcome our guests with something we have created ourselves, without having to spend precious hours in the kitchen. They allow us to be part of the party. Serving appetizers instead of a full meal not only is less stressful for us as hosts, but also allows our guests the opportunity to graze at will, making choices in terms of quantity and variety to suit their own tastes and dietary preferences.

The sharpened focus on diet and health also places a growing emphasis on a new ingredient list and smaller servings. Freshness is essential, and less is more. As old ways of eating are being replaced with more relaxed, more practical, and healthier strategies, no category of American food comes closer to being an ideal match for our rapidly changing, more mobile lifestyle than easy-to-prepare, lighter appetizers.

500 Low-Fat and Fat-Free Appetizers, Snacks, and Hors d'Oeuvres offers the contemporary cook a complete one-stop reference guide to creating simple yet elegant, exciting appetizers, snacks, and finger foods that are healthful. It is an up-to-date, nutritionally aware, ethnically diverse collection of simple, delicious, and versatile recipes that can be served as snacks, as first courses for a meal, or can be grouped together to create a miniature feast for any occasion when light fare is what's called for.

• ENTERTAINING WITH APPETIZERS •

Entertaining with appetizers can be an ideal answer for every occasion, from offering hospitality to a few friends who pop in unexpectedly, to preparing a buffet for a large group you've invited to a special celebration. In fact, you can serve appetizers to a large number of guests almost as easily as you can serve a few. Gatherings where appetizers are served are easier to prepare for, more informal, and more relaxing to host than sit-down meals.

As you select appetizers from the five hundred possibilities in this book, plan to prepare enough different dishes to give your guests plenty of choices. Choose a group of appetizers based not only on their individual appeal, but on how they will relate to each other in terms of appearance, texture, and taste.

Consider serving a choice of hot and cold appetizers. While this factor will be influenced by the season of the year as well as by your available refrigerator space and warming facilities, a balance between chilled and heated appetizers can add contrast to your menu.

Serve an array of appetizers that includes different textures and a variety of flavors. Remember to consider your guests' ages, special diet requirements, and food preferences. It's a good idea to include one or more of the fat-free recipes in this book for guests who are on restricted-fat diets. If you aren't aware of food preferences, you're safer serving mild-flavored appetizers. Strike a balance between lighter and heavier appetizer choices. When you are pressed for time, emphasize dips, dunks, and spreads, rather than individual items.

If your appetizers are to be served before dinner, they should be lighter fare than if your party is "just appetizers." If you are serving appetizers with dinner, try to coordinate your choices with your dinner menu. Appetizer flavors should differ from main-meal dishes, but should come from the same ethnic cuisine.

• ESTIMATING APPETIZER QUANTITIES •

Plan the quantity and variety of appetizers you will serve around the nature and expected length of your gathering.

- For two or three people before dinner, serve one or two different appetizers—possibly one dip and one hot appetizer—and estimate five to six pieces a person.
- Estimate eight to ten appetizers per person if the appetizers take the place of a meal.
- For ten guests, prepare five different types of appetizers. For twenty guests, prepare seven different types of appetizers.
- If you are passing foods on trays, be sure to also serve several appetizers your guests can help themselves to, such as dips and spreads.
- Consider the weather. Your guests may tend to eat more when it's cold and to drink more when it's hot.
- You can plan for less food if you are serving appetizers in the midafternoon than you'll need for early evening.

EQUIPMENT AND SUPPLIES
• FOR SERVING YOUR APPETIZERS •

The following items are useful for serving appetizers in a variety of settings. For a large gathering, you can secure items you don't own from a local rental center.

- Fondue pots, hot plates, electric hot trays, and chafing dishes for keeping hot appetizers hot
- Baskets and trays
- A variety of serving dishes (Since decorative plates may detract visually from the food you're serving, white plates are often the best choice for elaborate appetizers. Serve appetizers on smaller platters to refill as needed, instead of starting with larger platters that look empty when food is partially gone.)
- Nesting platters for serving cold appetizers over ice
- Paper doilies for lining serving trays
- Serving pieces, such as spoons or tongs, that require only one hand
- Small china or paper plates in scale with the appetizers you are serving
- Napkins, cocktail forks, and other eating utensils, as well as cups and glasses
- Ice bucket and tongs
- Punch bowl, ladle, coffee and tea urns, coasters
- Candles, candle holders, matches

- Centerpieces and table decorations
- Table coverings
- Decorative toothpicks (wooden or plastic) and skewers (wooden, plastic, or bamboo)
- Cups or bowls for discarding toothpicks and skewers

• SERVING APPETIZERS •

Avoid placing more than one kind of appetizer on a serving plate, and try not to crowd the appetizers together. Appetizers look better when they are well spaced, and they're also easier for guests to pick up. A guest should be able to remove one appetizer from a tray without touching another one. When serving in the living room, stick to bite-size appetizers, unless you are furnishing plates and cocktail forks.

When serving a larger group of guests, serve appetizers either on a buffet table or on smaller tables placed around the room. If using a buffet table, move it away from the wall so your guests can circulate around it. If you are serving a very large group, use more than one buffet table.

Serve hot appetizers directly from the oven when it's time to eat them, or use a form of heated dish to keep them warm. Serve cold offerings right from the refrigerator or on platters set on cracked ice. Be sure to choose foods that are easy to pick up quickly if serving from a buffet table, and keep those that must be spooned out, sliced, or spread to a minimum.

If you are using plates, stack them at the end of the table where you want your guests to begin serving themselves. Be sure to leave enough room between appetizer serving pieces so that guests can set their plates down to serve themselves. Beverages and silverware should be placed on the opposite side of the buffet table from the plates.

When serving appetizers on a buffet table, consider the collective color impact of the foods you are grouping together. Hollow out large tomatoes, bell peppers, pattypan squash, eggplant, small pumpkins, or cabbages and use them as containers for dips, sauces, and spreads. Elevate some appetizer platters and dishes on stands made from inverted bowls and other pedestals to provide height variation.

Decorate serving plates by adding interesting bases such as unusual lettuces, watercress, endive, kale, shredded carrots, curly parsley, or lemon leaves to enhance the appearance of less-vivid appetizers.

Garnishes and bases should complement the food being served and should include a variety of tastes, textures, and colors. Some easy garnishes for appetizers include:

- Carrot flowers created by cutting five or six grooves ¼ inch deep down the length of a carrot and then cutting the carrot crosswise into thin slices
- Three or four cranberries skewered on a toothpick and tucked into a bed of parsley
- Black or green pitted olives cut in half; pimento-stuffed olives sliced crosswise to create concentric rings of red and green, or small pimento-stuffed olives stuck into appetizers on cocktail sticks
- Blanched whole snow peas spread on a plate like the petals of a flower with an appetizer placed in the middle
- Parsley, dill, sage, tarragon, chives, and basil chopped and sprinkled on top of appetizers, or whole sprigs of these herbs arranged in small sprays
- Small fruits such as grapes and berries, small leaves such as mint, and edible flowers such as pansies, violets, and nasturtiums, frosted by dipping them into egg whites beaten until frothy, and then into superfine sugar, repeating process until the items are well coated, and then dried on a wire rack

• HELPFUL KITCHEN TOOLS •

- Blender and/or food processor
- Electric mixer
- Microwave oven (Most appetizers will reheat well on MEDIUM or MEDIUM-HIGH power. The microwave is a great way to bring foods to "room temperature." For example, 2 cups of eggplant dip that has been chilling in your refrigerator can be brought to room temperature by heating it on MEDIUM for 2 to 3 minutes.)
- Paring knife, 6-inch cook's knife, and serrated grapefruit knife for hollowing out vegetables before filling; apple corer
- Pastry brush
- Kitchen scissors; tongs for turning items in oven or on grill
- Chopping boards; graters; mixing bowls; colanders; strainers
- Pepper grinder
- Small forks for mashing small quantities of ingredients; spoons and spatulas for mixing and assembling

- Nonstick baking sheets; nonstick shallow baking pans; miniature muffin pans; cooling racks
- Parchment paper or foil for lining baking pans
- Small spritzer bottle for filling with oil
- Biscuit and canapé cutters in various sizes for cutting round bases and for making decorative pieces from thin slices of vegetables or fruit
- Measuring cups and spoons
- Yogurt strainer or cheesecloth for lining a colander
- Sauté pans and skillets with nonstick interiors
- Heavy saucepan with a snugly fitting lid and a steamer insert

· INSTANT APPETIZER PANTRY ·

By keeping the following items on your pantry shelves, you can always be ready to create appetizers on the spot.

Nonperishables

Canned, juice-packed pineapple chunks, pears, jellied cranberry sauce

Canned green chiles, water-packed artichoke hearts, beets, salsa, mango chutney, hot pepper sauce

Prepared bean dip, anchovy paste

Canned smoked oysters, clams, and fish; anchovies, sardines, herring; water-packed, white albacore tuna

Natural maple syrup, all-fruit preserves, nonfat or reduced-fat mayonnaise, light-flavored olive oil, nonfat or reduced-fat Italian dressing, honey, light soy sauce, cider vinegar, horseradish, mustard

Figs, capers, walnuts, hazelnuts, pecans

Black and green olives, pickled onions, low-sodium sweet pickles, marinated mushroom caps, pimentos, pickled vegetables

Nonfat or reduced-fat melba toast rounds, bagel thins, mini–rice cakes

Nonfat or reduced-fat corn chips, nonfat or reduced-fat crackers

Sugar, paprika, curry powder, cinnamon, rosemary, cumin, dried jalapeños, minced garlic, black peppercorns

Refrigerator

Nonfat or reduced-fat cream cheese, nonfat or reduced-fat cheddar and grated Parmesan cheese, nonfat or reduced-fat cottage cheese, nonfat

or reduced-fat plain yogurt, nonfat or reduced-fat sour cream, nonfat
or reduced-fat ricotta cheese, nonfat or reduced-fat mozzarella cheese
Eggs (for egg whites)
Onions, parsley, scallions, garlic
Prepared pesto sauce, prepared guacamole

Freezer

Whole-grain breads, pumpernickel, bagels, French baguettes, Italian
bread, Boboli, corn tortillas
Orange juice concentrate
Nonfat loaf cake
Tortellini
Gingerroot

Having stocked your shelves, refrigerator, and freezer with the above staples, supplement these with fresh foods from the deli, fish, and produce counters of your supermarket, including:

Reduced-fat roast and smoked turkey, nonfat or reduced-fat cheese,
chicken breasts
Cantaloupe or honeydew, red or green grapes, lemons, oranges, strawberries, bananas
Spinach, tomatoes, radishes, watercress, zucchini, cucumber, endive, avocado, cherry tomatoes, green bell peppers, red bell peppers, large mushrooms, fresh jalapeño peppers
Oysters, clams, smoked salmon, shrimp, fish fillets

Using these ingredients, you can instantly create the fifty appetizers that follow.

· FIFTY FAST, FAST, FAST APPETIZERS ·

Here are ideas for fifty fast appetizers to fix when you are short on preparation time or advance notice.

1. Skewer cubes of smoked or roast turkey, nonfat or reduced-fat cheese, olives, pickled onions, and chunks of sweet pickle on wooden or plastic party picks.

2. Skewer cubes of smoked or roast turkey and canned, juice-packed pineapple chunks on wooden party picks. Brush with maple syrup. Place under the broiler until lightly browned.

3. Wrap slices of smoked or roast turkey around figs, large pitted green olives, melon cubes, or chunks of canned pears. Fasten with a wooden or plastic party pick.

4. Trim the crust from slices of whole-grain bread. Cut rounds from the bread with a cookie or canapé cutter. Spread with nonfat or reduced-fat mayonnaise. Top with a slice of very thinly sliced smoked or roast turkey and a dab of canned, jellied cranberry sauce.

5. Place smoked or roast turkey slices on nonfat melba toast rounds, top with nonfat or reduced-fat grated cheese, and place under broiler until cheese melts.

6. Cut smoked or roast turkey slices with a biscuit cutter into 3-inch circles. Form into a cone, using a toothpick to secure. Spoon a little softened nonfat or reduced-fat cream cheese into each cone and press a red or green grape into the cream cheese.

7. Mash canned, smoked oysters into a paste and spread on rounds of nonfat melba toast.

8. Arrange freshly opened raw oysters or clams on a serving dish and drizzle with lemon. Sprinkle with freshly ground pepper.

9. Loosen raw oysters from their shells. Steam trimmed, fresh, large spinach leaves for 1½ minutes. Place a spinach leaf under each oyster inside shell. Top oyster with a few thin strips of fresh tomato. Sprinkle with olive oil. Bake at 350 degrees for 4 minutes.

10. Serve smoked fish, smoked oysters, sardines, herring, clams, or anchovy fillets on thin slices of pumpernickel, rye bread, toast, or bagel thins garnished with capers, onion slices, parsley, and lemon wedges.

11. Trim the crust from slices of pumpernickel bread. Cut rounds from the bread with a cookie or canapé cutter. Spread with nonfat or reduced-fat mayonnaise. Top with a slice of very thinly sliced smoked salmon and some chopped olives.

12. Combine white tuna, chopped scallions, nonfat or reduced-fat mayonnaise, and grated nonfat or reduced-fat cheddar cheese. Spread on crackers or toasted French bread. Place under the broiler until cheese melts.

13. Combine softened cream cheese, canned, boned sardines, lemon juice, and grated onion. Spread on crackers or toasted French bread and place under broiler until the tops brown slightly.

14. Wrap anchovy fillets around red radishes and secure with a toothpick.

15. Trim the crusts from slices of Italian bread. Cut rounds from the bread with a cookie or canapé cutter. Spread with nonfat or reduced-fat mayonnaise. Top with steamed, peeled shrimp (cut in half lengthwise) and watercress leaves.

16. Marinate cooked shrimp in a commercially prepared nonfat or reduced-fat Italian dressing spiced with canned green chiles and finely chopped garlic for 1 hour. Serve with toothpicks.

17. Open jars of marinated mushroom caps, pickled onions, and pimentos. Thread alternately on wooden or plastic party picks.

18. Place an array of commercially prepared pickled vegetables including cauliflower florets, carrot sticks, brussels sprouts, and baby corn on a platter. Sprinkle with finely chopped fresh parsley. Serve with wooden or plastic party picks.

19. Marinate canned and drained, water-packed artichoke hearts in commercially prepared nonfat or reduced-fat Italian dressing for an hour. Sprinkle with Parmesan cheese and serve with wooden or plastic party picks or cocktail forks.

20. Combine softened nonfat or reduced-fat cream cheese with chopped fresh parsley. Spread between thin slices of peeled cucumber or zucchini. Dust the edges with paprika.

21. Stuff endive leaves with a spoonful of softened nonfat or reduced-fat cream cheese and garnish with a sprig of fresh parsley.

22. Trim the crust from slices of dark rye bread. Cut rounds from the bread with a cookie or canapé cutter. Spread with nonfat or reduced-fat mayonnaise. Top with slices of very thinly sliced fresh tomato. Spread tomato slices with mashed avocado mixed with a small amount of lemon juice.

23. Trim the crust from slices of white bread. Cut rounds from the bread with a cookie or canapé cutter. Spread with nonfat or reduced-fat mayonnaise. Top with very thin cucumber slices and sprigs of fresh parsley.

24. Hollow out cherry tomatoes. Line the inside of the tomato shell with one or two anchovy fillets, and fill center with capers. Sprinkle with nonfat or reduced-fat Parmesan cheese.

25. Trim the crust from slices of whole-grain bread. Use a biscuit or canapé cutter to cut round slices from the bread. Top with a dab of nonfat or reduced-fat mayonnaise. Add a slice of hard-boiled egg or egg white, a slice of canned beet, and a small sprig of fresh parsley.

26. Combine prepared salsa, chopped fresh tomatoes, chopped onions, and chopped green bell peppers. Spread on mini–rice cakes or nonfat melba toast rounds.

27. Cut cherry tomatoes in a cross, not cutting all the way through the tomato, and spread into 4 sections. Stuff with a small cube of canned, jellied cranberry sauce and sprinkle with chopped fresh parsley or chives.

28. Cut cherry tomatoes in a cross, not cutting all the way through the tomato, and spread into 4 sections. Stuff with commercially prepared pesto sauce.

29. Cut stems from 12 large mushrooms. Spoon prepared pesto sauce into the mushrooms and place in a glass pie pan. Cover with vented plastic wrap and microwave on 100% HIGH for 3 minutes.

30. Cut large red and green bell peppers into eighths. Top each piece with a spoonful of nonfat or reduced-fat cottage cheese and a sprinkling of chopped fresh parsley.

31. Combine 1 cup nonfat or reduced-fat ricotta cheese with 1 tablespoon minced scallions and ½ teaspoon curry powder. Cut stems from mushroom caps. Fill caps with cheese mixture and sprinkle with paprika.

32. Peel an avocado. Cut into 6 slices. Fill the hollow at the base of each slice with mango chutney.

33. Serve skewers of fresh fruit with a dip made of 8 ounces of whipped nonfat or reduced-fat cream cheese, ¼ cup chopped hazelnuts, and honey to taste.

34. Add ½ teaspoon cinnamon to a container of nonfat or reduced-fat yogurt. Stir in 1 tablespoon orange juice concentrate, 2 tablespoons finely chopped walnuts or pecans, and 1 teaspoon grated orange rind. Serve with large, hulled strawberries or assorted fruit chunks as dippers.

35. Combine nonfat or reduced-fat softened cream cheese with chopped strawberries and honey. Spread on thin strips of nonfat loaf cake.

36. Combine all-fruit jam and mashed bananas. Spread on mini–rice cakes.

37. Sprinkle a corn tortilla with nonfat or reduced-fat cheddar cheese. Top with a tortilla and spread with salsa. Top with another tortilla and sprinkle with cheese. Top with a fourth tortilla and bake at 350 degrees until cheese melts. Top with prepared guacamole and nonfat or reduced-fat sour cream. Sprinkle with canned, sliced chiles. Cut into wedges.

38. In a large salad bowl, layer prepared bean dip, prepared guacamole, nonfat or reduced-fat sour cream, chopped tomatoes, chopped black olives, shredded nonfat or low-fat cheddar cheese, and chopped scallions. Serve with nonfat corn chips.

39. Cook tortellini, drain, and toss with prepared pesto sauce. Thread on wooden or plastic party picks.

40. Top mini-Boboli shells from the supermarket with thinly sliced nonfat or reduced-fat mozzarella, thinly sliced tomatoes, and dried rosemary. Bake at 400 degrees for 8 to 10 minutes or until cheese melts.

41. Top mini-Boboli shells with drained canned clams, olive oil, and nonfat or regular Parmesan cheese. Bake at 400 degrees for 8 to 10 minutes or until cheese melts.

42. Toast slices of whole wheat baguettes. Rub with cut garlic cloves and brush with olive oil. Top with a tomato slice, sprinkle with nonfat or reduced-fat cheddar cheese, and broil for 1 minute until the cheese melts.

43. Top crackers with grated nonfat or reduced-fat mozzarella cheese and a dot of anchovy paste. Place under broiler until cheese melts.

44. Combine softened nonfat or reduced-fat cream cheese with curry powder. Spread on melba toast rounds and broil for 1 to 2 minutes until tops brown slightly.

45. Combine ½ cup nonfat or reduced-fat sour cream with ½ cup nonfat or reduced-fat mayonnaise; add curry powder to taste. Serve with a bowl of hulled cherry tomatoes.

46. Make a quick garlic dip for raw vegetables by combining 1½ cups nonfat or reduced-fat plain yogurt with ¼ cup chopped scallions, 2 minced cloves garlic, and ½ teaspoon granulated sugar.

47. Combine 1 cup nonfat or reduced-fat yogurt with 2 tablespoons chopped tomatoes, 1 tablespoon chopped scallions, 1 seeded and minced fresh jalapeño pepper, and ½ teaspoon cumin. Serve with nonfat corn chips.

48. Make a dip of ½ cup light soy sauce, 2 teaspoons hot pepper sauce, 2 minced cloves garlic, and ⅛ teaspoon sugar to serve with chunks of cooked chicken breast on wooden or plastic party picks.

49. Make a dip of ½ cup cider vinegar and 1 teaspoon minced fresh gingerroot to serve with chunks of steamed fish on wooden or plastic party picks.

50. Make a dip of 1 teaspoon prepared horseradish, 1 tablespoon sugar, 4 teaspoons cider vinegar, and ½ cup light soy sauce to serve with steamed shrimp.

• SAMPLE APPETIZER MENUS •

Informal Party of 12 to 16 Guests

Chicken Dijon Bites
Garlic Shrimp
Meatballs Italia
Mushrooms Stuffed with Crab
White Wine–Eggplant Caviar
Olive-Carrot Sandwich Strips
Spicy Crunch Mix
Apples with Chutney Dip

Informal Spread for 6 to 8 Guests

Hot and Pungent Crab Dip
Zucchini Rounds with Red Pepper Filling
Boboli Bites
Tiny Turkey Burgers
Parmesan-Potato Wedges
Fruit Salad Kabobs with Pineapple Dip
Honey-Spice Popcorn

Southwestern Spread for 12 to 16 Guests

Pinto Bean Crostini
Nachos and Avocado with Taco Sauce
Salmon Tortillas
Mexican Chicken Wings
Baked Tomato-Jalapeño Clams
Coriander-Corn Guacamole
Potato Skins with Chile Salsa
Spiced Honeydew Chunks

Chinese Appetizer Feast for 12 to 16 Guests

Chicken-Leek Wontons with Apricot Dipping Sauce
Steamed Clams with Oriental Hot Sauce
Snow Peas with Crab

Spiced Shiitake Mushrooms
Skewered Turkey with Plum Sauce
Steamed Broccoli and Shrimp with Oyster Sauce
Sesame Wonton Snacks
Sugared-Pineapple Wedges

Italian Spread for 12 to 16 Guests

Vegetable Antipasto
Cannellini Bean Dip
Baked Oysters Parmesan
Tortellini with Spinach-Parsley Dip
Parmesan Chicken Nuggets
French Bread Pizza Slices
Wrapped Olives and Anchovies
Ricotta Sticks

Mediterranean Spread for 12 to 16 Guests

Spinach-Feta Dip
Artichokes Stuffed with Mussels
Garlic-Potato Canapés
Baked Stuffed Grape Leaves
Cherry Tomatoes Stuffed with Orzo
Chicken Kabobs
Greek Meatballs
Mediterranean Stuffed Lemons

Brunch Spread for 10 to 12 Guests

Lox and Minibagels
Horseradish-Egg Dip
Petite Potato Cakes
Sausage-Pizza Mushroom Caps
Pan Bagnat
Honey-Roasted Turkey Roll-ups
Berry Bites
Strawberry Melon Kabobs with Ginger-Honey Sauce

Formal Buffet for 18 to 22 Guests

Endive with Shrimp
Potato-Caviar Bites
Asparagus–Smoked Turkey Roll-ups
Cherry Tomatoes with Crab
Salmon Mousse
Scallops with Red Pepper–Orange-Tomato Salsa
Chicken-Mushroom Satay
Cheese-Stuffed Strawberries

• SHOPPING GUIDE TO INGREDIENTS • USED IN THE RECIPES

Anchovies   Anchovies are tiny fish that are usually filleted, salt-cured, and canned in oil. They're sold flat and rolled. They will be found either in the canned-seafood section or the gourmet foods section of your supermarket.

Apples   When buying apples, look for those that are bruise-free and firm to the touch. Choose crisp, crunchy, juicy apples, such as Granny Smith, Rome Beauty, or Gala, if you are going to serve them raw. Keep apples in a cool place. If you are storing them in the refrigerator, keep them in perforated plastic bags or containers to keep them from drying out. Apple corers and apple cutters make preparing apples quicker and easier. Since the flesh of apples turns brown quickly, dip slices or wedges in lemon juice mixed with water to preserve their color.

Applesauce   Buy natural applesauce without added sugar.

Apricots   Choose apricots that look ripe and glowing and are on the firm side. They should be smooth-skinned and blemish-free. Ripen them at room temperature, but refrigerate once ripe. When the fruit is soft to the touch, it is ready to eat. Cut them in half and remove the pit. They don't need to be peeled, but if you wish to remove the skin, plunge them in boiling water for 30 seconds, then in cold water. Dried apricots are available year-round. They should be soft and tender when purchased. They store extremely well.

Artichokes   The globe artichoke is the bud of a large plant from the thistle family and has tough, petal-shaped leaves. Once the leaves have been removed, the inedible prickly choke is scraped away and discarded. Then the tender artichoke heart and meaty bottom can be eaten. Artichoke hearts are available frozen and canned; artichoke bottoms are available canned. Canned artichoke hearts are baby artichokes with tender leaves and a bottom in which the bristly choke is undeveloped and therefore edible. Buy only artichoke hearts and bottoms packed in water. They can be stored unopened on a cool, dry pantry shelf for a year. Drain the water before using. Once opened, store canned artichokes in the refrigerator for up to 4 days.

Asparagus   Select firm, straight green spears with closed, compact tips or buds. The optimum size for an asparagus stalk is ½ inch in diameter. Purchase spears of uniform thickness. Refrigerate spears uncovered and use them as soon as possible. To prepare for recipes requiring cooked asparagus, lay stalks down in a frying pan, cover with boiling water, and cook for 5 to 7 minutes or until the tips droop. Plunge into ice water.

Avocados   Choose those with either smooth green skins or thick, pebbly, dark green skins that are free of bruises and damage spots. If you plan to use the avocado within 24 hours, buy one that is soft but not mushy. If you plan to use it within several days, buy a harder one. Soft avocados can be refrigerated for up to 5 days. Harder ones should be kept at room temperature. When a wooden toothpick can be inserted in the stem end, the fruit is ready to be eaten. Cut them immediately before using. Cut the fruit in half lengthwise around the seed with a sharp paring knife. Twist the 2 halves of the avocado in opposite directions and separate. Remove seed by gently tapping seed with the blade of a heavy knife such as a cleaver or butcher knife. Lift seed out. Dip cut surfaces in a mixture of lemon juice and water to preserve color.

Bagels   Look for "water" bagels and avoid those made with egg. Check labels on packaged bagels to find those with the lowest fat content. Minibagels, used in some of the recipes in this book, can be found with other packaged frozen bagels.

Baguette   A baguette is French bread that has been formed into a long, narrow, cylindrical loaf. It usually has a crisp brown crust and a light chewy interior.

Bamboo Shoots   Bamboo shoots are the edible portion of young bamboo plants. Once you have opened canned bamboo shoots, cover them with water and refrigerate. If you drain the shoots regularly and re-cover them with water, they will keep for 1 month.

Bananas   Bananas should be stored at room temperature until they are ripe. After ripening, they can be refrigerated for 3 or 4 days. Since bananas will discolor after cutting, dip cut bananas into a mixture of lemon juice and water to preserve color.

Beans   Keep the following beans and legumes on hand in dried and/or canned form: kidney, black, pinto, Great Northern, chickpeas (garbanzo beans), cannellini, lima, and navy beans; and lentils, split peas, and black-eyed peas. Read labels on canned beans carefully. Most beans contain some natural fat, which will be indicated on the label. However, avoid those that have meats like bacon or pork added. Look for low-sodium products and/or drain beans and rinse well before adding to a recipe. Rinsing can reduce the sodium in canned beans by half. When buying dried beans and legumes, look for those with shiny skins and bright colors. When beans and legumes are old, they take on a dull luster. Fresher beans take less time to cook. If you want to cook your own beans you can use either the stovetop or microwave method. When cooking with dried beans, 1 cup (8 ounces) is equal to 2 to 2½ cups cooked beans.

Stovetop Method: Wash and pick over beans, discarding cracked or shriveled ones. Bring the beans to a boil, cover tightly, remove from heat, and let sit for 1 hour. (You can skip this step with lentils and black-eyed peas.) To cook, discard the soaking water. Place 3 parts fresh water and 1 part beans in a large, heavy pan. You can add garlic cloves, as well as onion, celery, and carrot chunks, or a chile pepper or bay leaf. (Remove bay leaf before serving.) Partially cover the pan. Cook black beans, limas, and small white beans for 1½ hours; black-eyed peas, lentils, and split peas for 1 hour; and Great Northern, kidney, and pinto beans for 2 hours. Test for doneness by tasting. Beans should be cooked until they are soft. Avoid adding tomatoes or salt until the end of the cooking process, because these ingredients can prevent your beans from softening.

Microwave Method: Combine the washed and picked-over beans with water (1¼ cups dried beans to 1 to 3 quarts water) in a large bowl. Seal airtight with a double layer of unvented plastic wrap and microwave for 1¾ hours on HIGH. (Some very dry beans can take 2 hours.)

You can store cooked beans in the refrigerator for 1 week. They can be frozen in individual serving containers and quickly microwaved as needed. Slightly undercook beans you are planning to freeze.

Bean Sprouts   Sprouts are infant plants that grow out of beans in a warm, moist environment. Look for moist and crisp-looking sprouts with a fresh scent. The shorter the tendrils, the younger and tenderer the sprout. Fresh sprouts, which are now available in many supermarkets, will keep for 7 to 10 days in a plastic bag in the refrigerator. They should be kept moist, but don't allow too much free water to build up in the bag. Canned bean sprouts are also available in supermarkets.

Beets   Beets should be chosen on the basis of firmness and the smoothness of their skins. Leave 1 inch of beet greens attached to prevent loss of nutrients and color during cooking. Store in a plastic bag in the refrigerator for up to 3 weeks. Just before cooking, wash beets gently, taking care not to pierce the skin. Peel after cooking.

Belgian Endive   Belgian endive is a small cigar-shaped head of cream-colored, tightly packed, slightly bitter leaves. It is available from September until May. Buy crisp, firmly packed heads with pale, yellow-green tips. Belgian endive can become bitter when exposed to light. When using for appetizers, separate leaves of Belgian endive and wash well. Drain, wrap in a cotton kitchen towel, and refrigerate. Fill leaves just before serving.

Bing Cherries   Bing cherries are large cherries that range in color from a deep garnet to almost black. Their skin is smooth and glossy, and the flesh is firm and sweet. Often used in cooking, Bing cherries are available in canned form in your supermarket.

Boboli   Boboli are prepared Italian bread shells that can be used alone or as a base for pizzas. Boboli are available in supermarkets.

Broccoli   Select unwrapped broccoli and look for a firm head with tightly closed buds. The buds may show a bluish-purple cast but should not be open to show yellow flowers. Store in a perforated plastic bag, or spray broccoli lightly with cold water and wrap in a damp cotton kitchen towel. Broccoli will keep for 2 or 3 days in the refrigerator.

Brussels Sprouts   Shop for brussels sprouts that have firm, tight heads. The core end should have a clean, white appearance. Sprouts that are small, green, and firm will taste best. Store, unwashed, in perforated plastic bags in the refrigerator for several days. Cut an X in the base of each sprout before cooking.

Bulgur   Bulgur is made from whole wheat kernels. The wheat kernels are parboiled, dried, and partially debranned, then cracked into coarse fragments to make bulgur. You will find bulgur in the pasta and grain aisle of your supermarket or in the gourmet foods section.

Cantaloupe   A ripe melon should be firm but should give slightly when pressed at the stem end. Ripe cantaloupe should also have a fragrant, musky scent. Melons should be free of dents and bruises and should have dry rinds. If the melon is slightly unripe, keep it at room temperature for 1 to 2 days. Refrigerate ripe melons to use within a few days.

Capers   Capers are the flower bud of a bush native to the Mediterranean and parts of Asia. They are picked, sun-dried, and pickled in a vinegar brine. Capers should be rinsed before using. Look for capers near olives in your supermarket or in the gourmet foods section.

Carrots   Shop for carrots that are small to medium in size. They should be bright orange and firm. Carrots can be sealed without their tops in perforated plastic bags in the refrigerator for several weeks. When preparing carrots, scrub and scrape the skin if it seems tough.

Catsup   Shop for low-sodium catsup.

Cauliflower   Look for firm, compact, white or ivory heads that are surrounded by tender, green leaves. Avoid brown spots. Wrap cauliflower in perforated plastic bags and store, unwashed, in the refrigerator for 1 week.

Cayenne Pepper   Cayenne is a small, thin, hot red pepper usually found in a ground version on supermarket spice racks.

Celery   Choose firm bunches that are tightly formed. The leaves should be green and crisp. Store in a plastic bag in the refrigerator and leave ribs attached to stalk. When ready to use, wash well and trim leaves and base. To revive limp celery, trim ends and place in a jar of water in the refrigerator until crispy.

Cheeses   Both nonfat and reduced-fat cheeses are used in the recipes in this book. Mozzarella cheese, cheddar cheese, Swiss cheese, American cheese, cream cheese, ricotta cheese, Parmesan cheese, and cottage cheese are available in both nonfat and reduced-fat form. Most of these cheeses are made from skim milk.

Chicken Buy skinless chicken parts or skin them yourself at home. Look for the government grading stamp within a shield on the package wrapping. Buy Grade A chicken. Store chicken in the coldest part of your refrigerator. If it is packaged tightly in cellophane, loosely rewrap chicken in wax paper. Store raw chicken in the refrigerator up to 2 days, and cooked chicken for up to 3 days. Salmonella bacteria are present on most poultry, so raw chicken should be handled with care. Rinse it thoroughly before preparing. After cutting or working with chicken, thoroughly wash utensils, cutting tools, cutting board, and your hands.

Chicken Broth Look for nonfat or reduced-fat, low-sodium canned chicken broth. If you cannot find nonfat canned chicken broth, remove contents of can and refrigerate in a glass or plastic container overnight (or place in freezer for 30 minutes) until fat rises to the top and congeals. Skim fat off before using.

Chili Sauce A spicy blend of tomatoes, chile peppers or chili powder, onions, green peppers, vinegar, sugar, and spices.

Chinese Cabbage See Napa Cabbage.

Chutney Chutney is a spicy condiment that contains fruit, vinegar, sugar, and spices. It can range in texture from chunky to smooth and can range in degree of spiciness from mild to hot. Mango chutney, which is readily available in most supermarkets, is suggested in some of the recipes.

Clams When buying hard-shell clams in the shell, be sure the shells are tightly closed. Tap any slightly open shells. If they don't snap closed, the clam is dead and should be discarded. Store live clams for up to 2 days in a 40-degree refrigerator. Shucked clams should be plump and packaged in clear clam liquor. Store shucked clams in the refrigerator in their liquor for up to 4 days. Clams can also be purchased canned in the canned-fish section of your supermarket. Before steaming clams, scrub them thoroughly with a brush. Rinse several times. To steam clams, place ½ inch of water in the bottom of a steamer. Place clams on steamer rack. Cover the pot and steam the clams over medium heat for 5 to 10 minutes or until they open, but no longer. Discard any unopened clams.

Corn Chips   Nonfat corn chips are now widely available, and you can also create your own by cutting corn tortillas into chips and baking. See recipe on page 389.

Cornstarch   A dense, powdery "flour" obtained from the corn kernel, cornstarch is used as a thickening agent. You will find it with other flours in your supermarket.

Couscous   A precooked cracked-wheat product that is an alternative to rice, couscous is made from white durum wheat from which the bran and germ have been removed. Once cooked, it has a very light, airy quality and a silky texture. Couscous can be found with other grains such as rice, or in the international foods section of your supermarket.

Crabmeat   Crabmeat is sold fresh, frozen, canned, and pasteurized (heated in cans at a temperature high enough to kill bacteria, but lower than that used in canning). It may be in the form of cooked lump meat (whole pieces of the white body meat) or flaked meat (small bits of light and dark meat from the body and claws).

Crackers   Buy nonfat, low-sodium crackers.

Cranberry Sauce   Canned cranberry sauces are available year-round in the canned-fruit section of your supermarket.

Cucumbers   Choose firm, seedless cucumbers with smooth, brightly colored skins; avoid those with soft spots. Store whole cucumbers, unwashed, in a plastic bag in the refrigerator for up to 10 days. Wash well just before using. Since cucumbers tend to "weep" when they are sliced, you may want to take steps to prevent their giving off moisture that will dampen the bread for appetizer sandwiches. If so, place them in a colander with a light sprinkling of salt, toss, and let stand for 30 minutes. Rinse with cold water to wash off salt. With the back of a wooden spoon, press out as much moisture as you can, then pat dry with paper towels.

Curry Powder   Curry powder is a blend of different herbs and spices that vary according to the country of origin. Varieties can differ in intensity of flavor, so use carefully. Curry flavor becomes stronger in a dish that is refrigerated and then reheated.

Dijon Mustard   Dijon is a strong French mustard that is easy to find in supermarkets. Avoid varieties with added oil or eggs. It will keep in the refrigerator almost indefinitely.

Eggplant   Look for plump eggplants with very shiny skins that are firm to the touch and free of soft spots. Bright green caps indicate freshness. Store eggplant in a cool place, or wrap in plastic wrap and store in the refrigerator for up to 2 days.

Egg Roll Wrappers   See Wonton Wrappers.

Egg Whites   The recipes call for egg whites, but not for egg yolks, which are extremely high in cholesterol. Egg whites contain half the protein in an egg and no fat or cholesterol. You can substitute 2 egg whites for 1 whole egg.

Feta Cheese   Feta is a classic Greek cheese traditionally made from sheep's or goat's milk, now often made with cow's milk. It has a rich, tangy flavor and can range in texture from soft to semidry. White, crumbly, and rindless, feta can be found at the cheese counters in many supermarkets.

Flours   Use unbleached, all-purpose flour that has no chemicals added to whiten or to age the flour artificially. Unbleached flour has a creamy off-white color. All-purpose flour is a mixture of soft wheat and hard, high-gluten wheat.

Fruit Products:
  Canned Fruit: Buy fruit packed in unsweetened juice or water. Canned fruits used in the recipes include pineapples (crushed and chunk), mandarin oranges, pears, peaches, and apricots.
  Dried Fruit: Dried fruit can be plumped in your microwave by combining ½ cup dried fruit with 2 tablespoons orange juice and microwaving for 2 minutes on HIGH until juice is absorbed. Let stand 5 minutes.
  Frozen Fruit: Use frozen fruit when fresh fruit is not in season. Frozen fruit should be packed with no sugar added.
  Fruit Juice: Shop for natural juices without added sugar or syrup. Frozen fruit-juice concentrates are also used in some recipes.

Garam Masala   *Garam masala* is the Indian term for "warm," and this blend of dry-roasted, ground spices may include black pepper, cinnamon, cloves, coriander, cumin, cardamom, dried chiles, fennel, mace, nutmeg, and other spices. You can mix your own garam masala, or buy it in many supermarkets or Indian markets.

Garlic Buy fresh garlic, chopped garlic packed without oil, and minced dried garlic. When buying fresh garlic, look for bulbs with firm, large cloves. Store garlic in a cool, dry place.

Gelatin Gelatin is a dry, powdered protein made from animal by-products. Buy unflavored gelatin.

Ginger:
   Crystallized Ginger: Also called candied ginger, this form of ginger has been cooked in a sugar syrup and coated with coarse sugar. It can be found in many supermarkets and in oriental markets.
   Gingerroot: Fresh gingerroot, which adds a distinctive, spicy flavor to many dishes, can be found in the produce department of most supermarkets. To use, peel the tan skin and slice the root, then mince or grate. You can freeze leftover gingerroot wrapped in plastic freezer wrap until ready to use.

Goat Cheese Goat cheese or chèvre is pure, white, goat's-milk cheese with a tart flavor. Store tightly wrapped in the refrigerator for up to 2 weeks.

Grapes Buy grapes that are plump, full-colored, and firmly attached to their stems. Store grapes, unwashed, in a plastic bag in the refrigerator. Wash thoroughly and blot dry with a paper towel just before eating or using.

Grape Leaves Buy unstuffed grape leaves in the international foods section of your supermarket or in Greek or Middle Eastern markets.

Green Beans Buy thin beans without bulges; the skin should not feel tough or leathery. Avoid limp or spotted beans. Look for beans with good color, plumpness, and a fresh-looking velvety coat. Refrigerate beans in perforated plastic bags in the vegetable crisper and use within a few days.

Halibut Halibut meat is low-fat, white, firm, and mild-flavored. Fresh and frozen halibut are marketed as fillets and steaks.

Hearts of Palm Hearts of palm are the edible inner portions of the stems of the cabbage palm tree. They are thin, ivory-colored stalks about 4 inches in length with an artichokelike flavor. They are available fresh only in Florida and other areas where they are grown. Canned hearts of palm are packed in water and can be found in most supermarkets. Once opened, they should be transferred to a nonmetal container with an airtight cover. They can be refrigerated in their own liquid for up to a week.

Herbs   While fresh herbs are always preferable to dried herbs in terms of flavor, they are not always easy to obtain. Therefore, with the exception of parsley, which is widely available, I have suggested using dried herbs in the recipes. Keep dried herbs tightly covered in an airtight container. Don't expose them to extremely high heat or intense light. They are best if used within 6 months to a year, so it is wise to date containers at the time you purchase or store them. To maximize the flavor of dried herbs, soak them for several minutes in a liquid you will be using in the recipe, such as stock, lemon juice, or vinegar. Crush dried herbs before using by rubbing them between your fingers. If you can find fresh herbs at your supermarket or greengrocer (or can grow your own), after buying or picking them, wash them and place them in a jar of water. Cover with a plastic bag and place them in the refrigerator. They will keep for up to 2 weeks. They must be thoroughly patted dry with paper towels before you chop them or they will stick to the knife and each other. Use three parts fresh herbs for one part dried. The recipes in this book frequently call for basil, rosemary, thyme, dill, tarragon, bay leaves, chives, cilantro, mint, marjoram, oregano, and sage.

Hoisin Sauce   Also called Peking sauce, hoisin sauce is a mixture of soybeans, garlic, chile peppers, and various spices. It will keep indefinitely in the refrigerator once you have opened it. It can be found in the international foods section of your supermarket and at oriental markets.

Honey   Honey is sweeter than granulated sugar and easier to digest. Its flavor and sweetness vary, depending on what kind of nectar the bees were eating when they made the honey. You can store liquid honey in its jar for up to a year in a cool, dry, dark place. Be sure the cap is tightly closed. Thin honey that starts to crystallize by placing it in a pan of hot water, or microwave on HIGH for 10 seconds.

Honey Mustard   Mustard with honey added can be found commercially packaged at your supermarket and in gourmet food shops.

Honeydew Melons   A ripe honeydew should be firm, have a smooth depression at its stem end, and have a fragrant, musky scent at its blossom end. The melon should be free of dents and bruises and should have a dry rind. The skin should feel velvety and somewhat sticky. The deeper the color of the melon's flesh, the sweeter it will be. Refrigerate ripe melons to use within a few days.

Horseradish   Prepared horseradish is mixed with vinegar and packed in jars. You can store it in the refrigerator for 3 to 4 months, but it will lose pungency as it ages. Fresh horseradish is a woody-looking root with a fiery flavor. To use fresh horseradish, scrub or peel it and then grate. It can be stored in the refrigerator for 3 weeks.

Hot Pepper Sauce   Tabasco-type sauces are very hot purees of red chiles, vinegar, and numerous seasonings. The fiercely hot peppers used in Tabasco-type sauces are often 20 times hotter than jalapeño peppers. Hot pepper sauces are bright red when fresh. They will last up to a year at room temperature. When a bottle of hot pepper sauce turns brown, throw it out.

Italian Bread   Italian bread is almost identical to French bread, but it is shorter and plumper than the baguette. Italian bread is sometimes sprinkled with sesame seeds.

Jams and Jellies   Buy all-fruit jams, jellies, and marmalades that are sugar-free and made with fruit and fruit juices only.

Jicama   A large bulbous root vegetable, jicama has a thin brown skin and a white crunchy flesh. It should be stored in the refrigerator and will last for up to 5 days. The skin should be peeled just before using. It is available in most large supermarkets and at Mexican markets.

Kiwis   Look for firm, round or oval-shaped kiwis that are free from bruises and skin breaks. Kiwis are ripe when the skin gives slightly if pressed. Seal unripened kiwis in a plastic bag with an apple or two. The kiwis will be ready to eat in a few days. When ripe, place in the refrigerator for up to several days. Store away from other fruit to prevent overripening. To prepare kiwis, trim stem ends with a small paring knife and use a vegetable peeler to trim off the thin brown skin. If they are hard to peel, dip them in boiling water for 30 seconds, then peel.

Kohlrabi   Kohlrabi is a member of the turnip family, and both its purple-tinged, white, bulblike stem and its greens are edible. It tastes like a mild, sweet turnip. Choose kohlrabi that is heavy for its size with firm, deeply colored green leaves. Store tightly wrapped for up to 4 days in the refrigerator.

Leeks   Leeks should have crisp, brightly colored leaves and an unblemished white portion. Avoid leeks with withered or yellow-spotted leaves. The smaller the leek, the more tender it will be. Refrigerate leeks in a plastic bag for up to 5 days. Before using, trim rootlets and leaf ends. Slit leeks from top to bottom and wash thoroughly to remove all the dirt trapped between the leaf layers.

Lemons and Limes   Choose lemons that have fine-textured, unblemished skin. Choose limes that have glossy, fine-textured, bright-green or yellow-tinged skins. Store them in the crisper drawers of your refrigerator or in open containers on your refrigerator shelves. Don't keep them in airtight plastic bags, because mold develops quickly when air can't circulate. To extract more juice, microwave lemons and limes on HIGH for 30 seconds before cutting and squeezing. Or let sit in a pan of very hot water for 5 to 10 minutes before squeezing.

Lemon Peel   Either grate the peel of fresh lemons or buy grated lemon peel in the spice section of your supermarket.

Lettuces   Choose those that are crisp and free of blemishes. They should be washed and either drained completely or blotted with a paper towel to remove all traces of moisture. Never allow leaves to soak, because their minerals will leach out. Refrigerate washed and dried lettuce in an airtight plastic bag for 3 to 5 days.

Mandarin Oranges   Most of the canned mandarin oranges sold in the United States are Japanese satsuma oranges, a variety that is almost seedless. Buy canned mandarin oranges that are packed in juice.

Mangoes   Shop for mangoes with reddish-yellow skin that seems fairly firm when gentle pressure is applied. Avoid soft or bruised mangoes and green mangoes. A few brown spots on the skin are normal indicators of ripeness. Store still-firm mangoes at room temperature. Mangoes can be ripened in a paper bag at room temperature. When soft to the touch, store them in the refrigerator for up to 1 week. Don't cut until ready to use. Peel mangoes with a sharp knife, then slice down the mango on one side of the seed as close to it as possible. Repeat with the other side. Trim off any remaining flesh from around the seed.

Maple Syrup   Pure maple syrup is more expensive than pancake syrups made by mixing artificial maple flavoring with corn syrup. However, the taste of pure maple syrup is well worth the difference in price. Once opened, the syrup should be refrigerated. It will last a year in the refrigerator. Cold, pure maple syrup does not pour easily, so you should leave it at room temperature for an hour before serving.

Mayonnaise Dressings   A number of nonfat or reduced-fat mayonnaise products are available in which all or some of the fat has been replaced with starch and emulsifiers. Be aware of the rather high sodium content of these products.

Milk   Buy skim milk, 1% milk, and nonfat or reduced-fat buttermilk. Skim milk is best if you are concerned about the amount of fat you are consuming. Avoid 2% milk, which has almost as much fat as whole milk.

Mushrooms   Buy young, pale, button mushrooms. Brush them and wipe them with a damp cloth or paper towel. If you need to wash them, be sure to dry them thoroughly. When serving them raw, sprinkle with lemon juice or white wine to keep them light in color. Mushrooms that will be stuffed for appetizers can be steamed over boiling water for 1 or 2 minutes or served raw.

Shiitake Mushrooms: Also called forest mushrooms, fresh and dried shiitake mushrooms can be found in the produce sections of many supermarkets. They are parasol-shaped, colored brownish-black, and have a light garlic aroma. They contain B vitamins and minerals. To reconstitute dry shiitake mushrooms, soak them in enough hot water to cover for about 30 minutes, or until they are soft. Drain. Squeeze out excess water. Remove and discard stems.

Mussels   Buy mussels with tightly closed shells or those that snap shut when tapped. Avoid those with broken shells, that feel heavy, or that feel light and loose when shaken. Fresh mussels should be stored in the refrigerator and used within a day or two. Scrub to remove sand and dirt, scraping off any barnacles from the shell with a knife, and remove the beard. To get rid of grit inside the shells, place mussels in a pot with salted cold water to cover. Add 1 tablespoon flour for each gallon of water, and soak for 1 hour. To steam mussels, place ½ inch of water in the bottom of a steamer. Place mussels on steamer rack. Cover the pot, and steam over medium heat for 5 to 10 minutes or until they open, but no longer. Discard any unopened mussels.

Napa Cabbage (Chinese Cabbage)   Napa cabbage is available year-round. Choose firm, tightly packed heads with crisp, green-tipped leaves. Refrigerate tightly wrapped for up to 3 days.

Nectarines   Nectarines should be uniform in shape with a creamy yellow skin and no green at the stem end. Choose nectarines that yield to gentle pressure. Refrigerate ripe nectarines, and use within a few days. Dip cut nectarines in lemon juice mixed with water to preserve color.

Nuts   Buy dry-roasted, unsalted nuts. Most nuts will keep for 1 month at room temperature and for 3 months in the refrigerator. They can also be frozen for 6 to 12 months. Frozen nuts do not need to be thawed before using.

Oils   Light-flavored olive oil is suggested as the oil of choice, due to its high monounsaturated fat content. Canola oil is an acceptable substitute. For lightly oiling skillets, baking sheets and pans, and muffin cups, make your own olive oil cooking spray by filling a spritz bottle with oil.

Olives   Buy pitted green and black olives, and pimento-stuffed olives. Be sure to rinse them well to get rid of salty brine before using.

Onions   When buying onions, choose those that are heavy for their size, with dry skins that show no signs of spotting or moistness. Avoid those with soft spots. Store in a cool, dry place with good air circulation for up to 3 months.

Oranges   Look for firm heavy fruit with smooth skin. Avoid oranges with cuts or discolored areas of skin around the stem end. Store whole oranges in the crisper drawers of your refrigerator or in open containers on your refrigerator shelves. Don't put them in airtight plastic bags, because mold develops quickly when air can't circulate.

Orange Peel Either grate the peel of fresh oranges, or buy grated orange peel in the spice section of your supermarket.

Orzo Orzo is a tiny pasta that resembles elongated rice or barley.

Oysters Only buy live oysters with tightly closed shells or those that snap shut when tapped. The smaller the oyster (for its type), the younger and more tender it will be. Fresh, shucked oysters should be plump, uniform in size, have good color, smell fresh, and be packaged in clear oyster liquor. Live oysters should be covered with a damp towel and refrigerated (larger shell down) for up to 3 days. Refrigerate shucked oysters in their liquor, and use within 2 days. As an alternative to shucking oysters, you can open their shells by placing them in a 400-degree oven for 5 to 7 minutes. Then drop them briefly into ice water. They should open easily. To shuck, release the oyster from the shell with a knife.

Oyster Sauce A dark-brown sauce consisting of oysters, brine, and soy sauce cooked until thick and concentrated. It is available at many supermarkets in the international foods section and at oriental markets.

Papaya Select papayas that are at least half yellow and yield to gentle pressure. Look for bruise-free fruit with smooth, unwrinkled skin. Avoid very soft or bruised ones with a fermented aroma. Green papayas will ripen at home at room temperature away from sunlight in 3 or 4 days. They are ripe when they yield to pressure when squeezed gently between the palms of your hands. Refrigerate ripe fruit and use within a week. You can either spoon the fruit from a papaya or peel the skin and slice the fruit thinly to serve.

Parsley While other fresh herbs can be hard to find, parsley is widely available and should always be used in its fresh form, if possible. It will chop finely if it is thoroughly dried with a cotton kitchen towel before chopping.

Pasta Dried and fresh pastas are both made from flour and water or flour and eggs. If you are watching your cholesterol, you want to avoid pasta made with whole eggs. However, there are now a number of fresh and dried pastas made with flour and egg whites. Durum wheat, the hardest, or semolina, the coarsest grind of durum, makes the most flavorful and resilient pasta. A cup of cooked durum wheat macaroni or spaghetti (about 2 ounces dry) has barely a trace of fat or cholesterol. Stored in a cool, dry place, dried pasta keeps indefinitely. Be sure to store fresh pasta in the refrigerator until ready to cook. It should be used within 2 or 3 days of purchase or according to the date on the package. It can also be stored in the freezer.

Peaches Look for very fragrant fruit that gives slightly to pressure. Refrigerate ripe peaches for up to 5 days and bring to room temperature before serving. To peel, blanch peaches in boiling water for 30 seconds, and then plunge them into icy water.

Peanut Butter Buy commercially available peanut butter substitute or nonhydrogenated natural peanut butter with no added fats, stabilizers, salt, or sweeteners. If the oil rises to the top, stir it back in. Store in refrigerator for up to 6 months.

Pears Avoid pears with soft spots near the stem or bottom ends, and those with heavy bruises. If pears are still firm, ripen them at room temperature or place in a brown paper bag with a ripe apple until pears are soft to the touch. Ripe pears yield to gentle pressure at the stem end. Store ripe pears in the refrigerator and use in a few days. To keep cut pears from discoloring, drop them into a mixture of water and lemon juice.

Peppers:

Bell Peppers: Sweet, thick-fleshed bell peppers come in several colors. Red bell peppers were actually green peppers until a few days before picking. Their color indicates that they've matured and increased their vitamin A content ten times. The flavor of red peppers is slightly sweeter than the familiar green pepper taste. Yellow peppers are even sweeter and more mellow. Buy plump, brilliantly colored, well-shaped peppers with healthy-looking stems. Avoid those with soft spots, cracks, or soft stems. They should look crisp and be firm. Refrigerate bell peppers for up to several days in the crisper drawer. Red and yellow peppers will not keep as long as green peppers because of their high sugar content. When preparing bell peppers, halve them from the stem to the base. Remove seedy core, stems, and white pith along ribs. Roasted red bell peppers are also sold in jars.

Fresh Chile Peppers: Jalapeño peppers, frequently used in these recipes, are usually found green, but are sometimes red when ripe. They are small, blunt-tipped, and range from hot to fiery. They will contribute less heat to a recipe if the seeds are removed. Be sure to wear protective gloves when handling pepper seeds, or be careful to wash your hands immediately after handling them. Rinse off knives and cutting boards. Roasting the peppers will also lessen the heat and will concentrate the flavors.

Canned Chile Peppers: Canned green chiles are used in the recipes. They can be found in the international foods section of your supermarket or in Mexican markets.

Dried Chile Peppers: Whole jalapeños and other varieties of chile peppers can also be found in dried form. Store the peppers in a basket or by threading them on cotton string in a "necklace" and hanging them up. If kept cool and dry, they can be stored for a year.

Crushed Red Pepper: Crushed red pepper contains the seeds and flesh of the long, red, New Mexican chile. It's mildly hot and comes in shaker-top jars.

Pickle Relish   Sweet pickle relish is called for in several of the recipes. Look for brands that have no added salt.

Pimentos   Pimentos are large, heart-shaped, sweet red peppers that are often sliced and sold in jars.

Pine Nuts   Pine nuts or pignoli come from several varieties of pine trees. They have a thin shell with an ivory-colored nut meat. Italian pine nuts have a light delicate flavor and are more expensive than Chinese pine nuts, which have a pungent pine flavor. They can found in nut shops, health-food stores, Italian markets, and in many supermarkets. They can be stored in the refrigerator for up to 3 months or frozen for up to 9 months.

Pita Bread   Buy whole wheat, nonfat pita breads (also called pocket breads). Store in the refrigerator wrapped in tightly closed plastic bags.

Plum Sauce   Also called duck sauce, plum sauce is a thick, sweet-and-sour condiment made with plums, apricots, sugar, and seasonings. It is available in many supermarkets and at oriental markets.

Popcorn   Buy air-popped popcorn or pop your own without oil in a tightly closed brown paper bag in your microwave.

Potatoes   Choose potatoes that are firm, well shaped for their type, and blemish-free. Avoid potatoes that are wrinkled, sprouted, or cracked. Store potatoes in a cool, dark, well-ventilated place for up to 2 weeks. New potatoes should be used within 3 days of purchase. Refrigerating potatoes causes them to become sweet and turn dark when cooked. Always drop peeled potatoes in water immediately after peeling to prevent discoloration.

Potato Chips Baked, nonfat potato chips both with and without salt in regular and barbecue flavors can now be found in the supermarket or at health-food stores.

Pumpernickel A coarse, dark bread with a slightly sour taste, pumpernickel is made of rye and wheat flour. Molasses is used for color and flavor.

Raisins Buy dark seedless raisins.

Raspberries Look for firm, plump berries with a healthy color. Refrigerate them, unwashed, in a shallow plastic container covered with paper towels, and use within several days. Do not store raspberries in tin or aluminum containers or their red color may turn blue. Gently wash berries in a strainer or colander before using, and pat dry.

Rice Rice is classified by its size—long, medium, or short grain. The length of long-grain rice is four to five times that of its width. There are both white and brown varieties of long-grain rice that, when cooked, produce light, dry grains that separate easily. Perfumy East Indian basmati rice is a long-grain rice. Brown rice is the entire grain with only the inedible outer husk removed. The nutritious, high-fiber bran coating gives it a light tan color, nutlike flavor, and chewy texture. It takes slightly longer to cook than regular white, long-grain rice. Either white or brown rice can be used when rice is an ingredient in recipes in this book.

Rice Cakes Mini–rice cakes are used as an appetizer base. You will find them with regular-size rice cakes in the snacks and crackers section of your supermarket.

Salmon Recipes in this book call for canned salmon, smoked salmon, and salmon caviar. Smoked salmon is fresh salmon that has undergone a smoking process. Salmon caviar is medium-size, pale orange to deep red, sieved, and lightly salted fish roe.

Salsa   Prepared salsas, which are relishes made from chopped vegetables, can be found in the condiments aisle or with the international foods in your supermarket. Some fresh-vegetable salsas are also kept in the refrigerator case alongside fresh tortillas. You can also make your own by combining 2 diced fresh tomatoes, 1 diced green bell pepper, 1 diced medium onion, 2 cloves minced garlic, 2 teaspoons lemon juice, 1 teaspoon ground cumin, 1 teaspoon dried oregano, ¼ teaspoon black pepper, and ¼ teaspoon ground cayenne pepper in a blender or food processor. Process until chunky. Stir in 2 cups crushed canned tomatoes and 1 chopped green or red bell pepper. (Makes 4 cups.)

Sardines   A generic name used to describe various small, soft-boned saltwater fish that swim in huge schools near the water's surface. In America, sardines are usually sold canned in oil, mustard, or tomato sauce. Some are packed with bones, and some are skinned, boned, and sold as fillets.

Scallions   Choose those with crisp, bright green tops and a firm white base. Store, wrapped in a plastic bag, in the vegetable crisper of your refrigerator for up to 3 days.

Scallops   Scallops should have a sweet smell and a fresh, moist sheen. Because they perish quickly out of water, they're usually sold shucked. They should be refrigerated immediately after purchase and used within a day or two. Bay scallops average about 100 to the pound, and their meat is sweeter and more succulent than that of the sea scallop. Sea scallops average 1½ inches in diameter, and there are about 30 to the pound. Though slightly chewier, the meat of sea scallops is still sweet and moist.

Seeds   Buy raw, unsalted sesame and sunflower seeds.

Sesame Oil   This oil made from sesame seeds can be found in the international foods section of your supermarket or at oriental markets. Light sesame oil is milder than dark sesame oil, and is preferable in most of these recipes.

Shrimp   Raw shrimp should smell of the sea with no hint of ammonia. Cooked, shelled shrimp should look plump and succulent. Whether or not to devein shrimp is a matter of personal preference. Deveining small and medium shrimp is primarily cosmetic. However, in large shrimp, the intestinal vein may contain grit. There are usually 31 to 35 medium shrimp in a pound, and 21 to 30 large shrimp to a pound. To cook fresh shrimp, drop them into boiling water, reduce the heat at once, and simmer for 3 to 4 minutes. Remove them from the heat before they begin to curl up. Drain at once.

Snow Peas Choose bright, crisp-colored pods with small seeds. Refrigerate in a plastic bag for up to 3 days. To prepare snow peas to be stuffed for appetizers, trim ends of snow peas and remove strings. Blanch for 15 seconds in boiling water. Remove with a slotted spoon, plunge into ice water, drain, and pat dry with paper towels. With the top of a sharp, thin-bladed knife, carefully slit the rounded side of the pea, opening the pod to within ¼ inch of the end.

Sour Cream Buy nonfat or reduced-fat sour cream.

Soy Sauce Light soy sauce contains from 33 to 46 percent less sodium than regular soy sauce, with little or no difference in flavor resulting from the sodium reduction. Store in refrigerator.

Spices Keep dried spices tightly covered in an airtight container. Don't expose them to extremely high heat or intense light. Dried spices are best if used within 6 months to a year, so it is wise to date containers at the time you purchase or store them. During the summer months, store ground cayenne pepper, paprika, chile powder, and crushed red pepper in the refrigerator. Spices used in the recipes include ground black and white pepper, whole peppercorns, chili powder, ground and whole cloves, ground cayenne pepper, crushed red pepper, allspice, caraway seeds, celery seeds, dry mustard, dill seeds, mustard seeds, pickling spices, poppy seeds, ground and stick cinnamon, ground coriander, ground cumin, ground ginger, nutmeg, paprika, fennel seeds, cumin, cardamom, anise seeds, mace, and turmeric.

Spinach Buy fresh-looking, dark-green spinach with crisp leaves and thin stalks. Refrigerate unwashed spinach uncovered and wrapped in a cotton kitchen towel. Careful cleaning is essential, because spinach is very gritty. Dump unwashed spinach into a sink filled with warm water. Drain water and clean sink. Rinse leaves under cold running water until spinach is completely free of grit. To stem spinach, fold the leaf in half lengthwise and zip off the stem. Frozen spinach can be substituted for fresh in many of the recipes that call for chopped spinach.

Strawberries　Look for berries that are firm, deep red, and have a green cap attached. Store them, unwashed, in an open paper bag in the refrigerator, to use within several days. Gently wash berries in a strainer or colander before using, and pat dry. Wash before hulling to avoid losing any of the juices. Hull strawberries with a strawberry huller or a sharp paring knife.

Sugar　Table sugar is sucrose, a highly refined product made from sugar beets or sugar cane. It is so refined that it is nearly 100 percent pure and almost indestructible. Brown sugar is a variation on granulated sugar and shares its very long shelf life. Brown sugar contains granulated sugar coated with refined, colored, molasses-flavored syrup. Light brown sugar has less molasses flavor than dark brown sugar. To soften brown sugar that has turned hard, place in a sealed plastic bag with half an apple overnight. Store granulated sugar in an airtight container at room temperature. Store brown sugar in an airtight plastic bag inside a glass jar.

Sugar Substitutes　Sugar substitutes are not suggested in the recipes. If you choose to buy sugar substitutes, be aware of their particular chemical compositions and any resulting health implications.

Sweet Potatoes　Look for unblemished, firm sweet potatoes with no soft spots or bruises. Store them in a humid, well-ventilated spot with temperatures between 55 and 58 degrees. Wash well before cooking. Always drop peeled sweet potatoes in water immediately after peeling to prevent discoloration.

Swordfish　Swordfish is mild-flavored, with firm, dense, and meatlike flesh. It is available fresh from early spring to late fall and is also available frozen year-round. It is sold in steaks and chunks.

Tahini　Tahini, which is a thick paste made of ground sesame seed, can be found in the international foods sections of supermarkets, in health-food stores, and in Middle Eastern markets.

Tomatoes　Look for tomatoes with good color and firm flesh. They should be well formed and free of bruises. Ripe tomatoes feel tender and are heavy in relation to their size. They have a full red color. They will keep 2 or 3 days at room temperature. Don't refrigerate tomatoes unless necessary. Refrigerate only those that are extraripe. Dunking tomatoes into boiling water for 5 seconds will allow them to be easily peeled.

Tomato Products When buying canned tomatoes, tomato puree, and tomato paste, look for low-sodium products. Canned Italian plum tomatoes are the best substitute for fresh tomatoes. Do not keep unopened canned tomato products for more than 6 months. Store them on a cool, dry shelf. After opening, canned tomato products should be stored in clean, covered glass containers. They tend to take on a metallic flavor if left in their cans. You can keep them in the refrigerator for a week. Leftover tomato paste and tomato sauce can be frozen for up to 2 months in airtight containers. Drop leftover tomato paste by the tablespoon on a sheet of wax paper and freeze. When frozen, place in a plastic freezer bag and store in freezer until needed.

Sun-Dried Tomatoes These chewy, intensely flavored, sweet, dark red tomatoes are dried in the sun. They are either packed in oil or dry-packed in cellophane. Soak dry-pack sun-dried tomatoes in hot water until soft; soaking time will vary depending on tomatoes.

Tortellini Tortellini is small pasta stuffed with various fillings, folded over, and then shaped into a ring or hat shape. You can find dried, fresh, or frozen tortellini with a variety of fillings at your supermarket.

Tortillas Tortillas are made from either flour or corn. Corn tortillas usually do not contain oil or shortening. Tortillas can be warmed in the microwave by wrapping them in a damp paper towel and microwaving for 1 minute on HIGH.

Tuna:
   Canned Tuna: Buy white albacore tuna that is packed in water, not in oil. Cans marked *solid* or *fancy* contain large pieces of fish; those marked *chunk* contain smaller pieces.
   Fresh Tuna: Fresh tuna is available from late spring into early fall. Frozen tuna is available year-round and is sold as both steaks and fillets.

Turkey:
   Ground Turkey: Buy low-fat ground turkey breast with a fat content under 7 percent.
   Smoked or Roast Turkey: When buying smoked and roast turkey at your deli counter, look for products that are at least 97 percent fat-free. Buy sliced, fresh roast turkey breast whenever available.
   Turkey Sausage: Buy turkey sausage with the lowest percentage of calories from fat.

Vegetable Oil Spray Buy nonstick vegetable spray with the lowest fat count possible in case you need it to spray baking pans or other surfaces while cooking. You can also buy an inexpensive plastic spray bottle and fill it with light-flavored olive oil or canola oil.

Vinegars:

Vinegars are very sour liquids fermented from a distilled alcohol, often wine or apple cider. Tightly capped vinegar keeps up to a year at room temperature, or until sediment appears at the bottom of the bottle.

Wine Vinegar: Buy red and white wine vinegars.

Balsamic Vinegar: Balsamic vinegar adds an elegant, complex, sweet-and-sour taste to food. It is aged in Italy in wooden casks for about 4 years with the skins from grapes used to make red wine, which gives it a winelike sweetness. The longer it is aged, the more mellow it becomes. When replacing regular vinegar with balsamic, you can use a lot less because the balsamic is so flavorful.

Rice Vinegar: Japanese or Chinese vinegars made from fermented rice are milder than most Western vinegars. They can be found in many supermarkets and in oriental markets.

Cider Vinegar: Cider vinegar is made from fermented apple cider.

Water Chestnuts   The canned variety of water chestnut, which is round and woody and about the size of a cherry tomato, can be refrigerated, covered in its liquid, for 1 week after opening.

Watercress   Watercress has small, crisp, dark green leaves. Its pungent flavor is slightly bitter and has a peppery snap. Choose crisp leaves that have a deep color and show no sign of yellowing or wilting. Refrigerate in a plastic bag for up to 5 days. Wash and shake dry just before using. Watercress can be substituted for parsley in many recipes, and can be used as a garnish.

Watermelon   When a watermelon is ripe, it should sound dull, flat, and heavy when thumped. Store whole watermelon at room temperature. Cut melon should be wrapped and refrigerated.

Wine and Other Spirits   Dry white wine, red wine, sherry, brandy, and Grand Marnier are used as flavoring in some of the recipes. Nonalcoholic wines or grape juice can be substituted if desired.

Winter Squash   Buy winter squash (acorn, butternut, or Hubbard) that are hard, heavy, and clean. Avoid squash that have cracks, soft spots, or decayed spots. Store squash in a dry spot with low humidity and temperatures between 50 and 55 degrees.

Wonton Wrappers   Not only can wonton wrappers be used for wontons and dumplings, but they are a quick and easy way to prepare dishes often made with fresh pasta dough, such as ravioli. They can be baked and used as a substitute for crackers. Some are made with fat, so check the package labels. They can be found in the produce or frozen food sections of supermarkets and in oriental markets.

Worcestershire Sauce   So named because it was first bottled in Worcestershire, England, this thin, dark, piquant sauce is usually a blend of garlic, soy sauce, tamarind, onion, molasses, lime, anchovies, vinegar, and various seasonings. It is available in supermarkets.

Yellow Summer Squash (Crookneck)   Choose squash that are small, tender, and have thin skins. The skins should be free of bruises and should have a vibrant color. They can be refrigerated in a plastic bag for up to 5 days.

Yogurt   Yogurt is one of the most healthful foods you can eat. Eight ounces, or 1 cup, will provide you with 25 percent of the RDA for protein and 300 to 400 milligrams of calcium. It's a good source of riboflavin, phosphorus, and potassium. Buy only nonfat, plain yogurt, which has substantially fewer calories per ounce than regular or low-fat yogurt, and less than 1 gram of fat per serving.

Zucchini   Choose zucchini that are small, tender, and have thin skins. The skins should be free of bruises and should have a vibrant color. They can be refrigerated in a plastic bag for up to 5 days.

• ABOUT THE RECIPES •

The five hundred recipes in this book are either fat-free or extremely low in fat. Margarine and butter are not used in any of the recipes. When oil is used it is either monounsaturated, light-flavored olive oil or monounsaturated canola oil. Light sesame oil, which is highly flavored, is also occasionally called for in small amounts. If you are on an extremely low fat diet, you may wish to substitute water, nonfat or reduced-fat, low-sodium chicken or vegetable broth, juice, or wine for the oil in some of the recipes where olive oil or canola oil is used for sautéing.

Nonfat choices are often offered as the ingredient of choice, but the recipes can also be made with reduced-fat ingredients according to individual taste and diet needs. If you are on a very low sodium diet, be sure to check the sodium counts on the nonfat ingredients you purchase, since food manufacturers often compensate for the lack of fat in a product by adding a great deal of sodium.

Many of the recipes are vegetarian, but others include chicken, turkey, fish, and seafood. Recipes using beef, pork, ham, veal, or lamb are not included.

While the time you need to spend in the kitchen actively preparing the recipes is as pared down as possible, some of the recipes require marinating time or longer, slower cooking procedures. Be sure to check the time data at the top of each recipe to allow enough marinating and/or cooking time. Some of the recipes call for ingredients that can be purchased already cooked, such as beans or shrimp. If you prefer to buy these items uncooked, and to cook them yourself, allow more time.

• Nutritional Analysis •

The recipes in this book have been nutritionally analyzed using Nutritionist IV software. Among the important sources of the Nutritionist IV database are the USDA Handbooks No. 8, No. 16, and No. 81.

A nutritional analysis is given for each recipe on a per-serving-size basis. Serving size is indicated at the top of each recipe. The nutritional analysis includes calories; fat (in grams); cholesterol (in milligrams); protein (in grams); carbohydrates (in grams); dietary fiber (in grams); and sodium (in milligrams). Numbers in the analyses are rounded off to the nearest whole digit.

When the ingredient listing gives more than one option, the first ingredient listed is the one analyzed. Optional ingredients are not included in the analyses.

Due to inevitable variations in the ingredients you may select, nutritional analyses should be considered approximate.

500 LOW-FAT
AND FAT-FREE
APPETIZER RECIPES

Vegetable Appetizers

Asparagus Bites • Asparagus–Smoked Turkey Roll-ups • Asparagus Tips Wrapped in Salmon • Artichoke Cups with Egg Stuffing • Artichokes Stuffed with Mussels • Pickled Broccoli Stems • Steamed Broccoli and Shrimp with Oyster Sauce • Lemon Broccoli Florets • Baked Broccoli Bites • Broccoli-Tomato Hors d'Oeuvres • Garlic-Chile Brussels Sprouts • Dilled Brussels Sprouts • Cabbage Rolls • Sweet-and-Sour Carrots • Spicy Cauliflower Florets • Cauliflower with Parsley and Scallions • Cauliflower with Curry Sauce • Cold Cauliflower with Shrimp • Orange and Raisin–Stuffed Celery • Celery Boats Stuffed with Red Peppers • Pesto-Stuffed Celery • Three Cheese–Stuffed Celery • Cucumber-Crab Canapés • Cucumber–Salmon–Cream Cheese Slices • Cucumber-Tuna Boats • Cucumber Cups Stuffed with Lemon-Dill Shrimp • Cucumber Rounds with Walnut Chicken • Caponata • Sautéed Japanese Eggplant • Stuffed Eggplant • Balsamic Eggplant Coins • Eggplant-Zucchini Bundles • Endive with Curried Chicken • Endive with Shrimp • Endive-Beet Boats • Belgian Endive with Apples and Cream Cheese • Drizzled Green Beans • Tarragon Green Beans with Mustard Dressing • Jicama-Stuffed Mushrooms • Jicama Chips with Jalapeño-Bean Dip •

Spiced Jicama • Hearts of Palm with Vinaigrette • Kohlrabi Crudités • Spiced Shiitake Mushrooms • Mushrooms Stuffed with Crab • Mushrooms with Tuna • Mushrooms in Coriander-Wine Sauce • Sautéed Mushroom Caps in Garlic-Parsley Sauce • Mushrooms in Herb Sauce • Spinach Mushrooms • Potato-Tomato Delights • Garlic-Parsley New Potato Bites • Rosemary Potatoes • Stuffed New Potatoes • Corn-Stuffed Potatoes • New Potatoes Stuffed with Carrots • New Potatoes with Lemon-Mint Sauce • Lemon-Coriander Potatoes • Petite Potato Cakes • Potato-Caviar Bites • Potato-Carrot Minicakes • Parmesan-Potato Wedges • Tuna-Topped Potatoes • Potato-Cheese Slices • Potato Slices with Spinach Pesto • New Potato Rounds • Sweet Potato Slices • Petite Sweet Potato Pancakes with Applesauce • Potato Skins with Chile Salsa • Pizza Skins • Crispy Parmesan Potato Skins • Radicchio Bites • Snow Peas with Shrimp • Chicken Salad–Stuffed Snow Peas • Snow Peas with Crab • Sweet-and-Spicy Tomatoes • Parsley-Basil-Cheese–Stuffed Cherry Tomatoes • Parsley Pesto Tomatoes • Cherry Tomatoes with Artichoke Filling • Cherry Tomatoes with Green Pepper–Corn Filling • Spinach-Ricotta–Stuffed Cherry Tomatoes • Couscous Tomatoes • Cherry Tomatoes Stuffed with Orzo • Cherry Tomatoes with Pasta Stuffing • Cherry Tomatoes with Hummus • Cherry Tomato–Salmon Bites • Cherry Tomatoes with Crab • Cherry Tomatoes with Tuna • Cherry Tomatoes with Shrimp Stuffing • Cherry Tomatoes with Lemon-Oyster Stuffing • Olive-Stuffed Tomatoes • Feta-Stuffed Tomatoes • Green and Gold Slices • Yellow Squash Rounds with Green Pepper Filling • Zucchini Slices with Crumb Topping • Zucchini Rounds with Red Pepper Filling • Zucchini Rounds with Curried-Egg Topping • Carrot and Zucchini Rolls • Zucchini-Crab Bites • Zucchini-Shrimp Bites • Zucchini–Red Pepper Tastes • Vegetable Antipasto • Vegetable Antipasto II • Mixed Vegetable Platter • Bread and Veggie Kabobs • Veggie Roll-ups • Basil-Balsamic Vegetables • Mini–Vegetable Bundles • Mediterranean Stuffed Lemons • Baked Stuffed Grape Leaves • Vegetable Skewers

❧ *Asparagus Bites* ❦

YIELD: 18 servings (2 each) • *PREPARATION TIME: 10 minutes plus 20 minutes refrigeration time* • *COOKING TIME: 2 minutes*

Fresh asparagus is parboiled and marinated in soy sauce, sesame oil, and sugar.

1 pound fresh asparagus
1 teaspoon sugar
3 tablespoons light soy sauce

½ teaspoon light-flavored olive or
sesame oil

1. Cut asparagus on the diagonal in 1½-inch sections, discarding tough ends.
2. Drop cut asparagus in boiling water for 2 minutes. Remove with a slotted spoon, plunge into cold water, and drain.
3. Combine sugar, soy sauce, and oil.
4. Pour over asparagus in a bowl and toss well.
5. Cover and refrigerate for 20 minutes. Serve with wooden or plastic party picks.

Calories Per Serving: 10
Fat: 0 g
Cholesterol: 0 mg
Protein: 1 g

Carbohydrates: 1 g
Dietary Fiber: 0 g
Sodium: 96 mg

❧ *Asparagus—Smoked Turkey Roll-ups* ❦

YIELD: 12 servings (2 each) • *PREPARATION TIME: 15 minutes* • *COOKING TIME: 6 minutes*

Asparagus spears are rolled in smoked turkey slices spread with honey mustard.

24 small fresh or frozen whole aspara-
gus spears, stem ends trimmed
2½ cups nonfat or reduced-fat, low-
sodium chicken broth

2 tablespoons honey mustard
12 thin slices smoked turkey, cut in
half

1. Cook asparagus in chicken stock until just tender. Drain.
2. Spread honey mustard on smoked turkey slices.
3. Top each half slice of turkey with 1 spear of asparagus and roll up. Serve at once.

Calories Per Serving: 32
Fat: 1 g
Cholesterol: 3 mg
Protein: 6 g

Carbohydrates: 1 g
Dietary Fiber: 0 g
Sodium: 267 mg

Asparagus Tips Wrapped in Salmon

YIELD: 12 servings (2 each) • *PREPARATION TIME: 30 minutes* •
COOKING TIME: 3 minutes

Serve this tempting dish when asparagus is in season.

7 tablespoons Dijon mustard
6 tablespoons sugar
¼ cup red wine vinegar
1 tablespoon light-flavored olive oil

3-inch-long tips from 24 asparagus
   spears
8 ounces smoked salmon, thinly sliced

1. Place asparagus tips over boiling water in a steamer basket and steam for 3 minutes, or until tender-crisp. Immediately plunge into cold water.
2. Whisk together mustard, sugar, vinegar, and olive oil. Pour in a small serving bowl.
3. Wrap each asparagus tip in a 2-inch-wide slice of salmon.
4. Serve cold with the mustard sauce for dipping.

Calories Per Serving: 77
Fat: 3 g
Cholesterol: 5 mg
Protein: 5 g

Carbohydrates: 8 g
Dietary Fiber: 0 g
Sodium: 382 mg

❧ *Artichoke Cups with Egg Stuffing* ✒

YIELD: *10 servings (1 each)* • PREPARATION TIME: *25 minutes plus
1 hour refrigeration time*

Artichoke bottoms are stuffed with eggs, capers, and red peppers.

*10 hard-boiled egg whites, finely
  chopped
¼ cup fat-free mayonnaise
2 tablespoons white wine vinegar
½ red bell pepper, finely chopped
2 tablespoons capers, drained and
  chopped*

*2 tablespoons chopped fresh parsley
¼ teaspoon black pepper
14 ounces canned, water-packed artichoke bottoms, drained
Juice of ½ lemon
1 teaspoon ground coriander*

1. Combine cooked egg whites, mayonnaise, and vinegar. Stir in bell pepper, capers, parsley, and black pepper.
2. Place artichoke bottoms on a serving plate. Fill each with the egg mixture.
3. Combine lemon juice and coriander. Sprinkle on artichokes.
4. Chill for 1 hour before serving. Serve with plates and cocktail forks.

Calories Per Serving: 48
Fat: 0 g
Cholesterol: 0 mg
Protein: 5 g

Carbohydrates: 7 g
Dietary Fiber: 2 g
Sodium: 138 mg

❧ *Artichokes Stuffed with Mussels* ✒

YIELD: *10 servings (2 each)* • PREPARATION TIME: *20 minutes*

Canned artichoke hearts are topped with canned mussels and cream cheese.

*3 ounces nonfat or reduced-fat cream
  cheese, softened
2 tablespoons lemon juice
1 tablespoon dried dill*

*3 tablespoons minced onion
14 ounces canned, water-packed artichoke hearts, rinsed and drained
9 ounces canned mussels, drained*

1. Combine cream cheese, lemon juice, dill, and onion.
2. Drain the artichoke hearts and pat dry with paper towels.
3. Spread the drained, canned mussels on paper towels and pat dry. Put a mussel on each artichoke heart.
4. Cover the top of each mussel with ¼ teaspoon of the cheese mixture. Serve with plates and cocktail forks.

Calories Per Serving: 57
Fat: 1 g
Cholesterol: 16 mg
Protein: 7 g

Carbohydrates: 7 g
Dietary Fiber: 2 g
Sodium: 174 mg

❧ *Pickled Broccoli Stems* ❧

YIELD: 32 servings (2 tablespoons each) • *PREPARATION TIME: 20 minutes plus 2 hours refrigeration time*

Broccoli stems, an often-discarded portion of the vegetable, are delicious when peeled and tossed with rice vinegar, jalapeño pepper, and fresh gingerroot.

4 cups broccoli stems, peeled and cut into matchstick-size pieces
2 teaspoons rice vinegar

2 cloves garlic, minced
1 jalapeño pepper, seeded and minced
½ teaspoon minced fresh gingerroot

1. Blanch the julienned broccoli stems in boiling water for 20 seconds. Cool under cold running water and drain.
2. Whisk together the rice vinegar, garlic, jalapeño pepper, and gingerroot in a large glass bowl.
3. Toss the broccoli stems with the vinegar mixture and chill for 2 hours before serving. Serve with plates and cocktail forks.

Calories Per Serving: 6
Fat: 0 g
Cholesterol: 0 mg
Protein: 1 g

Carbohydrates: 1 g
Dietary Fiber: 1 g
Sodium: 5 mg

Steamed Broccoli and
◊ Shrimp with Oyster Sauce ◊

YIELD: 12 servings (2 each) ▪ *PREPARATION TIME: 25 minutes* ▪
COOKING TIME: 10 minutes

Broccoli florets are surrounded by shrimp, then steamed and served with a dipping sauce.

¼ teaspoon white pepper
¼ teaspoon sugar
1 egg white, lightly beaten
1 tablespoon cornstarch

24 medium shrimp, shelled and de-veined
24 broccoli florets with 2-inch stems

SAUCE

3 tablespoons oyster sauce
3 tablespoons water

1 teaspoon light-flavored olive or sesame oil

1. Combine white pepper, sugar, egg white, and cornstarch.
2. Paint each shrimp with some of the egg-cornstarch mixture.
3. Place a broccoli floret in the curve of each shrimp. Carefully place shrimp-wrapped broccoli florets on a plate.
4. Bring a quart of water to a boil in a wok or large pot with a steamer rack. Reduce heat to simmer.
5. Set plate with shrimp-wrapped broccoli on the rack. Cover and steam for 5 minutes. Shrimp will fit around broccoli more snugly after they cook.
6. While shrimp-wrapped broccoli are steaming, make the sauce by combining the oyster sauce, water, and oil in a small serving bowl.
7. Remove shrimp-wrapped broccoli, drain on paper towels, and arrange on a platter around the dipping sauce. Serve with wooden or plastic party picks.

Calories Per Serving: 61
Fat: 1 g
Cholesterol: 59 mg
Protein: 9 g

Carbohydrates: 4 g
Dietary Fiber: 1 g
Sodium: 210 mg

❧ *Lemon Broccoli Florets* ❧

YIELD: 16 servings (¼ cup each) • *PREPARATION TIME: 15 minutes plus 2 hours refrigeration time*

Fresh broccoli is marinated in an olive oil, olive, and lemon juice dressing.

4 cups broccoli florets
2 tablespoons light-flavored olive oil

12 stuffed green olives, halved
¼ cup lemon juice

1. Toss florets with olive oil, olives, and lemon juice.
2. Cover and chill for 2 hours before serving. Serve with wooden or plastic party picks.

Calories Per Serving: 25
Fat: 2 g
Cholesterol: 0 mg
Protein: 1 g

Carbohydrates: 2 g
Dietary Fiber: 1 g
Sodium: 67 mg

❧ *Baked Broccoli Bites* ❧

YIELD: 20 servings (2 each) • *PREPARATION TIME: 20 minutes* • *COOKING TIME: 20 minutes*

Try making this alternative to deep-fried vegetables with other vegetables as well.

1½ cups nonfat or reduced-fat sour cream
1 teaspoon Worcestershire sauce
1 clove garlic, minced

1 bunch broccoli, cut into florets with 1-inch stems
½ cup corn flakes or other flaked whole-grain cereal, crushed

1. Preheat oven to 400 degrees. Combine sour cream, Worcestershire sauce, and garlic.
2. Dip broccoli into sour cream mixture and roll in crushed corn flakes to coat. Place on a nonstick baking sheet.

3. Bake for 20 minutes or until tender-crisp. Serve warm.

Calories Per Serving: 72
Fat: 0 g
Cholesterol: 12 mg
Protein: 5 g

Carbohydrates: 12 g
Dietary Fiber: 3 g
Sodium: 95 mg

❧ *Broccoli-Tomato Hors d'Oeuvres* ☙

YIELD: 12 servings (½ cup each) • *PREPARATION TIME: 25 minutes plus
1 hour refrigeration time*

Broccoli stalks and tomatoes are served with a lemon-vinegar-Parmesan dressing.

*8 thick broccoli stalks, peeled and cut
 into matchstick-size pieces, 2 inches
 long
2 large tomatoes, seeded and chopped
2 cloves garlic, minced
4 teaspoons lemon juice*

*2 tablespoons red wine vinegar
3 tablespoons light-flavored olive oil
3 tablespoons grated nonfat or reduced-
 fat Parmesan cheese
¼ teaspoon black pepper*

1. Combine broccoli and tomatoes.
2. In a medium bowl, whisk together garlic, lemon juice, vinegar, olive oil, Parmesan cheese, and pepper.
3. Add broccoli and tomatoes to bowl with dressing and toss.
4. Chill for 1 hour. Serve with small plates and cocktail forks.

Calories Per Serving: 47
Fat: 4 g
Cholesterol: 1 mg
Protein: 2 g

Carbohydrates: 3 g
Dietary Fiber: 1 g
Sodium: 21 mg

❧ *Garlic-Chile Brussels Sprouts* ❧

YIELD: 8 servings (2 to 3 each) • *PREPARATION TIME: 15 minutes plus overnight refrigeration time* • *COOKING TIME: 15 minutes*

Brussels sprouts are simmered in a tangy sauce.

24 fresh brussels sprouts
1 cup white wine vinegar
½ cup water

2 cloves garlic, chopped
1 dried chile pepper

1. Remove outer leaves of brussels sprouts, cut an X in their bottoms, and soak in lukewarm water for 15 minutes.
2. Place brussels sprouts, vinegar, water, garlic, and chile pepper in a saucepan. Bring to a boil, lower the heat, and simmer for 10 minutes or until sprouts are tender-crisp.
3. Cool and place brussels sprouts and liquid from saucepan in a glass jar. Cover and refrigerate overnight. Serve with wooden or plastic party picks.

Calories Per Serving: 36
Fat: 0 g
Cholesterol: 0 mg
Protein: 4 g

Carbohydrates: 6 g
Dietary Fiber: 3 g
Sodium: 45 mg

❧ *Dilled Brussels Sprouts* ❧

YIELD: 12 servings (2 each) • *PREPARATION TIME: 15 minutes plus overnight refrigeration time* • *COOKING TIME: 10 to 15 minutes*

Steamed brussels sprouts are chilled overnight in a lemon-garlic marinade.

24 fresh brussels sprouts
3 tablespoons light-flavored olive oil
¼ cup lemon juice
2 tablespoons finely chopped onion

1 clove garlic, minced
½ teaspoon dried dill
¼ teaspoon black pepper

1. Remove outer leaves of brussels sprouts, cut an X in their bottoms, and soak in lukewarm water for 15 minutes.
2. Steam brussels sprouts until tender-crisp (about 10 to 15 minutes). Drain and rinse in cold water.
3. In a medium bowl, whisk together oil, lemon juice, onion, garlic, dill, and pepper.
4. Add brussels sprouts and toss.
5. Cover and chill overnight, tightly covered. Serve with wooden or plastic party picks.

Calories Per Serving: 65

Carbohydrates: 8 g

Fat: 3 g

Dietary Fiber: 4 g

Cholesterol: 0 mg

Sodium: 22 mg

Protein: 3 g

❧ *Cabbage Rolls* ❧

YIELD: *6 servings (2 each)* • PREPARATION TIME: *30 minutes plus 1 hour refrigeration time*

Napa cabbage leaves are filled with marinated vegetables, and rolled.

1 head napa cabbage

1 teaspoon sugar

1 carrot

1 tablespoon light-flavored olive or

1 stalk celery

   sesame oil

1 cup rice vinegar

2 tablespoons dried cilantro

1. Remove the leaves from the napa cabbage. Wash and set aside. Cut the root sections of the napa cabbage into 2½-inch lengths. Cut these sections into thin strips.
2. Cut carrot and celery into similar thin strips.
3. Combine vinegar, sugar, and oil in a large glass bowl. Add whole napa cabbage leaves and vegetable strips. Press down gently with a wooden spoon so that marinade covers all the vegetables. Refrigerate for 1 hour, occasionally stirring and re-covering vegetables with the marinade.
4. Remove napa cabbage leaves and drain.
5. Drain marinated vegetable strips and sprinkle with cilantro.

6. Place a spoonful of marinated vegetables in the bottom half of each cabbage leaf. Fold the two sides toward the middle, then roll from the bottom up. Serve with plates and cocktail forks.

Calories Per Serving: 53
Fat: 2 g
Cholesterol: 0 mg
Protein: 4 g

Carbohydrates: 3 g
Dietary Fiber: 1 g
Sodium: 27 mg

❧ *Sweet-and-Sour Carrots* ❧

YIELD: 10 servings (3 each) • *PREPARATION TIME: 15 minutes plus 2 days refrigeration time* • *COOKING TIME: 12 minutes*

Small, steamed carrots are marinated in a multiflavored dressing.

1 pound baby carrots
2 dried bay leaves
½ cup white wine vinegar
¼ cup water

3 tablespoons sugar
½ teaspoon dried dill
¼ teaspoon crushed red pepper
1 clove garlic, minced

1. Boil water in the bottom of a vegetable steamer. Place carrots in a steamer basket over boiling water, cover, and steam for 12 minutes or until tender-crisp.
2. Plunge into cold water and drain.
3. Combine bay leaves, vinegar, water, sugar, dill, crushed red pepper, and garlic and stir until sugar is dissolved. Pour over carrots in a glass jar, cover, and refrigerate for 2 days. Drain and serve with wooden or plastic party picks.

Calories Per Serving: 46
Fat: 0 g
Cholesterol: 0 mg
Protein: 1 g

Carbohydrates: 12 g
Dietary Fiber: 1 g
Sodium: 16 mg

❧ *Spicy Cauliflower Florets* ❧

YIELD: 16 servings (¼ cup each) • *PREPARATION TIME: 15 minutes* •
COOKING TIME: 10 minutes

Cauliflower florets are seasoned Indian-style and cooked in apple juice and lemon juice.

2 tablespoons light-flavored olive oil	*½ teaspoon turmeric*
4 cups cauliflower florets	*⅛ teaspoon ground cayenne pepper*
2 teaspoons minced fresh gingerroot	*½ cup natural apple juice*
1 teaspoon ground coriander	*2 tablespoons lemon juice*

1. Heat oil in a skillet over medium heat.
2. In a medium bowl, toss cauliflower florets with gingerroot, coriander, turmeric, and cayenne.
3. Add cauliflower and seasonings to skillet and stir several times.
4. Pour in apple juice and lemon juice. Cover and simmer for 5 minutes or until cauliflower is tender-crisp.
5. Serve warm or room temperature with wooden or plastic party picks.

Calories Per Serving: 29	Carbohydrates: 3 g
Fat: 2 g	Dietary Fiber: 1 g
Cholesterol: 0 mg	Sodium: 19 mg
Protein: 1 g	

❧ *Cauliflower with Parsley and Scallions* ❧

YIELD: 12 servings (⅓ cup each) • *PREPARATION TIME: 15 minutes plus
overnight refrigeration time*

Cauliflower florets are marinated overnight, then tossed with parsley and scallions.

4 cups cauliflower florets	¼ teaspoon black pepper
1 tablespoon dried basil	1 cup white wine vinegar
½ teaspoon dried oregano	2 tablespoons light-flavored olive oil
1 clove garlic, minced	3 tablespoons chopped fresh parsley
½ teaspoon mustard seeds	3 tablespoons chopped scallions

1. Place cauliflower in a steamer basket over boiling water and steam for 3 minutes.
2. Immediately plunge cauliflower into cold water. Drain, and transfer to a glass bowl.
3. Place basil, oregano, garlic, mustard seeds, black pepper, and vinegar in a saucepan and bring to a boil.
4. Pour vinegar mixture over cauliflower and toss gently. Cover and refrigerate overnight.
5. Drain cauliflower and sprinkle with oil.
6. Toss with parsley and scallions. Serve with wooden or plastic party picks.

Calories Per Serving: 37	Carbohydrates: 2 g
Fat: 2 g	Dietary Fiber: 0 g
Cholesterol: 0 mg	Sodium: 12 mg
Protein: 2 g	

❧ *Cauliflower with Curry Sauce* ❧

YIELD: 16 servings (¼ cup each) • *PREPARATION TIME: 10 minutes* • *COOKING TIME: 13 minutes*

Steamed cauliflower florets are served with a tomato-honey-curry sauce.

4 cups cauliflower florets	2 cups canned, low-sodium tomato
1 tablespoon light-flavored olive oil	puree
1 small onion, diced	1 tablespoon honey
1 stalk celery, diced	2 tablespoons curry powder

1. Place cauliflower florets in a steamer basket over boiling water and steam for 3 minutes, or until tender-crisp. Plunge into cold water, drain, and set aside.

2. Heat the olive oil in a skillet over medium heat. Add the onion and celery and sauté for 10 minutes or until tender.
3. Place onion-celery mixture, tomato puree, honey, and curry powder in a blender or food processor and blend for 30 seconds.
4. Pour the sauce into a serving bowl and surround with cauliflower florets. Serve with wooden or plastic party picks.

Calories Per Serving: 36
Fat: 1 g
Cholesterol: 0 mg
Protein: 1 g

Carbohydrates: 6 g
Dietary Fiber: 1 g
Sodium: 14 mg

❧ *Cold Cauliflower with Shrimp* ❧

YIELD: 14 servings (1 cauliflower floret, 1 shrimp each) • *PREPARATION TIME: 15 minutes plus 20 minutes refrigeration time* • *COOKING TIME: 4 minutes*

Cauliflower florets and steamed shrimp are marinated in soy sauce and sesame oil.

*1 small head cauliflower, separated into
   small florets
½ pound cooked medium shrimp,
   shelled and deveined*

*1 tablespoon light soy sauce
½ teaspoon canola or light-flavored
   sesame oil*

1. Place cauliflower florets in a steamer basket over boiling water and steam for 3 minutes. Rinse with cold water, and drain.
2. Place cauliflower and cooked shrimp in a bowl.
3. Add soy sauce and oil. Toss.
4. Refrigerate, covered, for 20 minutes. Serve with wooden or plastic party picks.

Calories Per Serving: 26
Fat: 0 g
Cholesterol: 24 mg
Protein: 5 g

Carbohydrates: 2 g
Dietary Fiber: 2 g
Sodium: 173 mg

❧ *Orange and Raisin–Stuffed Celery* ✍

YIELD: 20 servings (2 each) • *PREPARATION TIME: 25 minutes*

A cheese mixture with oranges, raisins, and scallions makes a festive filling for crisp celery sticks.

3 ounces nonfat or reduced-fat cream cheese
3 ounces nonfat or reduced-fat cheddar cheese
2 ounces raisins
1 orange, peeled, seeded, and chopped
1 teaspoon grated orange peel
1 tablespoon minced scallions
5 to 6 stalks celery, trimmed

1. Combine cream cheese, cheddar cheese, raisins, orange, orange peel, and scallions.
2. Spread filling into celery stalks.
3. Cut into 40 1½-inch segments.

Calories Per Serving: 24
Fat: 0 g
Cholesterol: 1 mg
Protein: 2 g

Carbohydrates: 4 g
Dietary Fiber: 0 g
Sodium: 99 mg

❧ *Celery Boats Stuffed with Red Peppers* ✍

YIELD: 12 servings (2 each) • *PREPARATION TIME: 25 minutes* •
COOKING TIME: 40 minutes

Celery segments, packed with a delectable combination of bread crumbs, mozzarella cheese, and red peppers, are baked and served piping hot.

2 tablespoons light-flavored olive oil
1 small onion, finely chopped
1 clove garlic, chopped
1 red bell pepper, seeded and finely chopped
2 tablespoons capers, drained
½ cup fresh bread crumbs
½ cup nonfat or reduced-fat mozzarella cheese, shredded
3 tablespoons chopped fresh parsley
¼ teaspoon black pepper
8 stalks celery, cut into 24 3-inch lengths
Olive oil cooking spray

1. Preheat oven to 375 degrees. Heat oil in a skillet over medium heat. Add onion, garlic, and red bell pepper and sauté for 3 minutes. Remove from heat.
2. Stir in capers, bread crumbs, cheese, parsley, and black pepper.
3. Spoon cheese mixture into celery boats. Spray a shallow baking dish with olive oil cooking spray. Arrange celery in dish. Cover with foil and bake for 20 minutes. Remove foil and bake for 10 minutes more until celery is tender. Serve immediately.

Calories Per Serving: 62
Fat: 3 g
Cholesterol: 2 mg
Protein: 4 g

Carbohydrates: 6 g
Dietary Fiber: 1 g
Sodium: 130 mg

❧ *Pesto-Stuffed Celery* ❧

YIELD: 12 servings (2 each) • *PREPARATION TIME: 20 minutes*

Celery stalks are filled with a pesto created from parsley, walnuts, and Parmesan cheese.

2 cups chopped fresh parsley
2 cloves garlic
½ cup grated nonfat or reduced-fat
  Parmesan cheese
¼ cup chopped walnuts

2 tablespoons light-flavored olive oil
2 tablespoons nonfat or reduced-fat,
  low-sodium chicken broth
8 stalks celery, trimmed

1. Place parsley, garlic, Parmesan cheese, walnuts, olive oil, and broth in a blender or food processor and process until smooth.
2. Stuff celery stalks with parsley pesto.
3. Cut stalks into 24 3-inch pieces.

Calories Per Serving: 49
Fat: 3 g
Cholesterol: 3 mg
Protein: 2 g

Carbohydrates: 3 g
Dietary Fiber: 1 g
Sodium: 63 mg

❧ *Three Cheese—Stuffed Celery* ❧

YIELD: 15 servings (2 each) • *PREPARATION TIME: 30 minutes*

Bite-size pieces of crisp celery are stuffed with a medley of cheeses.

*8 ounces nonfat or reduced-fat cream
  cheese, softened*
¼ cup blue cheese, crumbled
*½ cup nonfat or reduced-fat cheddar
  cheese*

½ teaspoon paprika
10 stalks celery, trimmed

1. Place cream cheese, blue cheese, cheddar cheese, and paprika in bowl of an electric mixer and beat at medium speed until well blended.
2. Fill celery stalks with cheese mixture.
3. Cut stalks into 30 3-inch pieces.

Calories Per Serving: 44
Fat: 1 g
Cholesterol: 4 mg
Protein: 6 g

Carbohydrates: 3 g
Dietary Fiber: 1 g
Sodium: 307 mg

❧ *Cucumber-Crab Canapés* ❧

YIELD: 18 servings (2 each) • *PREPARATION TIME: 25 minutes*

These crisp cucumber slices spread with a crabmeat—sour cream mixture make elegant appetizers.

6 ounces cooked crabmeat, drained
*2 tablespoons nonfat or reduced-fat
  sour cream*
2 tablespoons chopped scallions

⅛ teaspoon black pepper
2 medium seedless cucumbers
Paprika

1. Combine crabmeat, sour cream, scallions, and pepper.
2. Cut cucumber into slices ¼ inch thick.

3. Mound a small spoonful of crab mixture onto each cucumber round.
4. Sprinkle with paprika.

Calories Per Serving: 14   Carbohydrates: 1 g
Fat: 0 g   Dietary Fiber: 0 g
Cholesterol: 9 mg   Sodium: 33 mg
Protein: 2 g

❦ *Cucumber–Salmon–Cream Cheese Slices* ❦

YIELD: 20 servings (2 each) • *PREPARATION TIME: 30 minutes
plus 30 minutes refrigeration time*

Fresh cucumber slices are topped with a cream cheese and smoked salmon spread.

*8 ounces nonfat or reduced-fat cream   2 tablespoons skim or 1% milk
  cheese, softened   ⅛ teaspoon white pepper
2 ounces smoked salmon   2 medium seedless cucumbers
¼ teaspoon lemon juice*

1. Place cream cheese, smoked salmon, lemon juice, milk, and white pepper in a food processor or blender. Blend until smooth. Chill for 30 minutes.
2. Cut each cucumber into 20 slices approximately ¼ inch thick.
3. Place a dab of the chilled cream cheese mixture on each cucumber round.

Calories Per Serving: 20   Carbohydrates: 2 g
Fat: 0 g   Dietary Fiber: 0 g
Cholesterol: 3 mg   Sodium: 103 mg
Protein: 3 g

❧ *Cucumber-Tuna Boats* ❧

YIELD: 24 servings (4 each) • *PREPARATION TIME: 25 minutes
plus 4 hours refrigeration time*

This crowd-pleasing appetizer features cucumbers stuffed with a savory mixture of tuna, red peppers, and celery.

*6½ ounces canned, water-packed,
white albacore tuna, drained and
flaked
½ cup whole wheat bread crumbs
1 stalk celery, finely chopped
¼ cup finely chopped red bell
pepper
1 scallion, finely chopped
1 tablespoon minced fresh parsley
2 teaspoons lemon juice*

*2 tablespoons nonfat or reduced-fat
plain yogurt
2 tablespoons nonfat or reduced-fat
mayonnaise
1½ teaspoons light-flavored olive oil
1 teaspoon Dijon mustard
¼ teaspoon dried tarragon
⅛ teaspoon black pepper
4 medium cucumbers, cut into halves
lengthwise*

1. Mix together the tuna, bread crumbs, celery, red pepper, scallion, parsley, lemon juice, yogurt, mayonnaise, olive oil, mustard, tarragon, and black pepper.
2. Scoop out the centers of the cucumbers, leaving a ¼-inch shell.
3. Stuff the tuna mixture into each cucumber half, wrap in plastic wrap, and refrigerate for at least 4 hours.
4. Cut the stuffed cucumber halves into ½-inch slices.

Calories Per Serving: 31
Fat: 1 g
Cholesterol: 3 mg
Protein: 3 g

Carbohydrates: 4 g
Dietary Fiber: 0 g
Sodium: 66 mg

Cucumber Cups
❧ Stuffed with Lemon-Dill Shrimp ❧

YIELD: 12 servings (2 each) • *PREPARATION TIME: 20 minutes*
plus 1 hour refrigeration time

These little cucumber cups filled with a tangy shrimp mixture make simple but fancy appetizers.

4 small seedless cucumbers, peeled
¾ cup chopped cooked shrimp
½ teaspoon dried dill
1½ tablespoons nonfat or reduced-fat
  mayonnaise

½ teaspoon lemon juice
⅛ teaspoon black pepper

1. Trim ends of cucumbers. Cut each cucumber into 6 slices ¾ inch thick.
2. Using a melon-ball scoop, scoop out a hollow in the center of each cucumber slice, leaving a bottom layer.
3. Combine shrimp, dill, mayonnaise, lemon juice, and black pepper.
4. Top each cucumber cup with a small mound of the shrimp mixture. Chill 1 hour before serving.

Calories Per Serving: 15
Fat: 0 g
Cholesterol: 12 mg
Protein: 2 g

Carbohydrates: 2 g
Dietary Fiber: 0 g
Sodium: 72 mg

❧ Cucumber Rounds with Walnut Chicken ❧

YIELD: 20 servings (2 each) • *PREPARATION TIME: 25 minutes*

These delicious bites consist of chicken salad spread on crisp cucumber rounds.

1 cup shredded, cooked chicken breast
1 teaspoon dried tarragon
½ cup nonfat or reduced-fat mayon-
　　naise

¼ cup finely chopped celery
¼ cup chopped walnuts
¼ teaspoon black pepper
2 medium seedless cucumbers

1. Combine shredded chicken, tarragon, mayonnaise, celery, walnuts, and black pepper.
2. Slice cucumbers into 40 ¼-inch slices.
3. Spoon chicken salad on top of cucumber slices.

Calories Per Serving: 36
Fat: 1 g
Cholesterol: 7 mg
Protein: 3 g

Carbohydrates: 3 g
Dietary Fiber: 0 g
Sodium: 8 mg

＞ *Caponata* ＜

YIELD: 24 servings (¼ cup each) • PREPARATION TIME: 20 minutes plus overnight refrigeration time • COOKING TIME: 10 minutes

Serve this superb blend of vegetables in a glass bowl with a platter of toasted baguette slices that have been rubbed with garlic.

2 tablespoons light-flavored olive oil
1 small eggplant, peeled and cut into
　　½-inch cubes (approximately 4 cups)
¼ cup chopped onion
¼ cup chopped leek
¾ cup chopped fresh or canned, low-
　　sodium tomatoes

½ cup chopped green bell pepper
3 tablespoons red wine vinegar
1 teaspoon sugar
⅛ teaspoon ground cayenne pepper
½ cup sliced, pitted black olives
1 tablespoon chopped fresh parsley

1. Heat olive oil in a skillet over medium heat. Sauté eggplant, onion, and leek in oil for 6 minutes or until tender.
2. Add tomatoes, green pepper, vinegar, sugar, and cayenne. Cook for 3 minutes.
3. When eggplant mixture has cooled, stir in olives and parsley. Transfer to a glass bowl and refrigerate overnight. Bring to room temperature before serving.

Calories Per Serving: 21
Fat: 1 g
Cholesterol: 0 mg
Protein: 0 g

Carbohydrates: 2 g
Dietary Fiber: 0 g
Sodium: 2 mg

❧ *Sautéed Japanese Eggplant* ❧

YIELD: 20 servings (2 each) • *PREPARATION TIME: 10 minutes* •
COOKING TIME: 15 minutes

Narrow, straight Japanese eggplant ranges in color from solid purple to striated shades. It can be found in the gourmet produce section of your supermarket. It is especially well suited to appetizer dishes because it produces slices with small diameters and is quite tender and sweet.

5 small Japanese eggplants　　　　　*Black pepper*
¼ cup light-flavored olive oil

1. Cut eggplants into 40 slices ½ inch thick.
2. Heat part of the olive oil in a skillet over medium heat.
3. Sauté the eggplant slices for 3 minutes. Turn slices and sauté for 2 minutes more or until the slices have all been lightly browned. Add more oil as necessary.
4. Drain eggplant on paper towels. Sprinkle with pepper and transfer to serving plate. Serve with wooden or plastic party picks.

Calories Per Serving: 31
Fat: 3 g
Cholesterol: 0 mg
Protein: 0 g

Carbohydrates: 1 g
Dietary Fiber: 0 g
Sodium: 1 mg

❧ *Stuffed Eggplant* ❧

YIELD: 12 servings (½ eggplant each) • *PREPARATION TIME: 20 minutes* •
COOKING TIME: 45 minutes

Rice and spiced tomato sauce are spooned into eggplant shells.

6 narrow, purple Japanese eggplants	*2 medium tomatoes, seeded and*
3 tablespoons light-flavored olive oil	*chopped*
¼ cup water or nonfat or reduced-fat,	*1½ cups cooked rice*
low-sodium chicken broth	*½ cup chopped fresh parsley*
1 large onion, diced	*½ teaspoon dried mint*
4 cloves garlic, minced	*¼ teaspoon black pepper*

1. Preheat oven to 400 degrees. Slice each eggplant in half lengthwise and rub it inside and out with olive oil.
2. Place cut side down on a baking sheet and bake 20 minutes, or until the inside is soft. Remove from oven and cool to room temperature. Leave oven on.
3. When the eggplant has cooled, gently scoop out the flesh, leaving a ¼-inch shell. Place half of the scooped-out flesh in a bowl and set aside.
4. Heat the water or broth in a skillet over medium heat. Add onion and garlic and sauté until tender.
5. Add the tomatoes and cook for 4 minutes or until the juices have evaporated.
6. Stir in the reserved eggplant, rice, parsley, mint, and pepper.
7. Spoon the filling into the eggplant shells and place on a baking sheet.
8. Place in oven and heat for 10 minutes or until warmed through. Serve with plates and cocktail forks.

Calories Per Serving: 54	Carbohydrates: 9 g
Fat: 2 g	Dietary Fiber: 1 g
Cholesterol: 0 mg	Sodium: 13 mg
Protein: 1 g	

✎ *Balsamic Eggplant Coins* ✎

YIELD: *24 servings (2 each)* • PREPARATION TIME: *10 minutes* •
COOKING TIME: *15 minutes*

Slices of eggplant are served marinated in an oil and balsamic vinegar dressing flavored with herbs.

3 small eggplants
¼ cup light-flavored olive oil
4 cloves garlic, minced
1 teaspoon dried basil

1 teaspoon dried thyme
1 teaspoon dried oregano
1 tablespoon balsamic vinegar

1. Cut eggplant into 48 slices ⅓ inch thick.
2. Heat half of the oil in a skillet over medium heat. Sauté eggplant slices in oil until lightly golden and tender. Add more oil to skillet as needed.
3. Drain eggplant slices on paper towels.
4. Sauté garlic in skillet until lightly browned. Remove skillet from heat.
5. Add basil, thyme, oregano, and vinegar to skillet and whisk together with garlic.
6. Arrange eggplant slices on a platter and sprinkle with herb dressing. Serve with wooden or plastic party picks.

Calories Per Serving: 25
Fat: 2 g
Cholesterol: 0 g
Protein: 0 g

Carbohydrates: 1 g
Dietary Fiber: 0 g
Sodium: 1 mg

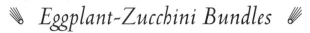 Eggplant-Zucchini Bundles

YIELD: 15 servings (2 each) • *PREPARATION TIME: 30 minutes* •
COOKING TIME: 55 minutes

Lettuce leaves wrapped around a Mediterranean vegetable mixture make up
these sumptuous bundles.

3 tablespoons light-flavored olive oil
2 large onions, diced
6 cloves garlic, minced
1 medium eggplant, diced
½ teaspoon dried thyme
½ teaspoon dried oregano
½ teaspoon dried basil
½ teaspoon dried marjoram
¼ teaspoon ground cayenne pepper

2 stalks celery, diced
1 zucchini, diced
½ cup balsamic vinegar
½ cup tomatoes, chopped
¼ teaspoon black pepper
½ cup chopped, pitted black olives
　(optional)
3 tablespoons capers, drained (optional)
30 large green leaf lettuce leaves

1. Heat the oil in a skillet over medium heat. Add the onions and garlic and
   sauté until tender.
2. Add the eggplant, thyme, oregano, basil, marjoram, and cayenne pepper
   and cook until the eggplant is tender, about 15 minutes.
3. Add the celery, zucchini, and balsamic vinegar and cook over high heat
   for 5 minutes, stirring constantly.
4. Add the tomatoes and black pepper and reduce the heat to low. Cook for
   20 minutes, until the mixture is thick and soft. Add the olives and capers,
   if using. Cool to room temperature.
5. Place 2 tablespoons of vegetable mixture on the bottom half of each lettuce leaf. Fold the bottom of the leaf over the filling, fold in the sides, and
   continue to roll the leaf. Serve with plates and cocktail forks.

Calories Per Serving: 57
Fat: 3 g
Cholesterol: 0 mg
Protein: 1 g

Carbohydrates: 7 g
Dietary Fiber: 1 g
Sodium: 12 mg

❧ *Endive with Curried Chicken* ❧

YIELD: *12 servings (2 each)* • PREPARATION TIME: *20 minutes*

Curried chicken with crunchy water chestnuts creates an exotic filling for Belgian endive leaves.

*1 cup finely chopped, cooked chicken
   breast*
¼ cup nonfat or reduced-fat mayonnaise
2 tablespoons chopped water chestnuts

2 teaspoons curry powder
⅛ teaspoon black pepper
*24 Belgian endive leaves (2 to 3
   heads), stem ends trimmed*

1. Combine chicken, mayonnaise, water chestnuts, curry powder, and black pepper.
2. Place a teaspoon of chicken mixture on each Belgian endive leaf.

Calories Per Serving: 33
Fat: 1 g
Cholesterol: 11 mg
Protein: 4 g

Carbohydrates: 2 g
Dietary Fiber: 1 g
Sodium: 15 mg

❧ *Endive with Shrimp* ❧

YIELD: *12 servings (2 each)* • PREPARATION TIME: *20 minutes*

Shrimp and pimento are served in Belgian endive leaves.

2 tablespoons light-flavored olive oil
1 tablespoon white wine vinegar
1 teaspoon dried tarragon
1 cup finely chopped cooked shrimp

*2 tablespoons chopped, drained
   pimento*
*24 Belgian endive leaves (2 to 3
   heads), stem ends trimmed*

1. In a medium bowl, whisk together the oil, vinegar, and tarragon. Stir in the shrimp and the pimento.
2. Spoon 1 teaspoon of the shrimp mixture onto each endive leaf and serve.

Calories Per Serving: 39
Fat: 2 g
Cholesterol: 14 mg
Protein: 3 g

Carbohydrates: 2 g
Dietary Fiber: 1 g
Sodium: 73 mg

✎ *Endive-Beet Boats* ✎

YIELD: 25 servings (2 each) • PREPARATION TIME: 20 minutes

A tangy beet mixture fills these endive leaves.

*2 medium, uncooked, fresh beets,
    peeled and grated*
3 tablespoons orange juice
*3 tablespoons light-flavored olive or
    canola oil*

2 tablespoons chopped scallions
⅓ cup nonfat or reduced-fat sour cream
*50 Belgian endive leaves (5 to 6
    heads), stem ends trimmed*

1. Combine beets, orange juice, oil, scallions, and sour cream.
2. When ready to serve, spoon about 2 teaspoons of the beet mixture into
   endive leaves.

Calories Per Serving: 33
Fat: 2 g
Cholesterol: 0 mg
Protein: 1 g

Carbohydrates: 3 g
Dietary Fiber: 1 g
Sodium: 20 mg

✎ *Belgian Endive with Apples and Cream Cheese* ✎

YIELD: 10 servings (2 each) • PREPARATION TIME: 20 minutes

Garlicky cream cheese and tangy apple complement one another in this easy
appetizer.

1 cup water
1 tablespoon lemon juice
*1 small apple, halved and cut into 20
    thin slices*
1 large clove garlic, minced

*8 ounces nonfat or reduced-fat cream
    cheese, softened*
*20 Belgian endive leaves (2 to 3
    heads), stem ends trimmed*

1. Combine water and lemon juice in a medium bowl. Toss apple slices in the lemon water and drain on paper towels.
2. Combine garlic and cream cheese.
3. Spoon about 1 tablespoon of the garlic–cream cheese onto endive leaves.
4. Garnish each stuffed leaf with an apple slice.

Calories Per Serving: 35
Fat: 0 g
Cholesterol: 4 mg
Protein: 5 g

Carbohydrates: 4 g
Dietary Fiber: 1 g
Sodium: 164 mg

❧ *Drizzled Green Beans* ❧

YIELD: 8 servings (½ cup each) • *PREPARATION TIME: 15 minutes* • *COOKING TIME: 8 minutes*

Fresh, whole green beans are drizzled with a sauce of lemon juice, parsley, and mint.

1 pound green beans, ends trimmed
¼ cup lemon juice
¼ cup chopped fresh parsley

1 teaspoon dried mint
¼ teaspoon black pepper
1 tablespoon light-flavored olive oil

1. Cook the beans in a large pot of boiling water for 5 minutes or until just tender. Plunge into cold water, drain, and transfer to a serving plate.
2. Combine lemon juice, parsley, mint, and black pepper in a blender or food processor and process until well combined.
3. Lightly toss beans with olive oil. Drizzle lemon sauce over them and serve at room temperature with plates and cocktail forks.

Calories Per Serving: 40
Fat: 2 g
Cholesterol: 0 mg
Protein: 1 g

Carbohydrates: 6 g
Dietary Fiber: 1 g
Sodium: 3 mg

Tarragon Green Beans
🖋 *with Mustard Dressing* 🖋

YIELD: *24 servings (⅓ cup each)* • PREPARATION TIME: *15 minutes* •
COOKING TIME: *8 minutes*

Select small, slender green beans for this dish, which pairs them with a
snappy mustard dressing.

2 pounds green beans, ends trimmed	*¼ cup light-flavored olive oil*
3 tablespoons Dijon mustard	*1 teaspoon dried tarragon*
3 tablespoons white wine vinegar	*¼ teaspoon black pepper*

1. Bring a large pot of water to a boil. Blanch beans in boiling water for 3
   minutes. Plunge beans into cold water and drain. Transfer to a serving
   platter.
2. Combine mustard, vinegar, olive oil, tarragon, and pepper until smooth.
3. Pour mustard dressing over beans. Serve with plates and cocktail forks.

Calories Per Serving: 40	Carbohydrates: 4 g
Fat: 3 g	Dietary Fiber: 1 g
Cholesterol: 0 mg	Sodium: 96 mg
Protein: 1 g	

🖋 *Jicama-Stuffed Mushrooms* 🖋

YIELD: *10 servings (2 each)* • PREPARATION TIME: *20 minutes* •
COOKING TIME: *15 minutes*

Mushroom caps are stuffed with a mixture of scallions, bread crumbs, and
jicama, which is often called "the Mexican potato."

2 tablespoons light-flavored olive oil	*¾ cup soft bread crumbs*
20 large mushrooms, stems removed	*3 tablespoons chopped scallions*
and chopped	*2 teaspoons light soy sauce*
¼ pound fresh jicama, peeled and	
finely chopped	

1. Preheat oven to 350 degrees. Heat oil in a skillet over medium heat. Sauté caps and chopped stems in the oil for 3 minutes. Remove skillet from heat. Remove caps and drain on paper towels.
2. In the skillet with mushroom stems, add jicama, bread crumbs, scallions, and soy sauce. Stir together until well combined.
3. Stuff mushroom caps with jicama mixture.
4. Place on a baking sheet and bake for 9 minutes. Serve at once.

Calories Per Serving: 70
Fat: 3 g
Cholesterol: 0 mg
Protein: 2 g

Carbohydrates: 9 g
Dietary Fiber: 1 g
Sodium: 116 mg

◈ *Jicama Chips with Jalapeño-Bean Dip* ◈

YIELD: *12 servings (⅓ cup each)* • PREPARATION TIME: *15 minutes*

Crisp vegetable dippers are served with a spicy red kidney bean dish.

1 teaspoon light-flavored olive or
   canola oil
½ cup chopped red onion
1 tablespoon seeded and chopped
   jalapeño pepper
2 cloves garlic, minced
1 teaspoon ground cumin
⅛ teaspoon ground cayenne pepper

½ cup nonfat or reduced-fat plain
   yogurt
16 ounces canned, red kidney beans,
   rinsed and drained
1 jicama, about ¾ pound, peeled and
   sliced into half moons, about ¼ inch
   thick
2 cups diagonally sliced carrots

1. Heat oil in a skillet over medium heat. Add onion, chopped jalapeño pepper, and garlic. Sauté 5 minutes. Add cumin and cayenne pepper. Cook for 1 minute. Remove from heat.
2. Place onion mixture, yogurt, and beans in a blender or food processor and process until smooth.
3. Serve with jicama and carrot dippers.

Calories Per Serving: 60
Fat: 1 g
Cholesterol: 0 mg
Protein: 3 g

Carbohydrates: 11 g
Dietary Fiber: 3 g
Sodium: 192 mg

❦ *Spiced Jicama* ❦

YIELD: 20 servings (2 slices each) • *PREPARATION TIME: 15 minutes*

Jicama is sliced and seasoned with lime juice and chili powder.

2 medium jicamas, peeled and cut into　　*Juice of 2 limes*
　¼-inch slices　　　　　　　　　　　*Chili powder*

1. Place jicama slices on a serving platter.
2. Sprinkle with lime juice and chili powder. Serve with wooden or plastic party picks.

Calories Per Serving: 7　　　　　　Carbohydrates: 2 g
Fat: 0 g　　　　　　　　　　　　　Dietary Fiber: 1 g
Cholesterol: 0 mg　　　　　　　　Sodium: 16 mg
Protein: 0 g

❦ *Hearts of Palm with Vinaigrette* ❦

YIELD: 30 servings (2 each) • *PREPARATION TIME: 10 minutes plus*
30 minutes refrigeration time

Hearts of palm are slender, ivory-colored stalks that resemble white asparagus without a tip. They contain no fat or cholesterol. In this recipe, hearts of palm are drizzled with vinaigrette.

2 scallions, finely chopped　　　　*¼ cup light-flavored olive oil*
1 tomato, finely chopped　　　　　*20 stalks canned hearts of palm,*
⅓ cup minced fresh parsley　　　　　*drained*
½ cup cider vinegar

1. Combine scallions, tomato, parsley, cider vinegar, and olive oil. Chill for 30 minutes.
2. Cut each heart of palm stalk into 3 sections. Arrange on a serving dish.
3. Spoon chilled vinaigrette over hearts of palm. Serve with wooden or plastic party picks.

Calories Per Serving: 20
Fat: 2 g
Cholesterol: 0 mg
Protein: 4 g

Carbohydrates: 1 g
Dietary Fiber: 3 g
Sodium: 55 mg

❧ *Kohlrabi Crudités* ❧

YIELD: 12 servings (⅓ cup each) • *PREPARATION TIME: 15 minutes*

Kohlrabi is an often neglected vegetable that tastes like a cross between a radish and a white turnip. Here, kohlrabi is cut into chunks and served with a sesame-soy dipping sauce.

½ cup light soy sauce
½ cup rice vinegar
1 teaspoon toasted sesame seeds

1 tablespoon minced scallions
4 cups raw kohlrabi chunks

1. Combine soy sauce, vinegar, sesame seeds, and scallions.
2. Serve in a bowl surrounded by kohlrabi chunks. Provide wooden or plastic party picks.

Calories Per Serving: 23
Fat: 0 g
Cholesterol: 0 mg
Protein: 2 g

Carbohydrates: 4 g
Dietary Fiber: 1 g
Sodium: 362 mg

❧ *Spiced Shiitake Mushrooms* ❧

YIELD: 10 servings (2 each) • *PREPARATION TIME: 20 minutes*

These tempting mushrooms are simmered in a sauce flavored with chiles and coriander.

1¼ cups white wine vinegar
1¼ cups water
2 small fresh red chiles, halved lengthwise and seeded
Grated peel of 1 lemon
2 dried bay leaves

2 teaspoons ground coriander
1 teaspoon ground cumin
1 teaspoon whole peppercorns
3 cloves garlic, sliced
1 pound medium-size shiitake mushrooms

1. Combine vinegar, water, chiles, lemon peel, bay leaves, coriander, cumin, peppercorns, and garlic in a saucepan. Bring to a boil.
2. Add the mushrooms and boil 7 to 8 minutes or until tender.
3. Drain mushrooms, cut off and discard stems, and serve with wooden or plastic party picks.

Calories Per Serving: 153
Fat: 1 g
Cholesterol: 0 mg
Protein: 6 g

Carbohydrates: 35 g
Dietary Fiber: 5 g
Sodium: 87 mg

❦ Mushrooms Stuffed with Crab ❦

YIELD: 10 servings (2 each) • *PREPARATION TIME: 25 minutes* •
COOKING TIME: 9 minutes

Mushroom caps are stuffed with a lemon-accented crab mixture, and broiled.

2 tablespoons nonfat or reduced-fat
  plain yogurt
2 egg whites, lightly beaten
2 teaspoons diced onion
1 clove garlic, minced
2 teaspoons minced fresh parsley

1 teaspoon Worcestershire sauce
1½ tablespoons lemon juice
½ pound cooked crabmeat
20 large mushroom caps
¼ cup grated nonfat or reduced-fat
  Parmesan cheese

1. Preheat oven to 425 degrees. Combine yogurt, egg whites, onion, garlic, parsley, Worcestershire sauce, lemon juice, and crabmeat.
2. Stuff mushroom caps with crabmeat mixture. Sprinkle with Parmesan cheese.

3. Arrange stuffed mushroom caps in a shallow baking dish. Bake for 9 minutes and serve at once.

Calories Per Serving: 44
Fat: 1 g
Cholesterol: 19 mg
Protein: 7 g

Carbohydrates: 2 g
Dietary Fiber: 0 g
Sodium: 133 mg

❧ *Mushrooms with Tuna* ❧

YIELD: 8 servings (2 each) • *PREPARATION TIME: 20 minutes* •
COOKING TIME: 12 minutes

A stuffing of albacore tuna, scallions, and carrot blended with whole-grain bread crumbs and nonfat mayonnaise is baked inside snowy-white mushroom caps.

6½ ounces canned, water-packed,
  white albacore tuna, drained
¼ cup soft, whole-grain bread crumbs
¼ cup nonfat or reduced-fat mayonnaise

1 tablespoon chopped scallion
3 tablespoons grated carrot
16 large mushroom caps

1. Preheat oven to 375 degrees. Place tuna, bread crumbs, mayonnaise, and scallion in a blender or food processor and blend until almost smooth.
2. Stir in grated carrot.
3. Mound 1 tablespoon of tuna mixture into each mushroom cap.
4. Place mushrooms in a shallow baking pan. Cover with foil. Bake for 12 minutes or until hot.

Calories Per Serving: 68
Fat: 1 g
Cholesterol: 9 mg
Protein: 8 g

Carbohydrates: 7 g
Dietary Fiber: 1 g
Sodium: 122 mg

Mushrooms in
Coriander-Wine Sauce

YIELD: 20 servings (2 each) • *PREPARATION TIME: 20 minutes plus overnight refrigeration time* • *COOKING TIME: 7 minutes*

These mushrooms are marinated in a combination of olive oil, white wine, lemon juice, garlic, fennel seeds, and ground coriander. While coriander seeds and coriander leaves (also called cilantro or Chinese parsley) come from the same plant, they have completely different flavors. Ground coriander is available on the spice rack at your supermarket.

⅓ cup light-flavored olive oil	¼ teaspoon black pepper
¼ cup dry white wine	1 teaspoon sugar
2 tablespoons lemon juice	¼ teaspoon fennel seeds
½ cup water	½ teaspoon ground coriander
1 clove garlic, minced	1 pound small mushrooms

1. Place oil, wine, lemon juice, water, garlic, pepper, sugar, fennel seeds, and coriander in a saucepan. Bring to a boil. Reduce heat and simmer for 2 minutes.
2. Place mushrooms in a nonaluminum heat-resistant bowl and pour marinade over them. Allow to reach room temperature.
3. Cover bowl and place in refrigerator overnight. Serve with wooden or plastic party picks.

Calories Per Serving: 33	Carbohydrates: 1 g
Fat: 3 g	Dietary Fiber: 0 g
Cholesterol: 0 mg	Sodium: 1 mg
Protein: 0 g	

Sautéed Mushroom Caps
🌿 in Garlic-Parsley Sauce 🌿

YIELD: *20 servings (3 each)* • PREPARATION TIME: *10 minutes* •
COOKING TIME: *10 minutes*

Fresh parsley and garlic flavor mushroom caps that are sautéed in olive oil.

2 tablespoons light-flavored olive oil
3 cloves garlic, 1 whole and 2 minced
1½ pounds small mushroom caps

1 tablespoon finely chopped fresh
  parsley
¼ teaspoon black pepper

1. Heat olive oil in a skillet over medium heat. Add whole garlic clove and mushroom caps. Sauté mushrooms for 1 minute.
2. Stir in minced garlic and chopped parsley.
3. Season with pepper. Serve warm with wooden or plastic party picks.

Calories Per Serving: 18
Fat: 2 g
Cholesterol: 0 mg
Protein: 1 g

Carbohydrates: 1 g
Dietary Fiber: 0 g
Sodium: 1 mg

🌿 Mushrooms in Herb Sauce 🌿

YIELD: *20 servings (2 each)* • PREPARATION TIME: *15 minutes plus overnight*
refrigeration time • COOKING TIME: *7 minutes*

Thyme, which has a pungent, minty, light-lemon aroma, is combined with garlic, oregano, onion, paprika, and red wine vinegar as a marinade for small white mushrooms.

1 pound small mushrooms
⅓ cup light-flavored olive oil
½ cup red wine vinegar
1 clove garlic, minced
¾ teaspoon dried thyme

¼ teaspoon dried oregano
¼ teaspoon black pepper
¼ teaspoon ground paprika
1 small onion, thinly sliced

1. Bring water to a boil in the bottom of a steamer. Place mushrooms in a steamer basket, cover, and steam for 1 minute.
2. Plunge mushrooms into cold water and drain.
3. Combine oil, vinegar, garlic, thyme, oregano, pepper, paprika, and onion in a large glass bowl.
4. Add steamed mushrooms and stir well.
5. Cover and place in refrigerator overnight. Serve with wooden or plastic party picks.

Calories Per Serving: 34
Fat: 3 g
Cholesterol: 0 mg
Protein: 1 g

Carbohydrates: 1 g
Dietary Fiber: 0 g
Sodium: 1 mg

☙ *Spinach Mushrooms* ❧

YIELD: 6 servings (2 each) • *PREPARATION TIME: 25 minutes* •
COOKING TIME: 20 minutes

Fresh chopped spinach cooked with garlic, oregano, and lemon juice is stuffed into large mushroom caps.

½ pound fresh spinach, stems trimmed
12 large mushrooms
1 tablespoon light-flavored olive oil
1 clove garlic, minced

¼ teaspoon dried oregano
1 tablespoon lemon juice
2 tablespoons dry bread crumbs
Olive oil cooking spray

1. Preheat oven to 400 degrees. Place spinach in a heavy saucepan with 2 tablespoons water. Cook over medium heat for 2 minutes or until wilted.
2. Cool, drain, and squeeze spinach to remove any remaining water. Finely chop and set aside.
3. Remove mushroom stems and finely chop.
4. Heat olive oil in a skillet over medium heat. Sauté garlic and chopped mushroom stems for 5 minutes or until lightly browned.
5. Stir in spinach and oregano. Sauté for 1 minute.
6. Stir in lemon juice. Remove from heat.
7. Fill mushroom caps with spinach mixture. Top with bread crumbs.

8. Spray a baking pan with olive oil cooking spray. Place mushrooms on pan. Bake for 12 minutes or until topping is lightly golden. Serve hot.

Calories Per Serving: 46
Fat: 3 g
Cholesterol: 0 mg
Protein: 2 g

Carbohydrates: 5 g
Dietary Fiber: 1 g
Sodium: 50 mg

❦ *Potato-Tomato Delights* ❦

YIELD: 15 servings (1 each) • *PREPARATION TIME: 15 minutes* •
COOKING TIME: 2 minutes plus potato-baking time

This hearty Italian-style appetizer features broiled baked potato slices topped with bubbling mozzarella cheese, sun-dried tomatoes, oregano, and parsley.

3 baking potatoes, baked until just tender, at room temperature
½ cup grated nonfat or reduced-fat mozzarella cheese
3 tablespoons finely chopped sun-dried tomatoes in oil

½ teaspoon dried oregano
1 tablespoon finely chopped fresh parsley

1. Preheat broiler. Slice unpeeled baked potatoes into 15 ½-inch slices.
2. Combine cheese, tomatoes, and oregano.
3. Arrange potato slices in a baking dish.
4. Top each potato slice with ½ tablespoon of the cheese mixture.
5. Broil for 2 minutes or until bubbly.
6. Sprinkle with chopped parsley and serve immediately.

Calories Per Serving: 57
Fat: 0 g
Cholesterol: 1 mg
Protein: 3 g

Carbohydrates: 11 g
Dietary Fiber: 1 g
Sodium: 71 mg

❧ Garlic-Parsley New Potato Bites ❧

YIELD: *16 servings (2 halves each)* • PREPARATION TIME: *15 minutes* •
COOKING TIME: *50 minutes*

Tiny new potatoes are roasted with olive oil, whole garlic cloves, and fresh parsley.

2 pounds tiny new potatoes, halved
2 tablespoons light-flavored olive oil
1 head garlic, cloves peeled

4 cups minced fresh parsley
¼ teaspoon black pepper

1. Preheat oven to 350 degrees. Toss the potatoes with the olive oil, whole garlic cloves, and 1½ cups of the parsley.
2. Transfer to a baking dish. Bake for 50 minutes or until potatoes are fork-tender, stirring several times.
3. Toss with remaining parsley and black pepper before serving. Serve with wooden or plastic party picks.

Calories Per Serving: 67
Fat: 2 g
Cholesterol: 0 mg
Protein: 2 g

Carbohydrates: 11 g
Dietary Fiber: 1 g
Sodium: 13 mg

❧ Rosemary Potatoes ❧

YIELD: *24 servings (2 halves each)* • PREPARATION TIME: *15 minutes* •
COOKING TIME: *50 minutes*

These fragrant potatoes can be served with a variety of dipping sauces such as a fresh tomato sauce with garlic or a yogurt-spinach sauce.

1 tablespoon light-flavored olive oil
24 small, red-skinned new potatoes

2 teaspoons dried rosemary
¼ teaspoon black pepper

1. Preheat oven to 350 degrees. Lightly coat a glass baking dish with the olive oil and place it in the oven to heat for 3 minutes.
2. Cut the potatoes in half, arrange them on the baking dish, sprinkle with rosemary, and bake for 45 minutes, or until tender.
3. Season with pepper and serve warm with wooden or plastic party picks.

Calories Per Serving: 34   Carbohydrates: 8 g
Fat: 0 g   Dietary Fiber: 1 g
Cholesterol: 0 mg   Sodium: 2 mg
Protein: 1 g

❦ *Stuffed New Potatoes* ❦

YIELD: 8 servings (1 each) • *PREPARATION TIME: 20 minutes* •
COOKING TIME: 20 minutes

These new potatoes filled with an herb-and-cheese stuffing make elegant appetizers.

8 small new potatoes   *2 tablespoons minced scallions*
½ cup nonfat or reduced-fat cottage   *1 teaspoon dried dill*
  cheese   *¼ teaspoon black pepper*
2 tablespoons minced fresh parsley

1. Bring water to a boil in the bottom of a steamer and set potatoes in steamer basket. Cover and steam for 10 to 12 minutes or until tender.
2. Place cottage cheese in a blender or food processor and blend until smooth.
3. Place blended cottage cheese in a small bowl and stir in parsley, scallions, dill, and black pepper.
4. Slice about ½ inch off the top of each potato, and trim bottoms so they will not tip. Scoop out a hollow in the top of each potato and fill the cavity with the cheese mixture.

Calories Per Serving: 77   Carbohydrates: 16 g
Fat: 0 g   Dietary Fiber: 1 g
Cholesterol: 1 mg   Sodium: 51 mg
Protein: 3 g

❧ *Corn-Stuffed Potatoes* ❧

YIELD: *20 servings (2 halves each)* • PREPARATION TIME: *30 minutes* •
COOKING TIME: *20 minutes*

Corn and red bell pepper provide the stuffing for these southwestern-style
potato hors d'oeuvres.

20 small new potatoes
1½ cups cooked fresh or canned,
drained corn
1 medium red bell pepper, seeded and
minced

2 teaspoons dried sage
4 teaspoons red wine vinegar
3 tablespoons light-flavored olive oil

1. Bring water to a boil in the bottom of a steamer and set the new potatoes
   in the steamer basket. Cover and steam until tender, approximately 15
   minutes.
2. Combine corn, pepper, sage, vinegar, and olive oil.
3. When potatoes are done, cut in half crosswise. Hollow out the potato
   halves with a melon baller.
4. Fill the hollows with the corn mixture.

Calories Per Serving: 72
Fat: 2 g
Cholesterol: 0 mg
Protein: 1 g

Carbohydrates: 13 g
Dietary Fiber: 1 g
Sodium: 3 mg

❧ *New Potatoes Stuffed with Carrots* ❧

YIELD: *10 servings (2 each)* • PREPARATION TIME: *35 minutes* •
COOKING TIME: *30 minutes*

Small new potatoes are hollowed out, stuffed with a carrot filling, and
warmed through in the oven. You can also make this recipe with other vegetable purees, such as spinach or broccoli-onion.

20 small new potatoes

2 carrots, scraped and chopped

¼ cup nonfat or reduced-fat sour cream

2 teaspoons chopped scallions

2 teaspoons lemon juice

1. Preheat oven to 350 degrees. Bring water to boil in the bottom of a steamer and set the new potatoes in steamer basket. Cover and steam until tender, approximately 15 minutes.
2. Place carrots in blender or food processor and puree until smooth.
3. Trim a tiny slice off the bottom of potatoes so they will stand up. Cut tops from potatoes. With a melon baller, scoop out potatoes, leaving a ¼-inch shell, and place potato flesh in a bowl. Mash.
4. Combine ⅓ of the mashed potato with carrot puree.
5. Stir in sour cream, scallions, and lemon juice.
6. Spoon carrot mixture into hollowed-out potatoes.
7. Place on a baking sheet and bake for 10 minutes until warmed through.

Calories Per Serving: 119

Fat: 0 g

Cholesterol: 2 mg

Protein: 3 g

Carbohydrates: 27 g

Dietary Fiber: 2 g

Sodium: 16 mg

☘ *New Potatoes with Lemon-Mint Sauce* ☘

YIELD: 14 servings (4 pieces each) • *PREPARATION TIME: 15 minutes* •
COOKING TIME: 12 minutes

Tiny, new red potatoes are steamed and then dipped in a lemon-mint sauce.

14 small, red-skinned new potatoes, quartered

½ cup nonfat or reduced-fat yogurt

½ cup nonfat or reduced-fat sour cream

1½ teaspoons lemon juice

¼ teaspoon black pepper

1 tablespoon dried mint

2 tablespoons chopped scallions

1. Bring water to boil in the bottom of a steamer and put potatoes in steamer basket. Steam, covered, for 10 to 12 minutes or until tender.
2. Combine yogurt, sour cream, lemon juice, pepper, mint, and scallions. Place in a serving bowl.

3. Place bowl of lemon-mint sauce in the center of a large serving platter surrounded by steamed potato quarters. Serve with wooden or plastic party picks.

Calories Per Serving: 71
Fat: 0 g
Cholesterol: 3 mg
Protein: 2 g

Carbohydrates: 15 g
Dietary Fiber: 1 g
Sodium: 17 mg

❧ *Lemon-Coriander Potatoes* ❧

YIELD: 10 servings (2 each) • *PREPARATION TIME: 15 minutes* •
COOKING TIME: 30 minutes

Serve these Greek-inspired potatoes with a yogurt dipping sauce.

20 tiny new potatoes
2 tablespoons light-flavored olive oil
⅓ cup red wine vinegar
¼ cup ground coriander

¼ teaspoon black pepper
¼ cup chopped fresh parsley
1 tablespoon capers, rinsed and drained
1 tablespoon grated lemon peel

1. Tap each potato with a heavy knife handle to slightly crack it, but not to break it apart.
2. Heat the olive oil in a skillet with a close-fitting lid. Add the cracked potatoes in a single layer, cover, and cook, shaking the pan frequently, over low heat until lightly browned, about 15 minutes.
3. Add the vinegar, coriander, and pepper. Cover and cook over low heat until potatoes are tender, about 15 minutes.
4. Combine the parsley, capers, and lemon peel and sprinkle over the potatoes. Serve warm with wooden or plastic party picks.

Calories Per Serving: 136
Fat: 3 g
Cholesterol: 0 mg
Protein: 3 g

Carbohydrates: 25 g
Dietary Fiber: 2 g
Sodium: 10 mg

⬚ *Petite Potato Cakes* ⬚

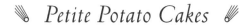

YIELD: 12 servings (2 each) ▪ *PREPARATION TIME: 35 minutes* ▪
COOKING TIME: 6 minutes

Potatoes, onion, and egg whites are combined to make these tiny pancakes. Serve with a bowl of nonfat or reduced-fat sour cream or yogurt and a choice of parsley or scallions to sprinkle on top.

2 medium baking potatoes, peeled, grated, and drained
2 tablespoons finely chopped onion
¼ teaspoon black pepper
2 egg whites, lightly beaten

1 tablespoon unbleached, all-purpose flour
¼ teaspoon baking powder
2 tablespoons light-flavored olive or canola oil

1. Combine potatoes, onion, and black pepper in a bowl.
2. Add egg whites, flour, and baking powder and toss well.
3. Heat 1 tablespoon of the oil in a skillet over medium heat. Drop a tablespoon of potato mixture into heated oil and flatten with the back of a wooden spoon. Repeat with as many tablespoons of batter as the skillet will hold, adding the remaining oil as needed.
4. Cook until potato pancakes are browned on both sides, about 6 minutes total. Drain on paper towels. Repeat process until batter is used up.
5. Transfer pancakes to serving platter. Serve with plates and cocktail forks.

Calories Per Serving: 61
Fat: 2 g
Cholesterol: 0 mg
Protein: 1 g

Carbohydrates: 9 g
Dietary Fiber: 1 g
Sodium: 19 mg

❧ *Potato-Caviar Bites* ✍

YIELD: *24 servings (2 each)* • PREPARATION TIME: *15 minutes* • COOKING TIME: *45 minutes*

New potatoes are roasted, then topped with nonfat sour cream, caviar, and scallions for a special occasion.

24 small new potatoes
1 cup nonfat or reduced-fat sour cream

1 5-ounce jar salmon caviar
Finely chopped scallion greens

1. Preheat oven to 350 degrees. Bake potatoes for 45 minutes or until done.
2. Cut each potato in half and top each half with ½ teaspoon sour cream and ¼ teaspoon caviar. Garnish with chopped scallion greens and serve warm.

Calories Per Serving: 38
Fat: 0 g
Cholesterol: 3 mg
Protein: 1 g

Carbohydrates: 8 g
Dietary Fiber: 1 g
Sodium: 9 mg

❧ *Potato-Carrot Minicakes* ✍

YIELD: *20 servings (1 each)* • PREPARATION TIME: *30 minutes* • COOKING TIME: *6 minutes per batch*

Tiny potato-carrot pancakes are an unexpected addition to an array of low-fat appetizers.

6 egg whites
3 tablespoons unbleached, all-purpose flour
¾ pound potatoes, peeled and grated

¾ pound carrots, peeled and grated
3 tablespoons minced onion
¼ teaspoon black pepper
¼ cup light-flavored olive or canola oil

1. Beat egg whites lightly in a bowl. Whisk in flour.
2. Add potatoes, carrots, onion, and pepper.

3. Heat half of the oil in a heavy skillet over medium heat. Using a table-spoon, drop batter by spoonfuls into skillet. Cook for about 3 minutes or until browned. Turn and brown on the other side for about 3 minutes. Repeat with remaining batter, adding oil as necessary. Drain on paper towels. Serve with plates and cocktail forks.

Calories Per Serving: 57
Fat: 3 g
Cholesterol: 0 mg
Protein: 2 g

Carbohydrates: 7 g
Dietary Fiber: 1 g
Sodium: 23 mg

⚘ *Parmesan-Potato Wedges* ⚘

YIELD: 16 servings (2 each) • *PREPARATION TIME: 15 minutes* •
COOKING TIME: 25 minutes

Serve these tasty potato wedges with a barbecue dipping sauce.

*4 large baking potatoes, unpeeled, and
  each cut into 8 wedges
1 tablespoon light-flavored olive oil*

*¼ cup grated nonfat or reduced-fat
  Parmesan cheese*

1. Preheat oven to 400 degrees. Brush potato wedges with oil; place on oiled baking sheet.
2. Sprinkle potato wedges with Parmesan cheese.
3. Bake for 25 minutes or until potatoes are tender and light golden brown.

Calories Per Serving: 66
Fat: 1 g
Cholesterol: 1 mg
Protein: 2 g

Carbohydrates: 13 g
Dietary Fiber: 1 g
Sodium: 15 mg

Tuna-Topped Potatoes

YIELD: *10 servings (2 each)* • PREPARATION TIME: *30 minutes* •
COOKING TIME: *30 minutes*

A mixture of tuna, lemon juice, cayenne pepper, anchovies, and capers tops steamed potatoes.

10 small new potatoes
2 tablespoons light-flavored olive oil
3 tablespoons nonfat or reduced-fat
  mayonnaise
1 tablespoon lemon juice
¼ teaspoon ground cayenne pepper

2 anchovy fillets, mashed
6½ ounces canned, water-packed,
  white albacore tuna, drained
1 tablespoon capers, drained
¼ cup chopped fresh parsley

1. Bring water to a boil in the bottom of a steamer and put whole potatoes in steamer basket. Cover and steam 10 to 12 minutes or until tender. Cool.
2. Place olive oil, mayonnaise, lemon juice, cayenne pepper, and anchovies in blender or food processor and blend until smooth.
3. Stir in tuna and capers and mix well.
4. Slice potatoes in half, trimming bottoms slightly so they do not tip. Scoop out a small hollow in the center of each potato half and top with tuna mixture. Sprinkle with parsley and serve.

Calories Per Serving: 141
Fat: 3 g
Cholesterol: 8 mg
Protein: 7 g

Carbohydrates: 21 g
Dietary Fiber: 2 g
Sodium: 107 mg

Potato-Cheese Slices

YIELD: *12 servings (2 each)* • PREPARATION TIME: *30 minutes* •
COOKING TIME: *25 minutes*

Potato slices are topped with a tangy cheese-and-scallion spread.

½ cup grated nonfat or reduced-fat
   Parmesan cheese
¼ cup crumbled goat cheese
2 tablespoons finely chopped scallions

⅛ teaspoon black pepper
1 tablespoon finely chopped fresh
   parsley
4 large baking potatoes

1. Preheat oven to 400 degrees. Combine Parmesan cheese, goat cheese, scallions, pepper, and parsley.
2. Cut each unpeeled potato lengthwise into 6 slices of equal thickness.
3. Spread cheese mixture on each potato slice.
4. Arrange potatoes in a lightly oiled baking pan. Bake for 25 minutes or until tender. Serve with plates and cocktail forks.

Calories Per Serving: 119
Fat: 3 g
Cholesterol: 11 mg
Protein: 5 g

Carbohydrates: 18 g
Dietary Fiber: 2 g
Sodium: 46 mg

❧ *Potato Slices with Spinach Pesto* ❧

YIELD: *18 servings (2 each)* • PREPARATION TIME: *25 minutes*

Lightly browned potato slices are spread with spinach pesto and served warm.

1 cup chopped spinach leaves
1 cup parsley sprigs, stems removed
2 tablespoons light-flavored olive oil
1 clove garlic, peeled and quartered

1 teaspoon dried basil
¼ cup grated nonfat or reduced-fat
   Parmesan cheese
6 medium baking potatoes

1. Preheat broiler. Place spinach, parsley, olive oil, garlic, basil, and Parmesan cheese in a blender or food processor. Blend until smooth.
2. Cut each unpeeled potato crosswise into 6 slices, ½ inch thick. Arrange potato slices in a single layer on a lightly oiled baking sheet.
3. Broil 5 ½ inches from heat for 12 minutes on each side, or until tender and lightly browned.
4. Place potato slices on a serving platter and top each warm slice with pesto.

Calories Per Serving: 82	Carbohydrates: 14 g
Fat: 2 g	Dietary Fiber: 2 g
Cholesterol: 1 mg	Sodium: 42 mg
Protein: 2 g	

❧ New Potato Rounds ❧

YIELD: *18 servings (2 each)* • PREPARATION TIME: *20 minutes*

Slices of new potatoes are topped with sour cream and served with a medley of garnishes.

1 pound small new potatoes, cooked, drained, and chilled

⅔ cup nonfat or reduced-fat sour cream

GARNISHES

⅓ cup chopped scallions
⅓ cup chopped black olives
⅓ cup chopped fresh parsley

⅓ cup chopped pimentos
⅓ cup shredded nonfat or reduced-fat cheddar cheese

1. Cut potatoes into ¾-inch-thick slices.
2. Spread each slice with sour cream.
3. Top slices with different combinations of scallions, olives, parsley, pimento, and cheddar cheese.

Calories Per Serving: 61	Carbohydrates: 11 g
Fat: 1 g	Dietary Fiber: 1 g
Cholesterol: 3 mg	Sodium: 157 mg
Protein: 3 g	

❧ Sweet Potato Slices ❧

YIELD: *15 servings (2 slices each)* • PREPARATION TIME: *20 minutes* •
COOKING TIME: *25 minutes*

Sweet potatoes are baked and topped with scallions and yogurt.

1 pound sweet potatoes, ends trimmed
2 tablespoons light-flavored olive oil
⅓ cup nonfat or reduced-fat plain yogurt
¾ cup chopped scallions

1. Preheat oven to 400 degrees. Slice unpeeled sweet potatoes crosswise into 30 1-inch slices.
2. Arrange slices on a lightly oiled baking sheet. Brush tops with the olive oil.
3. Bake for 15 minutes. Turn slices over and bake for 10 minutes more.
4. Place slices on a serving platter and top each slice with ½ teaspoon yogurt and a sprinkling of scallions.

Calories Per Serving: 50
Fat: 2 g
Cholesterol: 0 mg
Protein: 1 g
Carbohydrates: 8 g
Dietary Fiber: 1 g
Sodium: 7 mg

⧄ *Petite Sweet Potato Pancakes with Applesauce* ⧄

YIELD: 12 servings (2 each) • *PREPARATION TIME: 35 minutes* •
COOKING TIME: 6 minutes

Tiny sweet potato pancakes are flavored with honey and garlic and topped with applesauce.

2 egg whites
½ teaspoon lemon juice
¼ teaspoon black pepper
2 tablespoons honey
1 clove garlic, minced
2 sweet potatoes, peeled and grated
1 small onion, grated
1½ teaspoons unbleached, all-purpose flour
¼ teaspoon baking powder
2 tablespoons light-flavored olive or canola oil
¾ cup natural applesauce

1. Combine egg whites, lemon juice, and pepper in a bowl and beat until blended.
2. Add honey, garlic, sweet potatoes, onion, flour, and baking powder.
3. Heat half the oil in a heavy skillet over medium heat. Drop a tablespoon of potato mixture into heated oil and flatten with the back of a wooden spoon. Repeat with as many pancakes as the skillet will hold, adding the remaining oil between batches (allow time for oil to reheat) as needed.

4. Cook until potato pancakes are browned on both sides, about 6 minutes total. Drain on paper towels. Repeat until batter is used up.

5. Transfer pancakes to serving platter. Top each pancake with ½ tablespoon applesauce. Serve with plates and cocktail forks.

Calories Per Serving: 71

Fat: 2 g

Cholesterol: 0 mg

Protein: 1 g

Carbohydrates: 12 g

Dietary Fiber: 1 g

Sodium: 20 mg

⚫ *Potato Skins with Chile Salsa* ⚫

YIELD: 10 servings (2 each) • *PREPARATION TIME: 20 minutes* •
COOKING TIME: 15 minutes

Baked potato skins are topped with cheese and served with salsa.

5 large baking potatoes, baked and cooled

2 tablespoons light-flavored olive oil

8 ounces canned, low-sodium tomato sauce

4 ounces canned, mild green chiles

¼ cup chopped onion

1½ cups nonfat or reduced-fat cheddar cheese

1. Preheat oven to 500 degrees. Cut each baked potato lengthwise into quarters. Scoop flesh from skins, leaving a shell ⅛ inch thick.

2. Brush skins with olive oil and place in a single layer on a baking sheet. Bake for 12 minutes or until crisp.

3. Meanwhile, combine tomato sauce, chiles, and onion. Place in small serving bowl and chill until ready to use.

4. Remove potatoes from oven and sprinkle with cheese. Turn oven to broil.

5. Place baking sheet under broiler for 2 minutes or until cheese melts. Arrange around salsa on a serving platter.

Calories Per Serving: 96

Fat: 3 g

Cholesterol: 6 mg

Protein: 12 g

Carbohydrates: 6 g

Dietary Fiber: 1 g

Sodium: 258 mg

❧ *Pizza Skins* ❧

YIELD: 10 servings (2 each) ▪ *PREPARATION TIME: 20 minutes* ▪
COOKING TIME: 15 minutes

Baked potato skins are topped with an Italian-style tomato-mushroom sauce
and mozzarella cheese.

5 large baking potatoes, baked
2 tablespoons light-flavored olive oil
8 ounces canned, low-sodium tomato
  sauce
½ cup chopped mushrooms

½ teaspoon dried basil
½ teaspoon dried oregano
1½ cups nonfat or reduced-fat
  mozzarella cheese

1. Preheat oven to 500 degrees. Cut each baked potato lengthwise into
   quarters. Scoop flesh from skins, leaving a shell ⅛ inch thick.
2. Brush skins with olive oil and place in a single layer on a baking sheet.
   Bake for 12 minutes or until crisp.
3. Meanwhile, combine tomato sauce, mushrooms, basil, and oregano.
4. Remove potatoes from oven and lower heat to 350 degrees.
5. Top potato skins with tomato-mushroom sauce. Sprinkle with cheese.
6. Bake for 5 minutes or until cheese melts. Serve with plates and cocktail
   forks.

Calories Per Serving: 139
Fat: 3 g
Cholesterol: 6 mg
Protein: 13 g

Carbohydrates: 16 g
Dietary Fiber: 2 g
Sodium: 256 mg

❧ *Crispy Parmesan Potato Skins* ❧

YIELD: 16 servings (2 each) ▪ *PREPARATION TIME: 15 minutes* ▪
COOKING TIME: 10 minutes

Baked potato skins are crisped in the oven, then sprinkled with Parmesan
cheese and served with sour cream.

4 large baking potatoes, baked
3 tablespoons light-flavored olive oil
1 teaspoon dry mustard
½ teaspoon black pepper

½ cup nonfat or reduced-fat Parmesan cheese
1 cup nonfat or reduced-fat sour cream

1. Preheat oven to 400 degrees. Cut baked potatoes lengthwise into eighths. Scoop flesh out of potato segments, leaving a shell ⅛ inch thick.
2. Combine olive oil, dry mustard, and pepper. Brush over potato segments.
3. Place potato skins on a baking sheet, skin side up. Bake for 10 minutes or until crisp.
4. Sprinkle potato skins with Parmesan cheese while still hot, and serve with sour cream.

Calories Per Serving: 92
Fat: 2 g
Cholesterol: 7 mg
Protein: 3 g

Carbohydrates: 15 g
Dietary Fiber: 1 g
Sodium: 35 mg

❧ Radicchio Bites ❧

YIELD: 8 servings (2 each) • PREPARATION TIME: 20 minutes

Radicchio, a red-leafed Italian chicory, is stuffed with sour cream.

1 cup nonfat or reduced-fat sour cream
3 tablespoons minced green bell pepper
1 tablespoon dried basil
1 clove garlic, minced

¼ teaspoon white pepper
⅓ cup minced fresh parsley
16 small radicchio leaves

1. Combine sour cream, green pepper, basil, garlic, white pepper, and parsley.
2. Place a spoonful of sour cream mixture at the base of each radicchio leaf. Arrange leaves on a platter in a wheel-like pattern with their centers touching.

Calories Per Serving: 60
Fat: 0 g
Cholesterol: 1 mg
Protein: 5 g

Carbohydrates: 9 g
Dietary Fiber: 0 g
Sodium: 62 mg

❧ *Snow Peas with Shrimp* ❧

YIELD: 12 servings (3 each) • *PREPARATION TIME: 25 minutes* •
COOKING TIME: 5 minutes

Shrimp and snow peas make a quick and attractive appetizer. Serve with honey mustard for dipping.

36 fresh snow peas, ends trimmed and   *1 pound medium shrimp (approxi-*
strings removed   *mately 35 shrimp to a pound),*
                                            cooked, shelled, and deveined

1. Bring a pot of water to a boil and add snow peas. Return to a boil and blanch peas for 45 seconds. Run under cold water and drain.
2. Wrap a pea pod around each shrimp and secure with a wooden or plastic party pick.

Calories Per Serving: 64   Carbohydrates: 3 g
Fat: 0 g   Dietary Fiber: 1 g
Cholesterol: 85 mg   Sodium: 397 mg
Protein: 13 g

❧ *Chicken Salad–Stuffed Snow Peas* ❧

YIELD: 24 servings (2 each) • *PREPARATION TIME: 10 minutes plus 1 hour*
refrigeration time • *COOKING TIME: 5 minutes*

Crisp snow pea boats are filled with chicken salad.

48 fresh snow peas, ends trimmed and   *¼ cup finely chopped onion*
strings removed, split open   *¼ cup finely chopped fresh parsley*
2½ cups finely chopped cooked chicken   *1 tablespoon lemon juice*
breast   *⅛ teaspoon black pepper*
1 cup finely chopped celery   *½ cup nonfat or reduced-fat mayonnaise*

1. Bring 1½ quarts of water to a boil. Add snow peas, blanch 20 seconds, plunge peas into cold water, and drain.

2. Combine chicken, celery, onion, parsley, lemon juice, pepper, and mayonnaise.
3. Carefully fill each snow pea with chicken salad and refrigerate for 1 hour.

Calories Per Serving: 40
Fat: 1 g
Cholesterol: 14 mg
Protein: 6 g

Carbohydrates: 3 g
Dietary Fiber: 1 g
Sodium: 16 mg

 Snow Peas with Crab

YIELD: 12 servings (2 each) • *PREPARATION TIME: 10 minutes* •
COOKING TIME: 5 minutes

Fresh snow peas are stuffed with a rich-tasting cream cheese–crab mixture.

*24 snow peas, ends trimmed and
  strings removed, split open*
*4 ounces nonfat or reduced-fat cream
  cheese, softened*

¼ cup cooked crabmeat
Juice of 1 lemon
¼ teaspoon black pepper

1. Bring a quart of water to a boil. Blanch the snow peas in boiling water for 30 seconds. Cool in ice water and drain.
2. Combine cream cheese, crabmeat, lemon juice, and pepper.
3. Carefully stuff crabmeat mixture into each snow pea.

Calories Per Serving: 22
Fat: 0 g
Cholesterol: 4 mg
Protein: 3 g

Carbohydrates: 2 g
Dietary Fiber: 1 g
Sodium: 75 mg

Sweet-and-Spicy Tomatoes

YIELD: 12 servings (4 each) • *PREPARATION TIME: 20 minutes plus
overnight refrigeration time*

Cherry tomatoes are marinated overnight in a flavorful sauce.

48 cherry tomatoes (approximately
  2 pints)
2 cups red wine vinegar
¼ cup sugar

1 tablespoon whole cloves
6 dried bay leaves
1 cup low-sodium tomato juice

1. Lightly prick each tomato with a knife in several places.
2. Combine vinegar, sugar, cloves, bay leaves, and tomato juice in a glass bowl. Stir well.
3. Add tomatoes, cover, and refrigerate overnight.
4. Drain, and serve heaped in the center of a platter of sandwich appetizers.

Calories Per Serving: 48
Fat: 0 g
Cholesterol: 0 mg
Protein: 3 g

Carbohydrates: 9 g
Dietary Fiber: 1 g
Sodium: 13 mg

Parsley-Basil-Cheese— Stuffed Cherry Tomatoes

YIELD: 12 servings (2 each) • *PREPARATION TIME: 25 minutes*

Cherry tomatoes are stuffed with a cottage cheese, herb, and scallion mixture.

24 cherry tomatoes
¼ cup chopped fresh parsley
¼ cup chopped scallions
1 clove garlic, minced

1 teaspoon dried basil
1 cup nonfat or reduced-fat cottage
  cheese

1. Trim the bottom off each cherry tomato so it will not roll. Cut the top off each tomato and hollow out with a small spoon or melon baller.
2. Place parsley, scallions, garlic, basil, and cottage cheese in a blender or food processor and blend until smooth.
3. Fill hollowed-out cherry tomatoes with cheese mixture.

Calories Per Serving: 29
Fat: 0 g
Cholesterol: 7 mg
Protein: 3 g

Carbohydrates: 5 g
Dietary Fiber: 1 g
Sodium: 33 mg

❦ *Parsley Pesto Tomatoes* ❦

YIELD: 10 servings (2 each) ▪ *PREPARATION TIME: 30 minutes*

Cherry tomatoes are stuffed with a parsley pesto made with Parmesan and ricotta cheese.

20 cherry tomatoes
¾ cup fresh parsley
⅛ teaspoon black pepper
1 clove garlic, peeled and quartered

¼ cup grated nonfat or reduced-fat
*   Parmesan cheese*
½ cup nonfat or reduced-fat ricotta
*   cheese*

1. Trim the bottom off each tomato so it does not tip. Cut the top off each tomato and hollow out seeds and pulp with a small spoon or melon baller.
2. Place parsley, pepper, garlic, Parmesan, and ricotta in a blender or food processor. Process until well blended.
3. Spoon 2 teaspoons of pesto into each tomato.

Calories Per Serving: 39
Fat: 1 g
Cholesterol: 3 mg
Protein: 3 g

Carbohydrates: 7 g
Dietary Fiber: 1 g
Sodium: 51 mg

❦ *Cherry Tomatoes with Artichoke Filling* ❦

YIELD: 15 servings (2 each) ▪ *PREPARATION TIME: 25 minutes*

Artichoke hearts mixed with a medley of herbs make a delightful stuffing for ripe cherry tomatoes.

30 cherry tomatoes
16 ounces canned, water-packed arti-
*   choke hearts, drained*
Juice of ½ lemon
2 tablespoons white wine vinegar

1 tablespoon light-flavored olive oil
½ teaspoon dried tarragon
½ teaspoon dried dill
2 tablespoons chopped fresh parsley
¼ teaspoon black pepper

1. Trim the bottom off each cherry tomato so it does not tip. Cut the top off each tomato and hollow out seeds and pulp with a small spoon or melon baller.
2. Coarsely chop artichoke hearts in a blender, food processor, or by hand.
3. Combine artichoke hearts with lemon juice, vinegar, olive oil, tarragon, dill, parsley, and pepper.
4. Fill cherry tomatoes with artichoke mixture.

Calories Per Serving: 34
Fat: 1 g
Cholesterol: 0 mg
Protein: 1 g

Carbohydrates: 6 g
Dietary Fiber: 2 g
Sodium: 27 mg

Cherry Tomatoes 🖋️ *with Green Pepper–Corn Filling* 🖋️

YIELD: 10 servings (2 each) • *PREPARATION TIME: 25 minutes*

Cherry tomatoes are filled with a mixture of chopped green pepper, corn, red onion, and thyme.

20 cherry tomatoes
½ cup cooked fresh or canned, drained corn
1 tablespoon minced red onion

2 tablespoons minced green bell pepper
2 tablespoons light-flavored olive oil
½ teaspoon dried thyme
⅛ teaspoon white pepper

1. Trim the bottom off each tomato so it will not roll. Slice off the top and hollow out flesh and seeds with a small spoon or melon baller.
2. Combine corn, red onion, green pepper, olive oil, thyme, and white pepper.
3. Fill cherry tomatoes with vegetable mixture.

Calories Per Serving: 70
Fat: 3 g
Cholesterol: 0 mg
Protein: 1 g

Carbohydrates: 9 g
Dietary Fiber: 2 g
Sodium: 9 mg

❧ *Spinach-Ricotta–Stuffed Cherry Tomatoes* ✿

YIELD: 9 servings (2 each) • *PREPARATION TIME: 20 minutes*

A ricotta-spinach pesto filling is spooned into ripe cherry tomatoes.

18 cherry tomatoes
¾ cup chopped fresh spinach
¼ cup grated nonfat or reduced-fat
  Parmesan cheese
⅛ teaspoon black pepper

2 tablespoons light-flavored olive oil
1 clove garlic, peeled and quartered
½ cup nonfat or reduced-fat ricotta
  cheese

1. Trim the bottom off each tomato so it will not roll. Slice off the top and hollow out flesh and seeds with a small spoon or melon baller.
2. Place spinach, Parmesan cheese, pepper, oil, and garlic in a blender or food processor and process until smooth.
3. Add spinach mixture to ricotta cheese and mix well.
4. Fill cherry tomatoes with spinach-ricotta mixture.

Calories Per Serving: 50
Fat: 3 g
Cholesterol: 2 mg
Protein: 2 g

Carbohydrates: 5 g
Dietary Fiber: 1 g
Sodium: 29 mg

❧ *Couscous Tomatoes* ✿

YIELD: 12 servings (2 each) • *PREPARATION TIME: 25 minutes plus 1 hour
refrigeration time* • *COOKING TIME: 10 minutes*

Couscous, a basic ingredient of North African cuisine, is combined with curry, garlic, parsley, and scallions as a stuffing for cherry tomatoes.

24 cherry tomatoes
⅔ cup nonfat or reduced-fat, low-
  sodium chicken broth
½ teaspoon curry powder

⅛ clove garlic, minced
⅓ cup uncooked couscous
1 tablespoon chopped fresh parsley
1 tablespoon scallion, chopped

1. Trim bottom off of each cherry tomato so it will not roll. Slice top off of tomato and hollow out flesh and seeds with a small spoon or melon baller.
2. Place chicken broth in a pot, add curry powder and garlic, and bring to a boil.
3. Stir in couscous, parsley, and scallions. Cover, remove from heat, and let stand for 5 minutes. Fluff mixture with a fork.
4. Fill each tomato with about 2 teaspoons couscous mixture.
5. Cover and refrigerate for 1 hour.

Calories Per Serving: 35	Carbohydrates: 7 g
Fat: 0 g	Dietary Fiber: 2 g
Cholesterol: 0 mg	Sodium: 29 mg
Protein: 2 g	

❦ *Cherry Tomatoes Stuffed with Orzo* ❦

YIELD: 24 servings (2 each) • *PREPARATION TIME: 35 minutes* • *COOKING TIME: 6 minutes*

Orzo, a tiny rice-shaped pasta, is ideal for stuffing cherry tomatoes.

48 cherry tomatoes	*½ teaspoon dried oregano*
1 cup orzo	*½ teaspoon dried basil*
½ cup finely chopped scallions	*½ teaspoon dried thyme*
½ cup finely chopped orange or yellow	*¼ teaspoon black pepper*
bell pepper	*1 tablespoon light-flavored olive oil*
½ cup chopped fresh parsley	*1 teaspoon red wine vinegar*

1. Trim the bottom off of each tomato so it will not tip. Slice off top of tomato and hollow out flesh and seeds with a small spoon or melon baller.
2. Bring 4 cups of water to a boil. Add orzo and cook for 6 minutes or until tender. Drain.
3. Combine drained orzo, scallions, bell pepper, parsley, oregano, basil, thyme, pepper, olive oil, and vinegar.
4. Stuff the cherry tomatoes with the orzo mixture.

Calories Per Serving: 45

Carbohydrates: 8 g

Fat: 1 g

Dietary Fiber: 1 g

Cholesterol: 0 mg

Sodium: 5 mg

Protein: 1 g

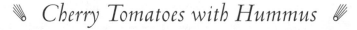

🌿 *Cherry Tomatoes with Pasta Stuffing* 🌿

YIELD: 10 servings (2 each)　•　PREPARATION TIME: 25 minutes

Cherry tomatoes are stuffed with cooked pasta that is flavored with garlic, basil, olive oil, and Parmesan cheese.

20 cherry tomatoes

½ cup cooked mini–bow ties or other small pasta

2 tablespoons light-flavored olive oil

1 teaspoon dried basil

1 garlic clove, minced

1 tablespoon nonfat or reduced-fat Parmesan cheese

⅛ teaspoon black pepper

1. Trim the bottom off each tomato so it will not roll. Slice off top of tomato and hollow out flesh and seeds with a small spoon or melon baller.
2. Combine cooked pasta, olive oil, basil, garlic, Parmesan cheese, and black pepper.
3. Fill cherry tomatoes with pasta mixture.

Calories Per Serving: 49

Carbohydrates: 5 g

Fat: 3 g

Dietary Fiber: 1 g

Cholesterol: 1 mg

Sodium: 11 mg

Protein: 1 g

🌿 *Cherry Tomatoes with Hummus* 🌿

YIELD: 25 servings (2 each)　•　PREPARATION TIME: 20 minutes

Cherry tomatoes are filled with a quickly prepared Middle Eastern mixture of chickpeas, tahini, and lemon juice.

50 cherry tomatoes
2 cups canned or home-cooked chickpeas, rinsed and drained
2 cloves garlic, quartered

3 tablespoons tahini (sesame seed
  paste)
¼ cup lemon juice

1. Trim the bottom off of each cherry tomato so it will not tip. Slice off top
   and hollow out flesh and seeds with a small spoon or melon baller.
2. Place chickpeas, garlic, tahini, and lemon juice in a blender or food
   processor and blend until smooth.
3. Spoon hummus into tomatoes.

Calories Per Serving: 67
Fat: 3 g
Cholesterol: 1 mg
Protein: 3 g

Carbohydrates: 9 g
Dietary Fiber: 2 g
Sodium: 72 mg

✎ *Cherry Tomato–Salmon Bites* ✎

YIELD: 15 servings (2 each) • *PREPARATION TIME: 25 minutes*

Plump, red cherry tomatoes are stuffed with a mixture of smoked salmon,
watercress, and nonfat cream cheese. Salmon is high in protein, as well as a
rich source of vitamin A, the B-group vitamins, and Omega-3 oils.

30 large cherry tomatoes
3 ounces smoked salmon, finely
  chopped
3 ounces nonfat or reduced-fat cream
  cheese, softened

1 teaspoon lemon juice
1 tablespoon minced watercress leaves
  or fresh parsley
⅛ teaspoon black pepper

1. Trim the bottom off of each tomato so it will not roll. Slice off top and
   hollow out flesh and seeds with a small spoon or melon baller.
2. Combine salmon, cream cheese, lemon juice, watercress, and pepper.
3. Fill tomato shells with salmon–cream cheese mixture.

Calories Per Serving: 22
Fat: 0 g
Cholesterol: 1 m
Protein: 2 g

Carbohydrates: 3 g
Dietary Fiber: 1 g
Sodium: 51 mg

✒ *Cherry Tomatoes with Crab* ✒

YIELD: 8 servings (2 each) ▪ *PREPARATION TIME: 30 minutes* ▪
COOKING TIME: 10 minutes

Cherry tomatoes are stuffed with a mixture of crabmeat, yogurt, parsley, and onion.

16 cherry tomatoes
¼ pound cooked crabmeat
2 teaspoons nonfat or reduced-fat plain
  yogurt
1 teaspoon chopped fresh parsley

½ teaspoon minced onion
½ teaspoon Worcestershire sauce
⅛ teaspoon white pepper
Paprika

1. Preheat oven to 375 degrees. Trim the bottom off each tomato so it will not roll. Slice off top and hollow out flesh and seeds with a small spoon or melon baller.
2. Combine crabmeat, yogurt, parsley, onion, Worcestershire sauce, and white pepper.
3. Spoon crabmeat mixture into tomatoes and sprinkle with paprika.
4. Arrange on a baking sheet. Bake for 10 minutes.

Calories Per Serving: 25
Fat: 0 g
Cholesterol: 11 mg
Protein: 3 g

Carbohydrates: 3 g
Dietary Fiber: 1 g
Sodium: 51 mg

✎ *Cherry Tomatoes with Tuna* ✎

YIELD: 8 servings (2 each) • *PREPARATION TIME: 30 minutes plus*
1 hour refrigeration time

Cherry tomatoes are stuffed with a mixture of tuna, red onion, garlic, parsley, and basil.

16 large cherry tomatoes
1 small red onion, finely chopped
1 clove garlic, finely minced
2 tablespoons chopped fresh parsley
2 teaspoons dried basil

1 tablespoon light-flavored olive oil
2 teaspoons red wine vinegar
4 ounces canned, water-packed, white
  albacore tuna, drained and flaked
¼ teaspoon black pepper

1. Trim the bottom off each tomato so it will not tip. Slice off top and hollow out flesh and seeds with a small spoon or melon baller.
2. Combine onion, garlic, parsley, basil, olive oil, vinegar, tuna, and pepper.
3. Stuff tomatoes with tuna mixture. Refrigerate for 1 hour or more before serving.

Calories Per Serving: 59
Fat: 2 g
Cholesterol: 6 mg
Protein: 5 g

Carbohydrates: 5 g
Dietary Fiber: 1 g
Sodium: 63 mg

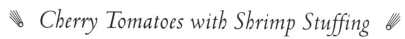

✎ *Cherry Tomatoes with Shrimp Stuffing* ✎

YIELD: 12 servings (2 each) • *PREPARATION TIME: 30 minutes plus*
3 hours refrigeration time

Cherry tomatoes are filled with a fancy mixture of shrimp, lemon juice, olive oil, and herbs.

24 cherry tomatoes
¼ pound cooked shrimp, peeled and
  deveined
2 tablespoons minced fresh parsley

2 tablespoons minced scallions
1 tablespoon lemon juice
1 tablespoon light-flavored olive oil
⅛ teaspoon black pepper

1. Trim the bottom off of each tomato so it will not roll. Slice off top and hollow out flesh and seeds with a small spoon or melon baller.
2. Place shrimp in a food processor or blender and process for 1 minute. Transfer to a bowl and mix in the parsley, scallions, lemon juice, olive oil, and pepper. Cover and refrigerate for 3 hours.
3. Fill tomatoes with the chilled shrimp mixture and serve.

Calories Per Serving: 34
Fat: 1 g
Cholesterol: 14 mg
Protein: 3 g

Carbohydrates: 4 g
Dietary Fiber: 1 g
Sodium: 73 mg

Cherry Tomatoes
❧ with Lemon-Oyster Stuffing ❧

YIELD: 20 servings (2 each) • *PREPARATION TIME: 30 minutes plus*
30 minutes refrigeration time

Cherry tomatoes are hollowed out and filled with a mixture of cream cheese, lemon juice, and smoked oysters.

40 cherry tomatoes
3½-ounce can smoked oysters,
  drained

3½-ounce package nonfat or reduced-
  fat cream cheese, softened
3 tablespoons lemon juice

1. Trim the bottom off of each tomato so it will not tip. Slice off top and hollow out flesh and seeds with a small spoon or melon baller.
2. Place oysters, cream cheese, and lemon juice in a blender or food processor and blend until smooth. Chill for 30 minutes.
3. Fill cherry tomatoes with oyster stuffing.

Calories Per Serving: 27

Fat: 0 g

Cholesterol: 6 mg

Protein: 2 g

Carbohydrates: 4 g

Dietary Fiber: 1 g

Sodium: 62 mg

❦ *Olive-Stuffed Tomatoes* ❦

YIELD: 24 servings (1 each) • *PREPARATION TIME: 35 minutes*

Cherry tomatoes are filled with a savory mixture of olives, anchovies, capers, and lemon juice.

24 cherry tomatoes
¾ cup pitted green olives, quartered
4 anchovy fillets, rinsed
1 clove garlic, peeled and quartered
2 tablespoons capers, drained

1 teaspoon dried basil
1 tablespoon chopped fresh parsley
1 tablespoon lemon juice
¼ cup light-flavored olive oil

1. Trim the bottom off of each tomato so it will not tip. Slice off top and hollow out flesh and seeds with a small spoon or melon baller.
2. Place olives, anchovies, garlic, capers, basil, parsley, and lemon juice in a blender or food processor. Process until finely chopped. Sprinkle with olive oil and process until smooth.
3. Fill each cherry tomato with olive mixture.

Calories Per Serving: 34

Fat: 3 g

Cholesterol: 1 mg

Protein: 1 g

Carbohydrates: 2 g

Dietary Fiber: 1 g

Sodium: 138 mg

❦ *Feta-Stuffed Tomatoes* ❦

YIELD: 20 servings (1 each) • *PREPARATION TIME: 35 minutes*

These Greek-style cherry tomatoes are stuffed with feta cheese and black olives.

20 cherry tomatoes

20 small, pitted black olives

6 ounces feta cheese

¼ teaspoon black pepper

2 teaspoons balsamic vinegar

1. Trim the bottom off of each tomato so it will not tip. Slice off top and hollow out flesh and seeds with a small spoon or melon baller.
2. Cut the tops from the black olives and set aside. Chop the rest of the olives and mix with the feta cheese.
3. Dry the insides of the tomatoes with paper towels, season each with black pepper, and place a couple of drops of balsamic vinegar in each tomato.
4. Fill the tomatoes with the cheese mixture. Place an olive top on each filled tomato and serve.

Calories Per Serving: 41

Fat: 2 g

Cholesterol: 7 mg

Protein: 2 g

Carbohydrates: 4 g

Dietary Fiber: 1 g

Sodium: 138 mg

❧ *Green and Gold Slices* ❧

YIELD: 12 servings (5 each) • *PREPARATION TIME: 10 minutes* •
COOKING TIME: 15 minutes

Slices of sautéed zucchini are served with an oil-and-vinegar dressing flavored with herbs.

2 medium zucchini

1 medium yellow summer squash

3 tablespoons light-flavored olive oil

4 cloves garlic, minced

1 teaspoon dried basil

1 teaspoon dried thyme

½ teaspoon dried mint

1 tablespoon red wine vinegar

1. Cut each zucchini and yellow summer squash into 20 slices ⅓ inch thick.
2. Heat half of the olive oil in a large skillet over medium heat. Sauté zucchini and yellow summer squash slices until lightly golden and tender. Add more oil to skillet as needed between each batch.
3. Remove zucchini and yellow summer squash slices from skillet and drain on paper towels.

4. Add garlic to skillet and quickly sauté until lightly browned, being careful not to overbrown.
5. Remove skillet from heat and add basil, thyme, mint, and vinegar; whisk together.
6. Arrange zucchini and yellow summer squash slices on a platter. Sprinkle garlic and herb dressing over slices. Serve with wooden or plastic party picks.

Calories Per Serving: 31
Fat: 3 g
Cholesterol: 0 mg
Protein: 1 g

Carbohydrates: 1 g
Dietary Fiber: 0 g
Sodium: 1 mg

Yellow Squash Rounds ❧ with Green Pepper Filling ❧

YIELD: 10 servings (2 each) • *PREPARATION TIME: 25 minutes* •
COOKING TIME: 8 minutes

Slices of yellow squash are steamed, stuffed with a green pepper–cheddar filling, and then baked.

20 slices yellow summer squash, ¾
 inch thick (about 2 medium squash)
½ cup minced green bell pepper
¼ cup nonfat or reduced-fat grated
 cheddar cheese

1 egg white, beaten
⅛ teaspoon black pepper
½ teaspoon dried basil

1. Preheat oven to 375 degrees. Hollow out an impression in the centers of the yellow squash slices with a melon-ball scoop or with a small, sharp knife.
2. Bring water to a boil in the bottom of a steamer. Place the squash slices in a steamer basket, cover, and steam for 3 minutes or just until tender.
3. Plunge steamed squash slices into cold water and drain.
4. Combine green pepper, cheese, egg white, black pepper, and dried basil.
5. Fill hollowed-out yellow squash slices with green pepper mixture.
6. Place on a baking sheet and bake for 5 minutes, or until cheese is melted.

Calories Per Serving: 22

Fat: 0 g

Cholesterol: 1 mg

Protein: 3 g

Carbohydrates: 3 g

Dietary Fiber: 1 g

Sodium: 48 mg

❧ Zucchini Slices with Crumb Topping ❧

YIELD: 20 servings (2 each)   ▪   PREPARATION TIME: 20 minutes   ▪
COOKING TIME: 30 minutes

Zucchini is baked with an herb-crumb topping, then sliced.

1½ cups bread crumbs made from
*   lightly toasted French bread*
1 tablespoon chopped fresh parsley
½ teaspoon dried basil
½ teaspoon dried rosemary

¼ teaspoon dried sage
½ teaspoon minced garlic
4 tablespoons light-flavored olive oil
4 medium zucchini, cut in half length-
*   wise*

1. Preheat oven to 350 degrees. Place bread crumbs, parsley, basil, rosemary, sage, garlic, and 2 tablespoons of the olive oil in a blender or food processor. Blend until well mixed.
2. Place squash in a shallow baking pan cut side up.
3. Sprinkle the bread crumb mixture over the cut sides of the zucchini.
4. Bake for 30 minutes, basting with the remaining olive oil.
5. When cool, cut zucchini halves into 5 slices each.

Calories Per Serving: 62

Fat: 3 g

Cholesterol: 0 mg

Protein: 1 g

Carbohydrates: 7 g

Dietary Fiber: 0 g

Sodium: 71 mg

✒ Zucchini Rounds with Red Pepper Filling ✒

YIELD: *10 servings (2 each)* • PREPARATION TIME: *25 minutes* •
COOKING TIME: *8 minutes*

Slices of zucchini are steamed, stuffed with a red pepper–Parmesan filling, and then baked.

20 slices zucchini, ⅓ inch thick (about
    1 medium zucchini)
½ cup minced red bell pepper
¼ cup nonfat or reduced-fat Parmesan
    cheese

1 egg white, beaten
⅛ teaspoon black pepper
½ teaspoon dried oregano

1. Preheat oven to 375 degrees. Scoop out a hollow in the centers of the zucchini slices with a melon-ball scoop or with a small, sharp knife.
2. Bring water to a boil in the bottom of a steamer. Place zucchini in steamer basket, cover, and steam for 2 to 3 minutes, or until just tender.
3. Plunge zucchini into cold water and drain.
4. Combine red pepper, cheese, egg white, black pepper, and dried oregano.
5. Fill hollowed-out zucchini slices with red pepper mixture.
6. Place zucchini slices on a baking sheet and bake for 5 minutes, or until cheese is melted.

Calories Per Serving: 15
Fat: 0 g
Cholesterol: 2 mg
Protein: 2 g

Carbohydrates: 2 g
Dietary Fiber: 0 g
Sodium: 25 mg

Zucchini Rounds
❧ with Curried-Egg Topping ❧

YIELD: 15 servings (2 each) • *PREPARATION TIME: 25 minutes plus*
2 hours refrigeration time

Slices of crisp zucchini are topped with an Indian-spiced egg spread.

½ cup nonfat or reduced-fat mayonnaise
½ teaspoon curry powder
¼ teaspoon dry mustard
¼ teaspoon hot pepper sauce
8 hard-boiled egg whites, finely
   chopped

½ cup finely chopped celery
2 tablespoons finely chopped onion
1 tablespoon chopped fresh parsley
30 slices zucchini, ¼ inch thick (about
   1 medium-large zucchini)
Paprika

1. Combine mayonnaise, curry powder, dry mustard, hot pepper sauce, egg whites, celery, onion, and parsley. Chill for 2 hours.
2. Spread curried egg mixture on zucchini slices. Sprinkle with paprika.

Calories Per Serving: 24
Fat: 0 g
Cholesterol: 0 mg
Protein: 2 g

Carbohydrates: 3 g
Dietary Fiber: 0 g
Sodium: 90 mg

❧ Carrot and Zucchini Rolls ❧

YIELD: 12 servings (1 each) • *PREPARATION TIME: 25 minutes*

Shredded carrot and zucchini are tossed with sour cream, scallions, and tarragon, then wrapped in lettuce leaves.

½ cup nonfat or reduced-fat sour cream
2 tablespoons chopped scallions
1 tablespoon chopped fresh parsley
½ teaspoon dried tarragon
⅛ teaspoon black pepper

2 teaspoons red wine vinegar
4 medium zucchini, shredded and
   drained
1 medium carrot, peeled and shredded
12 medium leaf lettuce leaves

1. Combine sour cream, scallions, parsley, tarragon, pepper, and vinegar.
2. Add zucchini and carrot; toss until well mixed.
3. Spoon 3 tablespoons mixture onto the bottom half of each lettuce leaf; roll up. Serve immediately with plates and cocktail forks.

Calories Per Serving: 22   Carbohydrates: 4 g
Fat: 0 g   Dietary Fiber: 1 g
Cholesterol: 3 mg   Sodium: 14 mg
Protein: 1 g

🌿 *Zucchini-Crab Bites* 🍴

Yield: 12 servings (2 each) • *Preparation Time: 20 minutes plus 1 hour refrigeration time* • *Cooking Time: 7 minutes*

Crabmeat is heaped into hollowed-out slices of steamed zucchini.

½ teaspoon lemon juice   *1½ tablespoons nonfat or reduced-fat*
¾ cup cooked crabmeat, drained   *mayonnaise*
2 small zucchini, about 6 inches each   *⅛ teaspoon black pepper*

1. Sprinkle lemon juice over crabmeat and let stand while zucchini are cooking.
2. Bring an inch of water to a boil in a medium saucepan. Drop zucchini in boiling water. When water returns to a boil, remove zucchini and plunge into ice water. Drain.
3. Trim ends of zucchini and cut them into 24 slices, approximately ½ inch thick.
4. Using a melon baller, scoop out a hollow in the center of each zucchini slice.
5. Combine crabmeat, mayonnaise, and pepper.
6. Top each hollowed-out zucchini slice with a small mound of crabmeat. Chill 1 hour before serving.

Calories Per Serving: 16   Carbohydrates: 2 g
Fat: 0 g   Dietary Fiber: 0 g
Cholesterol: 8 mg   Sodium: 43 mg
Protein: 2 g

❧ *Zucchini-Shrimp Bites* ❧

YIELD: 18 servings (2 each) • *PREPARATION TIME: 25 minutes*

Zucchini rounds are topped with a chutney-flavored spread and shrimp.

*8 ounces nonfat or reduced-fat cream
cheese, softened
2 tablespoons mango chutney
1½ teaspoons curry powder*

*36 zucchini slices, ¼ inch thick (about
2 medium zucchini)
36 small shrimp, cooked, shelled, and
chilled*

1. In a mixing bowl or by hand, combine cream cheese, chutney, and curry powder until well blended.
2. Spread cheese mixture on one side of each zucchini slice and top each with a shrimp.

Calories Per Serving: 52
Fat: 0 g
Cholesterol: 59 mg
Protein: 11 g

Carbohydrates: 3 g
Dietary Fiber: 0 g
Sodium: 353 mg

❧ *Zucchini—Red Pepper Tastes* ❧

YIELD: 18 servings (2 each) • *PREPARATION TIME: 25 minutes*

A zucchini puree with spices, garlic, and lemon juice is served on red pepper sections.

*6 medium zucchini, sliced and
steamed until soft
¼ teaspoon ground cayenne pepper
Juice of 2 lemons
5 cloves garlic, minced*

*1½ teaspoons ground coriander
1½ teaspoons ground caraway
6 large red bell peppers, halved and
seeded*

1. Puree steamed zucchini in a blender or food processor. Spoon puree into a fine sieve and press out excess liquid with the back of a wooden spoon.

2. Combine zucchini with cayenne, lemon juice, garlic, coriander, and caraway.
3. Cut each bell pepper half into 3 strips.
4. Spoon zucchini puree onto strips.

Calories Per Serving: 24
Fat: 0 g
Cholesterol: 0 mg
Protein: 1 g

Carbohydrates: 6 g
Dietary Fiber: 2 g
Sodium: 3 mg

❧ *Vegetable Antipasto* ✀

YIELD: *16 servings (½ cup each)* ▪ PREPARATION TIME: *35 minutes plus
approximately 1½ hours refrigeration time*

An array of vegetables is briefly marinated in a zesty dressing and then tossed
with olives, artichoke hearts, mushrooms, and cherry tomatoes.

¼ cup chili sauce
1 tablespoon light-flavored olive oil
2 tablespoons lemon juice
2 tablespoons red wine vinegar
2 cloves garlic, minced
¼ teaspoon dry mustard
½ teaspoon dried oregano
½ teaspoon dried basil
*1 cup carrots, cut into bite-size pieces,
steamed for 5 minutes*
*¾ cup zucchini, cut into bite-size
pieces, steamed for 2 minutes*

*3 cups cauliflower florets, steamed for
2 minutes*
*2 cups broccoli florets, steamed for 2
minutes*
*1 medium green pepper, cut into bite-
size pieces*
½ cup pitted green olives
*½ cup canned, water-packed artichoke
hearts, quartered*
¾ cup fresh mushrooms, halved
16 cherry tomatoes

1. Combine chili sauce, oil, lemon juice, vinegar, garlic, dry mustard, oregano, and basil in a saucepan. Bring to a boil. Turn heat off.
2. Place carrots, zucchini, cauliflower, broccoli, and green pepper in a bowl.
3. Pour hot dressing over vegetables, toss, and place in the refrigerator until no longer hot. Drain.

4. Stir in olives, artichoke hearts, mushrooms, and cherry tomatoes. Chill for 1 hour more. Serve in a large bowl with small plates and forks.

Calories Per Serving: 44
Fat: 2 g
Cholesterol: 0 mg
Protein: 2 g

Carbohydrates: 7 g
Dietary Fiber: 2 g
Sodium: 147 mg

❧ Vegetable Antipasto II ❧

YIELD: 16 servings (½ cup each) • PREPARATION TIME: 20 minutes plus overnight refrigeration time

Raw vegetables are marinated in a combination of white wine vinegar, olive oil, garlic, dry mustard, tarragon, and sugar.

3 tablespoons light-flavored olive oil
2 cups white wine vinegar
1 clove garlic, minced
1 teaspoon dry mustard
1 teaspoon dried tarragon
¼ teaspoon black pepper
2 tablespoons sugar

2 large carrots, scrubbed and cut into matchsticks
1 large cucumber, sliced
1 zucchini, sliced
1 yellow summer squash, sliced
1 small white onion, thinly sliced

1. Combine oil, vinegar, garlic, dry mustard, tarragon, pepper, and sugar in a large bowl.
2. Stir in carrots, cucumber, zucchini, yellow summer squash, and onion.
3. Cover and place in refrigerator overnight. Drain, and serve with small plates and cocktail forks.

Calories Per Serving: 50
Fat: 3 g
Cholesterol: 0 mg
Protein: 3 g

Carbohydrates: 5 g
Dietary Fiber: 1 g
Sodium: 7 mg

❧ *Mixed Vegetable Platter* ❧

YIELD: 16 servings (½ cup each) • *PREPARATION TIME: 20 minutes plus overnight refrigeration time*

This attractive combination of vegetables is a great way to savor the taste of fresh asparagus.

1 cup orange juice
2 tablespoons lemon juice
4 teaspoons minced fresh gingerroot
6 scallions, thinly sliced
5 tablespoons red wine vinegar
½ teaspoon black pepper
⅓ cup light-flavored olive oil
1 pound asparagus, trimmed and steamed until tender/crisp

1 pound green beans, trimmed and steamed until tender/crisp
1 small head cauliflower, cut into florets with 1 inch stems, steamed until tender/crisp
¾ cup pimento-stuffed green olives, drained
3 tomatoes, cut into wedges
1 large cucumber, peeled and sliced
¼ cup chopped fresh parsley

1. Place orange juice, lemon juice, gingerroot, scallions, wine vinegar, black pepper, and olive oil in a blender or food processor and process until smooth.
2. Place asparagus in a glass bowl. Cover with ⅔ cup of dressing. Cover and refrigerate overnight.
3. Place beans in a glass bowl. Cover with ⅔ cup of dressing. Cover and refrigerate overnight.
4. Place cauliflower in a glass bowl. Cover with ⅔ cup of dressing. Cover and refrigerate overnight.
5. Drain asparagus, beans, and cauliflower.
6. On a large serving platter, arrange asparagus, beans, and cauliflower with olives, tomatoes, and cucumber. Garnish with parsley. Serve with plates and cocktail forks.

Calories Per Serving: 45
Fat: 3 g
Cholesterol: 0 mg
Protein: 2 g

Carbohydrates: 4 g
Dietary Fiber: 1 g
Sodium: 96 mg

 Bread and Veggie Kabobs

YIELD: 8 servings (1 skewer each) • *PREPARATION TIME: 20 minutes* •
COOKING TIME: 10 minutes

Green and red bell peppers are broiled with marinated bread cubes. Serve
with a salsa.

*1 green bell pepper, cut into 1-inch
pieces
1 red bell pepper, cut into 1-inch pieces
1½ tablespoons light-flavored olive oil
1 clove garlic, minced*

*2 teaspoons chili powder
¼ teaspoon ground cumin
¼ teaspoon dried oregano
½ loaf Italian bread, cut into 1-inch
cubes*

1. Soak 8 8-inch wooden skewers in water for 30 minutes.
2. Boil 2 quarts of water in a large pot. Drop green and red pepper pieces in
   pot for 1 minute. Plunge into cold water and drain.
3. Preheat broiler. Heat olive oil in a large skillet over medium heat. Stir in
   garlic, chili powder, cumin, and oregano. Cook for 1 minute.
4. Add Italian bread cubes to skillet and stir until coated with oil and spices.
5. Thread the skewers, alternating pepper pieces and bread cubes.
6. Place kabobs on a rack 2 inches from broiler. Broil for several minutes,
   turning frequently, until the bread cubes are lightly toasted on all sides.

Calories Per Serving: 108
Fat: 3 g
Cholesterol: 0 mg
Protein: 3 g

Carbohydrates: 18 g
Dietary Fiber: 1 g
Sodium: 173 mg

Veggie Roll-ups

YIELD: 10 servings (2 each) • *PREPARATION TIME: 35 minutes* •
COOKING TIME: 10 minutes

Red bell pepper, mushrooms, zucchini, carrot, and scallions are tossed with
Parmesan cheese and rolled in red leaf lettuce bundles.

1 tablespoon light-flavored olive oil
1 red bell pepper, seeded and finely
    chopped
¾ cup finely chopped mushrooms
1 small zucchini, grated

1 carrot, grated
2 scallions, chopped
3 tablespoons grated nonfat or reduced-
    fat Parmesan cheese
20 red leaf lettuce leaves

1. Heat olive oil in skillet over medium heat. Add red bell pepper, mushrooms, zucchini, carrot, and scallions to skillet and stir-fry until vegetables
   are tender.
2. Add cheese to vegetables, toss, and set aside to cool.
3. Fill a large saucepan with water and bring to a boil. Fill a large bowl with
   water and ice.
4. Drop lettuce leaves in pan of boiling water and immediately plunge into
   the bowl of ice water. Pat dry with paper towels.
5. Place 1 tablespoon of the vegetable-cheese mixture in the bottom half of
   each leaf. Fold the sides of the leaf over the filling and roll up. Refrigerate
   until ready to serve.

Calories Per Serving: 53
Fat: 2 g
Cholesterol: 2 mg
Protein: 3 g

Carbohydrates: 7 g
Dietary Fiber: 1 g
Sodium: 35 mg

Basil-Balsamic Vegetables

YIELD: 16 servings (¼ cup each) • PREPARATION TIME: 25 minutes plus overnight
refrigeration time • COOKING TIME: 13 minutes

Bell peppers, cauliflower, and pearl onions are quick-cooked and pickled
overnight.

1 quart white wine vinegar
2⅔ cups water
3 tablespoons light-flavored olive
    oil
¼ cup sugar
½ teaspoon black pepper
½ teaspoon dried basil

3 medium red bell peppers, cut in ½-
    inch-wide strips
3 medium green bell peppers, cut in
    ½-inch-wide strips
½ medium cauliflower, cut into florets
10 pearl onions, peeled
⅓ cup balsamic vinegar

1. Combine white wine vinegar, water, olive oil, sugar, pepper, and basil in a large, heavy, nonaluminum saucepan. Bring to a boil and simmer for 3 minutes.
2. Place the peppers and cauliflower in the vinegar mixture and return to a boil. Cook for 3 minutes.
3. Remove the vegetables from the liquid with a slotted spoon. Place the vegetables in two 1-quart glass jars.
4. Add the onions to the hot liquid and cook for 5 minutes. Remove the onions from the cooking liquid with a slotted spoon and add them to the glass jars.
5. Boil the cooking liquid, uncovered, for 5 minutes. Remove from heat, add the balsamic vinegar, and pour the liquid over the vegetables. Add additional white wine vinegar if needed to cover the vegetables in the jars.
6. Cool, cover tightly, and refrigerate overnight.
7. Drain and serve with plates and cocktail forks.

Calories Per Serving: 77
Fat: 3 g
Cholesterol: 0 mg
Protein: 5 g

Carbohydrates: 9 g
Dietary Fiber: 2 g
Sodium: 17 mg

❦ *Mini—Vegetable Bundles* ❦

YIELD: 18 servings (2 each) • *PREPARATION TIME: 20 minutes*

Crisp, fresh celery, carrots, and tricolored bell peppers are tied together with scallion strips.

36 3-inch pieces of celery
1 carrot, cut into 3-inch-by-¼-inch matchsticks
½ green bell pepper, cut into 3-inch-by-⅛-inch matchsticks

½ red bell pepper, cut into 3-inch-by-⅛-inch matchsticks
½ yellow bell pepper, cut into 3-inch-by-⅛-inch matchsticks
36 6-inch-long green scallion sections

1. Fill center of each celery piece with 1 piece each of carrot and red, green, and yellow pepper.
2. Tie each bundle with a length of scallion. Arrange bundles on platter.

Calories Per Serving: 8
Fat: 0 g
Cholesterol: 0 mg
Protein: 0 g

Carbohydrates: 2 g
Dietary Fiber: 1 g
Sodium: 24 mg

❧ *Mediterranean Stuffed Lemons* ❧

YIELD: 18 servings (2 each) • *PREPARATION TIME: 40 minutes* •
COOKING TIME: 45 minutes

Lemon shells make beautiful vessels in which to serve this mixture of eggplant, zucchini, bell peppers, and onion.

½ cup red wine
1 medium onion, peeled and chopped
2 cloves garlic, minced
1 red bell pepper, seeded and diced
1 green bell pepper, seeded and diced
2 medium zucchini, cut into ½-inch cubes
1 medium eggplant, cut into ½-inch cubes

½ cup minced fresh parsley
1 teaspoon dried basil
1 teaspoon dried oregano
¼ teaspoon black pepper
2 cups canned, low-sodium tomatoes, drained and chopped
18 lemons, halved, flesh scooped out, bottoms trimmed

1. Heat ¼ cup of the red wine in a large skillet over medium heat. Sauté onion for 5 minutes. Add garlic and sauté 5 minutes more. Add bell peppers, zucchini, and the remaining ¼ cup wine. Simmer for 5 minutes.
2. Add eggplant, parsley, basil, oregano, pepper, and tomatoes. Simmer for 30 minutes. Remove from heat and allow to cool to room temperature.
3. Spoon ¼ cup of vegetable mixture into each lemon half. Serve with small plates and cocktail forks.

Calories Per Serving: 39
Fat: 0 g
Cholesterol: 0 mg
Protein: 1 g

Carbohydrates: 8 g
Dietary Fiber: 1 g
Sodium: 9 mg

Baked Stuffed Grape Leaves

YIELD: 25 servings (2 each) • *PREPARATION TIME: 30 minutes* •
COOKING TIME: 20 minutes

Grape leaves are stuffed with a mixture of rice, onion, parsley, and Parmesan cheese, then baked.

1½ cups uncooked rice
1 medium onion, chopped
½ cup chopped fresh parsley
5 ounces grated nonfat or reduced-fat
  Parmesan cheese

½ teaspoon black pepper
1-pint jar grape leaves
¼ cup light-flavored olive oil

1. Preheat oven to 350 degrees. Combine rice, onion, parsley, Parmesan cheese, and black pepper.
2. Spoon some of the rice mixture on the bottom half of each grape leaf. Fold up bottom, then sides, and then roll grape leaves into a bundle.
3. Place grape leave bundles, seam side down, in a shallow baking dish in one layer. Mix olive oil with enough water to cover leaves and bake for 20 minutes or until rice is tender, adding water if necessary. Bring to room temperature before serving.

Calories Per Serving: 91
Fat: 3 g
Cholesterol: 6 mg
Protein: 3 g

Carbohydrates: 10 g
Dietary Fiber: 1 g
Sodium: 232 mg

Vegetable Skewers

YIELD: 14 servings (1 skewer each) • *PREPARATION TIME: 25 minutes plus*
1 hour refrigeration time

Sun-dried tomatoes, potatoes, artichoke hearts, cucumbers, and bell peppers are marinated and threaded on skewers.

½ cup sun-dried tomatoes

1 pound small new potatoes, cooked
  and cut into 1-inch chunks

14½ ounces canned, water-packed
  artichoke hearts, drained

1 cup 1-inch cucumber chunks

1 cup 1-inch green bell pepper chunks

¾ cup prepared, nonfat or reduced-fat
  Italian dressing

1. Bring 1 cup of water to a boil and pour over tomatoes. Let sit for 10 minutes. Drain and blot dry on paper towels.
2. Combine sun-dried tomatoes, potatoes, artichoke hearts, cucumbers, and bell peppers in a glass bowl.
3. Pour dressing over vegetables and toss. Refrigerate for 1 hour.
4. Drain and then alternate vegetables on 14 wooden or plastic skewers.

Calories Per Serving: 56
Fat: 0 g
Cholesterol: 0 mg
Protein: 2 g

Carbohydrates: 13 g
Dietary Fiber: 2 g
Sodium: 250 mg

FRUIT APPETIZERS

Strawberry-Melon Kabobs with Ginger-Honey Dip • Watermelon Skewers • Watermelon Bites • Marinated Melon Skewers • Mangoes and Papayas with Pineapple Dip • Kiwi Kabobs with Apricot Dip • Pear-Shrimp Minikabobs • Strawberries, Pineapple, and Oranges with Banana Dip • Fall Fruit Medley with Pear-Yogurt Dip • Fruit Salad Kabobs with Pineapple Dip • Banana-Apple Skewers with Honey-Lime Dip • Elegant Orange Slices with Raspberries • Marinated Strawberries • Sugared-Pineapple Wedges • Almond-Ginger Apricots • Cheese-Stuffed Strawberries • Strawberries with Maple-Orange Liqueur • Peanut Butter–Fruit Bites • Fruit Bites • Papaya-Salmon Bites • Apples with Chutney Dip • Tropical Fruit Bites • Pineapple and Strawberries with Mango Sauce • Pineapple-Spice Bites • Spiced Honeydew Chunks

Strawberry-Melon Kabobs
with Ginger-Honey Dip

YIELD: 8 servings (1 skewer each) • *PREPARATION TIME: 25 minutes*

You can also make these kabobs using chunks of banana and pineapple.

3 cups 1-inch cantaloupe chunks
2 cups 1-inch honeydew melon chunks
¼ cup lemon juice
8 large strawberries, hulled
1 cup nonfat or reduced-fat plain yogurt

3 tablespoons natural peanut butter
¼ cup orange juice
1 teaspoon honey
1½ teaspoons grated fresh gingerroot

1. Sprinkle cantaloupe and honeydew chunks with lemon juice.
2. Thread 8 small wooden skewers, beginning with a strawberry and then alternating melon chunks.
3. Place yogurt, peanut butter, orange juice, honey, and gingerroot in a blender or food processor and process until smooth. Transfer to a serving bowl.
4. Serve fruit kabobs arranged around bowl of dip.

Calories Per Serving: 96
Fat: 3 g
Cholesterol: 5 mg
Protein: 4 g

Carbohydrates: 15 g
Dietary Fiber: 2 g
Sodium: 160 mg

Watermelon Skewers

YIELD: 12 servings (1 skewer each) • *PREPARATION TIME: 25 minutes plus
1 hour refrigeration time*

Watermelon and honeydew melon balls are marinated and then threaded on skewers.

3 cups seeded watermelon balls
3 cups honeydew melon balls
1 tablespoon lime juice
¼ cup orange juice
½ teaspoon finely grated lime peel

½ teaspoon finely grated orange peel
1 tablespoon honey
1 tablespoon thinly sliced fresh ginger-
root

1. Place melon balls in a bowl.
2. Combine the lime juice, orange juice, lime peel, orange peel, honey, and gingerroot slices.
3. Spoon the honey mixture over the melon balls. Cover and chill for 1 hour.
4. Drain and then put 4 melon balls on each of 12 small wooden or plastic skewers, alternating honeydew and watermelon.

Calories Per Serving: 36
Fat: 0 g
Cholesterol: 0 mg
Protein: 0 g

Carbohydrates: 9 g
Dietary Fiber: 1 g
Sodium: 5 mg

⬬ *Watermelon Bites* ⬬

YIELD: *20 servings (2 each)* • PREPARATION TIME: *25 minutes*

Watermelon chunks are served with a lime-tequila sauce.

1 cup lime juice
1 teaspoon tequila
¼ teaspoon salt

Several dashes hot pepper sauce
(optional)
5 cups 1-inch seeded watermelon chunks

1. Combine lime juice, tequila, salt, and hot pepper sauce, if using, in a small bowl.
2. Serve surrounded with watermelon chunks. Provide wooden or plastic party picks.

Calories Per Serving: 17
Fat: 0 g
Cholesterol: 0 mg
Protein: 0 g

Carbohydrates: 4 g
Dietary Fiber: 0 g
Sodium: 28 mg

❧ *Marinated Melon Skewers* ❧

YIELD: 25 servings (2 skewers each) • *PREPARATION TIME: 25 minutes plus 2 hours refrigeration time*

Small cantaloupe and honeydew melon balls are marinated in white wine, then skewered on wooden party picks.

75 small cantaloupe balls
75 small honeydew balls

Dry white wine

1. Place cantaloupe balls in a glass bowl. Place honeydew melon balls in a second glass bowl.
2. Pour enough dry white wine over the cantaloupe and honeydew melon balls to cover them. Cover with plastic wrap. Refrigerate for 2 hours.
3. Drain, and then place 3 balls on each of 50 plastic or wooden skewers, alternating cantaloupe and honeydew.

Calories Per Serving: 49
Fat: 0 g
Cholesterol: 0 mg
Protein: 1 g

Carbohydrates: 10 g
Dietary Fiber: 1 g
Sodium: 8 mg

❧ *Mangoes and Papayas with Pineapple Dip* ❧

YIELD: 16 servings (¼ cup each) • *PREPARATION TIME: 20 minutes plus 1 hour refrigeration time*

Chunks of tropical fruit are served with a creamy pineapple dip.

½ cup canned, juice-packed crushed
*   pineapple*
¼ cup finely chopped walnuts
¼ cup brown sugar, firmly packed
1 cup nonfat or reduced-fat cream
*   cheese, softened*

1¼ cups nonfat or reduced-fat plain
*   yogurt*
2 cups mango chunks
2 cups papaya chunks

1. Combine pineapple, walnuts, and sugar in a mixing bowl.
2. In a separate bowl, combine cream cheese and yogurt. Add cheese mixture to pineapple mixture and mix well.
3. Place in refrigerator to chill for 1 hour.
4. Serve dip surrounded by mango and papaya chunks. Provide wooden or plastic party picks.

Calories Per Serving: 80	Carbohydrates: 16 g
Fat: 1 g	Dietary Fiber: 1 g
Cholesterol: 9 mg	Sodium: 29 mg
Protein: 2 g	

✎ *Kiwi Kabobs with Apricot Dip* ✎

YIELD: 8 servings (2 skewers each) • *PREPARATION TIME: 20 minutes*

Kiwis, bananas, oranges, and strawberries are arranged on skewers and served with an apricot-honey dip.

¾ cup canned, water-packed apricots, crushed
¼ teaspoon grated orange peel
2 tablespoons honey
¼ teaspoon ground cinnamon
¼ teaspoon ground nutmeg
1¼ cups nonfat or reduced-fat plain yogurt

1 cup nonfat or reduced-fat cream cheese, softened
4 kiwis
2 large navel oranges
2 bananas
1 tablespoon lemon juice mixed with 1 tablespoon water
16 strawberries, hulled

1. Combine apricots, orange peel, honey, cinnamon, and nutmeg in a serving bowl.
2. Blend yogurt and cream cheese until smooth.
3. Add yogurt mixture to fruit mixture in bowl and stir until combined. Cover and chill until ready to serve.
4. Peel kiwis and cut into quarters lengthwise.
5. Peel oranges. Cut into 4 thick crosswise slices. Cut each slice in half.
6. Peel bananas; cut each into 8 chunks and dip into lemon water to prevent discoloration.

7. Alternate fruit on 16 wooden skewers, ending with a strawberry.
8. Arrange kabobs on a large serving platter around the bowl of apricot dip.

Calories Per Serving: 152
Fat: 0 g
Cholesterol: 6 mg
Protein: 9 g

Carbohydrates: 30 g
Dietary Fiber: 4 g
Sodium: 230 mg

🍴 *Pear-Shrimp Minikabobs* 🍴

YIELD: 12 servings (2 each) • *PREPARATION TIME: 20 minutes plus*
1 hour refrigeration time

Slices of fresh pear and cooked shrimp are marinated in lemon juice and fat-free Italian dressing.

2 large pears, peeled and cut into 24
   chunks
½ pound medium shrimp, cooked,
   peeled, and deveined

½ cup prepared nonfat or reduced-fat
   Italian dressing
¼ cup lemon juice

1. Combine the pears, shrimp, dressing, and lemon juice. Marinate for 1 hour in refrigerator.
2. Drain. Skewer a pear chunk and a shrimp on each of 24 wooden or plastic party picks.

Calories Per Serving: 37
Fat: 0 g
Cholesterol: 28 mg
Protein: 4 g

Carbohydrates: 5 g
Dietary Fiber: 1 g
Sodium: 272 mg

Strawberries, Pineapple, and Oranges with Banana Dip

YIELD: 16 servings (¼ cup each) • *PREPARATION TIME: 20 minutes plus 1 hour refrigeration time*

Juicy strawberries, pineapple chunks, and navel orange chunks are served with a banana-pecan dip. Substitute apple, pear, or banana chunks when strawberries are out of season.

¾ cup mashed banana
¼ cup finely chopped pecans
¼ cup brown sugar, firmly packed
1 cup nonfat or reduced-fat cream cheese, softened
1¼ cups nonfat or reduced-fat plain yogurt

¾ cup canned, juice-packed pineapple chunks, drained
¾ cup navel orange chunks
1 cup strawberries, hulled

1. Combine banana, pecans, and sugar in a mixing bowl.
2. In a separate bowl, combine cream cheese and yogurt. Add cheese mixture to banana mixture and mix well.
3. Place in refrigerator to chill for 1 hour.
4. Serve dip surrounded by pineapple chunks, orange chunks, and strawberries. Provide wooden or plastic party picks.

Calories Per Serving: 68
Fat: 1 g
Cholesterol: 3 mg
Protein: 4 g

Carbohydrates: 11 g
Dietary Fiber: 1 g
Sodium: 115 mg

Fall Fruit Medley with Pear-Yogurt Dip

YIELD: 20 servings (6 pieces each) • *PREPARATION TIME: 20 minutes*

Apples, tangerines, papaya, and red seedless grapes are sliced and served with a dip that combines chopped pears, almonds, honey, cream cheese, and yogurt.

2 tablespoons honey

¾ cup chopped fresh or canned, juice-
packed pears

¼ cup finely chopped toasted almonds

1¼ cups nonfat or reduced-fat plain
yogurt

1 cup nonfat or reduced-fat cream
cheese, softened

3 apples, cored and thinly sliced

2 tablespoons lemon juice mixed with
2 tablespoons water

3 tangerines or navel oranges, peeled,
sectioned, and seeded

1 papaya, peeled and sliced

1 large bunch red seedless grapes

1. Combine honey, pears, and almonds in a serving bowl.
2. Beat together yogurt and cream cheese until smooth.
3. Add yogurt mixture to fruit mixture in bowl and stir until combined.
4. Cover and chill until ready to serve.
5. When ready to serve, dip apple slices in lemon water to prevent discoloration. Arrange apple slices, tangerine sections, papaya slices, and grapes
   around pear dip in the center of a large platter.

Calories Per Serving: 73
Fat: 1 g
Cholesterol: 2 mg
Protein: 4 g

Carbohydrates: 14 g
Dietary Fiber: 1 g
Sodium: 106 mg

❧ *Fruit Salad Kabobs with Pineapple Dip* ❧

Yield: 15 servings (2 each) • *Preparation Time: 25 minutes*

Grapes, pineapple, mandarin oranges, strawberries, and cheese are threaded
on skewers and served with a yogurt-pineapple dip.

30 seedless red grapes

30 canned, juice-packed pineapple
chunks, drained

30 canned, juice-packed mandarin
orange segments, drained

15 strawberries, cut into halves

30 ¾-inch cubes nonfat or reduced-fat
cheddar cheese

1½ cups nonfat or reduced-fat plain
yogurt

¼ cup honey

2 teaspoons finely minced fresh gingerroot

8 ounces canned, juice-packed crushed
pineapple, drained

1. Place a grape, a pineapple chunk, a mandarin orange segment, a strawberry half, and a piece of cheese on each of 30 small wooden or plastic skewers.
2. Combine yogurt, honey, and gingerroot and mix until creamy. Stir in pineapple.
3. Serve fruit kabobs with ginger-honey dip.

Calories Per Serving: 75
Fat: 0 g
Cholesterol: 0 mg
Protein: 4 g

Carbohydrates: 15 g
Dietary Fiber: 1 g
Sodium: 182 mg

Banana-Apple Skewers
≫ with Honey-Lime Dip ≪

YIELD: 8 servings (1 skewer each) • *PREPARATION TIME: 20 minutes plus overnight refrigeration time*

Fresh fruit is skewered and served with a dip of yogurt mixed with honey, lime peel, and lime juice.

1 cup nonfat or reduced-fat plain yogurt
Grated peel of 1 lime
1 tablespoon lime juice
3 tablespoons honey
2 small bananas, each cut into 8 chunks

2 apples, cored, each cut into 8 wedges
2 tablespoons lemon juice mixed with 2 tablespoons water
2 kiwis, each cut into 8 chunks
8 large strawberries

1. Whisk together yogurt, lime peel, lime juice, and honey. Cover and refrigerate overnight.
2. When ready to serve, dip banana chunks and apple wedges into the lemon water to prevent discoloration.
3. Alternate bananas, apples, and kiwis on each of 8 wooden or plastic skewers, ending with a strawberry.
4. Place dip in bowl and arrange skewers around it.

Calories Per Serving: 199
Fat: 1 g
Cholesterol: 1 mg
Protein: 3 g

Carbohydrates: 48 g
Dietary Fiber: 8 g
Sodium: 55 mg

✎ *Elegant Orange Slices with Raspberries* ✐

YIELD: 18 servings (2 each) • *PREPARATION TIME: 15 minutes plus*
1 hour refrigeration time

Orange slices marinated in Grand Marnier, a brandy-based French liqueur flavored with orange peel, are served topped with raspberries. Serve as a classic accent with an appetizer buffet of hot and cold offerings.

6 navel oranges, peeled
3 tablespoons Grand Marnier

2 tablespoons sugar
1 pint raspberries

1. Slice oranges crosswise ¼ inch thick.
2. Place in glass bowl with Grand Marnier and sugar. Marinate in refrigerator for 1 hour.
3. Drain orange slices and arrange on a serving platter. Spoon a few raspberries on top of each orange slice. Serve with small plates and cocktail forks.

Calories Per Serving: 40
Fat: 0 g
Cholesterol: 0 mg
Protein: 1 g

Carbohydrates: 8 g
Dietary Fiber: 4 g
Sodium: 1 mg

✎ *Marinated Strawberries* ✐

YIELD: 8 servings (2 each) • *PREPARATION TIME: 5 minutes plus*
1 hour refrigeration time

Fresh strawberries are marinated in sugar and lemon juice. Serve with a creamy yogurt dip.

2 pints large strawberries, hulled
3 tablespoons sugar

3 tablespoons lemon juice

1. Sprinkle berries with the sugar and lemon juice; toss gently.
2. Refrigerate for 1 hour. Serve with plastic or wooden party picks.

Calories Per Serving: 29
Fat: 0 g
Cholesterol: 0 mg
Protein: 0 g

Carbohydrates: 7 g
Dietary Fiber: 1 g
Sodium: 0 mg

✎ Sugared-Pineapple Wedges ✎

YIELD: 8 servings (4 pieces each) • PREPARATION TIME: 15 minutes •
COOKING TIME: 25 minutes

Fresh pineapple is a special treat when baked and sprinkled with brown
sugar.

1 large ripe pineapple, top and bottom
  removed, cored, and cut into 8
  1-inch slices
2 teaspoons canola oil

¼ teaspoon black pepper
2 tablespoons brown sugar, firmly
  packed
Juice of 2 limes

1. Preheat oven to 500 degrees. Rub the pineapple slices with oil, sprinkle
   with pepper, and place in a single layer on a baking sheet.
2. Bake for 15 minutes, turn pineapple over, and bake for an additional 10
   minutes.
3. Remove from oven, sprinkle with brown sugar, and drizzle with lime
   juice. Cut each slice into quarters and serve with small plates and cocktail
   forks.

Calories Per Serving: 92
Fat: 2 g
Cholesterol: 0 mg
Protein: 1 g

Carbohydrates: 21 g
Dietary Fiber: 2 g
Sodium: 3 mg

❧ *Almond-Ginger Apricots* ❧

YIELD: 24 servings (1 each) • *PREPARATION TIME: 20 minutes*

Large dried apricots are stuffed with a cream cheese, orange marmalade, ginger, and almond filling.

*3 ounces nonfat or reduced-fat cream
  cheese, softened
½ teaspoon ground ginger
1½ tablespoons all-fruit orange marmalade*

*24 whole, large dried apricots
24 unsalted almonds*

1. Blend together cream cheese, ginger, and orange marmalade.
2. Spoon ½ teaspoon filling into each apricot.
3. Push an almond into the center of each and serve.

Calories Per Serving: 48
Fat: 2 g
Cholesterol: 1 mg
Protein: 2 g

Carbohydrates: 6 g
Dietary Fiber: 1 g
Sodium: 26 mg

❧ *Cheese-Stuffed Strawberries* ❧

YIELD: 14 servings (1 each) • *PREPARATION TIME: 25 minutes*

Fresh strawberries are stuffed with a cream cheese filling.

*2 ounces nonfat or reduced-fat cream
  cheese, softened
2 tablespoons nonfat or reduced-fat
  sour cream*

*14 large strawberries
2 tablespoons brown sugar, firmly
  packed*

1. Beat together cream cheese and sour cream.
2. Cut an X through each strawberry, starting at the pointy end and cutting through nearly to the stem end, being careful that berries remain in one piece.

3. Carefully stuff the berries with the cheese mixture and sprinkle with brown sugar.

Calories Per Serving: 17
Fat: 0 g
Cholesterol: 1 mg
Protein: 1 g

Carbohydrates: 3 g
Dietary Fiber: 1 g
Sodium: 31 mg

✎ Strawberries with Maple-Orange Liqueur ✎

YIELD: 18 servings (⅓ cup each) • *PREPARATION TIME: 30 minutes*

Fresh strawberries are combined with nutmeg, maple syrup, orange-flavored liqueur, vanilla, and mint.

½ teaspoon ground nutmeg
2½ tablespoons pure maple syrup
2 tablespoons orange-flavored liqueur

1 tablespoon vanilla extract
½ teaspoon dried mint
6 cups strawberries, hulled

1. Whisk together nutmeg, maple syrup, liqueur, vanilla, and mint.
2. Place liqueur mixture in a bowl with strawberries and toss well. Let stand for 20 minutes.
3. Arrange strawberries on a serving dish. Serve with wooden or plastic party picks.

Calories Per Serving: 27
Fat: 0 g
Cholesterol: 0 mg
Protein: 0 g

Carbohydrates: 6 g
Dietary Fiber: 1 g
Sodium: 1 mg

✎ Peanut Butter–Fruit Bites ✎

YIELD: 18 servings (1 each) • *PREPARATION TIME: 10 minutes*

Peanut butter, dried fruit, and shredded apple are combined and served on mini–rice cakes.

½ *cup low-fat peanut butter substitute*
¼ *cup chopped raisins, dried apricots, or*
  dried peaches

1 *small apple, peeled and shredded*
18 *mini–rice cakes*

1. Combine peanut butter, dried fruit, and apple.
2. Spread on rice cakes and serve.

Calories Per Serving: 46
Fat: 1 g
Cholesterol: 0 mg
Protein: 1 g

Carbohydrates: 10 g
Dietary Fiber: 0 g
Sodium: 17 mg

❧ *Fruit Bites* ❦

YIELD: 16 servings (2 pieces each) • *PREPARATION TIME: 15 minutes*

Pieces of oranges, apples, and peaches are dipped in a coating of sesame seeds
and chopped walnuts.

2 *tablespoons toasted sesame seeds*
2 *tablespoons finely chopped walnuts*
2 *navel oranges, peeled and sectioned*
1 *large apple, cored and cut into*
  wedges

1 *large peach or nectarine, pitted and*
  cut into wedges
½ *cup nonfat or reduced-fat plain*
  yogurt

1. Combine sesame seeds and walnuts in a shallow plate.
2. Dip each piece of fruit into yogurt and then roll in the sesame seed–
   walnut mixture.
3. Serve with wooden or plastic party picks.

Calories Per Serving: 51
Fat: 1 g
Cholesterol: 0 mg
Protein: 1 g

Carbohydrates: 10 g
Dietary Fiber: 2 g
Sodium: 13 mg

❦ *Papaya-Salmon Bites* ❦

YIELD: 12 servings (2 each) • *PREPARATION TIME: 15 minutes*

Thinly sliced smoked salmon is wrapped around papaya slices.

2 medium papayas
12 ounces smoked salmon, cut into
   24 slices

Juice of 3 limes

1. Seed papayas, peel, and cut into 24 slices.
2. Wrap a slice of salmon around each piece of papaya and secure with party pick.
3. Sprinkle with lime juice immediately before serving.

Calories Per Serving: 61
Fat: 1 g
Cholesterol: 7 mg
Protein: 6 g

Carbohydrates: 7 g
Dietary Fiber: 1 g
Sodium: 222 mg

❦ *Apples with Chutney Dip* ❦

YIELD: 16 servings (2 each) • *PREPARATION TIME: 20 minutes plus*
30 minutes refrigeration time

Apples are sliced and served with a curried dip.

1 cup nonfat or reduced-fat sour cream
2 tablespoons curry powder
½ teaspoon ground ginger
2 tablespoons mango chutney
3 Red Delicious apples, cored and
   sliced ¼ inch thick

3 Golden Delicious apples, cored and
   sliced ¼ inch thick
2 tablespoons lemon juice mixed with
   2 tablespoons water

1. Combine sour cream, curry powder, ground ginger, and chutney in a serving bowl. Cover and refrigerate for 30 minutes.

2. Toss apple slices in lemon water to prevent discoloration.
3. Place dip in the middle of a serving platter and surround with apple slices.

Calories Per Serving: 186   Carbohydrates: 44 g
Fat: 2 g   Dietary Fiber: 10 g
Cholesterol: 5 mg   Sodium: 62 mg
Protein: 3 g

❧ *Tropical Fruit Bites* ✍

YIELD: 16 servings (½ cup each) • *PREPARATION TIME: 25 minutes plus
1 hour refrigeration time*

Papaya, mango, and melon are marinated in apple juice and anise.

1⅓ cups natural apple juice
1 tablespoon plus 1 teaspoon corn-
   starch
1 teaspoon anise seeds, crushed
2 cups cantaloupe balls

2 cups fresh papaya chunks
2 cups fresh mango chunks
2 cups fresh or canned, water-packed
   pineapple chunks

1. Combine apple juice, cornstarch, and anise seeds in a small saucepan. Stir until blended. Bring to a boil over medium heat and cook for 1 minute, stirring constantly. Remove from heat. Cool to room temperature.
2. Place cantaloupe balls, papaya chunks, mango chunks, and pineapple chunks in a glass bowl.
3. Pour juice mixture over fruit. Cover and refrigerate for 1 hour.
4. Drain, and then serve with wooden or plastic party picks.

Calories Per Serving: 45   Carbohydrates: 11 g
Fat: 0 g   Dietary Fiber: 1 g
Cholesterol: 0 mg   Sodium: 4 mg
Protein: 1 g

❦ *Pineapples and Strawberries with Mango Sauce* ❦

YIELD: 18 servings (½ cup each) • *PREPARATION TIME: 15 minutes plus
30 minutes refrigeration time*

Pineapple chunks and strawberries are served with a mango-lime sauce.

2 cups peeled fresh mango
1 tablespoon lime juice

4 cups fresh or canned, water-packed
   pineapple chunks
3 cups strawberries, hulled

1. Place mango in a blender or food processor and puree.
2. Transfer mango puree to a serving bowl. Stir in lime juice. Chill for 30 minutes.
3. Serve mango puree in a bowl surrounded by pineapple chunks and strawberries. Serve with wooden or plastic party picks.

Calories Per Serving: 36
Fat: 0 g
Cholesterol: 0 mg
Protein: 0 g

Carbohydrates: 9 g
Dietary Fiber: 1 g
Sodium: 1 mg

❦ *Pineapple-Spice Bites* ❦

YIELD: 16 servings (¼ cup each) • *PREPARATION TIME: 10 minutes plus
overnight refrigeration time*

Pineapple is simmered in sugar, spices, and vinegar.

32 ounces canned, juice-packed
   pineapple, drained and juice reserved
⅔ cup cider vinegar

¾ cup sugar
2 whole cloves
1 cinnamon stick

1. Place ⅓ cup of reserved pineapple juice, vinegar, sugar, cloves, and cinnamon stick in a saucepan. Simmer for 8 minutes.
2. Add pineapple chunks and heat until sauce boils. Remove from heat.

3. Transfer to a bowl. Cover and refrigerate overnight.
4. Drain, and then serve with wooden or plastic party picks.

Calories Per Serving: 56   Carbohydrates: 15 g
Fat: 0 g   Dietary Fiber: 0 g
Cholesterol: 0 mg   Sodium: 1 mg
Protein: 0 g

▧ *Spiced Honeydew Chunks* ▧

YIELD: 12 servings (3 each) • *PREPARATION TIME: 15 minutes*

Honeydew melon is tossed with lime juice and chili powder.

Juice of 2 limes   *1 honeydew melon, seeded and cut*
2½ teaspoons chili powder   *into 36 1-inch chunks*

1. In a glass bowl, whisk together lime juice and chili powder. Add melon chunks and toss.
2. Serve with wooden or plastic party picks.

Calories Per Serving: 53   Carbohydrates: 14 g
Fat: 0 g   Dietary Fiber: 1 g
Cholesterol: 0 mg   Sodium: 20 mg
Protein: 1 g

CANAPÉS

CROSTINI AND CANAPÉS ON TOAST

Broccoli Crostini • Mushroom Crostini • Plum Tomato Puree Canapés • Sun-Dried Tomato and Feta Crostini • Green Olive Crostini • Pinto Bean Crostini • Sardine Crostini • White Bean and Tomato Crostini • Red Pepper Canapés • Garlic-Potato Canapés • Brandied-Crab Canapés • Mussel and Clam Canapés with Salsa • Tuna Canapés • Anchovy-Cheese Canapés

COLD CANAPÉS

Fruit-Topped Danish Canapés • Tomato Canapés • Cucumber-Watercress Canapés • Radish Delights • Radish-Cuke Slices • Salmon-Cucumber Minislices • Banana-Date Strips • Olive-Carrot Sandwich Strips • Tuna Toppers • Smoked Salmon–Pumpernickel Stacks • Tuna-Egg Ribbon Slices • Turkey, Cheese, and Watercress Ribbon Slices • Turkey-Chutney Tastes • Dijon Chicken Canapés • Chicken-Walnut Sandwiches • Apple-

Chicken Sandwiches • Gingered Chicken Salad Canapés • Roast Turkey Delights • Smoked Turkey Minisandwiches • Feta Bites • Garden Harvest Treats • Apple-Cheese Bites • Fruit Salad–Cheese Tastes • Salmon Canapés • Sardine Spread on Rye Crackers • Avocado-Shrimp Delights • Pineapple-Cheese Bites

CANAPÉ ROUNDS, DIAMONDS, AND CUPS

Very Veggie Rounds • Apple-Carrot Rounds • Tiny Turkey Burgers • Chicken-Cucumber Rounds • Roast Turkey–Ricotta– Cranberry Rounds • Tuna-Avocado Pinwheels • Watercress-Dill– Shrimp Rounds • Peking Rounds • Crab Delights • Honey- Baked Turkey–Red Pepper Diamonds • Sherried Cheese Rounds • Curried Olive-Cheese Rounds • Ricotta Rounds • Shrimp- Caper Rounds • Pepper Rounds • Crab Cups • Gingered Chicken Cups • Tuna Cups • Curried Chicken Cups • Oriental Chicken Salad Cups • Eggplant Toast Cups • Shiitake Toast Cups • Mozzarella-Mushroom Bread Baskets • Olive-Cheese Wonton Baskets • Basil–Goat Cheese Rounds

STUFFED SANDWICHES AND PITAS

Pan Bagnat • Salmon Slices • Stuffed Shrimp Loaf • Oyster Slices • Tuna–Egg Salad Loaf • Sun-Dried Tomato–Turkey– Cheese Treats • Stuffed Italian Rolls • Mini–Veggie Pitas • Artichoke Wedges • Lox and Minibagels • Red Pepper–Artichoke Delights • Minimuffins with Sun-Dried Tomato Filling • Mango Chutney Bites • Wrapped Olives and Anchovies

HOT CANAPÉS

Artichoke Toasts ▪ Crab Morsels ▪ Olive-Crab Melts ▪ Oysters
Wicomico ▪ Puffed Cheese-Shrimp Rounds ▪ Shrimp Toasts ▪
Seafood-Cheese Melts ▪ Tuna Biscuits ▪ Parmesan-Onion Puffs ▪
Ricotta Sticks ▪ Toasted Veggie Minibagels ▪ Mini–Baked Bean
Melts ▪ Zucchini Pita Pizza Bites

ABOUT CANAPÉS

⠿

Canapé is the French word for "couch." Canapés are small, decorative pieces of toasted or untoasted bread or crackers, topped with spreads, poultry, seafood, vegetables, and fruits. They can be simple or elaborate, hot or cold.

When toasting bread for toasted canapé bases, arrange slices or cutouts on a baking sheet and place in a preheated 400-degree oven just until bread turns golden. Remove from oven, transfer to a wire rack or flip over on the baking sheet, and let cool. Arrange topping on the untoasted side of the bread if serving immediately. If serving will be delayed, toast the bread on both sides.

Cold canapés can be cut into squares, triangles, or strips. They can be made in one layer or several layers to create ribbon, checkerboard, pinwheel, or double-decker sandwich effects. Canapé bases can be cut with canapé or cookie cutters with fluted or scalloped edges, or in the shape of diamonds, circles, hearts, and flowers.

Shop at your local bakery for a variety of breads to use for canapés for increased visual appeal. Open-faced canapés can be made on standard slices or thinly sliced sandwich bread. Decorative canapés are often made with lengthwise slices of bread cut from whole loaves. "Sandwich" bread is ideal because it has a uniform shape and squared ends, resulting in less waste. When using two different-colored loaves of breads for canapés such as ribbon canapés, be sure they are both the same size. When selecting breads for canapés, look for those that are neither too heavy nor too bland or crumbly.

When preparing a loaf of sandwich bread to use for canapé bases, partially freeze uncut loaves of sandwich bread to make cutting the crusts off easier. Use an extremely sharp, hot knife when removing the crusts. Cut off the tops and bottom before you cut off the ends. Then slice the bread horizontally into 5- to 7½-inch slices. Wrap unused bread slices in plastic wrap and freeze in an airtight freezer bag to use another time.

When preparing thin slices of standard bread or sandwich bread for rolling up, remove crusts and gently roll over each slice with a rolling pin before filling.

In traditional canapés, a light coating of butter on the base keeps the bread from absorbing moisture and becoming soggy. However, since recipes in *500 Low-Fat and Fat-Free Appetizers, Snacks, and Hors d'Oeuvres* don't use butter or margarine, you should compensate for the lack of a butter layer on your sandwiches by making cold appetizer sandwiches as close to serving time as possible.

• CROSTINI AND CANAPÉS ON TOAST •

Broccoli Crostini

YIELD: 16 servings (1 each) • *PREPARATION TIME: 15 minutes* •
COOKING TIME: 30 minutes

Whole wheat baguette slices are toasted, seasoned with garlic, and spread with a broccoli-tomato topping.

16 ½-inch slices whole wheat or regular baguette
4 garlic cloves, 2 peeled, 2 finely chopped
3 tablespoons light-flavored olive oil
2 cups chopped broccoli
¼ teaspoon black pepper
½ cup diced, fresh or low-sodium canned tomatoes

1. Preheat oven to 400 degrees. Arrange bread in a single layer on a baking sheet.
2. Bake for 12 minutes or until golden. Remove bread slices and rub lightly with the 2 whole garlic cloves.
3. Heat the olive oil in a skillet over medium heat. Sauté the broccoli, chopped garlic, and pepper for 5 minutes.
4. Add the tomatoes. Cover the skillet and cook for 15 minutes or until the broccoli is tender.
5. Let broccoli-tomato topping come to room temperature. Spoon on slices of crostini and serve.

Calories Per Serving: 86

Carbohydrates: 13 g

Fat: 3 g

Dietary Fiber: 1 g

Cholesterol: 0 mg

Sodium: 128 mg

Protein: 2 g

❧ *Mushroom Crostini* ❧

YIELD: 16 servings (1 each) • *PREPARATION TIME: 15 minutes* •
COOKING TIME: 8 minutes

Whole wheat baguette slices are toasted, seasoned with garlic, and spread
with a mushroom-parsley topping.

*16 ½-inch slices whole wheat or regu-
  lar baguette*

5 cups sliced mushrooms

*4 garlic cloves, 2 peeled, 2 finely
  chopped*

¼ teaspoon black pepper

2 tablespoons chopped fresh parsley

3 tablespoons light-flavored olive oil

*¼ cup nonfat or reduced-fat, low-
  sodium chicken broth*

1. Preheat oven to 400 degrees. Arrange bread in a single layer on a baking
   sheet.
2. Bake for 12 minutes or until golden. Remove bread slices and rub lightly
   with the 2 whole garlic cloves.
3. Heat the olive oil in a skillet over medium heat. Sauté the mushrooms for
   8 minutes.
4. Add the chopped garlic, pepper, parsley, and broth. Boil until the broth has
   evaporated.
5. Transfer the mushrooms to a cutting board and chop until they reach a
   consistency that you can spread.
6. Let mushroom-parsley topping come to room temperature. Spoon on
   slices of crostini and serve.

Calories Per Serving: 82

Carbohydrates: 13 g

Fat: 3 g

Dietary Fiber: 0 g

Cholesterol: 0 mg

Sodium: 127 mg

Protein: 3 g

❧ *Plum Tomato Puree Canapés* ❧

YIELD: 12 servings (1 each) • *PREPARATION TIME: 35 minutes* •
COOKING TIME: 50 minutes

Plum tomatoes and canned red peppers top thick slices of garlic bread.

12 1-inch-thick slices day-old Italian
   bread
3 cloves garlic, 2 peeled, 1 minced
1 tablespoon light-flavored olive oil
2 tablespoons minced onion
14 ounces canned, low-sodium Italian
   plum tomatoes

6 ounces canned roasted red peppers,
   rinsed, drained, and diced
¼ teaspoon dried oregano
¼ teaspoon dried thyme

1. Preheat oven to 400 degrees. Place bread in a single layer on a baking sheet.
2. Bake for 12 minutes, or until golden.
3. Rub the top of the toast with the whole garlic cloves.
4. Heat oil in a large skillet over medium heat. Sauté the onions for 4 minutes. Add the minced garlic and sauté for 1 minute.
5. Add the plum tomatoes, red peppers, oregano, and thyme. Bring to a boil. Reduce heat and simmer for 20 minutes.
6. Let tomato mixture cool. Place in a blender or food processor, process until smooth, and return to skillet. Simmer until very thick. Cool to room temperature.
7. Spread the tomato mixture on the toast.

Calories Per Serving: 152
Fat: 3 g
Cholesterol: 0 mg
Protein: 5 g

Carbohydrates: 27 g
Dietary Fiber: 0 g
Sodium: 316 mg

❧ Sun-Dried Tomato and Feta Crostini ✦

YIELD: 20 servings (2 each) ▪ PREPARATION TIME: 30 minutes ▪
COOKING TIME: 12 minutes

The intense flavor of sun-dried tomatoes is combined with olives and feta cheese.

1 loaf French bread, unsliced	3 ounces nonfat or reduced-fat cream
4 ounces sun-dried tomatoes, packed in	cheese, softened
olive oil	4 ounces feta cheese
1 clove garlic, minced	2 tablespoons skim or 1% milk
¼ cup chopped, pitted black olives	

1. Preheat oven to 300 degrees. Cut bread into 40 ¼-inch slices. Arrange slices on baking sheets.
2. Drain tomatoes and reserve oil. Lightly brush one side of each bread slice with some of the reserved oil.
3. Bake for 6 minutes. Turn and bake for an additional 6 minutes until lightly browned.
4. Finely chop sun-dried tomatoes. Combine tomatoes with garlic and olives.
5. Combine cream cheese, feta cheese, and milk until smooth.
6. Spread cheese mixture on oiled side of toasted bread slices.
7. Top with a spoonful of tomato mixture.

Calories Per Serving: 96	Carbohydrates: 15 g
Fat: 2 g	Dietary Fiber: 0 g
Cholesterol: 6 mg	Sodium: 278 mg
Protein: 4 g	

❧ Green Olive Crostini ✦

YIELD: 20 servings (2 each) ▪ PREPARATION TIME: 15 minutes plus
3 days refrigeration time ▪ COOKING TIME: 12 minutes

This olive-almond spread takes only a few minutes to prepare and needs to sit in the refrigerator for 3 days to give the flavors a chance to blend.

1 cup pitted green olives, rinsed and
   drained
2 tablespoons slivered, blanched
   almonds
2 teaspoons dried basil

1 teaspoon dried basil
1 teaspoon dried oregano
1 teaspoon dried thyme
1 tablespoon light-flavored olive oil
1 loaf Italian bread, unsliced

1. Place olives, almonds, basil, oregano, thyme, and olive oil in blender or food processor and puree.
2. Chill in refrigerator for 3 days.
3. When ready to serve, remove from refrigerator and let stand at room temperature while preparing crostini.
4. Preheat oven to 400 degrees. Slice bread into 40 ¼-inch slices.
5. Arrange bread on a baking sheet and bake for 12 minutes.
6. Spread toasted side of crostini with olive-almond spread.

Calories Per Serving: 80
Fat: 3 g
Cholesterol: 0 mg
Protein: 2 g

Carbohydrates: 12 g
Dietary Fiber: 0 g
Sodium: 308 mg

Pinto Bean Crostini

YIELD: 8 servings (2 each) • *PREPARATION TIME: 20 minutes plus
2 hours refrigeration time* • *COOKING TIME: 15 minutes*

A mixture of oil-cured black olives, pinto beans, lemon juice, and capers is spread on toast.

1 clove garlic, minced
¼ cup pitted, oil-cured black olives
1 cup canned or home-cooked pinto
   beans, rinsed and drained
2 teaspoons lemon juice

1 teaspoon capers, drained
¾ teaspoon sugar
16 ½-inch slices French bread
8 cherry tomatoes, halved

1. Place garlic, olives, beans, lemon juice, capers, and sugar in a blender or food processor. Blend until the mixture is smooth. Cover and chill for 2 hours.

2. Preheat oven to 400 degrees. Place bread in a single layer on a baking sheet.
3. Bake for 12 minutes or until crisp and lightly brown.
4. Spread garlic mixture on toast slices. Place a tomato half on each toast.

Calories Per Serving: 184

Fat: 3 g

Cholesterol: 0 mg

Protein: 6 g

Carbohydrates: 33 g

Dietary Fiber: 0 g

Sodium: 570 mg

✎ *Sardine Crostini* ✎

YIELD: 8 servings (1 each) • *PREPARATION TIME: 15 minutes* •
COOKING TIME: 2 minutes

Sardines and red onion are served on slices of toasted baguette rubbed with garlic.

1 8-inch section of a baguette, sliced lengthwise into two long halves
1 clove garlic, peeled

3¾ ounces canned, oil-packed sardines
½ small red onion, divided into rings

1. Preheat broiler. Place baguette halves on a baking sheet, cut side up. Broil for 2 minutes or until bread is lightly browned.
2. Remove bread from oven and rub with garlic.
3. Arrange sardines on bread halves and arrange onion slices over sardines.
4. Cut each baguette half into 4 pieces and serve.

Calories Per Serving: 114

Fat: 3 g

Cholesterol: 21 mg

Protein: 6 g

Carbohydrates: 16 g

Dietary Fiber: 0 g

Sodium: 248 mg

White Bean and Tomato Crostini

YIELD: 16 servings (1 each) • *PREPARATION TIME: 15 minutes* •
COOKING TIME: 8 minutes

Whole wheat baguette slices are toasted, seasoned with garlic, and spread with a white bean and tomato topping.

16 ½-inch slices whole wheat or regular baguette
3 garlic cloves, 2 peeled, 1 minced
1 tablespoon light-flavored olive oil
1 small onion, minced

¼ cup chopped fresh or canned, low-sodium plum tomatoes
2 cups canned or home-cooked white beans, drained and rinsed
¼ teaspoon black pepper

1. Preheat oven to 400 degrees. Arrange bread in a single layer on a baking sheet.
2. Bake for 12 minutes, or until golden. Remove bread slices and rub lightly with the 2 whole garlic cloves.
3. Heat the olive oil in a skillet over medium heat. Sauté the onion and minced garlic for 1 minute.
4. Add chopped tomatoes, white beans, and pepper. Simmer, crushing beans with the back of a spoon, until beans and tomatoes are warmed through.
5. Let tomato-bean topping come to room temperature. Spoon onto slices of crostini.

Calories Per Serving: 95
Fat: 2 g
Cholesterol: 0 mg
Protein: 4 g

Carbohydrates: 17 g
Dietary Fiber: 2 g
Sodium: 114 mg

Red Pepper Canapés

YIELD: 12 servings (1 each) • *PREPARATION TIME: 25 minutes* •
COOKING TIME: 10 minutes

A mixture of red bell pepper, black olives, olive oil, and balsamic vinegar is spread on garlic toast.

1 cup pitted black olives
5 tablespoons light-flavored olive oil
¼ teaspoon balsamic vinegar
¼ teaspoon black pepper

4 1-inch-thick slices Italian bread
½ clove garlic, crushed
1 red bell pepper, cut into ¼-inch strips

1. Preheat oven to 400 degrees. Place black olives, 2 tablespoons of the olive oil, balsamic vinegar, and pepper in blender or food processor and process until smooth.
2. Cut each slice of bread into thirds. Place on a baking sheet and bake for 12 minutes or until crisp.
3. Warm the remaining 3 tablespoons oil and the garlic in a small pot.
4. Brush oil over toasted bread. Spread with olive mixture, top with red pepper strips, and serve.

Calories Per Serving: 46
Fat: 3 g
Cholesterol: 0 mg
Protein: 1 g

Carbohydrates: 5 g
Dietary Fiber: 0 g
Sodium: 141 mg

❧ *Garlic-Potato Canapés* ❧

YIELD: 10 servings (2 each)　•　PREPARATION TIME: 15 minutes　•
COOKING TIME: 20 minutes

A traditional Greek spread rich in garlic flavor is served on baguette slices. The spread can be made in advance and refrigerated for 48 hours.

1 large baking potato, scrubbed and
quartered
4 large cloves garlic
3 tablespoons light-flavored olive oil

2 tablespoons lemon juice
20 baguette slices
⅓ cup chopped fresh parsley

1. Place potato in a saucepan and add just enough water to cover. Cover saucepan, bring water to a boil, lower heat, and cook approximately 20 minutes or until potato is tender.
2. Drain potato and chop coarsely.

3. Place potato, garlic, olive oil, and lemon juice in a blender or food processor and process until well combined.
4. Transfer to a bowl and refrigerate until serving time.
5. When ready to serve, spread mixture on 20 baguette slices and sprinkle with parsley.

Calories Per Serving: 97	Carbohydrates: 15 g
Fat: 3 g	Dietary Fiber: 0 g
Cholesterol: 0 mg	Sodium: 153 mg
Protein: 2 g	

❧ *Brandied-Crab Canapés* ❧

YIELD: 16 servings (2 each) ▪ *PREPARATION TIME: 15 minutes* ▪
COOKING TIME: 10 minutes

These elegant little appetizers feature crabmeat sautéed with parsley, brandy, lemon juice, and spices that is spread on baguette slices.

2 tablespoons canola oil	*⅛ teaspoon paprika*
¼ cup chopped fresh parsley	*Juice of 1 large lemon*
2 tablespoons brandy	*1 pound cooked crabmeat*
⅛ teaspoon white pepper	*1 16-inch French baguette, cut into*
⅛ teaspoon ground nutmeg	*½-inch slices*

1. Heat oil in a skillet over medium heat. Add parsley, brandy, white pepper, nutmeg, paprika, and lemon juice. Heat until hot.
2. Add crabmeat and toss lightly to coat. Heat through.
3. To serve, spread on baguette slices and serve warm.

Calories Per Serving: 91	Carbohydrates: 11 g
Fat: 2 g	Dietary Fiber: 0 g
Cholesterol: 17 mg	Sodium: 189 mg
Protein: 6 g	

❦ *Mussel and Clam Canapés with Salsa* ❦

YIELD: 10 servings (2 each) • *PREPARATION TIME: 30 minutes* •
COOKING TIME: 30 minutes

Fresh mussels and clams are steamed, served on French bread toast, and topped with salsa.

3 pounds mussels, scrubbed and debearded
1 cup dry white wine
1 cup water
2 tablespoons lemon juice
36 steamer clams, scrubbed
1 medium onion, finely chopped
2 medium tomatoes, finely chopped

2 cloves garlic, minced
3 tablespoons chopped fresh parsley
3 tablespoons white wine vinegar
¼ teaspoon dried oregano
¼ teaspoon black pepper
20 slices French bread, lightly toasted
1 cup prepared salsa

1. Place mussels, wine, water, and lemon juice in a 6- to 8-quart kettle. Cover and simmer over medium-high heat for 5 minutes or until mussels open. Remove mussels and allow to cool. Discard any unopened mussels.
2. Add clams to kettle about 12 at a time. Simmer until open. Lift out clams as they open. Cool.
3. Combine onion, tomatoes, garlic, parsley, vinegar, oregano, and pepper.
4. Remove mussels and clams from shells. Place on toasted French bread slices. Top with salsa and serve.

Calories Per Serving: 165
Fat: 2 g
Cholesterol: 23 mg
Protein: 12 g

Carbohydrates: 21 g
Dietary Fiber: 1 g
Sodium: 289 mg

❧ *Tuna Canapés* ❧

YIELD: *8 servings (2 each)* • PREPARATION TIME: *25 minutes* •
COOKING TIME: *5 minutes*

Tuna accented with pickle relish and onion is spread on sourdough toast.

*7 ounces canned, water-packed white
   albacore tuna, drained
2 stalks celery, chopped
2 tablespoons sweet pickle relish
1 hard-boiled egg white, chopped
1 teaspoon minced onion
2 tablespoons nonfat or reduced-fat
   plain yogurt*

*1 tablespoon nonfat or reduced-fat
   mayonnaise
¼ teaspoon dry mustard
¼ teaspoon black pepper
1 loaf sourdough bread*

1. Combine tuna, celery, relish, egg white, onion, yogurt, mayonnaise, dry
   mustard, and black pepper.
2. Slice bread into 16 ¼-inch slices.
3. Lightly toast bread on one side under broiler.
4. Spread tuna mixture on sourdough toasts.

Calories Per Serving: 180
Fat: 2 g
Cholesterol: 9 mg
Protein: 11 g

Carbohydrates: 28 g
Dietary Fiber: 0 g
Sodium: 449 mg

❧ *Anchovy-Cheese Canapés* ❧

YIELD: *24 servings (1 each)* • PREPARATION TIME: *15 minutes* •
COOKING TIME: *12 minutes*

Italian bread brushed with anchovy-parsley oil is topped with bubbling
mozzarella cheese and an anchovy fillet.

12 1-inch-thick slices Italian bread, halved

14 anchovy fillets, drained and cut in half

3 tablespoons light-flavored olive oil

1 teaspoon finely chopped fresh parsley

16 ounces nonfat or reduced-fat mozzarella cheese, cut into 24 pieces

1. Preheat broiler. Arrange bread on a baking sheet. Toast both sides until lightly browned.
2. With a fork, mash 4 of the anchovy fillet halves in the bottom of a small saucepan. Whisk in oil and parsley, combine well, and heat over low heat.
3. Spread anchovy-parsley oil over toasted bread slices and top each with piece of cheese.
4. Arrange bread slices on a baking sheet and broil for 3 minutes. Top each canapé with an anchovy fillet half.

Calories Per Serving: 87
Fat: 3 g
Cholesterol: 5 mg
Protein: 8 g

Carbohydrates: 8 g
Dietary Fiber: 0 g
Sodium: 308 mg

• COLD CANAPÉS •

✎ Fruit-Topped Danish Canapés ✎

YIELD: 20 servings (2 each) • PREPARATION TIME: 25 minutes plus 1 hour refrigeration time

These Danish-inspired sandwiches feature smoked turkey, pineapple, and mandarin orange sections.

10 slices whole wheat bread

6 ounces nonfat or reduced-fat cream cheese, softened

2 tablespoons skim or 1% milk

1 teaspoon grated orange peel

10 thin slices smoked turkey

40 canned, water-packed pineapple chunks

40 canned, water-packed mandarin orange segments

1. Trim crusts from bread.
2. Blend together cream cheese, milk, and orange peel. Set aside about ¼ cup of mixture.

3. Thinly spread remaining cream cheese mixture on bread slices.
4. Top each with a turkey slice. Cut each slice of bread into 4 quarters.
5. Place a small dollop of the reserved cream cheese mixture in center of each section. Top with a pineapple chunk and a mandarin orange segment.
6. Cover and refrigerate for 1 hour before serving.

Calories Per Serving: 62   Carbohydrates: 10 g
Fat: 1 g   Dietary Fiber: 2 g
Cholesterol: 5 mg   Sodium: 215 mg
Protein: 5 g

❧ *Tomato Canapés* ❧

YIELD: 12 servings (2 each) • *PREPARATION TIME: 20 minutes*

Make these sandwiches when fresh tomatoes and summer herbs are at their peak. Try substituting fresh oregano, thyme, dill, cilantro, or other fresh herbs.

24 thin slices sandwich bread   *4 ripe tomatoes, each cut in 12 slices*
½ cup nonfat or reduced-fat mayon-   *½ cup chopped fresh parsley*
*   naise*

1. Trim crusts from bread.
2. Spread mayonnaise on half of bread slices.
3. Top each mayonnaise-covered slice with 4 slices of tomato.
4. Sprinkle tomatoes with parsley.
5. Top with second slice of bread.
6. Cut each sandwich in half diagonally.

Calories Per Serving: 101   Carbohydrates: 19 g
Fat: 1 g   Dietary Fiber: 1 g
Cholesterol: 0 mg   Sodium: 180 mg
Protein: 3 g

❧ Cucumber-Watercress Canapés ✿

YIELD: *12 servings (2 each)* • PREPARATION TIME: *20 minutes*

Thin slices of cucumber are teamed up with chopped watercress in these traditional treats.

24 slices whole-grain bread
½ cup nonfat or reduced-fat mayonnaise

48 thin slices peeled cucumber
¾ cup chopped fresh watercress

1. Trim crusts from bread slices.
2. Spread half of the bread slices with mayonnaise.
3. Top mayonnaise-covered slices with 4 cucumber rounds, watercress, and top with a second slice of bread.
4. Cut each sandwich in half diagonally.

Calories Per Serving: 147
Fat: 2 g
Cholesterol: 0 mg
Protein: 5 g

Carbohydrates: 28 g
Dietary Fiber: 0 g
Sodium: 272 mg

❧ Radish Delights ✿

YIELD: *18 servings (2 each)* • PREPARATION TIME: *25 minutes*

Crunchy radishes are combined with cream cheese, herbs, and lemon juice.

6 slices rye bread
16 radishes
6 ounces nonfat or reduced-fat cream cheese, softened

1 tablespoon chopped fresh parsley
1 teaspoon chopped scallions
3 teaspoons lemon juice
¼ teaspoon black pepper

1. Trim crusts from rye bread.
2. Grate radishes. Place between paper towels and squeeze to remove as much moisture as possible.

3. Blend together cream cheese, parsley, scallions, lemon juice, pepper, and half of the radishes.
4. Spread the cream cheese mixture on the bread and cut each slice into 6 pieces.
5. Top each piece with a generous mound of the remaining grated radishes.

Calories Per Serving: 39   Carbohydrates: 6 g
Fat: 0 g   Dietary Fiber: 0 g
Cholesterol: 2 mg   Sodium: 138 mg
Protein: 3 g

Radish-Cuke Slices

YIELD: 12 servings (2 each) • *PREPARATION TIME: 30 minutes plus 4 hours refrigeration time*

This easy canapé combines the crunch of garden-fresh radishes with a creamy cucumber spread.

8 ounces nonfat or reduced-fat cream   2 tablespoons minced scallions
*   cheese, softened   24 slices party-size rye bread*
½ cup peeled, seeded, and chopped   12 radishes, thinly sliced
*   cucumber*

1. Blend together cream cheese, cucumber, and scallions.
2. Cover and refrigerate at least 4 hours.
3. Spread cheese mixture on bread slices and top with sliced radishes.

Calories Per Serving: 68   Carbohydrates: 12 g
Fat: 0 g   Dietary Fiber: 1 g
Cholesterol: 3 mg   Sodium: 240 mg
Protein: 6 g

❧ *Salmon-Cucumber Minislices* ❧

YIELD: 15 servings (2 each) • *PREPARATION TIME: 25 minutes*

Salmon, cucumber, and radishes are combined with mayonnaise, lemon juice, and dill, then served on minislices of rye bread.

*7½ ounces canned red salmon, skin
   and bones removed
1 small cucumber, seeded and diced
⅓ cup chopped radishes
½ cup nonfat or reduced-fat mayonnaise*

*2 teaspoons lemon juice
½ teaspoon dried dill
¼ teaspoon black pepper
30 slices party-size rye bread
1 cup fresh parsley sprigs*

1. Combine salmon, cucumber, radishes, mayonnaise, lemon juice, dill, and black pepper.
2. Spread salmon mixture on rye bread slices.
3. Garnish each slice with a sprig of parsley.

Calories Per Serving: 109
Fat: 2 g
Cholesterol: 4 mg
Protein: 5 g

Carbohydrates: 18 g
Dietary Fiber: 1 g
Sodium: 287 mg

❧ *Banana-Date Strips* ❧

YIELD: 12 servings (2 each) • *PREPARATION TIME: 15 minutes*

Bananas, dates, lemon juice, and orange peel are combined to make the filling for these sandwich strips.

*4 ripe bananas
16 dates, finely chopped
2 teaspoons lemon juice*

*½ teaspoon grated orange peel
16 slices whole-grain sandwich bread*

1. Mash bananas with a fork.
2. Combine with dates, lemon juice, and orange peel.

3. Spread mixture on 8 slices of bread.
4. Cover with remaining 8 slices. Trim crusts from bread. Cut each sandwich in thirds.

Calories Per Serving: 147 Carbohydrates: 32 g
Fat: 2 g Dietary Fiber: 5 g
Cholesterol: 0 mg Sodium: 213 mg
Protein: 4 g

⚘ *Olive-Carrot Sandwich Strips* ⚘

YIELD: 9 servings (2 each) • *PREPARATION TIME: 20 minutes plus 30 minutes refrigeration time*

A mixture of grated carrots, ripe olives, celery, scallion, and mayonnaise is spread between slices of light and dark bread to make these sandwich strips.

1¼ cups finely grated carrots *⅓ cup nonfat or reduced-fat mayon-*
½ cup chopped ripe olives *naise*
⅓ cup minced celery *6 slices white sandwich bread*
2 tablespoons minced scallion *6 slices whole wheat sandwich bread*

1. Combine carrots, olives, celery, scallion, and mayonnaise. Chill for 30 minutes.
2. Spread carrot mixture on white bread. Top with whole wheat bread. Trim off crusts. Cut sandwiches in thirds.

Calories Per Serving: 86 Carbohydrates: 13 g
Fat: 3 g Dietary Fiber: 2 g
Cholesterol: 0 mg Sodium: 333 mg
Protein: 2 g

❧ *Tuna Toppers* ❧

YIELD: 12 servings (1 each) • *PREPARATION TIME: 25 minutes plus 45 minutes refrigeration time*

A mixture of albacore tuna, tomatoes, scallions, and celery is spread on crusty French bread.

1 tablespoon light-flavored olive oil
4 scallions, white sections only, chopped
2 celery stalks, finely chopped
7 ounces canned, water-packed, white albacore tuna, drained
2 tomatoes, peeled, seeded, and chopped

2 tablespoons nonfat or reduced-fat mayonnaise
1 teaspoon lemon juice
1 teaspoon white wine vinegar
¼ teaspoon black pepper
12 slices crusty French bread

1. Heat oil in skillet over low heat. Sauté scallions and celery until soft. Let cool.
2. After vegetables have cooled, place in a blender or food processor with tuna, tomatoes, mayonnaise, lemon juice, vinegar, and pepper. Process until smooth.
3. Chill for 45 minutes.
4. Spread tuna mixture on French bread.

Calories Per Serving: 104
Fat: 3 g
Cholesterol: 7 mg
Protein: 7 g

Carbohydrates: 14 g
Dietary Fiber: 1 g
Sodium: 194 mg

❧ *Smoked Salmon–Pumpernickel Stacks* ❧

YIELD: 16 servings (1 each) • *PREPARATION TIME: 25 minutes*

Smoked salmon and a lemon–cream cheese spread with dill and capers are layered in these triple-decker party sandwiches.

7 ounces nonfat or reduced-fat cream
  cheese, softened
2 teaspoons lemon juice
½ teaspoon dried dill

¼ teaspoon capers, drained
12 slices thin-sliced pumpernickel
  bread
6 ounces smoked salmon

1. Place cream cheese, lemon juice, dill, and capers in a blender or food processor and blend well.
2. Spread 4 slices of pumpernickel with a quarter of the blended cream cheese. Layer with one-half of the salmon.
3. Spread 4 more slices of pumpernickel with a quarter of the blended cheese. Place cheese side down on top of salmon.
4. Spread tops of the four stacks with a quarter of the blended cheese. Add a layer of the remaining salmon.
5. Spread remaining 4 slices of pumpernickel with the remaining blended cheese mixture. Place cheese side down on top of salmon.
6. Trim crusts and cut each stack into 4 triangles.

Calories Per Serving: 114
Fat: 2 g
Cholesterol: 6 mg
Protein: 9 g

Carbohydrates: 16 g
Dietary Fiber: 0 g
Sodium: 443 mg

✎ *Tuna-Egg Ribbon Slices* ✎

YIELD: *20 servings (2 each)* • PREPARATION TIME: *30 minutes plus
2 hours refrigeration time*

These triple-decker sandwich slices feature layers of tuna and egg salad with scallion mayonnaise.

1 unsliced loaf white bread
1 unsliced loaf whole wheat bread
6½ ounces canned, water-packed,
  white albacore tuna, drained
¼ cup minced green bell pepper
2 tablespoons chopped scallions

⅔ cup nonfat or reduced-fat mayonnaise
8 hard-boiled egg whites, chopped
1 teaspoon Dijon mustard
⅛ teaspoon black pepper

1. Trim crusts from both loaves of bread. Cut each loaf into ½-inch horizontal slices. Set aside 2 layers white, 1 wheat. Save remaining slices for another use.
2. Combine tuna, green pepper, 1 tablespoon of the scallions, and ⅓ cup of the mayonnaise. Spread on a layer of white bread.
3. Place slice of wheat bread on top of white bread layer with tuna.
4. Combine egg whites, the remaining ⅓ cup mayonnaise, Dijon mustard, the remaining tablespoon of the scallions, and pepper. Spread on top of wheat bread.
5. Place the remaining slice of white bread on top.
6. Wrap in plastic wrap and refrigerate for 2 hours. Cut into 20 slices. Cut each slice in half.

Calories Per Serving: 148
Fat: 2 g
Cholesterol: 4 mg
Protein: 8 g

Carbohydrates: 24 g
Dietary Fiber: 3 g
Sodium: 331 mg

Turkey, Cheese, and
⚘ Watercress Ribbon Slices ⚘

YIELD: *20 servings (2 each)* • PREPARATION TIME: *30 minutes plus 2 hours refrigeration time*

These triple-decker sandwich slices feature turkey, cheese, and watercress fillings.

1 unsliced loaf white bread
1 unsliced loaf whole wheat bread
Dijon mustard
¼ pound sliced roast turkey
¼ cup minced watercress leaves

1 tablespoon minced scallions
½ cup nonfat or reduced-fat sour cream
¼ pound nonfat or reduced-fat Swiss cheese

1. Trim crusts from both loaves of bread. Cut each loaf into ½-inch horizontal slices. Set aside 2 layers white, 1 wheat. Reserve remaining slices for another use.

2. Spread a piece of white bread with Dijon mustard and layer with turkey.

3. Combine watercress, scallions, and sour cream. Spread on a slice of wheat bread. Place wheat bread with watercress spread facedown on top of white bread–turkey layer.

4. Layer Swiss cheese on top of wheat bread. Spread Dijon mustard on the remaining slice of white bread and place on top of Swiss cheese layer.

5. Wrap in plastic wrap and refrigerate for 2 hours. Cut into 20 slices. Cut each slice in half.

Calories Per Serving: 139   Carbohydrates: 23 g
Fat: 2 g   Dietary Fiber: 3 g
Cholesterol: 4 mg   Sodium: 413 mg
Protein: 7 g

❧ *Turkey-Chutney Tastes* ❧

YIELD: 16 servings (1 each) • *PREPARATION TIME: 20 minutes*

The autumn flavors of roast turkey, fruit chutney, and sweet onion slices are served on whole-grain bread.

¼ cup nonfat or reduced-fat mayon-   *8 slices roast turkey breast*
  naise   *½ cup fruit chutney*
8 slices whole-grain bread   *½ sweet onion, thinly sliced*

1. Spread mayonnaise on one side of all 8 bread slices.
2. Place 2 slices of turkey on each of 4 bread slices.
3. Spread chutney on turkey.
4. Top with thinly sliced onion.
5. Cover with remaining 4 pieces of bread.
6. Trim crusts and cut each sandwich into 4 quarters.

Calories Per Serving: 64   Carbohydrates: 11 g
Fat: 1 g   Dietary Fiber: 1 g
Cholesterol: 5 mg   Sodium: 123 mg
Protein: 4 g

✎ *Dijon Chicken Canapés* ✎

YIELD: 24 servings (2 each) • *PREPARATION TIME: 25 minutes plus*
2 hours refrigeration time

These easy-to-prepare layered chicken sandwiches are spiced with Dijon mustard.

1½ cups chopped, cooked chicken
   breast
½ cup nonfat or reduced-fat mayon-
   naise

⅓ cup chopped celery
2 teaspoons Dijon mustard
1 unsliced loaf whole wheat bread,
   crusts trimmed

1. Combine chicken, mayonnaise, celery, and mustard.
2. Cut 4 horizontal slices, each ½ inch thick, from whole wheat loaf. Set aside rest of loaf for another use.
3. Spread 3 slices with chicken mixture.
4. Stack slices, topping with fourth slice.
5. Wrap in plastic wrap and refrigerate for 2 hours.
6. Cut loaf into 24 ½-inch slices. Cut each slice in half.

Calories Per Serving: 92
Fat: 1 g
Cholesterol: 12 mg
Protein: 6 g

Carbohydrates: 17 g
Dietary Fiber: 2 g
Sodium: 375 mg

✎ *Chicken-Walnut Sandwiches* ✎

YIELD: 15 servings (2 each) • *PREPARATION TIME: 20 minutes*

Chicken, celery, walnuts, and yogurt are combined to make a filling for these layered sandwiches.

1½ cups chopped, cooked chicken
   breast
1 stalk celery, chopped

2 tablespoons nonfat or reduced-fat
   plain yogurt

3 tablespoons nonfat or reduced-fat
   mayonnaise

¼ cup chopped walnuts
15 slices whole-grain bread

1. Combine chicken, celery, yogurt, mayonnaise, and walnuts.
2. Spread 5 slices of bread with half of the chicken mixture.
3. Top each slice with another slice of bread.
4. Spread the second slices of bread with the remaining chicken mixture.
5. Top each with a third slice of bread.
6. Trim the crusts from the bread and cut each sandwich into thirds. Then cut each third in half.

Calories Per Serving: 79
Fat: 1 g
Cholesterol: 6 mg
Protein: 4 g

Carbohydrates: 13 g
Dietary Fiber: 1 g
Sodium: 157 mg

Apple-Chicken Sandwiches

YIELD: 12 servings (2 each) • *PREPARATION TIME: 25 minutes*

Tart apples and sweet apricot spread complement chicken in these open-faced sandwiches.

½ cup nonfat or reduced-fat mayonnaise
½ cup all-fruit apricot spread

2 cups chopped, cooked chicken breast
1 cup chopped apple
24 slices French bread

1. Combine mayonnaise, apricot spread, chicken breast, and apple.
2. Spoon chicken-apple mixture onto French bread slices.

Calories Per Serving: 253
Fat: 3 g
Cholesterol: 18 mg
Protein: 12 g

Carbohydrates: 46 g
Dietary Fiber: 2 g
Sodium: 329 mg

✺ *Gingered Chicken Salad Canapés* ✺

YIELD: 16 servings (2 each) • *PREPARATION TIME: 25 minutes*

A gingered chicken salad with crunchy vegetables is served on oatmeal bread.

⅓ cup nonfat or reduced-fat mayon-
naise
½ teaspoon ground ginger
⅛ teaspoon hot pepper sauce
2 cups chopped, cooked chicken breast

½ cup shredded green bell pepper
½ cup shredded carrot
¼ cup shredded celery
64 2-inch rounds cut from firm oat-
meal bread

1. Combine mayonnaise, ginger, hot pepper sauce, chicken, green pepper, carrot, and celery.
2. Spread the chicken filling on 32 of the 2-inch rounds.
3. Top with the remaining 32 rounds.

Calories Per Serving: 154
Fat: 1 g
Cholesterol: 7 mg
Protein: 7 g

Carbohydrates: 27 g
Dietary Fiber: 2 g
Sodium: 344 mg

✺ *Roast Turkey Delights* ✺

YIELD: 18 servings (2 each) • *PREPARATION TIME: 25 minutes*

Roast turkey, cream cheese, and avocado are layered between whole-grain bread in these sinless delights.

5 ounces nonfat or reduced-fat cream
cheese, softened
¼ teaspoon paprika

12 slices whole-grain bread
7 ounces sliced roast turkey
½ avocado, mashed

1. Combine cream cheese and paprika. Spread a third of the cream cheese on 4 slices of bread.

2. Top with a layer of roast turkey, using half of the turkey.
3. Spread a thin layer of avocado over turkey, using half of the avocado.
4. Spread 4 more slices of bread with another third of the cream cheese. Place cheese side down on top of avocado layer.
5. Carefully spread the top of bread slices with the remaining cheese, add a layer of the remaining turkey, and spread turkey with the remaining avocado.
6. Top with remaining 4 pieces of bread.
7. Trim crusts from bread. Cut sandwiches into 3 strips. Cut each strip in thirds.

Calories Per Serving: 72
Fat: 2 g
Cholesterol: 6 mg
Protein: 5 g

Carbohydrates: 9 g
Dietary Fiber: 2 g
Sodium: 248 mg

❧ Smoked Turkey Minisandwiches ❧

YIELD: 12 servings (2 each) • *PREPARATION TIME: 25 minutes*

Smoked turkey and cucumber are combined with scallions, Dijon mustard, and cream cheese in these fancy, triple-decker, whole-grain sandwiches.

2 ounces nonfat or reduced-fat cream cheese, softened
2 tablespoons minced scallions
6 slices whole-grain bread

1 small cucumber, thinly sliced
3 tablespoons Dijon mustard
3 slices white bread
4 ounces thinly sliced smoked turkey

1. Blend together cream cheese and scallions.
2. Spread cream cheese on 3 slices of whole-grain bread. Top with cucumber.
3. Spread mustard on the 3 slices of white bread. Top with smoked turkey.
4. Place white bread slices on top of whole-grain slices spread with cream cheese. Place remaining 3 whole-grain slices on top of turkey layer.
5. Trim crusts from bread. Cut each stack in half. Then cut each half into 4 strips.

Calories Per Serving: 70
Fat: 1 g
Cholesterol: 5 mg
Protein: 5 g

Carbohydrates: 10 g
Dietary Fiber: 2 g
Sodium: 311 mg

Feta Bites

YIELD: *24 servings (1 each)* • PREPARATION TIME: *10 minutes*

Feta cheese, chopped black olives, yogurt, and red bell pepper are spread on melba toast rounds.

4 ounces feta cheese
2 tablespoons chopped red bell pepper
½ cup nonfat or reduced-fat plain
* yogurt*

¼ cup chopped, pitted black olives
½ teaspoon dried oregano
1 tablespoon chopped scallions
24 nonfat melba toast rounds

1. Combine feta cheese, red pepper, yogurt, olives, oregano, and scallions in a bowl.
2. Spoon mixture onto melba toast rounds.

Calories Per Serving: 66
Fat: 3 g
Cholesterol: 6 mg
Protein: 4 g

Carbohydrates: 7 g
Dietary Fiber: 1 g
Sodium: 238 mg

Garden Harvest Treats

YIELD: *18 servings (2 each)* • PREPARATION TIME: *20 minutes*

A mixture of jicama, carrots, zucchini, and sour cream tops crunchy whole-grain crackers.

½ cup shredded jicama
½ cup shredded carrot
½ cup shredded zucchini

½ cup nonfat or reduced-fat sour cream
36 nonfat whole-grain crackers

1. Combine jicama, carrot, zucchini, and sour cream.
2. Spread on crackers.

Calories Per Serving: 86
Fat: 0 g
Cholesterol: 2 mg
Protein: 2 g

Carbohydrates: 19 g
Dietary Fiber: 1 g
Sodium: 65 mg

＊ *Apple-Cheese Bites* ＊

YIELD: 9 servings (2 each) • *PREPARATION TIME: 20 minutes*

A mixture of cottage cheese, fresh apple, and curry powder is served on crisp whole-grain crackers.

½ cup nonfat or reduced-fat cottage cheese
½ cup finely chopped apple
¼ teaspoon curry powder

18 round, nonfat whole-grain crackers
1 small apple, cut into 18 thin wedges
1 tablespoon lemon juice mixed with 1 tablespoon water

1. Combine cottage cheese, chopped apple, and curry powder.
2. Mound on crackers.
3. Toss apple wedges in lemon water to prevent discoloration.
4. Garnish each cracker with a small apple wedge.

Calories Per Serving: 111
Fat: 2 g
Cholesterol: 4 mg
Protein: 3 g

Carbohydrates: 23 g
Dietary Fiber: 5 g
Sodium: 108 mg

＊ *Fruit Salad–Cheese Tastes* ＊

YIELD: 18 servings (2 each) • *PREPARATION TIME: 20 minutes*

Mini–rice cakes are topped with a sweet mixture of fruit, ricotta cheese, and honey.

2 chopped peaches or nectarines
1 cup chopped strawberries
½ cup nonfat or reduced-fat ricotta
   cheese

2 tablespoons honey
36 mini–rice cakes

1. Combine chopped peaches, strawberries, ricotta cheese, and honey.
2. Spread on mini–rice cakes.

Calories Per Serving: 95
Fat: 1 g
Cholesterol: 0 mg
Protein: 3 g

Carbohydrates: 20 g
Dietary Fiber: 1 g
Sodium: 69 mg

Salmon Canapés

YIELD: 20 servings (2 each) • *PREPARATION TIME: 20 minutes plus 2 hours refrigeration time*

Lemon-accented salmon spread is served on rye crispbreads.

7½ ounces canned red salmon,
   drained, skin and bones removed
2 ounces smoked salmon, cut into pieces
3 tablespoons nonfat or reduced-fat
   mayonnaise
1 tablespoon lemon juice

¼ cup minced green bell pepper
2 tablespoons minced scallions
1 tablespoon chopped fresh parsley
¼ teaspoon black pepper
20 rye crispbread crackers, broken in
   half

1. Place canned salmon, smoked salmon, mayonnaise, and lemon juice in a blender or food processor and blend until smooth.
2. Transfer to a bowl and add green pepper, scallions, parsley, and black pepper.
3. Cover and chill for 2 hours.
4. Spread on rye crispbreads.

Calories Per Serving: 115
Fat: 3 g
Cholesterol: 1 mg
Protein: 12 g

Carbohydrates: 9 g
Dietary Fiber: 0 g
Sodium: 63 mg

❧ *Sardine Spread on Rye Crackers* ❧

YIELD: 10 servings (2 each) • *PREPARATION TIME: 20 minutes*

Rye crackers are covered with a tangy tomato-sardine spread and garnished with cucumber and tomato.

8 ounces canned, oil-packed sardines, mashed
¼ cup canned, low-sodium tomato puree
¼ cup red wine vinegar

2 tablespoons nonfat or reduced-fat mayonnaise
20 nonfat rye crackers
10 cucumber slices, halved
10 cherry tomatoes, halved

1. Blend together mashed sardines, tomato puree, red wine vinegar, and mayonnaise.
2. Spread sardine mixture on crackers and garnish each with a cucumber half and cherry tomato half.

Calories Per Serving: 229
Fat: 3 g
Cholesterol: 33 mg
Protein: 11 g

Carbohydrates: 43 g
Dietary Fiber: 0 g
Sodium: 540 mg

❧ *Avocado-Shrimp Delights* ❧

YIELD: 20 servings (1 each) • *PREPARATION TIME: 15 minutes*

A spicy parsley, lime juice, and avocado mixture is spread on crackers and topped with cooked shrimp. Select avocados that are firm, but not hard.

Juice of 2 limes
2 large avocados
2 tablespoons chopped fresh parsley
¼ teaspoon black pepper

Cayenne pepper to taste
20 round nonfat crackers
20 medium fresh or frozen shrimp,
  cooked, shelled, and deveined

1. Place lime juice in a mixing bowl. Add avocados, parsley, black pepper, and cayenne pepper to taste and mash.
2. Spoon some avocado mixture on each cracker and top with a shrimp. Sprinkle shrimp with more cayenne pepper.

Calories Per Serving: 87
Fat: 3 g
Cholesterol: 25 mg
Protein: 5 g

Carbohydrates: 12 g
Dietary Fiber: 1 g
Sodium: 146 mg

❦ *Pineapple-Cheese Bites* ❦

YIELD: 16 servings (2 each) ▪ *PREPARATION TIME: 15 minutes*

Whole-grain bread is spread with lemony, smooth cottage cheese, raisins, and pineapple.

2 cups nonfat or reduced-fat cottage
  cheese
2 teaspoons lemon juice
1 cup raisins

1 cup canned, juice-packed, crushed
  pineapple, drained
8 slices firm whole-grain bread, crusts
  trimmed

1. Place cottage cheese and lemon juice in a blender or food processor and process until smooth.
2. Combine cottage cheese, raisins, and pineapple.
3. Spread mixture on bread slices. Cut each slice into quarters.

Calories Per Serving: 87
Fat: 1 g
Cholesterol: 10 mg
Protein: 4 g

Carbohydrates: 17 g
Dietary Fiber: 2 g
Sodium: 119 mg

• CANAPÉ ROUNDS, DIAMONDS, AND CUPS •

❧ *Very Veggie Rounds* ❧

YIELD: 18 servings (2 each) • *PREPARATION TIME: 20 minutes*

A topping of broccoli, onion, tomato, and sour cream is spread on firm rounds of pumpernickel bread.

¾ cup chopped broccoli
½ cup chopped tomato
½ cup chopped onion

¾ cup nonfat or reduced-fat sour cream
36 2-inch rounds cut from firm
  pumpernickel bread

1. Combine broccoli, tomato, onion, and sour cream.
2. Spread on pumpernickel rounds.

Calories Per Serving: 98
Fat: 1 g
Cholesterol: 3 mg
Protein: 4 g

Carbohydrates: 19 g
Dietary Fiber: 1 g
Sodium: 238 mg

❧ *Apple-Carrot Rounds* ❧

YIELD: 18 servings (2 each) • *PREPARATION TIME: 20 minutes*

A combination of chopped apples, shredded carrots, yogurt, and walnuts top rounds of raisin bread.

1 cup chopped apples
½ cup shredded carrots
½ cup nonfat or reduced-fat plain
  yogurt

¼ cup finely chopped walnuts
36 2-inch rounds cut from firm raisin
  bread

1. Combine apples, carrots, yogurt, and walnuts.
2. Spread on raisin bread rounds.

Calories Per Serving: 102

Carbohydrates: 16 g

Fat: 3 g

Dietary Fiber: 0 g

Cholesterol: 0 mg

Sodium: 107 mg

Protein: 3 g

Tiny Turkey Burgers

Yield: 12 servings (2 each) • *Preparation Time: 30 minutes* •
Cooking Time: 15 minutes

Ground turkey burgers are topped with melted cheese and served on toast rounds.

½ pound low-fat ground turkey breast

1 small onion, minced

1 teaspoon Dijon mustard

1 tablespoon canola oil

24 1½-inch rounds cut from toasted whole-grain bread

2 tablespoons low-sodium tomato paste

⅓ cup nonfat or reduced-fat grated cheese

1. Combine ground turkey, onion, and Dijon mustard.
2. Shape into 24 tiny burgers, using 2 teaspoons ground turkey mixture for each burger.
3. Heat canola oil in a skillet and brown burgers on each side until done.
4. Drain on paper towels. Preheat broiler.
5. Spread each round with tomato paste. Top with a tiny burger. Sprinkle burgers with cheese.
6. Place rounds on a baking sheet and run them under the broiler until cheese melts.

Calories Per Serving: 87

Carbohydrates: 13 g

Fat: 1 g

Dietary Fiber: 1 g

Cholesterol: 14 mg

Sodium: 190 mg

Protein: 8 g

❧ *Chicken-Cucumber Rounds* ❧

YIELD: *12 servings (2 each)* ▪ PREPARATION TIME: *30 minutes plus*
2½ hours refrigeration time

These chicken salad–stuffed cucumber sandwiches can be assembled several hours in advance and refrigerated until ready to serve.

2 cucumbers	¼ teaspoon black pepper
1 large chicken breast, cooked, boned, and minced	3 tablespoons nonfat or reduced-fat mayonnaise
2 hard-boiled egg whites, finely chopped	24 2-inch rounds cut from Italian bread slices
2 tablespoons chopped fresh parsley	

1. Slice off ends of cucumbers and hollow out centers with an apple corer, removing seeds.
2. Combine chicken, egg whites, parsley, pepper, and 1 tablespoon of the mayonnaise. Fill hollowed cucumbers with mixture. Wrap in plastic wrap and chill for 2½ hours.
3. Spread Italian bread rounds with the remaining mayonnaise. Slice cucumbers in ¼-inch slices and place on bread rounds.

Calories Per Serving: 126	Carbohydrates: 17 g
Fat: 2 g	Dietary Fiber: 0 g
Cholesterol: 14 mg	Sodium: 197 mg
Protein: 8 g	

❧ *Roast Turkey–Ricotta–Cranberry Rounds* ❧

YIELD: *30 servings (2 each)* ▪ PREPARATION TIME: *25 minutes*

Thanksgiving isn't the only time to enjoy turkey with cranberries. These rounds combine those traditional flavors with ricotta cheese.

60 1½-inch rounds cut from whole-grain bread
10 ounces nonfat or reduced-fat ricotta cheese

10 ounces sliced roast turkey, cut into 1-inch pieces
⅓ cup cranberry sauce
Fresh parsley sprigs

1. Spread whole-grain bread rounds with ricotta cheese.
2. Top with pieces of roast turkey.
3. Before serving, garnish each round with a dab of cranberry sauce and a sprig of parsley.

Calories Per Serving: 43
Fat: 1 g
Cholesterol: 5 mg
Protein: 4 g

Carbohydrates: 6 g
Dietary Fiber: 1 g
Sodium: 145 mg

❧ *Tuna-Avocado Pinwheels* ❧

YIELD: 18 servings (2 slices each) • *PREPARATION TIME: 20 minutes plus 24 hours refrigeration time*

Tuna–avocado salad is spread on bread, rolled, and sliced.

1 unsliced loaf white bread
13 ounces canned, water-packed, white albacore tuna, drained and flaked
⅔ cup nonfat or reduced-fat mayonnaise

½ cup minced celery
1 ripe avocado, chopped
2 teaspoons lemon juice

1. Trim crusts from bread loaf. Cut loaf into 5 horizontal slices about ½ inch thick. Reserve 2 slices for another use.
2. Combine tuna, mayonnaise, celery, avocado, and lemon juice.
3. Spread tuna on 3 slices.
4. Beginning at one end, roll up jelly-roll fashion.
5. Wrap tightly in plastic wrap and refrigerate for 24 hours.
6. Unwrap and cut each roll into 12 slices, using a bread knife.

Calories Per Serving: 124
Fat: 3 g
Cholesterol: 8 mg
Protein: 8 g

Carbohydrates: 16 g
Dietary Fiber: 1 g
Sodium: 220 mg

 *Watercress-Dill-Shrimp Rounds*

YIELD: 16 servings (2 rounds) • *PREPARATION TIME: 20 minutes*

Shrimp are halved and placed on top of herb mayonnaise on pumpernickel rounds.

1½ tablespoons finely chopped fresh
    parsley
1½ tablespoons finely chopped fresh
    scallions
¼ cup chopped watercress
½ teaspoon dried dill
1 cup nonfat or reduced-fat mayonnaise

32 2-inch rounds cut from thin slices
    pumpernickel bread
16 medium fresh or frozen shrimp,
    cooked, shelled, deveined, and halved
    lengthwise
Small sprigs of fresh parsley

1. Place chopped parsley, scallions, watercress, dill, and mayonnaise in a blender or food processor and process until well blended.
2. Spread pumpernickel rounds with herbed mayonnaise. Place a shrimp half, cut side down, on each circle. Garnish with a small sprig of parsley.

Calories Per Serving: 107
Fat: 1 g
Cholesterol: 21 mg
Protein: 6 g

Carbohydrates: 18 g
Dietary Fiber: 0 g
Sodium: 314 mg

Peking Rounds

YIELD: 16 servings (2 each) • *PREPARATION TIME: 25 minutes*

Shrimp are served on toast with hoisin sauce, which is available at many supermarkets and oriental markets.

⅔ cup hoisin sauce

32 1½-inch rounds cut from toasted
   whole wheat sandwich bread

1 pound medium fresh or frozen
   shrimp, cooked, shelled, and deveined

1 bunch scallions, cut into ½-inch
   lengths

1. Spread a teaspoon of hoisin sauce over each toast round.
2. Put a shrimp and a piece of scallion in the center of each round.

Calories Per Serving: 72

Fat: 1 g

Cholesterol: 42 mg

Protein: 7 g

Carbohydrates: 9 g

Dietary Fiber: 0 g

Sodium: 299 mg

❧ *Crab Delights* ❧

YIELD: *24 servings (2 each)* • PREPARATION TIME: *20 minutes*

Crabmeat is combined with a spicy honey-lemon sauce and spread on
rounds of rye toast.

1½ cups nonfat or reduced-fat mayonnaise

3 tablespoons honey

2 tablespoons minced scallions

¼ teaspoon hot pepper sauce

2 tablespoons lemon juice

3 tablespoons low-sodium catsup

2 pounds cooked crabmeat

48 1½-inch rounds cut from toasted,
   thinly sliced rye bread

10 large radishes, minced

1. Combine mayonnaise, honey, scallions, hot pepper sauce, lemon juice, and
   catsup.
2. Add crabmeat to sauce and toss well.
3. Spoon a tablespoon of crab-sauce mixture onto each toast round and
   sprinkle with minced radishes.

Calories Per Serving: 147

Fat: 2 g

Cholesterol: 34 mg

Protein: 10 g

Carbohydrates: 21 g

Dietary Fiber: 0 g

Sodium: 355 mg

Honey-Baked
Turkey–Red Pepper Diamonds

YIELD: 16 servings (2 each) • *PREPARATION TIME: 20 minutes*

Slices of honey-baked turkey breast from the deli are placed on diamond-shaped rye bread slices spread with tarragon mayonnaise.

¾ tablespoon dried tarragon	1 cup nonfat or reduced-fat mayonnaise
1½ tablespoons finely chopped scallions	32 thin slices rye bread
¼ cup chopped fresh parsley	8 slices honey-baked turkey breast, cut
½ teaspoon dried thyme	in quarters
1 teaspoon Dijon mustard	32 small strips red bell pepper

1. Place tarragon, scallions, parsley, thyme, Dijon mustard, and mayonnaise in a blender or food processor and process until well blended.
2. Using a diamond-shaped cookie cutter, cut shapes from rye bread slices.
3. Spread rye bread diamonds with herbed mayonnaise. Place a piece of turkey on each diamond. Garnish with a strip of red bell pepper.

Calories Per Serving: 65	Carbohydrates: 14 g
Fat: 1 g	Dietary Fiber: 2 g
Cholesterol: 2 mg	Sodium: 242 mg
Protein: 3 g	

Sherried Cheese Rounds

YIELD: 24 (1 each) • *PREPARATION TIME: 15 minutes* •
COOKING TIME: 11 minutes

This simple-to-prepare, hot appetizer features the surprising flavors of Parmesan cheese combined with sherry, dry mustard, onion, lemon peel, and curry powder.

⅓ cup nonfat or reduced-fat mayonnaise

⅔ cup grated nonfat or reduced-fat
   Parmesan cheese

¼ teaspoon black pepper

1 teaspoon grated lemon peel

¼ teaspoon curry powder

1 teaspoon dry mustard

2 tablespoons minced onion

½ teaspoon dry sherry

1 egg white, stiffly beaten

24 2½-inch rounds cut from whole-
   grain bread

1. Preheat oven to 425 degrees. Combine mayonnaise, Parmesan cheese, pepper, lemon peel, curry powder, dry mustard, onion, and sherry.
2. Fold in beaten egg white.
3. Mound mixture on whole-grain bread rounds with a teaspoon.
4. Bake for 11 minutes or until lightly browned. Serve at once.

Calories Per Serving: 43

Fat: 1 g

Cholesterol: 2 mg

Protein: 2 g

Carbohydrates: 7 g

Dietary Fiber: 1 g

Sodium: 102 mg

❧ Curried Olive-Cheese Rounds ❧

YIELD: 20 servings (2 each) • PREPARATION TIME: 25 minutes •
COOKING TIME: 4 minutes

This cheese spread is accented with curry, green olives, and scallions.

½ pound nonfat or reduced-fat cheddar
   cheese, shredded

1 cup chopped green olives

6 scallions, chopped

1 cup nonfat or reduced-fat mayonnaise

1 teaspoon curry powder

40 nonfat melba toast rounds

1. Preheat broiler. Combine cheese, olives, scallions, mayonnaise, and curry powder.
2. Spread on melba toast rounds.
3. Broil for 4 minutes or until bubbly.

Calories Per Serving: 70
Fat: 1 g
Cholesterol: 0 mg
Protein: 5 g

Carbohydrates: 10 g
Dietary Fiber: 1 g
Sodium: 491 mg

 *Ricotta Rounds*

YIELD: 8 servings (2 each) • *PREPARATION TIME: 10 minutes*

A spread of ricotta cheese, almonds, honey, and cardamom lends a Middle Eastern flair to these appetizers. Top each with a slice of peach, nectarine, or apricot if desired.

*1 cup nonfat or reduced-fat ricotta
  cheese*
2 tablespoons chopped toasted almonds
2 tablespoons honey

⅛ teaspoon ground cardamom
16 nonfat melba toast rounds
*Sliced peach, nectarine, and apricot
  (optional)*

1. Place ricotta cheese, almonds, honey, and cardamom in a blender or food processor and process until smooth.
2. Spread ricotta mixture on melba toast rounds.
3. Garnish with fruit slices, if desired.

Calories Per Serving: 81
Fat: 1 g
Cholesterol: 3 mg
Protein: 6 g

Carbohydrates: 13 g
Dietary Fiber: 1 g
Sodium: 92 mg

Shrimp-Caper Rounds

YIELD: 8 servings (2 each) • *PREPARATION TIME: 15 minutes*

A lemon-accented cream cheese is spread on melba toast rounds, then topped with cooked shrimp and capers.

3 ounces nonfat or reduced-fat cream
  cheese, softened
1 teaspoon lemon juice
½ teaspoon grated lemon peel
½ teaspoon dried dill

16 nonfat melba toast rounds
16 medium shrimp, cooked, shelled,
  and deveined
1 teaspoon capers, drained

1. Blend together cream cheese, lemon juice, lemon peel, and dill.
2. Spread mixture on melba rounds, top each round with 1 shrimp, and garnish with capers.

Calories Per Serving: 90
Fat: 0 g
Cholesterol: 87 mg
Protein: 16 g

Carbohydrates: 7 g
Dietary Fiber: 1 g
Sodium: 530 mg

❧ Pepper Rounds ❧

YIELD: 18 servings (2 each)   •   PREPARATION TIME: 20 minutes

In these colorful bites, red, green, and yellow peppers are combined with sour cream and spread on rye melba toast rounds.

½ cup chopped red bell pepper
½ cup chopped green bell pepper
½ cup chopped yellow bell pepper

½ cup nonfat or reduced-fat sour cream
36 rye melba toast rounds

1. Combine red, green, and yellow bell peppers with sour cream.
2. Spread on rye melba toast rounds.

Calories Per Serving: 48
Fat: 0 g
Cholesterol: 2 mg
Protein: 2 g

Carbohydrates: 10 g
Dietary Fiber: 0 g
Sodium: 96 mg

☙ *Crab Cups* ৶

YIELD: 10 servings (2 each) ▪ *PREPARATION TIME: 20 minutes* ▪
COOKING TIME: 12 minutes

Crabmeat and avocado are combined with lemon juice, scallions, yogurt, and chili powder, and then spooned into toast cups.

5 slices whole wheat sandwich bread
6 ounces cooked crabmeat, flaked
1 avocado, mashed
1 tablespoon lemon juice

2 tablespoons minced scallions
2 tablespoons nonfat or reduced-fat
  plain yogurt
⅛ teaspoon chili powder

1. Preheat oven to 375 degrees. Trim crusts from bread. Cut each slice into 4 squares.
2. Gently press each square into a 2-inch muffin cup.
3. Bake for 10 to 12 minutes or until lightly browned. Remove from oven and cool.
4. Combine crabmeat, avocado, lemon juice, scallions, yogurt, and chili powder.
5. Spoon 1 tablespoon of filling into each toast cup.

Calories Per Serving: 84
Fat: 3 g
Cholesterol: 15 mg
Protein: 5 g

Carbohydrates: 9 g
Dietary Fiber: 2 g
Sodium: 140 mg

☙ *Gingered Chicken Cups* ৶

YIELD: 12 servings (2 each) ▪ *PREPARATION TIME: 20 minutes* ▪
COOKING TIME: 12 minutes

Chicken salad with ginger, water chestnuts, and scallions is spooned into toast cups.

6 slices whole wheat sandwich bread
2 cups finely chopped, cooked chicken
   breast
½ cup finely chopped water chestnuts
2 scallions, finely chopped

½ cup nonfat or reduced-fat mayonnaise
½ teaspoon dry mustard
¼ teaspoon ground ginger

1. Preheat oven to 375 degrees. Trim crusts from bread. Cut each slice into
   4 squares.
2. Gently press each square into a 2-inch muffin cup.
3. Bake for 10 to 12 minutes or until lightly browned. Remove from oven
   and cool.
4. Combine chicken, water chestnuts, scallions, mayonnaise, dry mustard,
   and ginger.
5. Spoon 1 tablespoon of filling into each toast cup.

Calories Per Serving: 81
Fat: 1 g
Cholesterol: 18 mg
Protein: 8 g

Carbohydrates: 9 g
Dietary Fiber: 2 g
Sodium: 95 mg

⚅ *Tuna Cups* ⚅

YIELD: *12 servings (2 each)* • PREPARATION TIME: *20 minutes* •
COOKING TIME: *12 minutes*

Kids of all ages love these appetizers, made with white albacore tuna, pickle
relish, celery, and mayonnaise, combined and spooned into toast cups.

6 slices whole wheat sandwich bread
2 cups canned, water-packed, white albacore tuna, flaked

½ cup nonfat or reduced-fat mayonnaise
½ cup minced celery
2 tablespoons sweet pickle relish

1. Preheat oven to 375 degrees. Trim crusts from bread. Cut each slice into
   4 squares.
2. Gently press each square into a 2-inch muffin cup.
3. Bake for 10 to 12 minutes or until lightly browned. Remove from oven
   and cool.

4. Combine tuna, mayonnaise, celery, and pickle relish.
5. Spoon 1 tablespoon of filling into each toast cup.

Calories Per Serving: 66   Carbohydrates: 9 g
Fat: 1 g   Dietary Fiber: 1 g
Cholesterol: 9 mg   Sodium: 164 mg
Protein: 5 g

❧ *Curried Chicken Cups* ❧

YIELD: 12 servings (2 each) • *PREPARATION TIME: 20 minutes* •
COOKING TIME: 12 minutes

A curried chicken filling with apples is served in toast cups.

6 slices whole wheat sandwich bread
2 cups finely chopped, cooked chicken
  breast
¼ cup finely chopped celery

1 small apple, peeled and grated
⅓ cup nonfat or reduced-fat mayon-
  naise
2 teaspoons curry powder

1. Preheat oven to 375 degrees. Trim crusts from bread. Cut each slice into 4 squares.
2. Gently press each square into a 2-inch muffin cup.
3. Bake for 10 to 12 minutes or until lightly browned. Remove from oven and cool.
4. Combine chicken, celery, apple, mayonnaise, and curry powder.
5. Spoon 1½ tablespoons of filling into each toast cup.

Calories Per Serving: 62   Carbohydrates: 10 g
Fat: 1 g   Dietary Fiber: 1 g
Cholesterol: 9 mg   Sodium: 131 mg
Protein: 5 g

❦ Oriental Chicken Salad Cups ❦

YIELD: 12 servings (2 each)   •   PREPARATION TIME: 20 minutes   •
COOKING TIME: 12 minutes

Soy sauce, rice vinegar, parsley, and scallions give these chicken appetizers a Far East flavor.

6 slices whole wheat sandwich bread
2 cups finely chopped, cooked chicken breast
2 tablespoons light soy sauce

1½ tablespoons rice vinegar
2 tablespoons light-flavored olive oil
¼ cup chopped fresh parsley
2 scallions, minced

1. Preheat oven to 375 degrees. Trim crusts from bread. Cut each slice into 4 squares.
2. Gently press each square into a 2-inch muffin cup.
3. Bake for 10 to 12 minutes or until lightly browned. Remove from oven and cool.
4. Combine chicken, soy sauce, rice vinegar, oil, parsley, and scallions. Spoon 1 tablespoon of filling into each toast cup.

Calories Per Serving: 75
Fat: 3 g
Cholesterol: 14 mg
Protein: 7 g

Carbohydrates: 6 g
Dietary Fiber: 1 g
Sodium: 161 mg

❦ Eggplant Toast Cups ❦

YIELD: 16 servings (2 each)   •   PREPARATION TIME: 20 minutes   •
COOKING TIME: 8 minutes

This appetizer features eggplant sautéed in olive oil with garlic, rosemary, and thyme.

8 slices whole wheat or white sandwich bread

3 tablespoons light-flavored olive oil
¾ pound eggplant, cut into tiny cubes

1 clove garlic, minced
½ teaspoon dried rosemary

½ teaspoon dried thyme
¼ teaspoon black pepper

1. Preheat oven to 375 degrees. Trim crusts from bread. Cut each slice into 4 squares.
2. Gently press each square into a 2-inch muffin cup.
3. Bake for 10 to 12 minutes or until lightly browned. Remove from oven and cool.
4. Heat olive oil in a skillet over medium heat. Sauté eggplant for 5 minutes or until pieces are browned on all sides and tender.
5. Add garlic, rosemary, thyme, and pepper. Sauté for 1 minute more.
6. Spoon 1½ tablespoons of filling into each toast cup.

Calories Per Serving: 61
Fat: 3 g
Cholesterol: 0 mg
Protein: 1 g

Carbohydrates: 8 g
Dietary Fiber: 0 g
Sodium: 68 mg

☙ *Shiitake Toast Cups* ☙

YIELD: 12 servings (2 each) • *PREPARATION TIME: 20 minutes* •
COOKING TIME: 8 minutes

Fresh shiitake mushrooms are chopped and sautéed in olive oil with parsley.

6 slices whole wheat or white sandwich
bread
3 tablespoons light-flavored olive oil

3 cups finely chopped fresh shiitake
mushroom caps
½ cup chopped fresh parsley

1. Preheat oven to 375 degrees. Trim crusts from bread. Cut each slice into 4 squares.
2. Gently press each square into a 2-inch muffin cup.
3. Bake for 10 to 12 minutes or until lightly browned. Remove from oven and cool.
4. Heat olive oil in a skillet over medium heat. Sauté mushroom caps for 10 minutes or until shiitakes are lightly browned and tender.

5. Toss shiitakes with chopped parsley.
6. Spoon 1½ tablespoons of filling into each toast cup.

Calories Per Serving: 57
Fat: 3 g
Cholesterol: 0 mg
Protein: 1 g

Carbohydrates: 7 g
Dietary Fiber: 0 g
Sodium: 52 mg

❧ Mozzarella-Mushroom Bread Baskets ☙

YIELD: 12 servings (2 each) • *PREPARATION TIME: 25 minutes* •
COOKING TIME: 35 minutes

Toast cups are baked with a mushroom and cheese filling.

24 thin slices whole wheat bread
1 cup fine, whole-grain bread crumbs
1 large clove garlic, chopped
¼ cup chopped fresh parsley
¼ teaspoon black pepper

4 teaspoons mild-flavored olive oil
⅔ cup grated nonfat or reduced-fat
  mozzarella cheese
24 medium mushrooms, stems
  removed

1. Preheat oven to 300 degrees. Using a 2½-inch biscuit or cookie cutter, cut out 24 rounds of bread. Gently press bread rounds into 2-inch muffin tins. Bake for 20 minutes or until lightly browned. Remove from oven and cool. Turn oven to 400 degrees.
2. Combine bread crumbs, garlic, parsley, pepper, and olive oil.
3. Spoon stuffing into bread baskets.
4. Sprinkle with mozzarella cheese.
5. Place one mushroom on top of each toast cup.
6. Place toast cups on a baking sheet. Bake for 9 minutes or until heated through.
7. Toast under broiler for 1 minute and serve at once.

Calories Per Serving: 138
Fat: 3 g
Cholesterol: 3 mg
Protein: 8 g

Carbohydrates: 20 g
Dietary Fiber: 2 g
Sodium: 354 mg

❧ *Olive-Cheese Wonton Baskets* ❧

YIELD: 12 servings (2 each) • *PREPARATION TIME: 20 minutes* •
COOKING TIME: 18 minutes

Wonton skins can be used in unexpected ways for low-fat appetizer bases. Here they are baked in minimuffin tins with a spicy olive, bell pepper, and cheese filling.

Olive oil cooking spray
24 round wonton skins (or square skins cut into circles with a 3-inch cookie or biscuit cutter)
1 cup shredded nonfat or reduced fat cheddar cheese

⅓ cup nonfat or reduced-fat ricotta cheese
¼ cup minced green bell pepper
½ teaspoon chili powder
¼ cup chopped green olives

1. Preheat oven to 350 degrees. Spray two minimuffin tins with olive oil spray. Place wonton skins in muffin cups, shaping them to fit. Spray wonton skins with olive oil spray.
2. Bake for 8 minutes or until lightly browned.
3. Blend together cheddar cheese, ricotta cheese, bell pepper, chili powder, and green olives.
4. Remove wontons from muffin cups and transfer to baking sheets. Leave oven on.
5. Fill wonton baskets with 2 teaspoons of cheese filling.
6. Bake for 10 minutes.

Calories Per Serving: 81
Fat: 1 g
Cholesterol: 2 mg
Protein: 7 g

Carbohydrates: 11 g
Dietary Fiber: 0 g
Sodium: 437 mg

❧ *Basil–Goat Cheese Rounds* ❧

YIELD: 7 servings (2 each) • *PREPARATION TIME: 10 minutes plus overnight refrigeration time*

Semisoft goat cheese is seasoned with basil and onion, shaped, sliced, and served on rye crackers.

3 ounces semisoft goat cheese
2 teaspoons skim or 1% milk
¼ teaspoon minced onion

½ teaspoon dried basil
¼ teaspoon black pepper
14 low-fat round rye crackers

1. Blend together goat cheese, milk, onion, basil, and pepper until thoroughly combined.
2. Shape into a log. Cover with plastic wrap and chill overnight. Slice into 14 slices and place each slice on a cracker.

Calories Per Serving: 213
Fat: 4 g
Cholesterol: 9 mg
Protein: 7 g

Carbohydrates: 41 g
Dietary Fiber: 0 g
Sodium: 461 mg

• STUFFED SANDWICHES AND PITAS •

Pan Bagnat

YIELD: 10 servings (2 slices each) • PREPARATION TIME: 20 minutes plus
1 hour standing time

A slice of this classic French sandwich is a feast in miniature.

1 baguette
1 garlic clove, minced
1 tablespoon light-flavored olive oil
1 tomato, thinly sliced
1 cucumber, thinly sliced
½ red onion, thinly sliced
1 green bell pepper, thinly sliced
1 cup canned, water-packed artichoke
   hearts, sliced

2 hard-boiled egg whites, sliced
¼ pound nonfat or reduced-fat sliced
   mozzarella cheese
½ cup chopped black olives (optional)
1 teaspoon dried basil
1 teaspoon dried oregano

1. Slice bread in half lengthwise, not quite all the way through.
2. Lay the loaf open on a large sheet of aluminum foil. Sprinkle the bottom of the loaf with minced garlic. Brush olive oil on both sides of loaf.

3. Layer tomato, cucumber, onion, green pepper, artichokes, egg whites, cheese, and black olives, if using, on the bottom layer of the loaf.
4. Sprinkle with basil and oregano.
5. Close loaf and wrap it tightly in foil.
6. Weight the loaf with several heavy books or comparable weights and let stand for 1 hour.
7. Unwrap and cut into 20 slices.

Calories Per Serving: 175	Carbohydrates: 30 g
Fat: 2 g	Dietary Fiber: 2 g
Cholesterol: 0 mg	Sodium: 453 mg
Protein: 8 g	

＊ *Salmon Slices* ＊

YIELD: 12 servings (2 each) • *PREPARATION TIME: 20 minutes plus 3 hours refrigeration time*

French bread is stuffed with salmon flavored with cucumber and horseradish, then sliced.

1 12-inch loaf French bread	*½ cup chopped scallions*
8 ounces nonfat or reduced-fat cream cheese, softened	*½ cup nonfat or reduced-fat sour cream*
7½ ounces canned salmon, drained and flaked with skin and bones removed	*1 teaspoon dried dill*
	1 teaspoon prepared horseradish
½ cup seeded and finely chopped cucumber	*1 teaspoon lemon juice*

1. Cut loaf in half lengthwise and remove center of each half, leaving a ½-inch-thick shell.
2. Blend together cream cheese, salmon, cucumber, scallions, sour cream, dill, horseradish, and lemon juice.
3. Stuff hollowed-out bread with salmon mixture, wrap in plastic wrap, and refrigerate 3 or more hours.
4. Cut into ½-inch slices and serve.

Calories Per Serving: 130
Fat: 2 g
Cholesterol: 14 mg
Protein: 11 g

Carbohydrates: 17 g
Dietary Fiber: 0 g
Sodium: 394 mg

❧ *Stuffed Shrimp Loaf* ❧

YIELD: 18 servings (2 each) • *PREPARATION TIME: 15 minutes plus
1 hour refrigeration time*

Italian bread is spread with a creamy shrimp filling, chilled, and sliced.

1 long loaf Italian bread
½ cup nonfat or reduced-fat cream
   cheese, softened
2 tablespoons nonfat or reduced-fat
   mayonnaise
2 tablespoons lime juice

¼ cup chopped fresh parsley
1½ pounds cooked medium shrimp,
   shelled, deveined, and chopped
½ cup finely chopped celery
1½ teaspoons dried dillweed

1. Cut bread in half lengthwise. Scoop out the center of each half, leaving a ½-inch-thick shell.
2. Combine cream cheese, mayonnaise, and lime juice.
3. Spread bread halves with ⅓ cup cream cheese mixture. Sprinkle with parsley.
4. Blend together remaining cream cheese with shrimp, celery, and dill. Spoon onto bread halves.
5. Press halves together. Wrap in plastic wrap and refrigerate for 1 hour.
6. Cut into ¾-inch-thick slices before serving.

Calories Per Serving: 109
Fat: 1 g
Cholesterol: 58 mg
Protein: 11 g

Carbohydrates: 14 g
Dietary Fiber: 0 g
Sodium: 470 mg

❧ *Oyster Slices* ❧

YIELD: 12 servings (1 slice each) • *PREPARATION TIME: 25 minutes plus 24-hour refrigeration time* • *COOKING TIME: 8 to 10 minutes*

A loaf of French bread is stuffed with an oyster-Parmesan filling, refrigerated overnight, and thinly sliced.

1-pound loaf French bread
1 medium tomato, finely diced
4 scallions, finely sliced
¼ cup stuffed green olives (optional)
6 cloves garlic, minced
2 tablespoons chopped fresh parsley
¼ teaspoon dried thyme
¼ teaspoon black pepper

Juice of 1 lemon
⅛ teaspoon hot pepper sauce
2 tablespoons light-flavored olive oil, plus more for brushing bread
2 cups extra-small shucked oysters
1 tablespoon dry sherry
½ cup nonfat or reduced-fat Parmesan cheese

1. Cut French bread in half lengthwise and scoop out inside of both halves.
2. Grind bread from insides of loaf into fine crumbs in blender or food processor.
3. Combine crumbs with tomato, scallions, olives, if using, garlic, parsley, thyme, pepper, lemon, hot pepper sauce, and olive oil, mixing well.
4. Place oysters and sherry in a large pot with enough water to cover oysters. Bring to a boil. Cook for 4 minutes and drain at once.
5. Chop oysters and add to bread mixture, mixing well. Add Parmesan cheese to mixture.
6. Brush hollowed-out centers and edges of bread with olive oil.
7. Pack the oyster mixture into the hollowed-out space of both bread halves. It should be even with the sides, but can be mounded toward the center.
8. Carefully put halves of bread back together. Wrap in plastic wrap and refrigerate for 24 hours.
9. Cut into ½-inch slices to serve.

Calories Per Serving: 92
Fat: 3 g
Cholesterol: 13 mg
Protein: 4 g

Carbohydrates: 12 g
Dietary Fiber: 0 g
Sodium: 195 mg

❧ *Tuna–Egg Salad Loaf* ❧

YIELD: *10 servings (1 slice each)* • PREPARATION TIME: *25 minutes* •
COOKING TIME: *20 minutes*

Tuna and egg-white salads are layered on a baguette, which is baked and sliced.

1 20-inch whole wheat baguette	*6½ ounces canned, water-packed,*
8 hard-boiled egg whites, chopped	*white albacore tuna, drained*
¼ cup chopped black olives	*¼ cup nonfat or reduced-fat mayonnaise*
½ cup nonfat or reduced-fat cheddar	*2 tablespoons chopped scallions*
cheese	*2 tablespoons chopped celery*

1. Preheat oven to 375 degrees. Slice baguette horizontally into 3 equal slices.
2. Combine egg whites, olives, and cheese.
3. Spread egg mixture on the bottom slice of baguette. Top with middle slice of baguette.
4. Combine tuna, mayonnaise, scallions, and celery. Spread on top of middle slice of baguette. Top with remaining slice of baguette.
5. Wrap baguette in foil. Bake for 20 minutes.
6. Cut into 2-inch slices. Serve at once.

Calories Per Serving: 122	Carbohydrates: 20 g
Fat: 3 g	Dietary Fiber: 0 g
Cholesterol: 2 mg	Sodium: 242 mg
Protein: 4 g	

❧ *Sun-Dried Tomato–Turkey–Cheese Treats* ❧

YIELD: *10 servings (1 slice each)* • PREPARATION TIME: *20 minutes plus*
2 hours refrigeration time

Ricotta and mozzarella cheeses are layered with sun-dried tomatoes and roast turkey in a delicious sandwich, which is chilled and cut into serving-size strips.

1-pound loaf Italian bread

1 cup nonfat or reduced-fat ricotta cheese

½ cup chopped sun-dried tomatoes in oil, drained

2 tablespoons chopped fresh parsley

¼ teaspoon black pepper

4 slices nonfat or reduced-fat mozzarella cheese

¼ pound smoked turkey, chopped

2 tablespoons chopped scallions

⅓ cup nonfat or reduced-fat Parmesan cheese

1. Cut off top ½ inch of Italian bread. Scoop out center of bread, leaving ½-inch shell at the bottom and sides. Reserve bread crumbs for another use.
2. Combine ricotta cheese, sun-dried tomatoes, parsley, and pepper in a bowl.
3. Spread half of the ricotta mixture on the bottom of the bread shell.
4. Top with the mozzarella slices.
5. Combine the chopped turkey and the scallions.
6. Cover mozzarella slices with half of the turkey and scallions.
7. Top turkey with the remaining ricotta mixture.
8. Add a final layer of turkey and scallions.
9. Place top of bread over final layer.
10. Wrap tightly in plastic wrap and chill for 2 hours. Cut crosswise in 1½-inch slices.

Calories Per Serving: 178
Fat: 2 g
Cholesterol: 7 mg
Protein: 12 g

Carbohydrates: 28 g
Dietary Fiber: 1 g
Sodium: 576 mg

 *Stuffed Italian Rolls*

YIELD: 12 servings (2 slices each) • *PREPARATION TIME: 30 minutes plus 2 hours refrigeration time*

Italian rolls are stuffed with a combination of cheeses, vegetables, and spices, then chilled and sliced.

3 7-inch Italian rolls

8 ounces nonfat or reduced-fat cream
cheese, softened

1 cup grated nonfat or reduced-fat
cheddar cheese

½ cup pitted green olives (optional)

⅓ cup chopped celery

¼ cup chopped fresh parsley

¼ cup shredded carrot

¼ cup minced red bell pepper

¼ cup chopped scallions

1 teaspoon chili powder

½ teaspoon ground cumin

1. Cut a thin slice off the ends of each of the three rolls. Hollow out each roll, leaving a ½-inch shell.
2. Blend together cream cheese, cheddar cheese, olives, celery, parsley, carrot, red pepper, scallions, chili powder, and cumin.
3. Stuff cheese mixture into rolls. Wrap rolls tightly in plastic wrap. Chill for 2 hours.
4. Cut each roll into 8 slices.

Calories Per Serving: 193
Fat: 2 g
Cholesterol: 2 mg
Protein: 10 g

Carbohydrates: 33 g
Dietary Fiber: 0 g
Sodium: 586 mg

⚘ Mini–Veggie Pitas ⚘

YIELD: 16 servings (1 each) • PREPARATION TIME: 30 minutes

Small whole-grain pitas are halved and stuffed with a mixture of Parmesan cheese, sour cream, and vegetables.

⅓ cup grated nonfat or reduced-fat
Parmesan cheese

¼ cup nonfat or reduced-fat sour cream

1 teaspoon lemon juice

1 clove garlic, minced

⅛ teaspoon black pepper

⅓ cup nonfat or reduced-fat mayonnaise

1 cup chopped fresh or canned tomatoes

1 cup shredded carrots

½ cup chopped celery

½ cup chopped scallions

½ cup peeled and chopped cucumber

⅓ cup chopped radishes

⅓ cup chopped green bell pepper

¼ cup chopped fresh parsley

8 small whole-grain pita breads, cut in
half

1. Combine cheese, sour cream, lemon juice, garlic, pepper, and mayonnaise.
2. Add tomatoes, carrots, celery, scallions, cucumber, radishes, green pepper, and parsley. Toss to combine.
3. Fill pita halves with vegetable mixture.

Calories Per Serving: 156
Fat: 3 g
Cholesterol: 3 mg
Protein: 6 g

Carbohydrates: 29 g
Dietary Fiber: 1 g
Sodium: 256 mg

Artichoke Wedges

YIELD: 16 servings (2 each) • *PREPARATION TIME: 25 minutes* •
COOKING TIME: 12 minutes

These delectable pita bread wedges are spread with an artichoke mixture, sprinkled with Parmesan cheese, and then baked.

*4 ounces canned, water-packed arti-
choke hearts, drained
¼ cup minced green bell pepper
½ cup chopped smoked turkey
2 tablespoons minced onion
2 tablespoons chopped black olives
½ cup nonfat or reduced-fat cottage
cheese*

*2 tablespoons nonfat or reduced-fat
mayonnaise
1 teaspoon lemon juice
4 small whole wheat pitas
½ cup grated nonfat or reduced-fat
Parmesan cheese*

1. Preheat oven to 400 degrees. Place artichokes, green pepper, turkey, onion, and olives in a blender or food processor. Process until spreadable. Transfer to bowl.
2. Puree cottage cheese in a blender or food processor. Combine with artichoke mixture, mayonnaise, and lemon juice.
3. Slit the pitas all around to form circular halves. Spread inside of each half with artichoke–cottage cheese mixture. Sprinkle with Parmesan cheese.
4. Cut each pita circle into 4 wedges. Place wedges on a baking sheet.
5. Bake for 12 minutes.

Calories Per Serving: 73
Fat: 1 g
Cholesterol: 9 mg
Protein: 5 g

Carbohydrates: 12 g
Dietary Fiber: 0 g
Sodium: 240 mg

❧ *Lox and Minibagels* ❧

YIELD: 15 servings (2 halves each) • *PREPARATION TIME: 15 minutes*

Spread this tasty lox and cream cheese spread on lightly toasted minibagels.

½ cup nonfat or reduced-fat sour cream
3 ounces nonfat or reduced-fat cream cheese, softened
3 ounces smoked salmon (lox), cut in small pieces

½ teaspoon dried dill
1 teaspoon lemon juice
1 teaspoon chopped scallion
15 minibagels, halved and lightly toasted

1. Place sour cream, cream cheese, lox, dill, lemon juice, and scallions in a blender or food processor and process until well combined.
2. Spread mixture on minibagels.

Calories Per Serving: 108
Fat: 1 g
Cholesterol: 5 mg
Protein: 6 g

Carbohydrates: 18 g
Dietary Fiber: 1 g
Sodium: 262 mg

❧ *Red Pepper–Artichoke Delights* ❧

YIELD: 20 servings (1 half each) • *PREPARATION TIME: 10 minutes* •
COOKING TIME: 5 minutes

These tiny artichoke, red pepper, and cheese muffin bites are as quick as they are delicious.

10 miniature English muffins, split
6 ounces canned artichoke hearts,
    drained and halved
½ cup canned, roasted sweet red pep-
    pers, finely chopped

¾ cup finely shredded nonfat or
    reduced-fat mozzarella cheese
¼ cup grated nonfat or reduced-fat
    Parmesan cheese

1. Preheat broiler. Place muffins, split side up, on a baking sheet. Broil 2½ minutes, until muffins are lightly browned.
2. Place an artichoke half on each muffin half, then a piece of red pepper, then mozzarella cheese, then Parmesan cheese. Broil 2 minutes or until cheese melts.

Calories Per Serving: 81
Fat: 3 g
Cholesterol: 3 mg
Protein: 13 g

Carbohydrates: 12 g
Dietary Fiber: 0 g
Sodium: 209 mg

Minimuffins with
❧ *Sun-Dried Tomato Filling* ☙

YIELD: *10 servings (2 halves each)* • PREPARATION TIME: *40 minutes* •
COOKING TIME: *7 minutes*

Mini–English muffins make a delicious base for a sun-dried tomato spread.

10 miniature English muffins, split
Boiling water
6 tablespoons chopped sun-dried
    tomatoes

12 ounces nonfat or reduced-fat cream
    cheese, softened
2 scallions, minced
6 tablespoons shredded carrot

1. Preheat broiler. Place muffin halves, split side up, on a baking sheet. Broil 2½ minutes, or until lightly browned.
2. Pour boiling water over dried tomatoes. Let sit for 5 minutes, then drain.
3. Blend together tomatoes, cream cheese, scallions, and carrot.
4. Spread muffins with cheese-tomato mixture.

Calories Per Serving: 110
Fat: 1 g
Cholesterol: 6 mg
Protein: 10 g

Carbohydrates: 17 g
Dietary Fiber: 0 g
Sodium: 416 mg

❦ Mango Chutney Bites ❦

YIELD: 16 servings (2 quarters each) • PREPARATION TIME: 15 minutes •
COOKING TIME: 6 minutes

Prepared mango chutney, cream cheese, and cumin are spread on English muffins.

4 English muffins, split
1 cup mango chutney
½ cup nonfat or reduced-fat cream
    cheese, softened

¼ teaspoon ground cumin

1. Preheat broiler. Place muffin halves on a baking sheet and lightly toast both sides under the broiler.
2. Blend together mango chutney, cream cheese, and cumin.
3. Spread on muffins.
4. Broil until topping is hot.
5. Cut muffins into quarters.

Calories Per Serving: 81
Fat: 0 g
Cholesterol: 1 mg
Protein: 3 g

Carbohydrates: 17 g
Dietary Fiber: 0 g
Sodium: 120 mg

❦ Wrapped Olives and Anchovies ❦

YIELD: 20 servings (2 each) • PREPARATION TIME: 20 minutes •
COOKING TIME: 7 minutes

You can create a quick tray of assorted appetizers with a can of refrigerator biscuit dough and a variety of bite-size morsels such as olives or anchovies.

1 10-ounce container low-fat refrigerator biscuit dough
13 large pitted green olives
13 large pitted black olives

14 anchovies, rinsed
1 cup grated nonfat or reduced-fat
  Parmesan cheese

1. Preheat oven to 375 degrees. Cut each biscuit in quarters, stretch the dough into a small rope, and wrap each piece around an olive or an anchovy.
2. Roll each olive or anchovy in Parmesan cheese.
3. Place on a lightly oiled baking sheet and bake for 7 minutes or until lightly browned. Serve hot.

Calories Per Serving: 55
Fat: 2 g
Cholesterol: 6 mg
Protein: 3 g

Carbohydrates: 8 g
Dietary Fiber: 0 g
Sodium: 356 mg

• Hot Canapés •

Artichoke Toasts

YIELD: 12 servings (2 each) • *PREPARATION TIME: 15 minutes* •
COOKING TIME: 17 minutes

Water-packed artichoke hearts are combined with mozzarella and Parmesan cheeses, and oregano.

24 slices French bread, ¼ inch thick
2 cloves garlic, minced
6 ounces canned, water-packed artichoke hearts, drained and chopped
½ cup grated nonfat or reduced-fat
  mozzarella cheese

½ teaspoon dried oregano
¼ teaspoon black pepper
¼ cup nonfat or reduced-fat grated
  Parmesan cheese

1. Preheat oven to 400 degrees. Arrange bread slices on a baking sheet. Bake for 6 minutes. Turn and toast until evenly browned.
2. Remove toast from oven and reduce temperature to 375 degrees.
3. Combine garlic, chopped artichoke hearts, mozzarella cheese, oregano, and pepper.

4. Spoon the artichoke mixture on the toast slices.
5. Sprinkle with Parmesan cheese.
6. Bake for 7 minutes or until cheese is melted. Serve at once.

Calories Per Serving: 165
Fat: 2 g
Cholesterol: 3 mg
Protein: 9 g

Carbohydrates: 29 g
Dietary Fiber: 1 g
Sodium: 400 mg

❧ Crab Morsels ❧

YIELD: 12 servings (2 each) • *PREPARATION TIME: 25 minutes* •
COOKING TIME: 8 minutes

These flavorful mini–crab sandwiches have a golden crust.

6 slices sandwich bread, crusts trimmed
6 ounces cooked crabmeat
¼ cup nonfat or reduced-fat mayonnaise

1 teaspoon minced scallion
1 teaspoon Worcestershire sauce
1 egg white

1. Preheat broiler. Toast bread on one side under the broiler and cut each slice into quarters.
2. Combine crabmeat, mayonnaise, scallion, and Worcestershire sauce.
3. Beat egg white until stiff, but not dry. Fold into crab mixture.
4. Spoon crab mixture on untoasted side of toast squares.
5. Arrange squares on a large baking sheet. Broil 5 inches from heat for 5 minutes or until lightly browned.

Calories Per Serving: 52
Fat: 1 g
Cholesterol: 13 mg
Protein: 4 g

Carbohydrates: 7 g
Dietary Fiber: 0 g
Sodium: 115 mg

❧ *Olive-Crab Melts* ✿

YIELD: 8 servings (2 each) • *PREPARATION TIME: 20 minutes* •
COOKING TIME: 30 minutes

These sandwiches can be made several hours ahead and refrigerated before
baking.

*4 slices thin-sliced bread, quartered,
 crusts trimmed
6½ ounces cooked crabmeat, drained
¼ cup nonfat or reduced-fat mayonnaise
3 tablespoons finely chopped celery*

*2 tablespoons finely chopped green
 olives
1 tablespoon lemon juice
1 clove garlic, minced
4 slices nonfat or reduced-fat Swiss
 cheese, quartered*

1. Preheat oven to 350 degrees. Place bread quarters on a baking sheet and
   bake 10 minutes, turn, and bake for an additional 5 minutes.
2. Combine crabmeat, mayonnaise, celery, olives, lemon juice, and garlic.
3. Spread crab mixture on toast and place a cheese square on top of each
   sandwich.
4. Place the squares on a baking sheet and bake for 15 minutes.
5. Turn oven to broil. Place under the broiler for 1 minute to brown.

Calories Per Serving: 84
Fat: 1 g
Cholesterol: 24 mg
Protein: 9 g

Carbohydrates: 10 g
Dietary Fiber: 1 g
Sodium: 424 mg

❧ *Oysters Wicomico* ✿

YIELD: 8 servings (2 each) • *PREPARATION TIME: 20 minutes* •
COOKING TIME: 10 minutes

Oysters with a topping of cheese, bread crumbs, scallions, and onions are
baked on party-size bread slices.

16 slices party-size rye bread
1 pint uncooked shucked oysters,
   rinsed, drained, and cut in thirds
2 scallions, chopped
2 tablespoons finely minced onion

Black pepper
2 tablespoons bread crumbs
Worcestershire sauce
2 ounces nonfat or reduced-fat cheddar
   cheese, finely grated

1. Preheat oven to 350 degrees. Place bread slices on a large baking sheet.
2. Place 2 to 3 pieces of oyster on each slice.
3. Sprinkle with scallions, onion, pepper, bread crumbs, Worcestershire sauce, and cheese.
4. Bake for 10 minutes or until cheese melts.

Calories Per Serving: 119
Fat: 2 g
Cholesterol: 7 mg
Protein: 6 g

Carbohydrates: 19 g
Dietary Fiber: 0 g
Sodium: 393 mg

❧ Puffed Cheese-Shrimp Rounds ❧

YIELD: 12 servings (2 each) • PREPARATION TIME: 25 minutes •
COOKING TIME: 5 minutes

Steamed shrimp halves with a cheese sauce are broiled on crackers.

12 large shrimp, cooked, shelled, and
   deveined
1 egg white
¼ cup grated nonfat or reduced-fat
   Parmesan cheese

⅛ teaspoon paprika
⅛ teaspoon ground cayenne pepper
½ cup nonfat or reduced-fat mayonnaise
24 nonfat round crackers

1. Preheat broiler. Cut shrimp in half lengthwise.
2. Beat egg white until stiff. Fold in cheese, paprika, cayenne pepper, and mayonnaise.
3. Spread mixture on crackers.
4. Top each with a shrimp half.
5. Broil for 2 minutes or until lightly browned. Serve immediately.

Calories Per Serving: 87
Fat: 3 g
Cholesterol: 58 mg
Protein: 9 g

Carbohydrates: 6 g
Dietary Fiber: 0 g
Sodium: 337 mg

❧ Shrimp Toasts ❧

YIELD: 16 servings (2 each) • PREPARATION TIME: 20 minutes •
COOKING TIME: 10 minutes

These shrimp toasts are baked instead of fried and are a great way to enjoy a Chinese favorite without the added fat calories.

2 scallions, chopped
1 tablespoon chopped water chestnuts
1½ teaspoons chopped fresh gingerroot
1½ teaspoons arrowroot or cornstarch
1 clove garlic, minced
1 egg white

1½ teaspoons dry sherry
½ pound medium uncooked shrimp,
    shelled and deveined
8 thin slices white bread, crusts
    trimmed

1. Preheat oven to 375 degrees. Place scallions, water chestnuts, gingerroot, cornstarch, and garlic in a blender or food processor and process until well mixed.
2. Add egg white and sherry and process for 4 seconds.
3. Add shrimp and process only until mixture reaches a spreadable consistency.
4. Spread shrimp mixture over 1 side of each slice of bread. Cut bread in half. Cut halves into triangles.
5. Place shrimp toast on baking sheet and bake for 10 minutes.

Calories Per Serving: 57
Fat: 1 g
Cholesterol: 21 mg
Protein: 4 g

Carbohydrates: 8 g
Dietary Fiber: 0 g
Sodium: 190 mg

❦ *Seafood-Cheese Melts* ❦

YIELD: 36 servings (2 each) • *PREPARATION TIME: 35 minutes* •
COOKING TIME: 5 minutes

A combination of minced clams and flaked crabmeat is spread on toast rounds and broiled.

8 ounces nonfat or reduced-fat cream
   cheese, softened
7½ ounces canned minced clams,
   drained
¾ cup cooked crabmeat, flaked
2 teaspoons grated onion
2 tablespoons minced scallions

1 teaspoon Worcestershire sauce
½ teaspoon white pepper
⅛ teaspoon hot pepper sauce
1 clove garlic, minced
72 2-inch rounds cut from firm rye
   bread, lightly toasted
Paprika

1. Blend together cream cheese, clams, crabmeat, onion, scallions, Worcestershire sauce, pepper, hot pepper sauce, and garlic.
2. Spread cheese mixture on untoasted side of bread, sprinkle with paprika, and broil until just crusty. Serve at once.

Calories Per Serving: 57
Fat: 1 g
Cholesterol: 7 mg
Protein: 4 g

Carbohydrates: 8 g
Dietary Fiber: 0 g
Sodium: 148 mg

❦ *Tuna Biscuits* ❦

YIELD: 10 servings (2 each) • *PREPARATION TIME: 20 minutes* •
COOKING TIME: 10 to 12 minutes (per package instructions)

Use refrigerator biscuit dough for these curried tuna treats.

10 refrigerator biscuit dough sections
3½ ounces canned, water-packed,
   white albacore tuna
3 tablespoons finely chopped scallions

2 tablespoons nonfat or reduced-fat
   mayonnaise
1½ teaspoons curry powder

1. Preheat oven according to biscuit package directions. Split biscuits in half. Flatten the dough with your hand.
2. Combine tuna, scallions, mayonnaise, and curry powder. Put 1 teaspoon of tuna mixture in the center of each biscuit half. Fold the dough over to enclose the filling, and press the edges together.
3. Place on a baking sheet. Bake as biscuit package directs or until biscuits are golden brown.

Calories Per Serving: 81 Carbohydrates: 12 g
Fat: 1 g Dietary Fiber: 0 g
Cholesterol: 4 mg Sodium: 365 mg
Protein: 4 g

⚘ *Parmesan-Onion Puffs* ⚘

YIELD: 10 servings (2 each) • *PREPARATION TIME: 25 minutes* •
COOKING TIME: 2 minutes

These little toasted onion-cheese rounds are best served warm from the oven.

¼ cup grated nonfat or reduced-fat   *2 small yellow onions, thinly sliced*
  Parmesan cheese   *20 2-inch rounds cut from firm,*
¼ cup nonfat or reduced-fat mayonnaise   *whole-grain bread*

1. Combine cheese and mayonnaise.
2. Place an onion slice on each piece of bread.
3. Top the onion with a teaspoon of cheese mixture.
4. Place the bread rounds on a baking sheet and broil for 3 minutes, or until puffed.

Calories Per Serving: 95 Carbohydrates: 16 g
Fat: 2 g Dietary Fiber: 1 g
Cholesterol: 2 mg Sodium: 217 mg
Protein: 4 g

❧ *Ricotta Sticks* ❧

YIELD: 12 servings (4 each) ▪ *PREPARATION TIME: 15 minutes* ▪
COOKING TIME: 5 minutes

Tiny bread sticks have a topping of herbed ricotta cheese.

1-pound loaf Italian bread, unsliced
1 clove garlic, minced
½ cup nonfat or reduced-fat ricotta cheese

1 teaspoon dried oregano
¼ cup chopped fresh parsley
2 tablespoons grated nonfat or reduced-fat Parmesan cheese

1. Preheat broiler. Cut bread in half lengthwise.
2. Cut bread slices into 4-inch sections. Cut each section into 4-inch by 1-inch sticks, 48 in all.
3. Broil bread sticks for 2 minutes.
4. Combine garlic, ricotta, oregano, parsley, and Parmesan.
5. Spread on toasts.
6. Broil 3 more minutes.

Calories Per Serving: 115
Fat: 0 g
Cholesterol: 2 mg
Protein: 5 g

Carbohydrates: 23 g
Dietary Fiber: 1 g
Sodium: 234 mg

❧ *Toasted Veggie Minibagels* ❧

YIELD: 18 servings (2 halves each) ▪ *PREPARATION TIME: 20 minutes* ▪
COOKING TIME: 10 minutes

Minibagels are topped with a mixture of cottage cheese, vegetables, and herbs.

1½ cups nonfat or reduced-fat cottage cheese
¼ cup chopped radishes

¼ cup chopped green bell pepper
½ cup chopped celery

2 tablespoons chopped fresh parsley
1 clove garlic, minced
½ cup minced scallions

¼ teaspoon black pepper
18 minibagels, split and lightly toasted

1. Preheat broiler. Place cottage cheese in a blender or food processor and blend until smooth.
2. Combine cottage cheese, radishes, bell pepper, celery, parsley, garlic, scallions, and black pepper.
3. Spread mixture on bagels.
4. Broil for 8 to 10 minutes, watching to be sure they don't burn.

Calories Per Serving: 112
Fat: 1 g
Cholesterol: 7 mg
Protein: 6 g

Carbohydrates: 20 g
Dietary Fiber: 0 g
Sodium: 218 mg

✎ *Mini–Baked Bean Melts* ✎

YIELD: 16 servings (2 halves each) ▪ *PREPARATION TIME: 10 minutes* ▪
COOKING TIME: 6 minutes

Baked beans are accented with scallions and Dijon mustard, then spooned onto mini–English muffins and broiled with a cheese topping.

2 cups vegetarian baked beans
⅓ cup chopped scallions
2 teaspoons Dijon mustard
¼ teaspoon white pepper
16 mini–English muffins, split and
  lightly toasted

16 cherry tomatoes, halved
½ cup plus 2 tablespoons grated nonfat
  or reduced-fat cheese

1. Preheat broiler. Combine beans, scallions, Dijon mustard, and white pepper.
2. Place a tablespoon of bean mixture on each muffin half.
3. Place a cherry tomato on each muffin half, and sprinkle with grated cheese.

4. Place under broiler for 6 minutes or until cheese has melted. Serve with small plates and cocktail forks.

Calories Per Serving: 114

Fat: 1 g

Cholesterol: 2 mg

Protein: 6 g

Carbohydrates: 21 g

Dietary Fiber: 3 g

Sodium: 355 mg

❦ *Zucchini Pita Pizza Bites* ❦

YIELD: 24 servings (1 each) • PREPARATION TIME: 25 minutes •
COOKING TIME: 22 minutes

Pitas are toasted, split, and topped with zucchini, onions, thyme, tomato, and cheese.

¼ cup light-flavored olive oil
2 cups finely chopped onions
2 teaspoons dried thyme
4 cups grated zucchini

2 large tomatoes, diced
6 6-inch pita breads
3 cups nonfat or reduced-fat grated
  mozzarella cheese

1. Preheat oven to 450 degrees. Heat olive oil in a skillet over medium heat. Sauté onions and thyme for 5 minutes or until onions are tender.
2. Add zucchini and cook for 2 more minutes.
3. Raise heat and add tomatoes; cook, stirring, for 2 minutes more. Remove from heat.
4. Bake pita bread in the oven for 3 minutes. Remove and split around the edge into two rounds. Cut rounds in half.
5. Spoon topping onto pita half-circles. Sprinkle with cheese.
6. Place on baking sheet and bake for 10 minutes until cheese bubbles.

Calories Per Serving: 114

Fat: 3 g

Cholesterol: 5 mg

Protein: 11 g

Carbohydrates: 12 g

Dietary Fiber: 1 g

Sodium: 286 mg

DUMPLINGS, TORTILLAS, PIZZAS, AND NACHOS

Turkey Wontons • Steamed Chicken Wontons with Soy-Vinegar Dressing • Chicken–Leek Wontons with Apricot Dipping Sauce • Vegetable Wontons • Chicken in Double Wonton Wrappers • Steamed Turkey Dumplings • Crab Wontons with Plum Sauce • Curried Wontons • Chicken Shaomai • Shrimp-Bamboo Wontons • Ginger-Crab Potstickers • Chinese Shrimp Dumplings • Steamed Spinach Dumplings • Lettuce-Shrimp Rolls • Chicken Rolls with Dijon Dipping Sauce • Little Pinto Burritos • Salmon Tortillas • Bean Tortillas • Tortellini with Spinach-Parsley Dip • Dijon Chicken Salad–Stuffed Shells • Tuna-Stuffed Shells • Vegetable-Tortellini Skewers • Nachos and Avocados with Taco Sauce • Nachos with Mozzarella-Tomato Sauce • Southwestern Pinto Bean Chips • Parmesan-Artichoke Pita Bites • Petite Pizza Bites • French Bread Pizza Slices • Boboli Bites

❦ *Turkey Wontons* ❦

YIELD: *24 servings (1 each)* ▪ PREPARATION TIME: *30 minutes* ▪
COOKING TIME: *10 minutes*

These wontons are baked until lightly browned and crisp. Serve with your favorite Chinese dipping sauces.

1 tablespoon canola oil	*1 tablespoon dry sherry*
8 ounces low-fat ground turkey breast	*2 teaspoons cornstarch*
½ cup shredded carrot	*2 teaspoons grated fresh gingerroot*
¼ cup finely chopped celery	*24 square wonton wrappers*
1 tablespoon light soy sauce	*Olive oil cooking spray*

1. Heat canola oil in a skillet over medium heat. Sauté turkey until no pink remains.
2. Stir in carrot, celery, soy sauce, sherry, cornstarch, and gingerroot.
3. Preheat oven to 375 degrees. Spoon 1 rounded teaspoon of mixture into a wonton wrapper.
4. Brush edges of wonton with water. Bring two opposite corners of wrapper up over the filling; pinch together in center. Bring two remaining corners to center and pinch together. Pinch all edges together to seal. Repeat with the remaining filling and wrappers, keeping filled wontons under a damp cloth until ready to bake.
5. Spray baking sheet with olive oil spray. Place wontons on baking sheet. Lightly spray wontons with oil spray and bake for 8 to 10 minutes or until light brown and crisp. Serve immediately.

Calories Per Serving: 41
Fat: 1 g
Cholesterol: 8 mg
Protein: 3 g

Carbohydrates: 5 g
Dietary Fiber: 0 g
Sodium: 77 mg

Steamed Chicken Wontons
with Soy-Vinegar Dressing

YIELD: 24 servings (2 each)   •   PREPARATION TIME: 35 minutes plus 30 minutes standing time   •   COOKING TIME: 10 minutes per batch

Wonton wrappers are filled with a mixture of shredded chicken, minced water chestnuts, celery, and bamboo shoots, and then steamed.

2 cups shredded, cooked chicken breast
½ cup minced water chestnuts
½ cup minced celery
½ cup minced bamboo shoots
1 minced scallion

1 tablespoon light soy sauce
2 cloves garlic, minced
48 square wonton wrappers
Lettuce leaves

DRESSING

1½ teaspoons sugar
3 tablespoons light soy sauce
3 tablespoons rice vinegar
1 teaspoon dry sherry

Several drops canola or light sesame oil
½ teaspoon dry mustard
¼ teaspoon paprika

1. Combine chicken, water chestnuts, celery, bamboo shoots, scallion, soy sauce, and garlic. Let stand for 30 minutes.
2. Place 1 teaspoon of the chicken-vegetable mixture slightly below the center of a wonton wrapper.
3. Brush the edges of the wrapper with water.
4. Fold the wrapper over the filling diagonally to form a triangle, pressing the edges together to seal and pressing out air pockets around the filling.
5. Brush a small amount of water on the front of the triangle's right corner and on the back of the left corner.
6. Fold the corners so that the brushed sides meet each other, and press together to seal.
7. Repeat with the remaining wrappers and filling, keeping filled wontons under a damp cloth until ready to steam.
8. Line the steamer with lettuce leaves to keep wontons from sticking. Place a single layer of filled wontons on the rack of the steamer. Place over boiling water, cover, and steam for 10 minutes. Repeat until all the wontons have been steamed.

9. To make the dressing, whisk together sugar, soy sauce, and vinegar. Whisk in sherry, canola or sesame oil, dry mustard, and paprika.
10. Transfer wontons to a serving platter and serve with dressing in a bowl.

Calories Per Serving: 58
Fat: 1 g
Cholesterol: 7 mg
Protein: 3 g

Carbohydrates: 11 g
Dietary Fiber: 0 g
Sodium: 203 mg

Chicken-Leek Wontons
❧ with Apricot Dipping Sauce ❧

YIELD: 18 servings (2 each) • *PREPARATION TIME: 25 minutes* •
COOKING TIME: 15 minutes per batch

Wonton wrappers are filled with shredded cooked chicken and leeks.

2 cups shredded, cooked chicken breast
1 cup minced leeks
¼ cup chopped fresh parsley
2 scallions, minced
2 garlic cloves, minced
¼ teaspoon black pepper

1 tablespoon light soy sauce
36 round wonton wrappers (can be cut from square wrappers with a 3-inch biscuit cutter)
Lettuce leaves

SAUCE
1 cup all-fruit apricot preserves
1½ tablespoons grated fresh gingerroot

1 teaspoon Dijon mustard
1 tablespoon rice vinegar

1. Combine chicken, leeks, parsley, scallions, garlic, pepper, and soy sauce.
2. Place 1 teaspoon of the chicken-leek filling slightly below the center of a wrapper.
3. Brush the edge of the wrapper with water.
4. Fold the wrapper in half; press the edge together to seal and press out air pockets around filling.
5. Repeat with remaining filling and wrappers, keeping filled wontons under a damp cloth until ready to steam.
6. Line the steamer with lettuce leaves to keep wontons from sticking. Place a single layer of filled wontons on the rack of the steamer. Place over boil-

ing water, cover, and steam for 15 minutes. Repeat until all wontons have been steamed.

7. For sauce, whisk together apricot preserves, gingerroot, mustard, and vinegar. Transfer to a serving bowl.

8. Arrange wontons around dipping sauce on a serving platter.

Calories Per Serving: 82	Carbohydrates: 16 g
Fat: 1 g	Dietary Fiber: 0 g
Cholesterol: 8 mg	Sodium: 154 mg
Protein: 4 g	

❧ *Vegetable Wontons* ❧

YIELD: 18 servings (2 each) • PREPARATION TIME: 25 minutes •
COOKING TIME: 15 minutes per batch

Minced vegetables in wonton wrappers are steamed and served with a pungent dipping sauce.

½ cup minced celery
½ cup minced mushrooms
½ cup minced onion
½ cup minced carrot
½ cup minced green bell pepper
½ cup minced water chestnuts
¼ cup chopped fresh parsley
2 scallions, minced
2 cloves garlic, minced

¼ teaspoon black pepper
1 tablespoon light soy sauce
1 tablespoon dry sherry
1 teaspoon minced fresh gingerroot
36 round wonton wrappers (can be cut
*   from square wrappers with a 3-inch*
*   biscuit cutter)*
Lettuce leaves

SAUCE

⅓ cup light soy sauce
⅓ cup rice vinegar

1 scallion, minced

1. Combine celery, mushrooms, onion, carrot, green bell pepper, water chestnuts, parsley, scallions, garlic, black pepper, soy sauce, sherry, and gingerroot.

2. Place 1 teaspoon of the vegetable filling slightly below the center of a wrapper.

3. Brush the edges of the wrapper with water.

4. Fold the wrapper in half; press the edge together to seal, and press out air pockets around filling.
5. Repeat with remaining filling and wrappers, keeping filled wontons under a damp cloth until ready to steam.
6. Line a steamer with lettuce leaves to keep wontons from sticking. Place a single layer of filled wontons on the rack of the steamer. Place over boiling water, cover, and steam for 15 minutes. Repeat until all wontons have been steamed.
7. For the sauce, whisk together soy sauce, rice vinegar, and scallions. Transfer to a serving dish.
8. Arrange wontons around dipping sauce on a serving platter.

Calories Per Serving: 63   Carbohydrates: 12 g
Fat: 0 g   Dietary Fiber: 0 g
Cholesterol: 2 mg   Sodium: 288 mg
Protein: 3 g

❦ *Chicken in Double Wonton Wrappers* ✏

YIELD: 18 servings (1 each) • *PREPARATION TIME: 30 minutes* •
COOKING TIME: 10 minutes per batch

Wonton wrappers are filled with a mixture of chicken, mushrooms, and red pepper, and then sautéed.

2 cups diced cooked chicken breast   *⅛ teaspoon hot pepper sauce*
2 tablespoons chopped scallions   *⅛ teaspoon black pepper*
1 cup chopped mushrooms   *36 round wonton wrappers (can be cut*
1 clove garlic, chopped   *from square wrappers with a 3-inch*
½ cup chopped celery   *biscuit cutter)*
¼ cup chopped red bell pepper   *4 teaspoons canola oil*

1. Place chicken, scallions, mushrooms, garlic, celery, red pepper, hot pepper sauce, and black pepper in a blender or food processor and process until well blended.
2. Spoon about 2 tablespoons mixture onto center of 18 wonton wrappers. Lightly brush edges with water. Top each with another wonton wrapper; press edges together to seal.

3. Heat oil in a skillet over medium heat. Place a single layer of filled wontons in hot skillet. Brown lightly on both sides. Remove, and repeat with remaining wontons. Serve immediately.

Calories Per Serving: 84

Fat: 2 g

Cholesterol: 20 mg

Protein: 7 g

Carbohydrates: 10 g

Dietary Fiber: 0 g

Sodium: 112 mg

❦ *Steamed Turkey Dumplings* ❦

YIELD: 10 servings (2 each) • *PREPARATION TIME: 25 minutes* •
COOKING TIME: 30 minutes

Ground turkey is combined with scallions, gingerroot, soy sauce, and sesame oil and steamed in round wonton wrappers.

½ pound low-fat ground turkey breast
2 scallions, minced
2 tablespoons minced fresh gingerroot
1 tablespoon light soy sauce
1 teaspoon canola or sesame oil
¼ teaspoon black pepper

½ teaspoon sugar
2 tablespoons cornstarch
20 round wonton wrappers (can be cut
from square wrappers with a 3-inch
biscuit cutter)
Lettuce leaves

1. Combine turkey, scallions, gingerroot, soy sauce, oil, pepper, sugar, and cornstarch.
2. Place a teaspoon of filling in the center of each wonton wrapper. Lightly brush the edges with water. Press the edges of the wrappers together, keeping filled wontons under a damp cloth until ready to steam.
3. Line a steamer basket with lettuce leaves to keep dumplings from sticking and place dumplings on top of lettuce leaves over simmering water. Cover and steam for 30 minutes or until centers of dumplings are no longer pink. Serve hot in the steamer.

Calories Per Serving: 66

Fat: 1 g

Cholesterol: 15 mg

Protein: 3 g

Carbohydrates: 9 g

Dietary Fiber: 0 g

Sodium: 188 mg

❧ *Crab Wontons with Plum Sauce* ✔

YIELD: *12 servings (2 each)* • PREPARATION TIME: *30 minutes* •
COOKING TIME: *10 minutes*

These steamed wontons are filled with crabmeat, ginger, plum sauce, and water chestnuts. Plum sauce can be found in the international foods section of your supermarket or at oriental markets.

1½ cups cooked crabmeat
½ teaspoon grated fresh gingerroot
2 egg whites, beaten
2 tablespoons plum sauce
2 tablespoons chopped scallions
¼ cup chopped water chestnuts

⅛ teaspoon black pepper
24 round wonton wrappers (can be cut
from square wrappers with a 3-inch
biscuit cutter)
1 teaspoon toasted sesame seeds
Lettuce leaves

1. Combine crabmeat, gingerroot, egg whites, plum sauce, scallions, water chestnuts, and pepper.
2. Spoon 2 teaspoons crab mixture onto center of each wonton wrapper. Bring edge up around filling on all sides. Leave top open. Sprinkle top with toasted sesame seeds.
3. Bring 2 cups water to a boil in a covered skillet.
4. Line the steamer with lettuce leaves to keep wontons from sticking. Arrange dumplings, open side up, on a steamer rack in skillet. Cover and steam over low heat for 10 minutes. Serve immediately.

Calories Per Serving: 55
Fat: 0 g
Cholesterol: 2 mg
Protein: 2 g

Carbohydrates: 11 g
Dietary Fiber: 0 g
Sodium: 102 mg

❧ *Curried Wontons* ✔

YIELD: *10 servings (2 each)* • PREPARATION TIME: *25 minutes* •
COOKING TIME: *15 minutes*

Ground turkey is combined with garlic, curry, ginger, chutney, and yogurt as a filling for wonton wrappers. Use your favorite chutney with this recipe.

2 tablespoons light-flavored olive or
    canola oil
½ pound low-fat ground turkey breast
1 clove garlic, minced
1 teaspoon minced fresh gingerroot
1 tablespoon finely chopped mango
    chutney

¼ teaspoon black pepper
2 tablespoons nonfat or reduced-fat
    yogurt
20 round wonton wrappers (can be cut
    from square wrappers with a 3-inch
    biscuit cutter)
Lettuce leaves

1. Heat the oil in a skillet over medium heat. Add turkey and garlic, and
   sauté until turkey is no longer pink. Drain.
2. Combine turkey, gingerroot, chutney, pepper, and yogurt.
3. Place 2 teaspoons of filling on half of each wonton wrapper.
4. Brush edge of wrapper with water. Fold wrapper over. Press to seal.
5. Line a steamer basket with lettuce leaves to keep wontons from sticking.
   Add wontons and steam for 6 to 8 minutes. Serve at once.

Calories Per Serving: 55
Fat: 2 g
Cholesterol: 11 mg
Protein: 4 g

Carbohydrates: 6 g
Dietary Fiber: 0 g
Sodium: 56 mg

❧ Chicken Shaomai ❧

*YIELD: 30 servings (2 each) • PREPARATION TIME: 25 minutes •
COOKING TIME: 6 minutes*

This is a variation of a Chinese dim sum made with cooked, minced
chicken, cooked rice, and oriental seasonings.

1 cup cooked rice
1 cup minced cooked chicken breast
1 tablespoon light sesame oil
1 tablespoon light soy sauce

¼ teaspoon minced fresh gingerroot
¼ teaspoon white pepper
¼ teaspoon sugar
60 round or square wonton wrappers

1. Combine rice, chicken, sesame oil, soy sauce, gingerroot, white pepper,
   and sugar.
2. Place 1 teaspoon of filling in the middle of each wonton wrapper. Gather
   up the edges to enclose the filling, letting the dough pleat naturally. Pat

the sides of the wrapper to work out air, and squeeze to seal. Tap the bottom of the shaomai to flatten.

3. Place assembled shaomai on a plate covered with a damp cloth until ready to steam.

4. Bring a quart of water to a boil in a large wok or large pot with a steamer rack.

5. Place plate on rack and steam over high heat for 6 minutes. Serve at once.

Calories Per Serving: 68
Fat: 1 g
Cholesterol: 7 mg
Protein: 3 g

Carbohydrates: 11 g
Dietary Fiber: 0 g
Sodium: 114 mg

⍋ *Shrimp-Bamboo Wontons* ⍋

YIELD: 18 servings (2 each) • *PREPARATION TIME: 25 minutes* •
COOKING TIME: 15 minutes per batch

Shrimp, celery, onion, green pepper, and bamboo shoots are combined with sherry and scallions to fill round wonton wrappers.

1½ cups minced cooked shrimp
½ cup minced celery
¼ cup minced onion
½ cup minced bamboo shoots
2 scallions, minced
2 garlic cloves, minced
¼ teaspoon black pepper
2 tablespoons dry sherry

1 teaspoon minced fresh gingerroot
36 round wonton wrappers (can be cut
*   from square wrappers with a 3-inch*
*   biscuit cutter)*
2 egg whites beaten with 1 tablespoon
*   water*
Lettuce leaves

SAUCE

¼ cup light soy sauce
3 tablespoons rice vinegar
½ teaspoon canola or light sesame oil

1 scallion, minced
¼ teaspoon sugar

1. Combine shrimp, celery, onion, bamboo shoots, scallions, garlic, pepper, sherry, and gingerroot.

2. Place 1 teaspoon of the shrimp filling slightly below the center of each wrapper.
3. Brush the edges of a wrapper with egg-water mixture.
4. Fold the wrapper in half. Press the edge together to seal and press out air pockets around filling.
5. Repeat with remaining wontons and filling, keeping filled wontons under a damp cloth until ready to steam.
6. Line a steamer basket with lettuce leaves to keep wontons from sticking. Place a single layer of filled wontons on the lettuce leaves. Place over boiling water, cover, and steam for 15 minutes. Repeat until all wontons have been steamed.
7. For sauce, whisk together soy sauce, rice vinegar, oil, scallion, and sugar. Transfer to a serving dish.
8. Arrange wontons around dipping sauce on a platter.

Calories Per Serving: 71
Fat: 0 g
Cholesterol: 23 mg
Protein: 5 g

Carbohydrates: 11 g
Dietary Fiber: 0 g
Sodium: 362 mg

◟ Ginger-Crab Potstickers ◞

YIELD: 18 servings (2 each) • PREPARATION TIME: 25 minutes •
COOKING TIME: 15 minutes per batch

Cooked crabmeat is combined with oriental seasonings in these steamed wontons.

1½ cups cooked crabmeat
¼ cup chopped fresh parsley
2 scallions, minced
2 garlic cloves, minced
¼ teaspoon black pepper
½ teaspoon sugar

2 tablespoons light soy sauce
1 teaspoon minced fresh gingerroot
36 round wonton wrappers
2 egg whites beaten with 1 tablespoon
  water
Lettuce leaves

SAUCE

¼ cup light soy sauce
¼ cup rice vinegar

1 scallion, minced

1. Combine crabmeat, parsley, scallions, garlic, pepper, sugar, soy sauce, and gingerroot.
2. Place 1 teaspoon of the crab filling slightly below the center of each wrapper.
3. Brush the edges of the wrapper with egg-water mixture.
4. Fold the wrapper in half and press the edges together to seal, pressing out air pockets around filling. Keep filled wontons under a damp cloth until ready to steam.
5. Line a steamer basket with lettuce leaves to keep wontons from sticking. Place a single layer of filled wontons on the lettuce leaves. Place over boiling water, cover, and steam for 15 minutes. Repeat until all wontons have been steamed.
6. For the sauce, combine soy sauce, vinegar, and scallion. Transfer to a serving dish.
7. Arrange wontons around dipping sauce on a serving platter.

Calories Per Serving: 62	Carbohydrates: 10 g
Fat: 1 g	Dietary Fiber: 0 g
Cholesterol: 13 mg	Sodium: 189 mg
Protein: 4 g	

◊ *Chinese Shrimp Dumplings* ◊

YIELD: 14 servings (2 each) • *PREPARATION TIME: 30 minutes* •
COOKING TIME: 20 minutes

These steamed shrimp dumplings are quick and easier to shape than wontons.

1 pound uncooked shrimp, shelled, deveined, and coarsely chopped	*1 teaspoon cornstarch*
¼ cup finely chopped bamboo shoots	*1 tablespoon dry sherry*
4 scallions, finely chopped	*1 teaspoon canola or light sesame oil*
3 tablespoons nonfat or reduced-fat, low-sodium chicken broth or water	*½ teaspoon sugar*
1 tablespoon light soy sauce	*28 round wonton wrappers (can be cut from square wrappers with a 3-inch biscuit cutter)*

1. Combine shrimp, bamboo shoots, scallions, chicken broth, soy sauce, cornstarch, sherry, oil, and sugar.

2. Place about 1 tablespoon of the shrimp mixture on the center of each wonton skin. Shape the sides around the filling to form a cup, pleating as needed. Flatten the bottoms of the wontons enough that they will stand upright. Keep filled wontons under a damp cloth until ready to steam.

3. Arrange the dumplings on a lightly oiled plate, not letting them touch each other. Pour about 2 inches of water into a large pot. Place a small inverted heat-proof bowl into the pot and place the plate on the inverted bowl, so that the plate is above the water in the pot.

4. Cover the pot, bring the water to a boil, and steam for 20 minutes.

Calories Per Serving: 46   Carbohydrates: 6 g
Fat: 0 g   Dietary Fiber: 0 g
Cholesterol: 29 mg   Sodium: 211 mg
Protein: 5 g

❧ *Steamed Spinach Dumplings* ❧

YIELD: 24 servings (2 each) • PREPARATION TIME: 35 minutes •
COOKING TIME: 5 minutes per batch

Wonton wrappers are filled with a mixture of carrots, spinach, and onion, and then steamed.

1 tablespoon light-flavored olive oil   *48 square wonton wrappers*
½ cup minced onion   *2 egg whites beaten with 1 tablespoon*
2 cloves garlic, minced   *water*
1 cup cooked carrots, pureed in blender   *Lettuce leaves*
or food processor
1 pound fresh or frozen chopped
spinach, drained and chopped

1. Heat olive oil in a skillet over medium heat and sauté the onion and garlic until tender.

2. Blend together sautéed onion and garlic, carrot puree, and spinach.

3. Place 1 teaspoon of the vegetable mixture slightly below the center of each wrapper.

4. Brush the edges of the wrapper with the egg-water mixture.

5. Fold the wrapper over the filling diagonally to form a triangle, pressing the edges together to seal, and press out air pockets around the filling.

6. Repeat with the remaining wrappers and filling, keeping filled wontons under a damp cloth until ready to steam.

7. Line a steamer basket with lettuce leaves. Place a single layer of filled wontons on the lettuce leaves. Place over boiling water, cover, and steam for 5 minutes. Repeat until all the wontons have been steamed.

Calories Per Serving: 65
Fat: 1 g
Cholesterol: 2 mg
Protein: 3 g

Carbohydrates: 12 g
Dietary Fiber: 1 g
Sodium: 124 mg

❦ *Lettuce-Shrimp Rolls* ❦

YIELD: *12 servings (2 each)* • PREPARATION TIME: *30 minutes* •
COOKING TIME: *15 minutes*

Lettuce leaves are wrapped around shrimp, turkey sausage, Chinese cabbage, and bean sprouts.

1 tablespoon light-flavored olive oil
¼ pound fresh turkey sausage
1 clove garlic, minced
1 medium onion, diced
2 cups minced Chinese cabbage
1 cup fresh bean sprouts

¼ teaspoon black pepper
6 ounces cooked shrimp, shelled,
deveined, and finely chopped
24 Bibb lettuce leaves (or other small
crisp lettuce), rinsed and dried

1. Heat oil in a skillet over medium heat. Sauté sausage, garlic, and onion for 10 minutes until sausage is done. Break sausage up with a spoon while cooking.

2. Add Chinese cabbage, bean sprouts, and pepper. Sauté 5 more minutes, until vegetables are tender-crisp. Stir in shrimp and heat through. Remove from heat and cover skillet.

3. Steam lettuce leaves for 30 seconds. Divide mixture among lettuce leaves, placing a mound of filling in the bottom half of each leaf. Fold bottom of leaf over filling, bring sides of leaf to the center, then roll up. Place seam side down on serving platter.

Calories Per Serving: 59   Carbohydrates: 3 g
Fat: 3 g   Dietary Fiber: 1 g
Cholesterol: 33 mg   Sodium: 99 mg
Protein: 6 g

✎ *Chicken Rolls with Dijon Dipping Sauce* ✎

YIELD: 16 servings (½ spring roll each) • *PREPARATION TIME: 25 minutes* • *COOKING TIME: 20 minutes*

Chicken breast, mushrooms, scallions, and parsley make the filling for these baked spring rolls. Baking cuts down on their fat content. You could also use this mixture to fill 36 wonton-size wrappers.

1 chicken breast half, boned and   *2 tablespoons chopped fresh parsley*
  skinned, cut into small pieces   *¼ teaspoon black pepper*
6 mushrooms, halved   *4 tablespoons light-flavored olive oil*
1 scallion, chopped   *8 spring roll or egg roll wrappers*

SAUCE

¼ cup light soy sauce   *½ teaspoon honey*
1 tablespoon Dijon mustard   *1 teaspoon rice vinegar*

1. Preheat oven to 400 degrees. Place chicken, mushrooms, scallion, parsley, and pepper in a blender or food processor and process until finely chopped.
2. Heat 2 tablespoons of the olive oil in a skillet over medium heat. Stir-fry chicken mixture for 5 minutes or until chicken is done.
3. Lay 1 spring roll wrapper out on the counter with one point toward you. Put about ¼ cup of filling across the middle of the wrapper. Fold bottom point of skin over filling. Fold side corners over, forming an envelope shape. Roll up spring roll toward remaining corner. Moisten point with water and press firmly to seal. Repeat with remaining 7 wrappers and filling.
4. Place rolls, seam side down, on baking sheet. Brush with remaining 2 tablespoons olive oil. Bake for 7 minutes and turn. Bake for 8 more minutes or until lightly browned.

5. For the sauce, combine soy sauce, mustard, honey, and vinegar in a small serving bowl.
6. Cut each spring roll in half. Serve with dipping sauce.

Calories Per Serving: 53
Fat: 3 g
Cholesterol: 4 mg
Protein: 2 g

Carbohydrates: 5 g
Dietary Fiber: 0 g
Sodium: 218 mg

❧ *Little Pinto Burritos* ❧

Yield: 24 servings (1 each) • *Preparation Time: 20 minutes* •
Cooking Time: 15 minutes

Pinto beans are cooked with garlic, cumin, onion, and jalapeño peppers and rolled in tortillas. Serve with nonfat sour cream and prepared salsa.

12 6-inch flour tortillas
1 tablespoon light-flavored olive or canola oil
1 onion, chopped
2 cloves garlic, minced
2 fresh jalapeño peppers, seeded and minced

2 cups canned or home-cooked pinto beans, rinsed and drained
½ cup grated nonfat or reduced-fat cheese
½ teaspoon ground cumin

1. Preheat oven to 325 degrees. Stack tortillas and cut in half. Wrap tortillas in foil and warm in the oven for 15 minutes.
2. Heat oil in a skillet over medium heat. Sauté onion until tender.
3. Add garlic and jalapeño peppers and sauté for 30 seconds more.
4. Reduce heat to low and stir in pinto beans, cheese, and cumin. Cook for 6 minutes, stirring several times.
5. Place 1½ tablespoons of pinto bean mixture in middle of each tortilla half and roll up. Serve warm.

Calories Per Serving: 86
Fat: 2 g
Cholesterol: 0 mg
Protein: 6 g

Carbohydrates: 14 g
Dietary Fiber: 0 g
Sodium: 206 mg

❧ *Salmon Tortillas* ❧

YIELD: *20 servings (2 each)*　•　PREPARATION TIME: *25 minutes plus*
2 hours refrigeration time

Canned salmon is combined with cream cheese, tomato puree, chili powder, and parsley and then rolled in small, soft flour tortillas.

2 cups canned salmon, drained and
*　flaked*
8 ounces nonfat or reduced-fat cream
*　cheese, softened*

¼ cup canned low-sodium tomato puree
¼ teaspoon chili powder
1 tablespoon minced fresh parsley
10 8-inch flour tortillas

1. Combine salmon, cream cheese, tomato puree, chili powder, and parsley.
2. Spread 2 tablespoons of the salmon mixture on each tortilla, and roll up.
3. Chill, covered, for 2 hours.
4. Cut each tortilla into quarters with a bread knife.

Calories Per Serving: 105
Fat: 3 g
Cholesterol: 12 mg
Protein: 9 g

Carbohydrates: 11 g
Dietary Fiber: 0 g
Sodium: 287 mg

❧ *Bean Tortillas* ❧

YIELD: *14 servings (1 each)*　•　PREPARATION TIME: *25 minutes*

Black beans, pinto beans, jalapeño peppers, and spices are combined in this filling for small flour tortillas.

1 cup canned or home-cooked black
*　beans, rinsed and drained*
1 cup canned or home-cooked pinto
*　beans, rinsed and drained*
½ cup minced red onion
1 tablespoon dried cilantro

½ teaspoon black pepper
1 teaspoon dried oregano
1 garlic clove, minced
1 jalapeño pepper, seeded and minced
14 small flour tortillas

1. Preheat oven to 325 degrees. Combine the black beans, pinto beans, onion, cilantro, black pepper, oregano, garlic, and jalapeño in a bowl.
2. Spoon 1½ tablespoons of black bean mixture onto the bottom half of each tortilla.
3. Roll tortilla once, then fold sides in. Roll the rest of the tortilla. Place seam side down in a baking dish.
4. Bake for 15 minutes or until warmed through.

Calories Per Serving: 148   Carbohydrates: 26 g
Fat: 3 g   Dietary Fiber: 1 g
Cholesterol: 0 mg   Sodium: 239 mg
Protein: 5 g

✎ *Tortellini with Spinach-Parsley Dip* ✎

YIELD: 20 servings (2 skewers each) • *PREPARATION TIME: 25 minutes plus 1 hour refrigeration time*

Tortellini are skewered with cherry tomatoes, green olives, and mushrooms, and served with a spinach-parsley dip.

¼ cup grated nonfat or reduced-fat Parmesan cheese   *¾ cup chopped fresh parsley*
1 cup nonfat or reduced-fat sour cream   *40 cooked tortellini*
1 clove garlic   *40 cherry tomatoes*
¾ cup chopped fresh spinach leaves   *40 small mushrooms*
          40 pitted green olives

1. Place Parmesan cheese, sour cream, garlic, spinach, and parsley in a blender or food processor and process until smooth.
2. Place in a serving bowl, cover, and refrigerate for 1 hour.
3. Place 1 tortellini, 1 cherry tomato, 1 mushroom, and 1 olive on each of 40 small wooden or plastic skewers.
4. Arrange tortellini skewers around dip on a platter.

Calories Per Serving: 67   Carbohydrates: 9 g
Fat: 2 g   Dietary Fiber: 1 g
Cholesterol: 9 mg   Sodium: 317 mg
Protein: 4 g

❧ *Dijon Chicken Salad–Stuffed Shells* ❧

YIELD: 12 servings (1 each) • *PREPARATION TIME: 25 minutes* •
COOKING TIME: 10 minutes

Chicken mixed with Dijon mustard, sour cream, scallions, egg whites, and sun-dried tomatoes is stuffed into giant shells.

12 giant pasta shells
¼ cup nonfat or reduced-fat sour cream
¼ cup nonfat or reduced-fat mayonnaise
1 tablespoon finely chopped scallion
1 teaspoon Dijon mustard
2 hard-boiled egg whites, chopped

2 tablespoons chopped oil-packed sun-dried tomatoes, drained
⅛ teaspoon black pepper
1 cup dried cooked chicken breast
½ cup dried nonfat or reduced-fat mozzarella cheese

1. Bring 3 quarts water to a boil in a large pot.
2. Add pasta shells; cook 10 minutes or until barely tender. Rinse with cold water and drain on paper towels.
3. Combine sour cream, mayonnaise, scallion, mustard, egg whites, sun-dried tomatoes, and pepper. Stir in chicken and cheese.
4. Spoon into cooked shells.

Calories Per Serving: 109
Fat: 2 g
Cholesterol: 16 mg
Protein: 11 g

Carbohydrates: 13 g
Dietary Fiber: 1 g
Sodium: 109 mg

❧ *Tuna-Stuffed Shells* ❧

YIELD: 8 servings (2 each) • *PREPARATION TIME: 30 minutes plus 2 hours refrigeration time* • *COOKING TIME: 15 minutes*

Pasta shells are stuffed with a mixture of tuna, sautéed vegetables, and spices.

16 giant pasta shells

1 tablespoon light-flavored olive oil

½ cup finely chopped zucchini

½ cup finely chopped green bell pepper

1 clove garlic, minced

½ cup nonfat or reduced-fat plain yogurt

¼ cup nonfat or reduced-fat mayonnaise

½ teaspoon dried dill

¼ cup shredded carrot

¼ cup seeded and finely chopped cucumber

8 ounces canned, water-packed, white albacore tuna

1. Bring 3 quarts water to a boil in a large pot. Add pasta shells and cook 10 minutes or until just tender. Rinse with cold water; drain on paper towels.
2. Heat oil in skillet over medium heat. Sauté zucchini, green pepper, and garlic until just tender. Cool.
3. Combine yogurt, mayonnaise, dill, carrot, cucumber, tuna, and zucchini–green pepper mixture in a bowl.
4. Fill each shell with 2 tablespoons of tuna mixture.
5. Arrange in a shallow dish, cover, and chill for 2 hours before serving.

Calories Per Serving: 174

Fat: 3 g

Cholesterol: 12 mg

Protein: 11 g

Carbohydrates: 17 g

Dietary Fiber: 1 g

Sodium: 175 mg

☙ *Vegetable-Tortellini Skewers* ❧

YIELD: *8 servings (2 each)* • PREPARATION TIME: *20 minutes plus 20 minutes refrigeration time* • COOKING TIME: *10 minutes*

Cut down on your kitchen time by using prepared, nonfat Italian dressing as a marinade for fresh tortellini and peppers.

32 cooked cheese-filled tortellini

1 cup prepared, nonfat or reduced-fat Italian dressing

¼ cup water

1 tablespoon light-flavored olive oil

16 1-inch squares red bell pepper

16 1-inch squares green bell pepper

16 small mushrooms

16 cherry tomatoes

1. Arrange tortellini in a shallow dish. Combine dressing and water. Pour over the tortellini and toss.
2. Heat oil in a skillet over medium heat. Sauté the peppers about 5 minutes or until they begin to soften. Cool.
3. Add peppers, mushrooms, and tomatoes to the tortellini and toss gently. Cover and refrigerate for 20 minutes.
4. Thread 2 tortellini and 1 each of the vegetables on each of 16 wooden or plastic skewers.

Calories Per Serving: 89
Fat: 3 g
Cholesterol: 4 mg
Protein: 3 g

Carbohydrates: 13 g
Dietary Fiber: 2 g
Sodium: 459 mg

❧ *Nachos and Avocados with Taco Sauce* ❧

YIELD: 24 servings (4 each) • *PREPARATION TIME: 20 minutes* •
COOKING TIME: 40 minutes

Corn tortillas are baked with taco sauce, avocado, and cheese.

SAUCE

1 tablespoon light-flavored olive or
  canola oil
1 small onion, diced
1 green bell pepper, diced
1 stalk celery, diced
2 cloves garlic, minced

2 cups low-sodium tomato juice
1 tablespoon chili powder
½ teaspoon ground cumin
⅛ teaspoon ground cayenne pepper
½ jalapeño pepper, seeded and minced

NACHOS

24 corn tortillas
1 avocado, diced

2 cups grated nonfat or reduced-fat
  cheddar cheese

1. For the sauce, heat olive oil in a skillet over medium heat. Sauté the onion, green pepper, celery, and garlic for 10 minutes.
2. Add tomato juice, chili powder, cumin, cayenne, and jalapeño. Lower heat and simmer for at least 15 minutes.

3. Preheat oven to 400 degrees. For the nachos, cut each tortilla into quarters. Arrange in shallow baking dish. Bake for 10 minutes or until crisp.
4. Spread sauce over tortillas.
5. Sprinkle avocado and cheese over sauce.
6. Broil for 5 minutes or until cheese bubbles. Serve hot with small plates and cocktail napkins.

Calories Per Serving: 105
Fat: 2 g
Cholesterol: 3 mg
Protein: 7 g

Carbohydrates: 16 g
Dietary Fiber: 1 g
Sodium: 164 mg

❧ *Nachos with Mozzarella-Tomato Sauce* ❧

YIELD: 12 servings (2 each) • *PREPARATION TIME: 15 minutes* •
COOKING TIME: 15 minutes

Corn tortillas are baked and topped with tomato sauce, jalapeños, and mozzarella cheese.

4 6-inch corn tortillas, cut in sixths
1 tablespoon light-flavored olive oil
½ cup canned, low-sodium tomato sauce
1 clove garlic, minced
½ teaspoon chili powder
¼ teaspoon cinnamon

¼ teaspoon ground cloves
2 jalapeño peppers, seeded and minced
½ cup shredded nonfat or reduced-fat mozzarella cheese
3 tablespoons grated nonfat or reduced-fat Parmesan cheese
2 tablespoons minced fresh parsley

1. Preheat oven to 400 degrees. Brush both sides of tortilla chips with oil and place on a baking sheet. Bake for 10 minutes or until crisp.
2. Combine tomato sauce, garlic, chili powder, cinnamon, and cloves in a saucepan. Cover and bring to a boil. Reduce heat and remove cover. Simmer for 5 minutes or until sauce thickens slightly.
3. Top tortilla chips with sauce and sprinkle with jalapeños, mozzarella, and Parmesan. Bake for 3 minutes, until cheese has melted. Sprinkle with parsley and serve hot with small plates and cocktail napkins.

Calories Per Serving: 53   Carbohydrates: 7 g
Fat: 1 g   Dietary Fiber: 0 g
Cholesterol: 1 mg   Sodium: 253 mg
Protein: 4 g

✎ *Southwestern Pinto Bean Chips* ✎

YIELD: 15 servings (2 each) • *PREPARATION TIME: 25 minutes* •
COOKING TIME: 5 minutes

Tortilla chips are topped with pinto beans, salsa, and cheese, then broiled.

30 triangular nonfat tortilla chips   *1 tablespoon finely chopped fresh*
  (unbroken)   *cilantro or parsley*
15 ounces canned or home-cooked   *1½ cups shredded nonfat or reduced-fat*
  pinto beans, rinsed and drained   *cheese*
¼ cup prepared salsa   *½ cup nonfat or reduced-fat sour cream*

1. Preheat broiler. Place tortilla chips in single layer on ungreased baking sheets.
2. Combine pinto beans, salsa, and cilantro or parsley.
3. Place about 2 teaspoons of bean mixture on center of each chip.
4. Sprinkle cheese over each chip.
5. Broil until cheese is melted. Top each chip with a dab of sour cream. Serve hot with small plates and cocktail napkins.

Calories Per Serving: 93   Carbohydrates: 13 g
Fat: 2 g   Dietary Fiber: 1 g
Cholesterol: 3 mg   Sodium: 379 mg
Protein: 6 g

❧ *Parmesan-Artichoke Pita Bites* ✌

YIELD: 12 servings (2 each) • *PREPARATION TIME: 20 minutes* •
COOKING TIME: 5 minutes

A mixture of artichoke hearts, Parmesan cheese, mayonnaise, jalapeño pepper, and lime juice is spread on pita halves and broiled.

*6 ounces canned, water-packed arti-
choke hearts, drained and finely
chopped*
*½ cup grated nonfat or reduced-fat
Parmesan cheese*
½ cup nonfat or reduced-fat mayonnaise

*2 tablespoons seeded and finely
chopped jalapeño peppers*
1 teaspoon lime juice
1 teaspoon grated onion
2 6-inch pita breads

1. Preheat broiler. Blend together chopped artichoke hearts, cheese, mayonnaise, jalapeño pepper, lime juice, and onion.
2. Split pita breads into 2 circles. Spread artichoke mixture on cut sides of each round.
3. Place pitas on a baking sheet. Broil until bubbly and golden. Cut each pita round into 6 wedges and serve hot.

Calories Per Serving: 53
Fat: 0 g
Cholesterol: 3 mg
Protein: 3 g

Carbohydrates: 10 g
Dietary Fiber: 1 g
Sodium: 114 mg

❧ *Petite Pizza Bites* ✌

YIELD: 16 servings (2 each) • *PREPARATION TIME: 15 minutes* •
COOKING TIME: 6 minutes

These fresh-tasting appetizers are best in summer when garden tomatoes are in season. You can also use summer-fresh herbs instead of dried.

4 English muffins, split
1 cup canned, low-sodium tomato
*   sauce*
8 slices fresh tomato

1 cup nonfat or reduced-fat mozzarella
*   cheese*
½ teaspoon dried oregano
½ teaspoon dried basil

1. Preheat broiler. Lightly toast or broil bottoms and tops of muffin halves.
2. Spread tomato sauce on muffin halves. Place a slice of tomato on top of each muffin half.
3. Sprinkle with cheese, oregano, and basil.
4. Broil until cheese is melted.
5. Cut in quarters and serve hot.

Calories Per Serving: 65
Fat: 0 g
Cholesterol: 3 mg
Protein: 6 g

Carbohydrates: 10 g
Dietary Fiber: 1 g
Sodium: 174 mg

❧ *French Bread Pizza Slices* ❧

YIELD: 20 servings (1 each) • *PREPARATION TIME: 15 minutes* •
COOKING TIME: 10 minutes

Crusty French bread slices are topped with cheese, vegetables, and tomato slices, then baked.

3 cups canned, low-sodium tomato
*   sauce*
1¼ cups coarsely chopped onions,
*   lightly steamed*
1¼ cups coarsely chopped green bell
*   peppers, lightly steamed*
1¼ cups chopped, canned, water-
*   packed artichoke hearts*

20 1-inch slices French bread
10 ounces grated nonfat or reduced-fat
*   mozzarella cheese*
¼ cup grated nonfat or reduced-fat
*   Parmesan cheese*

1. Preheat oven to 350 degrees. Combine tomato sauce with onion, green bell pepper, and artichoke hearts.
2. Spoon tomato-vegetable sauce over French bread slices.

3. Sprinkle first with mozzarella cheese, then with Parmesan.
4. Place on a baking sheet and bake for 10 minutes or until cheese melts. Serve hot.

Calories Per Serving: 116
Fat: 1 g
Cholesterol: 4 mg
Protein: 8 g

Carbohydrates: 19 g
Dietary Fiber: 1 g
Sodium: 282 mg

◊ *Boboli Bites* ◊

YIELD: 8 servings (1 each) • *PREPARATION TIME: 25 minutes* •
COOKING TIME: 10 minutes

Goat cheese, red pepper, red onion, and black olives top small Boboli, which are Italian bread shells. You can find these versatile Italian breads in your supermarket.

2 ounces goat cheese
8-ounce package small Boboli shells
  (2 shells)

½ small red bell pepper, finely chopped
¼ medium red onion, slivered
6 pitted black olives, slivered

1. Preheat oven to 450 degrees. Crumble cheese; sprinkle the cheese over the Boboli shells.
2. Top with red pepper, onion, and olives.
3. Bake in oven for 10 minutes, until cheese is slightly melted. Cut each Boboli into 4 wedges and serve hot.

Calories Per Serving: 104
Fat: 3 g
Cholesterol: 9 mg
Protein: 5 g

Carbohydrates: 18 g
Dietary Fiber: 0 g
Sodium: 202 mg

POULTRY
APPETIZERS

NUGGETS, BITES, AND MEATBALLS

Cumin-Chili Chicken Nuggets ▪ Sweet-and-Sour Chicken Cubes ▪ Chicken Dijon Bites ▪ Cayenne Chicken Cubes ▪ Turkey Tidbits ▪ Rice Balls ▪ Mediterranean Turkey Meatballs ▪ Tangy Turkey Meatballs ▪ Spiced Meatballs ▪ Turkey Meatballs in Sweet-Sour Sauce ▪ Broiled Spiced Meatballs ▪ Sherried Meatballs ▪ Dijon-Honey Turkey Bites ▪ Meatballs Italia ▪ Gingered Turkey Meatballs ▪ Greek Meatballs

BAKED OR BROILED

Skewered Lemon-Chicken Bites ▪ Broiled Chicken Chunks with Apricot Dip ▪ Dijon Chicken in Marmalade Sauce ▪ Parmesan Chicken Nuggets ▪ Chicken Savories ▪ Chicken-Turkey-Cheese Slices ▪ Lemon-Yogurt Drumsticks ▪ Turkey Morsels

KABOBS

Chicken-Fruit Kabobs • Bell Pepper–Sesame Chicken Kabobs •
Gingered-Chicken Kabobs • Chicken-Mushroom Skewers •
Mini–Chicken Kabobs • Skewered Turkey with Plum Sauce •
Ground Turkey Sticks with Herb Dip

ROLL-UPS

Turkey–Potato Salad Bundles • Smoked Turkey–Fruit Wraparounds
• Honey-Roasted Turkey Roll-ups • Chicken-Prune Roll-ups •
Chicken Whirls

WINGS

Mexican Chicken Wings • Ginger-Garlic Teriyaki Wings • Sweet-
and-Sour Roast Chicken Wings • Chinese Simmered Wings •
Broiled Wings with Buttermilk Sauce • Orange Wings

• NUGGETS, BITES, AND MEATBALLS •

❧ *Cumin-Chili Chicken Nuggets* ❧

YIELD: 12 servings (2 each)   •   PREPARATION TIME: 30 minutes   •   COOKING TIME: 10 minutes

These spicy chicken nuggets are served with a mustard-accented sauce.

*½ pound chicken cutlets, cut into
   1-inch cubes
½ teaspoon chili powder
¼ teaspoon ground cumin
¼ teaspoon hot pepper sauce
3 cloves garlic, minced
1 tablespoon minced scallion*

*1½ teaspoons red wine vinegar
¼ cup nonfat or reduced-fat, low-
   sodium chicken broth
½ cup nonfat or reduced-fat plain
   yogurt
½ teaspoon Dijon mustard*

1. Place chicken in a blender or food processor with the chili powder, cumin, hot pepper sauce, garlic, scallion, and vinegar. Process until finely chopped.
2. Wet palms and shape the mixture into 24 nuggets.
3. Heat chicken broth in a skillet over medium heat. Add the chicken nuggets and cook until lightly browned and cooked through, about 5 minutes on each side.
4. In a small bowl, combine the yogurt and mustard. Serve as a dip with the warm nuggets and provide wooden or plastic party picks.

Calories Per Serving: 25
Fat: 1 g
Cholesterol: 12 mg
Protein: 5 g

Carbohydrates: 1 g
Dietary Fiber: 0 g
Sodium: 28 mg

❧ *Sweet-and-Sour Chicken Cubes* ❧

YIELD: 16 servings (2 each)   •   PREPARATION TIME: 15 minutes   •   COOKING TIME: 15 minutes

Dijon mustard, plum jam, and horseradish flavor these tasty chicken appetizers.

2 tablespoons light-flavored olive oil
2 boneless, skinless chicken breast
   halves, cut into 32 1-inch pieces
⅛ teaspoon black pepper

½ cup all-fruit plum or apricot jam
2 teaspoons Dijon mustard
2 teaspoons prepared horseradish
1 teaspoon lemon juice

1. Heat oil in a skillet over medium heat. Add chicken and sauté 5 minutes or until done.
2. Combine pepper, plum jam, mustard, horseradish, and lemon juice in a pan. Heat and stir until well blended.
3. Add cooked chicken; heat and stir until coated with sauce. Transfer to a serving platter with a slotted spoon. Serve warm with wooden or plastic party picks.

Calories Per Serving: 44
Fat: 2 g
Cholesterol: 7 mg
Protein: 2 g

Carbohydrates: 5 g
Dietary Fiber: 0 g
Sodium: 27 mg

≫ *Chicken Dijon Bites* ≪

Yield: 16 servings (2 each)   •   *Preparation Time: 15 minutes*   •
Cooking Time: 10 minutes

Chicken cubes are sautéed in olive oil, and combined with Dijon mustard, garlic, parsley, lemon juice, and sprinkled with Parmesan cheese.

2 tablespoons light-flavored olive oil
1 tablespoon Dijon mustard
1 clove garlic, minced
1 tablespoon minced fresh parsley
1 teaspoon lemon juice

2 boneless, skinless chicken breast
   halves, cut into 32 1-inch pieces
¼ cup grated nonfat or reduced-fat
   Parmesan cheese

1. Heat olive oil in a medium skillet over medium heat. Stir in mustard, garlic, parsley, and lemon juice.
2. Add chicken and sauté, turning until chicken is well coated, lightly browned on all sides, and no longer pink.
3. Transfer to a serving platter and sprinkle with Parmesan cheese. Serve with wooden or plastic party picks.

Calories Per Serving: 26
Fat: 2 g
Cholesterol: 7 mg
Protein: 2 g

Carbohydrates: 0 g
Dietary Fiber: 0 g
Sodium: 28 mg

❧ *Cayenne Chicken Cubes* ❧

YIELD: 25 servings (2 each) • *PREPARATION TIME: 15 minutes* •
COOKING TIME: 20 minutes

Chicken breast cubes are sautéed in olive oil and spices.

3 tablespoons light-flavored olive oil
1 teaspoon ground cayenne pepper
½ cup Dijon mustard
⅓ cup white wine vinegar
*2 tablespoons brown sugar, firmly
    packed*

3 tablespoons honey
1 tablespoon light soy sauce
*2 pounds chicken cutlets, cut into 50
    1-inch cubes*

1. Heat olive oil in a skillet over medium heat. Add cayenne pepper, Dijon
   mustard, vinegar, brown sugar, honey, and soy sauce. Simmer for 5 minutes.
2. Add chicken and sauté for 15 minutes or until chicken is lightly browned.
   Transfer chicken to a serving platter with a slotted spoon and serve warm
   with wooden or plastic party picks.

Calories Per Serving: 66
Fat: 2 g
Cholesterol: 23 mg
Protein: 8 g

Carbohydrates: 3 g
Dietary Fiber: 0 g
Sodium: 160 mg

❧ *Turkey Tidbits* ❧

YIELD: 16 servings (2 each) • *PREPARATION TIME: 10 minutes* •
COOKING TIME: 5 minutes

Chunks of turkey cutlet are sautéed in olive oil and simmered in a honey-
mustard sauce.

2 tablespoons light-flavored olive or
  canola oil
1 pound turkey cutlets, cut into 32
  1-inch chunks
2 tablespoons honey

2 tablespoons Dijon mustard
1 teaspoon lemon juice
1 teaspoon curry powder
1 clove garlic, minced
½ cup chopped scallions

1. Heat olive oil in a skillet over medium heat. Sauté turkey chunks for 2 or
   3 minutes until turkey is opaque.
2. Combine honey, mustard, lemon juice, curry powder, and garlic. Add to
   skillet.
3. Cook and stir for 2 minutes.
4. Transfer to a serving platter and sprinkle with scallions.
5. Serve hot with wooden or plastic party picks.

Calories Per Serving: 51
Fat: 2 g
Cholesterol: 21 mg
Protein: 8 g

Carbohydrates: 2 g
Dietary Fiber: 0 g
Sodium: 54 mg

＊ Rice Balls ＊

YIELD: 12 servings (2 each) • PREPARATION TIME: 30 minutes plus 30 minutes rice-
soaking time • COOKING TIME: 25 minutes

These Thai-inspired meatballs, made with ground turkey, green bell pepper,
scallions, and fresh gingerroot, are rolled in rice and cooked.

MEATBALLS

6 ounces uncooked long-grain white rice
14 ounces low-fat ground turkey breast
1 cup chopped scallions
½ cup diced green bell pepper

2 egg whites
1 tablespoon light soy sauce
¾ teaspoon chopped fresh gingerroot
⅛ teaspoon black pepper

DIPPING SAUCE

¼ cup light soy sauce
1 tablespoon rice vinegar

2 cloves garlic, minced

1. For the meatballs, place rice in a small bowl. Cover with hot water. Soak
   for 30 minutes. Drain and spread on a baking sheet.

2. Combine turkey, scallions, green bell pepper, egg whites, soy sauce, gingerroot, and pepper.
3. Shape mixture into 24 equal balls. Roll balls one at a time in rice, until evenly coated and all rice is used.
4. Bring enough water to cover bottom of a large skillet to a boil. Reduce heat to low and add rice balls.
5. Simmer, covered, until rice is tender (about 20 to 25 minutes).
6. For the sauce, combine soy sauce, vinegar, and garlic. Serve in a small bowl as a dipping sauce with the rice balls arranged around it. Serve with wooden or plastic party picks.

Calories Per Serving: 92
Fat: 1 g
Cholesterol: 17 mg
Protein: 10 g

Carbohydrates: 13 g
Dietary Fiber: 0 g
Sodium: 285 mg

✎ *Mediterranean Turkey Meatballs* ✎

YIELD: 15 servings (2 each) ▪ *PREPARATION TIME: 25 minutes* ▪
COOKING TIME: 55 minutes

Ground turkey is combined with bulgur, onion, egg whites, and oregano, then simmered in tomato juice. Bulgur, a nutritious staple in the Middle East, consists of wheat kernels that have been steamed, dried, and crushed. It has a tender, chewy texture and makes these meatballs very light.

¾ pound low-fat ground turkey breast
½ cup uncooked bulgur
2 tablespoons minced onion
2 egg whites, beaten

½ teaspoon dried oregano
¼ teaspoon black pepper
2 tablespoons light-flavored olive oil
1 cup low-sodium tomato juice

1. Combine ground turkey, bulgur, onion, egg whites, oregano, and black pepper.
2. Shape the mixture into 30 small meatballs.
3. Heat the oil in a skillet over medium heat. Add meatballs. After they have browned on all sides, add tomato juice and cover pan. Simmer for 45 minutes. Add more juice or water if needed.
4. Transfer to a serving platter with a slotted spoon. Serve warm with wooden or plastic party picks.

Calories Per Serving: 61
Fat: 2 g
Cholesterol: 17 mg
Protein: 7 g

Carbohydrates: 4 g
Dietary Fiber: 1 g
Sodium: 16 mg

✎ *Tangy Turkey Meatballs* ✎

YIELD: 24 servings (2 each) • *PREPARATION TIME: 25 minutes* •
COOKING TIME: 20 minutes

Ground turkey, onion, garlic, and Worcestershire sauce are combined to create tiny meatballs that are served in a sweet-and-tangy tomato sauce.

MEATBALLS

2 pounds low-fat ground turkey breast
1½ cups bread crumbs
1 onion, minced
2 teaspoons Worcestershire sauce

1 clove garlic, minced
¼ teaspoon black pepper
2 tablespoons light-flavored olive oil

SAUCE

1 cup low-sodium tomato sauce
1 cup all-fruit grape jelly

1. For the meatballs, combine turkey, bread crumbs, onion, Worcestershire sauce, garlic, and pepper. Shape into 48 tiny meatballs.
2. Heat olive oil in a skillet over medium heat. Sauté meatballs until browned on all sides. Drain.
3. Combine tomato sauce and jelly in a saucepan. Heat through.
4. Serve meatballs in sauce with plates and cocktail forks.

Calories Per Serving: 105
Fat: 2 g
Cholesterol: 29 mg
Protein: 11 g

Carbohydrates: 12 g
Dietary Fiber: 0 g
Sodium: 75 mg

❧ *Spiced Meatballs* ❧

YIELD: *15 (2 each)* • PREPARATION TIME: *20 minutes* •
COOKING TIME: *25 minutes*

These meatballs are made with garam masala, a blend of spices that can be found on many supermarket spice racks, and in Indian markets and gourmet shops.

MEATBALLS

1 tablespoon ground coriander
2 teaspoons ground cumin
2 teaspoons paprika
5 teaspoons garam masala
1 teaspoon sugar

1 tablespoon minced fresh gingerroot
1 pound low-fat ground turkey breast
2 tablespoons light-flavored olive oil
½ cup nonfat or reduced-fat, low-sodium chicken broth

SAUCE

2 cups nonfat or reduced-fat plain yogurt

1 teaspoon ground cumin

1. For the meatballs, combine coriander, cumin, paprika, garam masala, sugar, gingerroot, and turkey. Wet palms and form mixture into 30 1-inch balls.
2. Place oil in skillet over medium heat. Lightly brown meatballs. Add broth and simmer for 15 minutes or until meatballs are done. Drain meatballs on paper towels.
3. For the sauce, combine yogurt and cumin in a saucepan. Heat through, being careful not to bring to a boil.
4. Pour sauce over meatballs and serve hot with plates and cocktail forks.

Calories Per Serving: 69
Fat: 2 g
Cholesterol: 24 mg
Protein: 11 g

Carbohydrates: 3 g
Dietary Fiber: 0 g
Sodium: 43 mg

Turkey Meatballs
❧ in Sweet-Sour Sauce ❧

YIELD: 12 servings (2 each) • *PREPARATION TIME: 20 minutes* •
COOKING TIME: 20 minutes

Sage-accented turkey meatballs are served in a pineapple-pepper sauce.

2 egg whites
⅓ cup skim or 1% milk
½ cup soft bread crumbs
⅛ teaspoon black pepper
¼ teaspoon dried sage
¼ cup minced onion
1 pound low-fat ground turkey breast
8 ounces canned, juice-packed pineapple chunks, juice reserved

2 tablespoons cornstarch
2 tablespoons light soy sauce
1 cup nonfat or reduced-fat, low-sodium chicken broth
¼ cup rice vinegar
¼ cup honey
1 green bell pepper, cut into 1-inch squares

1. Preheat oven to 350 degrees. Whisk together egg whites, milk, bread crumbs, black pepper, sage, onion, and ground turkey. Shape into 24 1-inch balls.
2. Bake for 20 minutes or until lightly browned.
3. While meatballs are cooking, heat reserved pineapple juice. Stir cornstarch into juice until dissolved.
4. Add soy sauce, broth, vinegar, and honey. Cook and stir over low heat until sauce thickens. Stir in pineapple chunks and green pepper squares. Cook for 2 minutes more.
5. Drain meatballs. Add to sauce and serve hot with plates and cocktail forks.

Calories Per Serving: 85
Fat: 1 g
Cholesterol: 29 mg
Protein: 12 g

Carbohydrates: 11 g
Dietary Fiber: 0 g
Sodium: 144 mg

❦ *Broiled Spiced Meatballs* ❦

YIELD: *8 servings (2 each)* • PREPARATION TIME: *25 minutes* •
COOKING TIME: *10 minutes*

These broiled turkey meatballs are spiced with Middle Eastern–style flavors.

2 pounds low-fat ground turkey breast
¼ teaspoon ground cloves
¼ teaspoon ground cardamom
¼ teaspoon black pepper
¼ teaspoon ground cumin

¼ teaspoon ground ginger
¼ teaspoon ground cayenne pepper
1 tablespoon nonfat or reduced-fat
   plain yogurt
1 onion, minced

1. Preheat broiler. Mix turkey, cloves, cardamom, pepper, cumin, ginger, cayenne, yogurt, and onion.
2. Form mixture into 16 small balls.
3. Arrange on a baking sheet and broil approximately 3 inches from heat for 5 minutes on each side. Serve hot with wooden or plastic party picks.

Calories Per Serving: 120
Fat: 1 g
Cholesterol: 86 mg
Protein: 31 g

Carbohydrates: 2 g
Dietary Fiber: 0 g
Sodium: 31 mg

❦ *Sherried Meatballs* ❦

YIELD: *20 servings (2 each)* • PREPARATION TIME: *25 minutes* •
COOKING TIME: *20 minutes*

Sherry, ginger, soy sauce, and garlic are mixed with ground turkey to create these out-of-the-ordinary meatballs.

1½ pounds low-fat ground turkey
   breast
2 tablespoons light soy sauce
2 tablespoons dry sherry

1 tablespoon minced fresh gingerroot
5 cloves garlic, minced
2 tablespoons sugar

1. Preheat oven to 350 degrees. Combine ground turkey, soy sauce, sherry, gingerroot, garlic, and sugar.
2. Shape mixture into 40 small balls.
3. Place on baking sheet and bake for 20 minutes. Serve hot with wooden or plastic party picks.

Calories Per Serving: 47	Carbohydrates: 2 g
Fat: 1 g	Dietary Fiber: 0 g
Cholesterol: 25 mg	Sodium: 9 mg
Protein: 9 g	

❧ *Dijon-Honey Turkey Bites* ❧

Yield: 18 servings (2 each) • *Preparation Time: 30 minutes plus
1 hour refrigeration time* • *Cooking Time: 20 minutes*

Turkey is combined with zucchini, onion, and green pepper in these baked meatballs, which are served in a hot honey-mustard sauce.

Sauce

¼ cup honey	*1 tablespoon Dijon mustard*
2 tablespoons light soy sauce	*1 tablespoon lemon juice*

Meatballs

2 teaspoons light-flavored olive or canola oil	*½ cup fine bread crumbs*
	½ cup coarsely shredded zucchini
1 cup minced onion	*¼ teaspoon black pepper*
1 cup finely chopped green bell pepper	*2 teaspoons Dijon mustard*
2 cloves garlic, minced	*2 teaspoons lemon juice*
1½ pounds low-fat ground turkey breast	*1 teaspoon light soy sauce*

1. For the sauce, combine honey, soy sauce, mustard, and lemon juice.
2. For the meatballs, heat oil in a skillet over medium heat. Add onion, bell pepper, and garlic, and sauté for 5 minutes.
3. Combine sautéed vegetables, turkey, bread crumbs, zucchini, pepper, mustard, lemon juice, and soy sauce. Chill for 1 hour.

4. Preheat oven to 400 degrees. With wet hands, form chilled mixture into 36 1-inch balls.
5. Arrange meatballs, not touching one another, on a rack on a baking sheet. Bake for 15 to 20 minutes, turning every 5 minutes.
6. Place baked meatballs in skillet and pour sauce over meatballs. Cook over medium heat for 3 minutes or until sauce has thickened.
7. Serve hot with small plates and party picks.

Calories Per Serving: 73
Fat: 1 g
Cholesterol: 28 mg
Protein: 11 g

Carbohydrates: 8 g
Dietary Fiber: 0 g
Sodium: 147 mg

⚘ *Meatballs Italia* ⚘

YIELD: 12 servings (2 each) • *PREPARATION TIME: 20 minutes plus 1 hour refrigeration time* • *COOKING TIME: 20 minutes*

These tiny meatballs are flavored with garlic, basil, oregano, parsley, nutmeg, and Parmesan cheese.

1 pound low-fat ground turkey breast
2 cloves garlic, finely minced
¼ teaspoon black pepper
½ teaspoon dried basil
½ teaspoon dried oregano

1 tablespoon minced fresh parsley
¼ teaspoon ground nutmeg
2 tablespoons grated nonfat or reduced-fat Parmesan cheese
2 egg whites, beaten
2 tablespoons fine bread crumbs

1. Combine turkey, garlic, pepper, basil, oregano, parsley, nutmeg, Parmesan cheese, egg whites, and bread crumbs. Chill mixture for 1 hour.
2. Preheat oven to 350 degrees. With wet hands, form mixture into 24 1-inch balls.
3. Arrange meatballs, not touching, on a rack in a shallow baking pan.
4. Bake for 20 minutes, turning every 5 minutes.
5. Serve hot with wooden or plastic party picks.

Calories Per Serving: 115

Fat: 1 g

Cholesterol: 29 mg

Protein: 13 g

Carbohydrates: 14 g

Dietary Fiber: 0 g

Sodium: 180 mg

☙ *Gingered Turkey Meatballs* ☙

YIELD: 12 servings (2 each) • *PREPARATION TIME: 30 minutes plus
2 hours refrigeration time* • *COOKING TIME: 15 minutes*

These meatballs are made from lean ground turkey and are accented with ginger, garlic, scallions, water chestnuts, and tofu.

1 pound low-fat ground turkey breast
½ cup minced water chestnuts
½ cup minced scallions
2 garlic cloves, minced

½ teaspoon ground ginger
¼ teaspoon white pepper
3 tablespoons fine bread crumbs
¼ cup mashed soft tofu

1. Combine turkey, water chestnuts, scallions, garlic, ginger, pepper, bread crumbs, and tofu. Chill mixture for 2 hours.
2. Preheat oven to 400 degrees. With wet hands, form mixture into 24 1-inch balls.
3. Arrange meatballs, not touching, on a rack in a shallow baking pan.
4. Bake for 15 to 20 minutes, turning every 5 minutes.

Variation: For softer, moister meatballs, place meatballs on a large shallow dish and steam in a large steamer for 10 minutes or until meatballs are done.

Calories Per Serving: 57

Fat: 1 g

Cholesterol: 29 mg

Protein: 11 g

Carbohydrates: 3 g

Dietary Fiber: 0 g

Sodium: 25 mg

✎ *Greek Meatballs* ✎

YIELD: *16 servings (2 each)*   ▪   PREPARATION TIME: *20 minutes plus*
1 hour refrigeration time   ▪   COOKING TIME: *20 minutes*

Red wine, oregano, mint, and lemon give a Greek accent to these turkey meatballs.

2 slices firm bread, crusts removed
½ cup red wine
1 pound low-fat ground turkey breast
½ cup minced onion
2 cloves garlic, minced
2 tablespoons chopped fresh parsley

1 teaspoon dried oregano
2 teaspoons dried mint
¼ teaspoon black pepper
1 teaspoon grated lemon peel
2 egg whites, beaten

1. Crumble the bread and soak in the wine for 10 minutes.
2. Combine the soaked bread and wine with the turkey, onion, garlic, parsley, oregano, mint, black pepper, lemon peel, and egg whites in a large bowl.
3. Cover the bowl with plastic wrap and chill for 1 hour.
4. Preheat oven to 350 degrees. With wet hands, form mixture into 32 1-inch balls.
5. Arrange meatballs, not touching, on a rack in a shallow baking pan.
6. Bake for 20 minutes, turning every 5 minutes.
7. Serve hot with wooden or plastic party picks.

Calories Per Serving: 46
Fat: 1 g
Cholesterol: 21 mg
Protein: 9 g

Carbohydrates: 3 g
Dietary Fiber: 0 g
Sodium: 36 mg

• BAKED OR BROILED •

Skewered Lemon-Chicken Bites

YIELD: 12 servings (2 each) • PREPARATION TIME: 15 minutes plus
1 hour refrigeration time • COOKING TIME: 14 minutes

This appetizer has the flavor of Chinese lemon chicken without the added calories.

⅓ cup lemon juice
2 tablespoons light soy sauce plus more
* for basting*
2 tablespoons Dijon mustard

1 teaspoon light-flavored olive oil
⅛ teaspoon ground cayenne
2 boneless, skinless chicken breasts, cut
* into 24 ¾-inch cubes*

1. Combine the lemon juice, soy sauce, mustard, oil, and cayenne pepper. Add the chicken and toss well to coat. Cover and refrigerate, tossing occasionally, at least 1 hour. Meanwhile, soak 12 wooden party picks in water for 30 minutes.
2. Preheat broiler and lightly oil a broiler pan. Place 2 cubes of chicken on each wooden pick. Arrange the skewered chicken, not touching, on broiler pan and broil 4 inches from heat for 3 minutes.
3. Baste with soy sauce. Broil for 4 more minutes.
4. Turn, and broil another 3 minutes.
5. Baste with soy sauce. Broil for 4 more minutes. Serve hot.

Calories Per Serving: 21
Fat: 1 g
Cholesterol: 9 mg
Protein: 3 g

Carbohydrates: 1 g
Dietary Fiber: 0 g
Sodium: 172 mg

Broiled Chicken Chunks with Apricot Dip

YIELD: 30 servings (2 each) • PREPARATION TIME: 25 minutes •
COOKING TIME: 7 minutes

Chicken breasts are cut into chunks, broiled, and served with a tangy apricot dip.

4 boneless, skinless chicken breast halves, cut into 60 1-inch chunks
6 tablespoons all-fruit apricot preserves
¾ cup nonfat or reduced-fat mayonnaise

2 teaspoons rice vinegar
⅓ cup chopped celery
¼ cup walnuts

1. Preheat broiler. Combine chicken chunks and 4 tablespoons of the apricot preserves in a bowl. Toss well to coat chicken.
2. Place chicken on broiler pan and broil 4 to 6 inches from the heat for 7 minutes.
3. While chicken is cooking, place the remaining 2 tablespoons apricot preserves, mayonnaise, rice vinegar, celery, and walnuts in a blender or food processor and process until smooth.
4. Place the apricot-walnut dip in a bowl in the middle of a platter. Skewer a chicken chunk on each of 60 wooden or plastic party picks and arrange around the dip.

Calories Per Serving: 28
Fat: 1 g
Cholesterol: 7 mg
Protein: 3 g

Carbohydrates: 3 g
Dietary Fiber: 0 g
Sodium: 49 mg

Dijon Chicken in Marmalade Sauce

YIELD: 24 servings (2 each) • *PREPARATION TIME: 20 minutes plus 1 hour refrigeration time* • *COOKING TIME: 12 minutes*

Chicken chunks are marinated in a mustard-marmalade sauce and then baked.

1 cup Dijon mustard
¼ cup all-fruit orange marmalade
1 teaspoon dried basil

1½ tablespoons light-flavored olive oil
4 skinless, boneless chicken breast halves, cut into 12 pieces each

1. Combine mustard, marmalade, and basil in a bowl. Reserve ¼ cup.
2. Add oil to mustard-marmalade mixture in bowl.
3. Add chicken to bowl and toss well to coat. Refrigerate for 1 hour.
4. Preheat oven to 350 degrees. Place chicken in baking dish and bake for 10 minutes.
5. Place baking dish under broiler just long enough to brown top of the chicken.

6. Serve with reserved mustard-marmalade mixture from step 1. Provide wooden or plastic party picks.

Calories Per Serving: 28
Fat: 1 g
Cholesterol: 2 mg
Protein: 1 g

Carbohydrates: 2 g
Dietary Fiber: 0 g
Sodium: 239 mg

✺ *Parmesan Chicken Nuggets* ✺

YIELD: 24 servings (2 each) • *PREPARATION TIME: 25 minutes* •
COOKING TIME: 15 minutes

Chicken chunks are dipped in a Parmesan coating and baked.

2 cups bread crumbs
¼ cup grated nonfat or reduced-fat
Parmesan cheese
¼ cup chopped fresh parsley
½ teaspoon dried oregano

½ teaspoon dried basil
⅛ teaspoon black pepper
2 boneless, skinless chicken breasts, cut
into 48 bite-size pieces
2 egg whites, lightly beaten

1. Preheat oven to 400 degrees. Combine bread crumbs, Parmesan cheese, parsley, oregano, basil, and pepper.
2. Dip chicken first into egg white, then into bread-crumb mixture.
3. Place nuggets on shallow baking pans and bake for 15 minutes. Serve with wooden or plastic party picks.

Calories Per Serving: 45
Fat: 1 g
Cholesterol: 5 mg
Protein: 3 g

Carbohydrates: 7 g
Dietary Fiber: 0 g
Sodium: 90 mg

🌿 Chicken Savories 🍴

YIELD: 8 servings (2 each) • PREPARATION TIME: 30 minutes plus
5 minutes chilling time • COOKING TIME: 8 minutes

These hot little morsels are laced with cheese and dill.

1 cup finely chopped cooked chicken
breast
⅓ cup shredded nonfat or reduced-fat
cheese
¼ cup finely chopped celery
3 tablespoons nonfat or reduced-fat
mayonnaise

1 tablespoon chopped fresh parsley
⅛ teaspoon hot pepper sauce
¼ teaspoon dried dill
¼ teaspoon black pepper

1. Preheat oven to 350 degrees. Combine chicken, cheese, celery, mayonnaise, parsley, hot pepper sauce, dill, and pepper in a small bowl.
2. Chill mixture for 5 minutes in the freezer.
3. Roll mixture into 16 1-inch balls and place them on a lightly oiled baking sheet. Bake for 8 to 10 minutes or until lightly browned. Serve with wooden or plastic party picks.

Calories Per Serving: 25
Fat: 1 g
Cholesterol: 7 mg
Protein: 4 g

Carbohydrates: 2 g
Dietary Fiber: 0 g
Sodium: 128 mg

🌿 Chicken-Turkey-Cheese Slices 🍴

YIELD: 24 servings (1 each) • PREPARATION TIME: 20 minutes plus
1 hour refrigeration time • COOKING TIME: 40 minutes

Pounded chicken breasts are topped with smoked turkey and cheese, then rolled, baked, and sliced.

2 boneless, skinless chicken breasts,
  split
4 slices smoked turkey
4 thin slices nonfat or reduced-fat cheese
¼ teaspoon white pepper

¼ teaspoon dried sage
1 clove garlic, minced
¼ cup dry white wine
¼ cup nonfat or reduced-fat, low-
  sodium chicken broth

1. Preheat oven to 350 degrees. Place the chicken breasts between wax paper and pound to about ¼ inch thick.
2. Place 2 slices of smoked turkey and 2 slices of cheese on each piece of chicken. Sprinkle with pepper, sage, and garlic.
3. Roll up and fasten with toothpicks. Place in a baking dish and pour the wine and broth over the rolls.
4. Cover with foil. Bake for 40 minutes.
5. Chill for 1 hour. Cut each roll into 12 slices.

Calories Per Serving: 17
Fat: 1 g
Cholesterol: 6 mg
Protein: 3 g

Carbohydrates: 1 g
Dietary Fiber: 0 g
Sodium: 85 mg

❧ Lemon-Yogurt Drumsticks ❧

YIELD: 8 servings (1 each) • PREPARATION TIME: 15 minutes •
COOKING TIME: 50 minutes

Chicken drumsticks are dipped in a spiced lemon-yogurt mixture, rolled in bread crumbs, and then baked.

1 cup nonfat or reduced-fat plain
  yogurt
1 teaspoon curry powder
½ teaspoon ground cumin
2 cloves garlic, minced

2 tablespoons lemon juice
¼ teaspoon ground cayenne pepper
1¼ cups fine bread crumbs
8 chicken drumsticks, skinned

1. Preheat oven to 375 degrees. Combine yogurt, curry powder, cumin, garlic, lemon juice, and cayenne pepper.
2. Place bread crumbs in a small bowl.

3. Dip drumsticks into yogurt mixture, then into bread crumbs.
4. Place coated chicken in a lightly oiled baking pan, bake for 30 minutes, and turn drumsticks over. Continue baking 20 minutes or until golden brown.

Calories Per Serving: 119
Fat: 3 g
Cholesterol: 41 mg
Protein: 14 g

Carbohydrates: 8 g
Dietary Fiber: 0 g
Sodium: 126 mg

Turkey Morsels

YIELD: 24 servings (2 each) • *PREPARATION TIME: 25 minutes plus 1 hour refrigeration time* • *COOKING TIME: 30 minutes*

Serve these flavorful turkey bites warm or cold.

1½ cups minced onion
½ cup water
1 pound ground low-fat turkey breast
1 large potato, peeled and grated
½ cup bread crumbs
3 egg whites, lightly beaten

1 tablespoon red wine vinegar
¼ cup finely chopped fresh parsley
¼ teaspoon black pepper
1 tablespoon ground cumin
Flour for dredging
Olive oil for brushing

1. Place the onion and ½ cup of water in a small saucepan, bring to a boil, and simmer for 5 minutes or until liquid has evaporated.
2. Combine the onion, turkey, potato, bread crumbs, egg whites, vinegar, parsley, pepper, and cumin in a large bowl and mix until well blended.
3. Preheat oven to 325 degrees. Form the turkey mixture into 48 ¾-inch balls, flatten slightly, and dredge with flour.
4. Lightly oil 2 baking sheets and arrange the patties an inch apart on the sheets. Brush the turkey bites lightly with olive oil and bake for 25 minutes, turning once. Drain.
5. Serve with wooden or plastic party picks.

Calories Per Serving: 51
Fat: 1 g
Cholesterol: 14 mg
Protein: 6 g

Carbohydrates: 6 g
Dietary Fiber: 0 g
Sodium: 80 mg

• KABOBS •

Chicken-Fruit Kabobs

YIELD: 10 servings (2 each) • *PREPARATION TIME: 25 minutes plus 2 hours refrigeration time* • *COOKING TIME: 15 minutes*

Marinated chicken chunks are skewered with fruit chunks and then broiled.

⅔ cup red wine vinegar
2 tablespoons light-flavored olive oil
¼ teaspoon black pepper
2 teaspoons curry powder
2 boneless, skinless chicken breast
    halves, cut into 10 pieces each

2 bananas
1 medium papaya, peeled, halved,
    seeded, and cut into 1-inch cubes
2 cups canned, juice-packed pineapple
    chunks
⅓ cup honey

1. Combine vinegar, olive oil, black pepper, and curry powder.
2. Place chicken in a bowl and cover with ⅓ cup of the marinade mixture from step 1. Cover bowl and marinate in refrigerator for 2 hours. While chicken is marinating, soak 20 wooden skewers in water for 30 minutes.
3. Peel bananas and cut into 1-inch chunks. Coat with marinade.
4. Thread each skewer, alternating chicken chunks, banana chunks, papaya chunks, and pineapple chunks.
5. Preheat broiler. Stir honey into reserved dressing and brush over kabobs.
6. Broil kabobs 3 to 4 inches from heat for 8 minutes, basting with honey-dressing mixture. Turn and continue broiling, basting several times, for 7 additional minutes.

Calories Per Serving: 122
Fat: 3 g
Cholesterol: 11 mg
Protein: 4 g

Carbohydrates: 22 g
Dietary Fiber: 1 g
Sodium: 9 mg

❦ *Bell Pepper–Sesame Chicken Kabobs* ❦

YIELD: 12 servings (2 each) • *PREPARATION TIME: 25 minutes plus 3 hours refrigeration time* • *COOKING TIME: 5 minutes*

Chicken breasts are pounded thin, marinated in a sherry-flavored marinade, and broiled with red peppers.

Olive oil cooking spray
¼ cup minced onion
½ teaspoon ground cayenne pepper
2 tablespoons brown sugar, firmly packed
½ teaspoon black pepper
3 tablespoons white wine vinegar
3 tablespoons light soy sauce

3 tablespoons dry sherry
3 boneless, skinless chicken breast halves, flattened to ¼-inch thickness by pounding between layers of wax paper, and cut into 16 pieces each
3 red bell peppers, each cut into 16 pieces
2 teaspoons sesame seeds

1. Coat a skillet with cooking spray. Place over medium heat until hot. Add onion and cayenne pepper and sauté until onion is tender. Remove from heat.
2. Stir in brown sugar, black pepper, white wine vinegar, soy sauce, and sherry.
3. Place chicken in a bowl and cover with onion mixture. Cover and marinate in refrigerator for 3 hours. While chicken is marinating, soak 24 wooden skewers in water for 30 minutes.
4. Drain chicken, reserving marinade. Thread each skewer, alternating with 2 chicken pieces and 2 bell pepper pieces.
5. Place skewers on a rack over a broiler pan. Brush with reserved marinade, and sprinkle with 1 teaspoon sesame seeds. Broil for 2 minutes.
6. Turn skewers, brush with marinade, and sprinkle evenly with the remaining 1 teaspoon sesame seeds. Broil an additional 3 minutes or until chicken is done. Serve hot.

Calories Per Serving: 44
Fat: 1 g
Cholesterol: 14 mg
Protein: 5 g

Carbohydrates: 5 g
Dietary Fiber: 1 g
Sodium: 176 mg

❧ *Gingered-Chicken Kabobs* ❧

YIELD: 16 servings (1 each) • *PREPARATION TIME: 30 minutes plus 4½ hours refrigeration time* • *COOKING TIME: 10 minutes*

Chicken is marinated in ginger, lemon juice, garlic, cumin, cardamom, cloves, cayenne pepper, paprika, and yogurt.

4 skinless, boneless chicken breast halves, each cut into 8 1-inch squares
3 tablespoons lemon juice
3 large cloves garlic, finely chopped
1 tablespoon minced fresh gingerroot
1 teaspoon ground cumin
¼ teaspoon ground cardamom
¼ teaspoon ground cloves
¼ teaspoon ground cayenne
1 teaspoon ground paprika
½ cup nonfat or reduced-fat plain yogurt

1. Toss chicken squares with lemon juice in a glass bowl. Marinate for 30 minutes.
2. Combine garlic, gingerroot, cumin, cardamom, cloves, cayenne, paprika, and yogurt. Stir into chicken. Marinate in refrigerator for 4 hours. Meanwhile, soak 16 wooden skewers in water for at least 30 minutes.
3. Preheat oven to 500 degrees. Place 2 chicken cubes on each skewer. Place skewers on rack in a shallow baking pan. Roast for 10 minutes or until chicken is done. Serve hot.

Calories Per Serving: 26
Fat: 1 g
Cholesterol: 14 mg
Protein: 5 g

Carbohydrates: 1 g
Dietary Fiber: 0 g
Sodium: 15 mg

❧ *Chicken-Mushroom Skewers* ❧

YIELD: 20 servings (1 each) • *PREPARATION TIME: 20 minutes plus 30 minutes refrigeration time* • *COOKING TIME: 12 minutes*

Chunks of chicken breast, green pepper, and mushrooms are marinated and then broiled.

20 mushrooms

5 boneless, skinless chicken breast
  halves, each cut into 8 pieces

2 green bell peppers, cut into 20 pieces

2 tablespoons light-flavored olive oil

2 tablespoons lemon juice

¼ teaspoon black pepper

⅛ teaspoon ground cayenne pepper

½ teaspoon ground cumin

1 teaspoon minced garlic

1. Place mushrooms in a steamer basket over boiling water and steam, covered, for 2 minutes.
2. Thread 2 chicken chunks, 1 pepper piece, and 1 mushroom on each of 20 wooden skewers. Place in a shallow glass baking dish.
3. Combine the olive oil, lemon juice, pepper, cayenne, cumin, and garlic and pour mixture over the skewers to coat the kabobs evenly. Refrigerate for 30 minutes. Drain, and reserve marinade.
4. Preheat broiler. Broil skewers for 5 minutes, turn, and broil for an additional 5 minutes. Baste several times while broiling. Serve hot.

Calories Per Serving: 38
Fat: 2 g
Cholesterol: 14 mg
Protein: 5 g

Carbohydrates: 2 g
Dietary Fiber: 0 g
Sodium: 10 mg

❧ *Mini–Chicken Kabobs* ❧

YIELD: *24 servings (1 each)* • PREPARATION TIME: *20 minutes* •
COOKING TIME: *10 minutes*

Serve a platter of these tiny chicken kabobs with a tray of assorted vegetables.

6 tablespoons light-flavored olive oil

1 scallion, minced

2 cloves garlic, minced

1 teaspoon lemon juice

1 teaspoon dried oregano

¼ teaspoon black pepper

¼ teaspoon ground paprika

1 skinless, boneless chicken breast, cut
  into ½-inch cubes

1. Preheat broiler. Heat oil in a small saucepan over medium heat. Add scallion, garlic, lemon juice, oregano, pepper, and paprika.
2. Place several chicken cubes on each of 24 wooden skewers that have been soaked in water for 30 minutes.

3. Roll the chicken sticks in garlic–oil mixture, coating them well.
4. Broil 4 inches from heat for 5 minutes, turn, and broil 5 more minutes.

Calories Per Serving: 37

Carbohydrates: 0 g

Fat: 3 g

Dietary Fiber: 0 g

Cholesterol: 5 mg

Sodium: 3 mg

Protein: 2 g

✎ *Skewered Turkey with Plum Sauce* ✎

YIELD: 12 servings (1 each) • *PREPARATION TIME: 20 minutes* •
COOKING TIME: 4 to 6 minutes

Chunks of turkey cutlet are brushed with a tangy plum sauce while broiling.

*2½ pounds turkey cutlets, cut into
1¼-inch cubes
2 tablespoons light-flavored olive oil
2 tablespoons Dijon mustard
2 tablespoons Worcestershire sauce*

*½ cup all-fruit plum or apricot jam
2 teaspoons grated fresh gingerroot
2 cloves garlic, finely minced
2 tablespoons lemon juice*

1. Thread 4 to 5 turkey cubes onto each of 12 wooden skewers that have soaked in water for 30 minutes. Place skewers in a shallow baking pan. Brush turkey with olive oil.
2. Combine mustard, Worcestershire sauce, plum jam, gingerroot, garlic, and lemon juice.
3. Broil turkey kabobs for 2 minutes.
4. Brush kabobs with mustard sauce; broil an additional 1 to 2 minutes, or until done.
5. Brush with sauce again. Serve hot.

Calories Per Serving: 146

Carbohydrates: 7 g

Fat: 3 g

Dietary Fiber: 0 g

Cholesterol: 72 mg

Sodium: 111 mg

Protein: 26 g

Ground Turkey
🌿 *Sticks with Herb Dip* 🌿

YIELD: 20 servings (2 each) • *PREPARATION TIME: 30 minutes* •
COOKING TIME: 10 minutes

Ground turkey is combined with onion, garlic, and a variety of spices, shaped around the end of skewers, and broiled. The turkey sticks are served hot with a garlic-parsley-yogurt dip.

*1½ pounds low-fat ground turkey
   breast
1 onion, minced
1 clove garlic, minced
2 teaspoons ground paprika*

*2 teaspoons ground cumin
¼ teaspoon chili powder
¼ cup chopped fresh parsley
2 tablespoons dry red wine*

SAUCE

*2 cups nonfat or reduced-fat plain
   yogurt
2 cloves garlic, minced*

*2 tablespoons chopped fresh parsley
1 tablespoon chopped scallions*

1. Preheat broiler. Combine turkey, onion, garlic, paprika, cumin, chili powder, parsley, and red wine in a bowl.
2. Shape a tablespoon of turkey mixture around the end of each of 40 wooden skewers that have been soaked in water for 30 minutes.
3. Broil skewers. Cook for about 10 minutes, turning several times until meat is cooked through and well browned on all sides.
4. For the sauce, combine yogurt, garlic, parsley, and scallions.
5. Serve turkey sticks hot, with dip on side.

Calories Per Serving: 48
Fat: 1 g
Cholesterol: 26 mg
Protein: 11 g

Carbohydrates: 3 g
Dietary Fiber: 0 g
Sodium: 27 mg

• ROLL-UPS •

❧ *Turkey–Potato Salad Bundles* ❧

YIELD: 20 servings (1 each) • *PREPARATION TIME: 25 minutes plus
2 hours refrigeration time*

Cheese-potato salad is enclosed in a smoked turkey wrapping.

*3 medium potatoes, cooked, peeled,
  and cut into matchsticks ¼ inch by
  2 inches*
½ cup nonfat or reduced-fat cheese
½ cup diced celery
½ cup nonfat mayonnaise

1 tablespoon Dijon mustard
1 teaspoon prepared horseradish
2 tablespoons red wine vinegar
1 teaspoon sugar
¼ teaspoon black pepper
20 large slices smoked turkey

1. Combine potato strips, cheese, and celery.
2. Combine mayonnaise, mustard, horseradish, vinegar, sugar, and pepper.
3. Toss mayonnaise mixture with potato mixture. Cover and refrigerate at least 2 hours.
4. Spoon 2 liberal tablespoons of potato salad into each slice of turkey. Roll up and secure with a wooden or plastic party pick.

Calories Per Serving: 77
Fat: 1 g
Cholesterol: 5 mg
Protein: 7 g

Carbohydrates: 12 g
Dietary Fiber: 1 g
Sodium: 293 mg

❧ *Smoked Turkey–Fruit Wraparounds* ❧

YIELD: 18 servings (2 each) • *PREPARATION TIME: 20 minutes*

Smoked turkey slices are brushed with melted preserves and wrapped around fruit chunks. Serve with a curried-yogurt dip.

3 tablespoons all-fruit apricot or peach
  preserves
12 thin slices smoked turkey breast,
  each cut into thirds

1 tart apple, cut into 12 wedges
½ papaya, cut lengthwise into 12
  ⅛-inch slices
12 strawberries

1. Melt preserves in a small saucepan over medium heat.
2. Brush one side of each turkey slice with preserves.
3. Wrap a slice of turkey around each piece of fruit, trimming the meat to fit.
   Fasten each slice of turkey in place with a wooden or plastic party pick.

Calories Per Serving: 27
Fat: 0 g
Cholesterol: 6 mg
Protein: 3 g

Carbohydrates: 4 g
Dietary Fiber: 1 g
Sodium: 9 mg

Honey-Roasted Turkey Roll-ups

YIELD: 10 servings (2 each) • *PREPARATION TIME: 20 minutes* •
COOKING TIME: 5 minutes

Honey-roasted turkey from the deli counter is seasoned with mustard and
mango chutney, and rolled in leaf lettuce.

¼ pound honey-roasted or smoked
  turkey breast, chopped
1 tablespoon mango chutney
3 tablespoons nonfat or reduced-fat
  mayonnaise

1 teaspoon Dijon mustard
20 leaf lettuce leaves

1. Combine chopped turkey, chutney, mayonnaise, and mustard.
2. Fill a large saucepan with water and bring to a boil. Fill a large bowl with
   water and ice.
3. Drop lettuce leaves in pan of boiling water and remove at once. Plunge
   lettuce leaves into the bowl of ice water. Pat dry with paper towels.
4. Place a teaspoon of turkey-chutney mixture in the bottom half of each
   leaf. Fold bottom over filling, then fold the sides of the leaf over the filling
   and roll up the leaf in a bundle. Refrigerate until ready to serve.

Calories Per Serving: 28

Fat: 0 g

Cholesterol: 3 mg

Protein: 3 g

Carbohydrates: 3 g

Dietary Fiber: 0 g

Sodium: 164 mg

❧ *Chicken-Prune Roll-ups* ❧

YIELD: 10 servings (2 each) · PREPARATION TIME: 25 minutes plus
15 minutes prune-soaking time and 3 hours refrigeration time ·
COOKING TIME: 15 minutes

Chicken breasts and prunes are the unexpected partners in this rolled appetizer, which can be made 24 hours in advance. Prunes, which can be used in
a variety of sweet and savory dishes, have been traced back to Roman times.

⅔ cup pitted prunes
2 boneless, skinless chicken breast
  halves

2 cups nonfat or reduced-fat, low-
  sodium chicken broth

1. Pour boiling water over prunes, enough to soak. Let stand for 15 minutes.
   Drain.
2. Place prunes in a blender or food processor and puree until smooth.
3. Pound chicken between two sheets of wax paper until thin.
4. Spread prune mixture over chicken and roll up tightly. Wrap rolled
   chicken breasts tightly in foil.
5. Bring chicken broth to a boil in a large saucepan. Place foil-wrapped rolls
   in broth. Cover pan and simmer for 18 minutes or until chicken is
   cooked.
6. Remove rolls from broth, leaving foil wrapping in place.
7. Refrigerate for 3 hours. When ready to serve, unwrap rolls and cut each
   into 10 ½-inch slices. Provide wooden or plastic party picks.

Calories Per Serving: 46

Fat: 1 g

Cholesterol: 11 mg

Protein: 5 g

Carbohydrates: 6 g

Dietary Fiber: 1 g

Sodium: 75 mg

❦ *Chicken Whirls* ✿

YIELD: 24 servings (1 each) • *PREPARATION TIME: 25 minutes* •
COOKING TIME: 10 minutes

Serve these chicken-mustard slices with a bowl of chutney for dipping.

2 boneless, skinless chicken breast
  halves
1 tablespoon Dijon mustard

2 tablespoons light-flavored olive oil
⅛ teaspoon black pepper

1. Lightly pound chicken breasts between sheets of wax paper until they are about ¼ inch thick.
2. In a small bowl, combine mustard, 1 tablespoon of the oil, and pepper.
3. Spread one side of chicken pieces with mustard mixture.
4. Starting with long edge, tightly roll chicken pieces like a jelly roll. Secure with wooden picks.
5. Heat remaining tablespoon oil in a skillet over medium heat. Add chicken rolls; cook until all sides are done, about 10 minutes.
6. Remove chicken from heat; cool. Cut each roll crosswise into 12 pieces. Insert a wooden or plastic party pick into each slice.

Calories Per Serving: 17
Fat: 1 g
Cholesterol: 5 mg
Protein: 2 g

Carbohydrates: 0 g
Dietary Fiber: 0 g
Sodium: 19 mg

• WINGS •

❦ *Mexican Chicken Wings* ✿

YIELD: 24 servings (1 each) • *PREPARATION TIME: 15 minutes plus 4 hours
refrigeration time* • *COOKING TIME: 50 minutes*

Chicken wings are marinated in lime juice and cilantro for a special fajita flavor.

24 chicken wings, skinned, tips
  trimmed and discarded
¼ cup lime juice
2 tablespoons light-flavored olive oil
3 tablespoons chopped fresh cilantro or
  1 tablespoon dried cilantro

1 clove garlic, minced
1 teaspoon ground cumin
½ teaspoon dried oregano
¼ teaspoon ground cayenne pepper

1. Place chicken, lime juice, olive oil, cilantro, garlic, cumin, oregano, and cayenne in a glass bowl. Toss well, cover, and refrigerate for 4 hours. Turn chicken several times.
2. Preheat oven to 375 degrees. Drain chicken wings, reserving marinade. Place chicken on broiler pan. Bake for 50 minutes or until chicken is no longer pink. Brush twice with reserved marinade.
3. Drain wings and serve warm with small plates and cocktail napkins.

Calories Per Serving: 54
Fat: 3 g
Cholesterol: 18 mg
Protein: 6 g

Carbohydrates: 0 g
Dietary Fiber: 0 g
Sodium: 19 mg

✺ *Ginger-Garlic Teriyaki Wings* ✺

YIELD: 12 servings (2 each) • PREPARATION TIME: 15 minutes plus 4 hours refrigeration time • COOKING TIME: 50 minutes

These wings are marinated in soy sauce, wine, sugar, ginger, and garlic, and then baked.

¼ cup light soy sauce
¼ cup dry white wine
2 tablespoons sugar
½ teaspoon grated fresh gingerroot

1 garlic clove, minced
24 chicken wings, skinned, tips
  trimmed and discarded

1. Place soy sauce, white wine, sugar, gingerroot, garlic, and chicken wings in a glass bowl. Toss well, cover, and refrigerate for 4 hours, turning wings several times.
2. Preheat oven to 375 degrees. Drain chicken wings, reserving marinade. Place chicken on broiler pan.

3. Bake for 50 minutes or until chicken is no longer pink, brushing twice with reserved marinade.
4. Drain wings and serve immediately with small plates and cocktail napkins.

Calories Per Serving: 98
Fat: 3 g
Cholesterol: 36 mg
Protein: 13 g

Carbohydrates: 3 g
Dietary Fiber: 0 g
Sodium: 246 mg

❧ *Sweet-and-Sour Roast Chicken Wings* ❧

YIELD: 16 servings (1 each) • *PREPARATION TIME: 15 minutes plus 2 hours refrigeration time* • *COOKING TIME: 50 minutes*

Chicken wings are marinated in a sweet-and-sour sauce and then baked.

½ cup low-sodium catsup
½ cup brown sugar, firmly packed
¼ cup rice vinegar
3 tablespoons light soy sauce

2 tablespoons light sesame oil
4 cloves garlic, minced
16 chicken wings, skinned, tips trimmed and discarded

1. Combine catsup, brown sugar, rice vinegar, soy sauce, sesame oil, and minced garlic in a bowl.
2. Add chicken wings and toss to coat.
3. Cover with plastic wrap and refrigerate for 2 hours, turning several times in the marinade mixture.
4. Preheat oven to 375 degrees. Drain chicken wings, reserving marinade. Place the chicken wings on a foil-lined baking pan. Bake for 25 minutes, brush with marinade, turn the wings, and bake for an additional 25 minutes. Serve with small plates and cocktail napkins.

Calories Per Serving: 96
Fat: 3 g
Cholesterol: 18 mg
Protein: 7 g

Carbohydrates: 10 g
Dietary Fiber: 0 g
Sodium: 140 mg

❧ Chinese Simmered Wings ❧

YIELD: *10 servings (4 pieces each)* • PREPARATION TIME: *20 minutes plus
1 hour refrigeration time* • COOKING TIME: *45 minutes*

Chicken wings are simmered in a sauce of soy sauce, sherry, scallions, and brown sugar.

*20 chicken wings, skinned, cut into 2
pieces each, tips trimmed and discarded
4 scallion stalks, cut in 1-inch sections
½ cup light soy sauce*

*½ cup dry sherry
½ cup water
3 tablespoons brown sugar, firmly
packed*

1. Place wing sections and scallions in a pan with soy sauce, sherry, water, and brown sugar. Bring to a boil, then simmer, covered, for 30 minutes.
2. Remove cover and simmer for 15 more minutes, stirring and spooning sauce over wings.
3. Refrigerate for 1 hour before serving. Serve with small plates and cocktail napkins.

Calories Per Serving: 127
Fat: 3 g
Cholesterol: 36 mg
Protein: 14 g

Carbohydrates: 6 g
Dietary Fiber: 0 g
Sodium: 538 mg

❧ Broiled Wings with Buttermilk Sauce ❧

YIELD: *16 servings (2 pieces each)* • PREPARATION TIME: *20 minutes* •
COOKING TIME: *20 minutes*

Broiled chicken wings are dipped in a buttermilk–blue cheese–yogurt sauce.

*1 teaspoon canola or light-flavored
olive oil
1 teaspoon ground cayenne pepper*

*16 chicken wings, skinned, cut into
2 pieces each, tips trimmed and
discarded*

½ cup nonfat or reduced-fat plain yogurt

¼ cup nonfat or reduced-fat buttermilk

¼ cup blue cheese, crumbled

½ small onion, grated

1 teaspoon cider vinegar

1. Preheat broiler. Combine the oil and cayenne pepper in a medium bowl, add chicken wing segments, and turn until wings are coated.
2. Place the chicken wings on a broiler pan rack and broil, turning several times, about 20 minutes.
3. Combine the yogurt, buttermilk, blue cheese, onion, and vinegar in a serving bowl. Serve broiled wings hot with sauce on side. Provide small plates and cocktail napkins.

Calories Per Serving: 66
Fat: 3 g
Cholesterol: 21 mg
Protein: 8 g

Carbohydrates: 1 g
Dietary Fiber: 0 g
Sodium: 78 mg

⚘ *Orange Wings* ⚘

YIELD: 16 servings (1 each) • *PREPARATION TIME: 10 minutes plus overnight refrigeration time* • *COOKING TIME: 1 hour and 10 minutes*

Chicken wings are broiled and baked in an orange sauce, then refrigerated overnight.

1 6-ounce can frozen orange juice concentrate

¾ cup light soy sauce

⅓ cup Dijon mustard

16 chicken wings, skinned, tips trimmed and discarded

1. Combine orange juice, soy sauce, and mustard.
2. Place chicken wings in a single layer in shallow baking dish. Pour orange mixture over chicken.
3. Place under broiler until both sides of chicken are brown, turning as necessary.
4. Turn oven to 300 degrees. Bake for 1 hour or until most of sauce is gone.

5. Refrigerate overnight, then reheat before serving. Provide small plates and cocktail napkins.

Calories Per Serving: 67
Fat: 2 g
Cholesterol: 18 mg
Protein: 8 g

Carbohydrates: 7 g
Dietary Fiber: 0 g
Sodium: 549 mg

SEAFOOD APPETIZERS

OYSTERS AND CRABS

Oysters on the Half Shell with Horseradish Sauce •
Steamed Oysters • Oysters Rockefeller • Scalded Oysters
Maryland with Vinegar Sauce • Marinated Oysters •
Baked Oysters Parmesan • Oyster Crisps • Crabmeat in Petite
Shells • Spicy Crab Cakes

CLAMS AND MUSSELS

Steamed Clams Annapolis • Mediterranean Baked Clams •
Baked Tomato-Jalapeño Clams • Clams Parmesan • Steamed
Clams with Oriental Hot Sauce • Heavenly Mussels • Tomato-
Cheese Mussels • Greek Stuffed Mussels • Sherried Mussels •
Mussels Italiano

SCALLOPS AND FISH

Scallops in Lemon-Mustard Sauce • Scallop and Shrimp Dunk •
Scallops with Tartar Sauce • Scallops with Red Pepper–Orange–
Tomato Salsa • Tuna Tastes • Marinated Tuna-Stuffed Eggs •
Pineapple-Halibut Skewers • Greek Fish Kabobs

SHRIMP

Chinese Steamed Shrimp • Spicy Shrimp • Parsley-Garlic Baked
Shrimp • Jalapeño Shrimp • Garlic Shrimp • Broiled Shrimp
with Barbecue Sauce • Pineapple Shrimp • Steamed Shrimp with
Pineapple-Orange Salsa • Tarragon Shrimp • Mini–Ginger
Shrimp • Shrimp Delights • Shrimp with Dijon Marmalade Dip

Oysters on the Half Shell
with Horseradish Sauce

YIELD: 12 servings (2 each) · *PREPARATION TIME: 20 minutes*

Fresh oysters on the half shell are best served during the fall and winter months, since they spawn during the summer months and become soft and fatty.

24 fresh oysters, well scrubbed
1 cup low-sodium catsup
2 tablespoons low-sodium tomato
   paste

2 tablespoons lemon juice
⅓ cup prepared horseradish, drained
¼ teaspoon hot pepper sauce

1. Open oysters using a short knife with a thick blade. Place oyster in a towel with the deeper part of the shell toward your palm. Work the knife into the shell, to one side of the hinge, and ease it into the hinge. Run knife along the top inside of the shell to remove it. Use knife to loosen muscle that connects oyster to shell.
2. Combine catsup, tomato paste, lemon juice, horseradish, and hot pepper sauce in a serving bowl.
3. Place a bowl of the sauce in center of a large platter. Surround with oysters. Serve with plates and cocktail forks or long wooden or plastic party picks.

Calories Per Serving: 64
Fat: 1 g
Cholesterol: 27 mg
Protein: 4 g

Carbohydrates: 10 g
Dietary Fiber: 1 g
Sodium: 122 mg

Steamed Oysters

YIELD: 18 servings (2 each) · *PREPARATION TIME: 5 minutes* ·
COOKING TIME: 5 minutes

These simply prepared oysters are ready in 5 minutes. Serve with seafood cocktail sauce and small toast slices.

2 tablespoons light-flavored olive oil
1 pint shucked oysters, oyster liquor
   reserved
¼ teaspoon lemon juice

¼ teaspoon black pepper
1 teaspoon minced fresh parsley
1 clove garlic, minced
⅛ teaspoon dried tarragon

1. Heat oil in a skillet. Add oysters, reserved oyster liquor, lemon juice, pepper, parsley, garlic, and tarragon.
2. Simmer until edges of oysters curl, about 5 minutes. Serve with plates and cocktail forks or wooden or plastic party picks.

Calories Per Serving: 33
Fat: 2 g
Cholesterol: 15 mg
Protein: 2 g

Carbohydrates: 1 g
Dietary Fiber: 0 g
Sodium: 31 mg

﹨ *Oysters Rockefeller* ﹨

YIELD: 36 servings (1 each) • *PREPARATION TIME: 25 minutes* •
COOKING TIME: 10 minutes

Fresh oysters are baked with a topping of spinach, bread crumbs, and Parmesan cheese.

36 fresh oysters, well scrubbed
1 10-ounce package frozen spinach,
   cooked according to package directions, drained, and finely chopped
1 tablespoon minced fresh parsley
¼ teaspoon black pepper
2 tablespoons finely chopped celery

⅛ teaspoon hot pepper sauce
1 tablespoon minced onion
½ cup bread crumbs
⅓ cup light-flavored olive oil
Grated nonfat or reduced-fat Parmesan
   cheese

1. Preheat oven to 400 degrees. Open oysters using a short knife with a thick blade. Place oyster in a towel with the deeper part of the shell toward your palm. Work the knife into the shell, to one side of the hinge, and ease it into the hinge. Run knife along the top inside of the shell to remove it. Use knife to loosen muscle that connects oyster to shell. Leave oysters in the half shell.

2. Mix spinach with parsley, pepper, celery, hot pepper sauce, onion, bread crumbs, and olive oil.

3. Spread spinach mixture on top of oysters, sprinkle with cheese, and arrange in a single layer in a shallow baking pan.

4. Bake for 10 minutes or until bubbles begin to form on top. Serve with plates and cocktail forks.

Calories Per Serving: 38
Fat: 3 g
Cholesterol: 9 mg
Protein: 2 g

Carbohydrates: 2 g
Dietary Fiber: 0 g
Sodium: 38 mg

❦ *Scalded Oysters Maryland* ❦ *with Vinegar Sauce*

YIELD: 15 servings (2 each) · *PREPARATION TIME: 15 minutes plus 2 hours standing time for the sauce* · *COOKING TIME: 5 to 7 minutes*

Serve this traditional favorite with vinegar or cocktail sauce.

1 cup white wine vinegar
1 small onion, very thinly sliced

Coarse-ground pepper
30 oysters, scrubbed

1. Combine vinegar, onion, and pepper. Let stand at room temperature for 2 hours.

2. Put oysters in wire basket and place in rapidly boiling water. Cook until shells just begin to open. Discard any unopened oysters.

3. Serve oysters in shells immediately, with vinegar sauce on the side for dipping. Provide plates and cocktail forks or long wooden or plastic party picks.

Calories Per Serving: 25
Fat: 1 g
Cholesterol: 8 mg
Protein: 2 g

Carbohydrates: 4 g
Dietary Fiber: 0 g
Sodium: 58 mg

❦ *Marinated Oysters* ❦

YIELD: 20 servings (2 each) • *PREPARATION TIME: 10 minutes plus
3 hours refrigeration time* • *COOKING TIME: 15 minutes*

These simmered oysters are marinated in a vinegar-tarragon sauce. Serve with crackers.

*2 pints shucked, fresh oysters, oyster
   liquor reserved
1 cup white wine vinegar
¼ cup sugar*

*2 teaspoons dried tarragon
3 tablespoons pickling spice
¼ cup dry sherry*

1. Simmer oysters in their own liquor until curled. Add water if necessary. Set aside.
2. Combine vinegar, sugar, tarragon, pickling spice, and sherry in a small saucepan and cook over medium heat for 10 minutes.
3. Drain oysters thoroughly and transfer to a bowl.
4. Strain sauce and pour liquid over oysters.
5. Cover and refrigerate for 3 hours. Serve with plates and cocktail forks or wooden or plastic party picks.

Calories Per Serving: 44
Fat: 1 g
Cholesterol: 12 mg
Protein: 3 g

Carbohydrates: 6 g
Dietary Fiber: 0 g
Sodium: 86 mg

❦ *Baked Oysters Parmesan* ❦

YIELD: 24 servings (2 each) • *PREPARATION TIME: 25 minutes* •
COOKING TIME: 13 minutes

Oysters are baked with a delicious crumb topping.

*¼ cup nonfat or reduced-fat, low-
   sodium chicken broth*

*2 tablespoons light-flavored olive oil
1½ cups bread crumbs*

1½ teaspoons minced garlic
¼ cup minced fresh parsley
48 medium shucked oysters

⅓ cup grated nonfat or reduced-fat
Parmesan cheese

1. Preheat oven to 400 degrees. Heat chicken broth and olive oil in a skillet over medium heat. Add bread crumbs and garlic and toss until crumbs are golden brown, about 3 minutes. Stir in the parsley.
2. Spread two thirds of the bread-crumb mixture in a shallow, lightly oiled baking dish. Place oysters on the crumbs.
3. Mix cheese with the remaining crumbs and dab the mixture over the oysters.
4. Bake for 10 minutes or until the juices are bubbling and the mixture is heated through. Serve immediately with plates and cocktail forks.

Calories Per Serving: 67
Fat: 3 g
Cholesterol: 22 mg
Protein: 4 g

Carbohydrates: 7 g
Dietary Fiber: 0 g
Sodium: 157 mg

Oyster Crisps

YIELD: 12 servings (2 each) • PREPARATION TIME: 15 minutes •
COOKING TIME: 12 minutes

These oysters are breaded, baked, and served with tartar sauce. (For tartar sauce recipe, see page 301.)

24 shucked oysters, drained
2 tablespoons unbleached, all-purpose
  flour
4 egg whites

3 teaspoons water
½ teaspoon hot pepper sauce
1 cup bread crumbs
Olive oil cooking spray

1. Preheat oven to 450 degrees. Dredge oysters in flour.
2. Combine egg whites, water, and hot pepper sauce.
3. Dip each oyster in the egg mixture, then dredge in the bread crumbs.
4. Spray a baking sheet with the olive oil spray. Arrange the oysters on the baking sheet and mist lightly with the cooking spray.

5. Bake 10 to 15 minutes or until the coating becomes crisp. Serve hot with wooden or plastic party picks.

Calories Per Serving: 81
Fat: 2 g
Cholesterol: 27 mg
Protein: 6 g

Carbohydrates: 10 g
Dietary Fiber: 0 g
Sodium: 205 mg

❧ *Crabmeat in Petite Shells* ❧

YIELD: 20 servings (2 each) • *PREPARATION TIME: 20 minutes* •
COOKING TIME: 3 minutes

Crabmeat is baked in littleneck clam shells.

½ pound cooked crabmeat
40 littleneck clam shell halves
¼ cup nonfat or reduced-fat plain
 yogurt
3 tablespoons low-sodium catsup

1 ½ teaspoons lemon juice
1 teaspoon Worcestershire sauce
⅛ teaspoon white pepper
2 tablespoons chopped fresh parsley
¼ cup bread crumbs

1. Preheat broiler. Pack crabmeat into clam shells.
2. Combine yogurt, catsup, lemon juice, Worcestershire sauce, and pepper.
3. Spoon ⅔ teaspoon sauce over each shell, covering the crabmeat.
4. Sprinkle with parsley and bread crumbs.
5. Broil 3 minutes and serve hot.

Calories Per Serving: 15
Fat: 0 g
Cholesterol: 3 mg
Protein: 2 g

Carbohydrates: 1 g
Dietary Fiber: 0 g
Sodium: 27 mg

Spicy Crab Cakes

YIELD: 15 servings (2 each) • *PREPARATION TIME: 20 minutes* •
COOKING TIME: 20 minutes

Crab cakes don't have to be loaded with fat to be delicious.

¼ cup nonfat or reduced-fat plain yogurt	2 egg whites, beaten
2 tablespoons Worcestershire sauce	1 pound cooked crabmeat
1 teaspoon dry mustard	¼ cup cracker crumbs
¼ teaspoon black pepper	1½ tablespoons light-flavored olive oil

1. Combine yogurt, Worcestershire sauce, mustard, pepper, and egg whites.
2. Pour mixture over crabmeat, add cracker crumbs, and toss gently to mix. Shape into 30 patties.
3. Sauté half of the patties in half of the oil until golden brown, add the remaining oil and sauté the remaining patties. Serve with wooden or plastic party picks.

Calories Per Serving: 51	Carbohydrates: 2 g
Fat: 2 g	Dietary Fiber: 0 g
Cholesterol: 0 mg	Sodium: 128 mg
Protein: 6 g	

• CLAMS AND MUSSELS •

Steamed Clams Annapolis

YIELD: 18 (2 each) • *PREPARATION TIME: 10 minutes* •
COOKING TIME: 20 minutes

Clams are simply steamed and served in their own cooking liquid.

3 dozen cherrystone clams in shell, well scrubbed	¼ teaspoon black pepper
	½ cup water

1. Place clams, pepper, and water in a pan. Cover tightly and bring to a boil.
2. Reduce heat, and steam for 15 minutes or until shells open wide. Discard any unopened clams.
3. Drain clams, reserving liquid. Strain liquid.
4. Serve clams hot in shells with clam cooking liquid for dipping. Provide small plates and cocktail forks.

Calories Per Serving: 20
Fat: 0 g
Cholesterol: 9 mg
Protein: 3 g

Carbohydrates: 1 g
Dietary Fiber: 0 g
Sodium: 15 mg

❧ *Mediterranean Baked Clams* ✣

YIELD: 24 servings (2 each)   •   PREPARATION TIME: 25 minutes   •
COOKING TIME: 30 minutes

Italian bread cubes, sautéed with onions and garlic in olive oil, are combined with canned clams.

¼ cup light-flavored olive oil
1 large onion, chopped
3 cloves garlic, finely minced
1 cup chopped fresh parsley
2 teaspoons dried oregano
¼ teaspoon black pepper
8 slices Italian bread, crusts trimmed, and cubed

30 ounces (2 15-ounce cans) canned, minced clams, drained (liquid from cans reserved)
48 clam shell halves
¼ cup nonfat or reduced-fat Parmesan cheese

1. Preheat oven to 375 degrees. Heat oil in skillet over medium heat. Sauté onion and garlic until onion is transparent.
2. Add parsley, oregano, and pepper. Stir to mix.
3. Add bread cubes and toss until oil is absorbed and bread is coated.
4. Add clams and reserved liquid.
5. Fill shells with clam mixture and sprinkle with cheese. Place on shallow baking pan and bake for 30 minutes, or until lightly brown and bubbly. Provide plates and cocktail forks.

Calories Per Serving: 66

Fat: 3 g

Cholesterol: 13 mg

Protein: 6 g

Carbohydrates: 6 g

Dietary Fiber: 0 g

Sodium: 60 mg

✎ *Baked Tomato-Jalapeño Clams* ✐

YIELD: 12 servings (1 each) • *PREPARATION TIME: 20 minutes* •
COOKING TIME: 15 minutes

These pungent clams get their heat from jalapeño chiles, which are named after Jalapa, the capital of Veracruz, Mexico.

*4 jalapeño peppers, seeded and
    chopped*
1 tomato, chopped
1 small onion, minced

2 cloves garlic, minced
1 tablespoon lime juice
12 fresh clams, well scrubbed
Chopped fresh parsley for garnish

1. Preheat oven to 400 degrees. Place jalapeños, tomato, onion, garlic, and lime juice in a blender or food processor and puree.
2. Open the clams, remove the top shells, and leave the clam meat in the bottom shells.
3. Place clams in a shallow baking pan. Top each clam with a small portion of the jalapeño mixture. Bake for 15 minutes.
4. Sprinkle with parsley and serve with plates and cocktail forks.

Calories Per Serving: 26

Fat: 0 g

Cholesterol: 7 mg

Protein: 3 g

Carbohydrates: 3 g

Dietary Fiber: 0 g

Sodium: 153 mg

✎ *Clams Parmesan* ✐

YIELD: 12 servings (1 each) • *PREPARATION TIME: 30 minutes* •
COOKING TIME: 30 minutes

Canned clams are combined with vegetables, topped with Parmesan cheese, and baked.

2 tablespoons light-flavored olive oil
2 tablespoons nonfat or reduced-fat,
   low-sodium chicken broth
½ cup finely chopped onion
½ cup finely chopped celery
½ cup finely chopped green bell pepper
2 tablespoons unbleached, all-purpose
   flour
2 tablespoons grated nonfat or reduced-
   fat Parmesan cheese
¼ teaspoon black pepper
½ teaspoon Worcestershire sauce
¾ cup cracker crumbs
7½ ounces canned, minced clams
12 clam-size shells (real or ceramic)

1. Preheat oven to 350 degrees. Heat olive oil and chicken broth over medium heat. Sauté onion, celery, and green pepper until tender.
2. Stir in flour, cheese, black pepper, and Worcestershire sauce.
3. Add ½ cup of the cracker crumbs and mix well.
4. Stir in undrained, minced clams. Cook and stir until mixture thickens.
5. Fill shells. Sprinkle remaining crackers on top of shells.
6. Bake for 20 minutes or until lightly browned. Serve with plates and cocktail forks.

Calories Per Serving: 60
Fat: 3 g
Cholesterol: 6 mg
Protein: 1 g

Carbohydrates: 8 g
Dietary Fiber: 0 g
Sodium: 65 mg

Steamed Clams with Oriental Hot Sauce

YIELD: 12 servings (2 each) • PREPARATION TIME: 20 minutes

Littleneck clams are steamed and served with soy-chile sauce.

24 littleneck clams, scrubbed
3 tablespoons light soy sauce
1½ teaspoons canola or light sesame
   oil
2 cloves garlic, minced
2 scallions, finely chopped
1 tablespoon toasted sesame seeds
1 teaspoon sugar
1 small chile pepper, seeded and finely
   chopped

1. Heat 1 cup of water until boiling. Drop in clams. Cover and steam until shells open, about 7 minutes. Discard any unopened clams.

2. Remove clams and set aside to cool.
3. Remove top shells. Loosen clams in shells and arrange on a platter.
4. Combine soy sauce, oil, garlic, scallions, sesame seeds, sugar, and chile pepper.
5. Spoon a little bit of sauce onto each clam. Serve with plates and cocktail forks.

Calories Per Serving: 50
Fat: 2 g
Cholesterol: 1 mg
Protein: 1 g

Carbohydrates: 6 g
Dietary Fiber: 0 g
Sodium: 60 mg

❧ *Heavenly Mussels* ❧

YIELD: 10 servings (2 each) • *PREPARATION TIME: 20 minutes* •
COOKING TIME: 12 minutes

Mussels are simmered in a tomato-wine-vegetable sauce and then served on the half shell.

¼ cup water, or nonfat or reduced-fat, low-sodium chicken broth
1 clove garlic, minced
2 tablespoons minced onion
2 tablespoons minced green bell pepper
¼ teaspoon ground cayenne pepper

1 cup low-sodium tomato sauce
½ cup dry white wine
2 pounds medium mussels (approximately 20 mussels, scrubbed and debearded)
½ cup chopped fresh parsley

1. Heat water or broth in a large pot over medium heat. Sauté garlic, onion, and green pepper until lightly browned.
2. Add cayenne pepper, tomato sauce, wine, and mussels. Cover pot and simmer for 5 minutes or until all of the mussels have opened. Discard any unopened mussels.
3. Remove mussels from pot with a slotted spoon and remove meat from shells. Discard bottom half of each shell. Return mussel meat to pot and bring sauce to a boil. Cook for 1 minute.
4. Place 1 mussel and some sauce in each half shell. Sprinkle with parsley and serve. Provide small plates and cocktail forks.

Calories Per Serving: 42

Carbohydrates: 3 g

Fat: 1 g

Dietary Fiber: 0 g

Cholesterol: 7 mg

Sodium: 84 mg

Protein: 4 g

❧ Tomato-Cheese Mussels ❧

YIELD: *18 servings (2 each)* • PREPARATION TIME: *20 minutes* •
COOKING TIME: *20 minutes*

Steamed mussels are baked with a topping of tomato, onion, garlic, and cheese.

½ cup dry white wine
36 small mussels, scrubbed and de-bearded
3 tablespoons light-flavored olive oil
1 onion, minced
2 cloves garlic, minced

½ cup chopped fresh or canned low-sodium tomatoes
1 teaspoon dried basil
½ cup grated nonfat or reduced-fat Parmesan cheese

1. Heat wine in a large pan. Add mussels and steam over high heat for 5 minutes or until the shells open. Discard any unopened mussels.
2. Drain mussels. Place each mussel in half a shell and arrange on a baking sheet.
3. Heat olive oil in a skillet over medium heat. Add onion and garlic, and cook until onion is soft.
4. Add tomatoes and basil. Simmer for 10 minutes.
5. Preheat broiler. Spoon tomato mixture over mussels and sprinkle with Parmesan cheese.
6. Broil mussels until cheese is lightly browned. Serve with plates and cocktail forks.

Calories Per Serving: 46

Carbohydrates: 3 g

Fat: 1 g

Dietary Fiber: 0 g

Cholesterol: 9 mg

Sodium: 93 mg

Protein: 4 g

❧ *Greek Stuffed Mussels* ❧

YIELD: *10 servings (2 each)* ▪ PREPARATION TIME: *30 minutes* ▪
COOKING TIME: *30 minutes*

Steamed, chopped mussels are combined with rice, oregano, and lemon peel, and then broiled.

1 tablespoon light-flavored olive oil
¼ cup lemon juice
¼ cup water
2 cloves garlic, finely chopped
20 mussels, scrubbed and debearded

½ cup rice
½ teaspoon dried oregano
½ teaspoon grated lemon peel
2 tablespoons chopped fresh parsley

1. Place the olive oil, lemon juice, water, and garlic in a large pot over medium-high heat. Bring to a boil.
2. Add the mussels and cover the pot.
3. Cook, shaking the pot occasionally, until all the mussels open, about 4 minutes. Discard any unopened mussels.
4. Remove the mussels with a slotted spoon, reserving liquid in pot.
5. Add enough water to mussel broth from pot to make 1 cup. Place in a saucepan. Bring to a boil.
6. Add rice, reduce heat, and simmer for 15 minutes or until rice is cooked. Remove from heat.
7. Preheat broiler. Remove mussels from shells. Wash and dry 20 half shells.
8. Chop mussels. Add to rice. Add oregano, lemon peel, and parsley.
9. Stuff mussel mixture into shells. Broil for 3 minutes. Serve with plates and cocktail forks.

Calories Per Serving: 75
Fat: 2 g
Cholesterol: 8 mg
Protein: 4 g

Carbohydrates: 9 g
Dietary Fiber: 1 g
Sodium: 87 mg

❧ *Sherried Mussels* ❧

YIELD: 30 servings (2 each) • *PREPARATION TIME: 20 minutes plus
1 hour refrigeration time* • *COOKING TIME: 30 minutes*

Mussels are steamed and served on the half shell with a sherry–lemon sauce.

*3 tablespoons canned, low-sodium
tomato sauce
1 tablespoon lemon juice
2 tablespoons dry sherry
1 clove garlic, minced
½ onion, minced
½ cup water
1½ cups nonfat or reduced-fat mayonnaise*

*1½ tablespoons nonfat or reduced-fat
sour cream
1 tablespoon grated fresh or prepared
horseradish
5 dozen large mussels, scrubbed and
debearded
2 cups water
Minced scallions for garnish*

1. Place tomato sauce, lemon juice, sherry, garlic, onion, and ½ cup water in a saucepan. Bring to a boil, reduce heat, and simmer until sauce is reduced by two-thirds.
2. Remove from heat and stir in mayonnaise, sour cream, and horseradish. Chill sauce for 1 hour.
3. Steam mussels in 2 cups of water until shells open, approximately 5 to 7 minutes. Discard any unopened mussels.
4. Leave bottom shell on mussels, top with 1 teaspoon of sauce, and garnish with scallions. Serve with plates and cocktail forks.

Calories Per Serving: 37
Fat: 1 g
Cholesterol: 7 mg
Protein: 3 g

Carbohydrates: 4 g
Dietary Fiber: 0 g
Sodium: 78 mg

❧ *Mussels Italiano* ❧

YIELD: 30 servings (2 each) • *PREPARATION TIME: 25 minutes* •
COOKING TIME: 7 minutes

Mussels are steamed in wine and stuffed with an herb–bread crumb mixture.

*3 pounds medium mussels in their
    shells, scrubbed and debearded*
⅓ cup dry white wine
½ cup fresh bread crumbs

3 tablespoons light-flavored olive oil
3 tablespoons chopped fresh parsley
1 teaspoon dried oregano
2 cloves garlic, minced

1. Place mussels in a large pot with white wine. Cover and boil for 4 to 5 minutes, until shells open. Discard any unopened mussels.
2. Discard top half of each shell, leaving mussels connected on bottom half.
3. Preheat broiler. Combine bread crumbs, half of the olive oil, parsley, oregano, and garlic.
4. Place mussels on half shell on baking sheet and top with bread crumb mixture. Sprinkle with remaining olive oil, and cook for 2 minutes or until the crumb mixture is crisp. Serve with plates and cocktail forks.

Calories Per Serving: 60
Fat: 3 g
Cholesterol: 13 mg
Protein: 6 g

Carbohydrates: 3 g
Dietary Fiber: 0 g
Sodium: 146 mg

· SCALLOPS AND FISH ·

☙ *Scallops in Lemon-Mustard Sauce* ❧

YIELD: *8 servings (2 each)* · PREPARATION TIME: *15 minutes plus
3 hours refrigeration time* · COOKING TIME: *5 minutes*

Scallops are cooked in wine with bay leaves and mixed with a tangy sauce.

*1 cup nonfat or reduced-fat mayon-
    naise*
2 teaspoons Dijon mustard
Dash of lemon juice
2 small cloves garlic, minced
1 tablespoon capers, drained

1½ teaspoons dried tarragon
¼ teaspoon hot pepper sauce
½ teaspoon paprika
1½ cups dry white wine
4 dried bay leaves
1 pound fresh sea scallops

1. Combine mayonnaise, mustard, lemon juice, garlic, capers, tarragon, hot pepper sauce, and paprika. Cover and chill at least 1 hour.
2. Place wine and bay leaves in a nonaluminum saucepan and bring to a boil. Add the scallops. Cover the saucepan and cook over medium heat for 2 minutes.

3. Drain scallops, discard bay leaves, and allow scallops to cool.
4. Fold scallops into sauce and chill for 2 hours before serving. Serve with small plates and cocktail forks.

Calories Per Serving: 114
Fat: 1 g
Cholesterol: 19 mg
Protein: 10 g

Carbohydrates: 8 g
Dietary Fiber: 0 g
Sodium: 336 mg

❧ *Scallop and Shrimp Dunk* ❧

YIELD: 15 servings (1 scallop, 1 shrimp each) • *PREPARATION TIME: 25 minutes* • *COOKING TIME: 20 minutes*

Scallops and shrimp are simmered in a fragrant sauce, then served in a chafing dish.

2 tablespoons light-flavored olive oil
1 small onion, chopped
1 clove garlic, crushed
¼ teaspoon dried basil
¼ teaspoon black pepper
¼ teaspoon dried marjoram
1 teaspoon lemon juice

1 cup canned, low-sodium tomato sauce
1 cup nonfat or reduced fat, low-sodium chicken broth
½ pound small scallops
½ pound shrimp, shelled and deveined

1. Heat olive oil in a skillet over medium heat. Sauté onion until tender.
2. Add garlic, basil, pepper, marjoram, lemon juice, tomato sauce, and chicken broth. Reduce heat and simmer for 10 minutes.
3. Add scallops and shrimp to sauce. Simmer for 5 minutes or until scallops and shrimp are fork-tender.
4. Transfer to a chafing dish. Serve with wooden or plastic party picks.

Calories Per Serving: 52
Fat: 2 g
Cholesterol: 28 mg
Protein: 6 g

Carbohydrates: 2 g
Dietary Fiber: 0 g
Sodium: 157 mg

❧ *Scallops with Tartar Sauce* ❧

YIELD: 15 servings (2 each) · *PREPARATION TIME: 15 minutes plus 2 hours refrigeration time*

Scallops are served with a tartar sauce that combines mayonnaise, yogurt, pickle relish, onion, and red bell pepper.

¾ cup nonfat or reduced-fat mayonnaise
¾ cup nonfat or reduced-fat plain yogurt

½ cup sweet pickle relish
¼ cup minced onion
½ cup minced red bell pepper
30 steamed sea scallops

1. Stir together mayonnaise, yogurt, relish, onion, and red pepper.
2. Cover and chill for 2 hours.
3. Serve tartar sauce in a bowl on a platter surrounded by scallops. Provide wooden and plastic party picks.

Calories Per Serving: 59
Fat: 0 g
Cholesterol: 15 mg
Protein: 7 g

Carbohydrates: 7 g
Dietary Fiber: 0 g
Sodium: 301 mg

Scallops with ❧ *Red Pepper–Orange–Tomato Salsa* ❧

YIELD: 15 servings (2 each) · *PREPARATION TIME: 20 minutes*

Scallops are served with a dipping sauce that combines tomatoes, oranges, red peppers, honey, scallions, lemon juice, and red wine vinegar.

¼ cup red wine vinegar
½ cup sliced scallions
1 tablespoon honey
2 cups finely chopped fresh or canned, low-sodium tomatoes

2 navel oranges, finely chopped
1 tablespoon lemon juice
2 tablespoons finely chopped red bell pepper
30 steamed sea scallops

1. Heat vinegar over medium heat and add the scallions. Cook for 1 minute.
2. Mix in the honey. Cook for 1 minute. Remove from heat.
3. Stir in the tomatoes, oranges, lemon juice, and red pepper. Heat sauce gently and serve in a bowl on a platter surrounded by scallops. Serve with wooden or plastic party picks.

Calories Per Serving: 52
Fat: 1 g
Cholesterol: 15 mg
Protein: 7 g

Carbohydrates: 5 g
Dietary Fiber: 1 g
Sodium: 78 mg

☙ *Tuna Tastes* ☙

YIELD: 15 servings (2 each) • *PREPARATION TIME: 20 minutes* •
COOKING TIME: 12 minutes

These little morsels of tuna and pickle relish are sautéed in canola oil.

6½ ounces canned, water-packed, white albacore tuna, drained
2 egg whites, lightly beaten
¼ cup fine bread crumbs
2 tablespoons nonfat or reduced-fat mayonnaise

1 tablespoon sweet pickle relish, drained
3 tablespoons canola or light-flavored olive oil

1. Combine tuna with egg whites, bread crumbs, mayonnaise, and pickle relish.
2. Shape into 30 1-inch balls.
3. Heat oil in a skillet over medium heat. Sauté tuna balls until they have firmed up and are lightly golden on all sides.
4. Serve immediately with wooden or plastic party picks.

Calories Per Serving: 53
Fat: 3 g
Cholesterol: 5 mg
Protein: 4 g

Carbohydrates: 2 g
Dietary Fiber: 0 g
Sodium: 93 mg

❧ *Marinated Tuna-Stuffed Eggs* ❧

YIELD: 8 servings (2 each) • *PREPARATION TIME: 15 minutes plus overnight refrigeration time* • *COOKING TIME: 15 minutes*

Hard-boiled egg whites are stuffed with white albacore tuna that has been marinated in vinegar, onion, and black pepper.

6½ ounces canned, water-packed,
white albacore tuna
1 tablespoon white wine vinegar
¼ teaspoon black pepper

½ small onion, sliced
8 eggs
Chopped fresh parsley

1. Place tuna in a glass bowl. Add vinegar, black pepper, and sliced onion, and toss well. Place in refrigerator to marinate overnight.
2. Bring a pan of water to a boil and boil eggs for 10 minutes. Remove from heat and place under cold running water.
3. Peel eggs and slice in half. Scoop yolks out and discard.
4. Stuff egg whites with marinated tuna mixture and sprinkle with chopped parsley.

Calories Per Serving: 53
Fat: 1 g
Cholesterol: 9 mg
Protein: 10 g

Carbohydrates: 1 g
Dietary Fiber: 0 g
Sodium: 146 mg

❧ *Pineapple-Halibut Skewers* ❧

YIELD: 12 servings (1 each) • *PREPARATION TIME: 15 minutes plus 1 hour refrigeration time* • *COOKING TIME: 9 minutes*

Halibut is marinated in soy sauce, orange juice, scallions, canola oil, fresh gingerroot, and sesame seeds, and then broiled with pineapple chunks and cherry tomatoes.

⅓ cup light soy sauce
1 tablespoon orange juice
2 tablespoons chopped scallions
1 tablespoon canola oil
1 tablespoon grated fresh gingerroot
1 tablespoon toasted sesame seeds
1 teaspoon honey

¼ teaspoon black pepper
1½ pounds halibut, cut into 1-inch
  chunks
12 canned, juice-packed pineapple
  chunks, drained
12 cherry tomatoes

1. Place soy sauce, orange juice, scallions, oil, gingerroot, sesame seeds, honey, and black pepper in a blender and process until well combined.
2. Place fish pieces in a glass bowl and pour marinade over them. Toss well, then cover and refrigerate for 1 hour. Meanwhile, soak 12 wooden skewers in water for 30 minutes.
3. Preheat broiler. Reserving the marinade, thread skewers with fish chunks, alternating with pineapple chunks and cherry tomatoes.
4. Broil for 6 minutes, turn, and brush with marinade.
5. Broil for 3 minutes more or until fish flakes with a fork.

Calories Per Serving: 98
Fat: 3 g
Cholesterol: 18 mg
Protein: 13 g

Carbohydrates: 5 g
Dietary Fiber: 1 g
Sodium: 267 mg

❧ Greek Fish Kabobs ❧

YIELD: 18 servings (1 each) • *PREPARATION TIME: 20 minutes plus 30 minutes refrigeration time* • *COOKING TIME: 8 minutes*

Chunks of swordfish steak are marinated in a lemon-oregano sauce and broiled with green olives.

¼ cup lemon juice
2 teaspoons dried oregano
2 pounds swordfish steaks, 1 inch
  thick

1 tablespoon light-flavored olive oil
18 large pimento-stuffed olives
Olive oil for basting

1. Combine lemon juice and oregano. Rub into swordfish steaks. Let stand for 30 minutes. Soak 18 wooden skewers in water for 30 minutes.

2. Brush fish with olive oil. Cut fish into 36 1-inch chunks.
3. Place 2 fish chunks and 1 olive on each skewer.
4. Broil for 8 minutes, turning to brown evenly and basting with olive oil. Cook only until fish flakes easily with a fork.

Calories Per Serving: 75
Fat: 3 g
Cholesterol: 20 mg
Protein: 10 g

Carbohydrates: 1 g
Dietary Fiber: 0 g
Sodium: 153 mg

• SHRIMP •

Chinese Steamed Shrimp

YIELD: 15 servings (2 each) • *PREPARATION TIME: 30 minutes* •
COOKING TIME: 15 minutes

Shrimp are steamed with ginger, soy sauce, and sherry.

4 slices fresh gingerroot, minced
1 tablespoon light soy sauce
1 tablespoon dry sherry

1 pound medium shrimp, shelled and deveined

1. Combine gingerroot, soy sauce, and sherry.
2. Add soy sauce mixture to shrimp and toss. Let stand for 15 minutes, turning twice.
3. Place shrimp and marinade in a shallow heat-proof dish.
4. Place water to boil in a steamer. Place heat-proof dish on a steamer rack and steam shrimp over low heat for 15 minutes or until they are no longer pink.
5. Drain, and serve with wooden or plastic party picks.

Calories Per Serving: 29
Fat: 0 g
Cholesterol: 45 mg
Protein: 6 g

Carbohydrates: 0 g
Dietary Fiber: 0 g
Sodium: 248 mg

❧ *Spicy Shrimp* ❧

YIELD: 12 servings (2 each) · *PREPARATION TIME: 20 minutes plus 2 hours refrigeration time* · *COOKING TIME: 18 minutes*

These flavorful shrimp are easy to prepare and make an elegant addition to a selection of dips and vegetable-based appetizers.

12 whole peppercorns	*1 stalk celery, chopped*
4 whole cloves	*3 slices lemon*
1 dried bay leaf	*3 cloves garlic, chopped*
½ teaspoon ground cayenne pepper	*2 tablespoons red wine vinegar*
½ teaspoon mustard seeds	*24 large shrimp, peeled and deveined*
½ teaspoon dried thyme	*2 tablespoons lemon juice*
½ teaspoon ground coriander	*1 tablespoon light-flavored olive oil*
4 cups water	*Dash of hot pepper sauce*
1 medium onion, chopped	

1. Place peppercorns, cloves, bay leaf, cayenne pepper, mustard seeds, thyme, and coriander in a cheesecloth square and tie with cotton string or thread.
2. Bring 4 cups of water to a boil. Add spice bundle, onion, celery, lemon slices, garlic, and vinegar. Lower heat and simmer for 15 minutes.
3. Add shrimp and cook 3 minutes or until shrimp are pink. Drain shrimp and refrigerate for 2 hours.
4. Combine lemon juice, olive oil, and hot pepper sauce. Toss with shrimp. Serve with wooden or plastic party picks.

Calories Per Serving: 67
Fat: 1 g
Cholesterol: 85 mg
Protein: 12 g

Carbohydrates: 3 g
Dietary Fiber: 0 g
Sodium: 400 mg

Parsley-Garlic Baked Shrimp

YIELD: 15 servings (2 each) • *PREPARATION TIME: 10 minutes plus 4 hours refrigeration time* • *COOKING TIME: 10 minutes*

Fresh shrimp are marinated in garlic, oil, and parsley before being baked.

3 tablespoons light-flavored olive oil
1 clove garlic, minced
1 pound medium shrimp, shelled and deveined

1 tablespoon minced fresh parsley

1. Place oil, garlic, and shrimp in a shallow baking dish. Toss to coat the shrimp with the oil and garlic, and sprinkle with parsley.
2. Cover and refrigerate for 4 hours.
3. Preheat oven to 375 degrees. Bake shrimp, uncovered, for 10 minutes or until shrimp turn pink.
4. Serve hot with wooden or plastic party picks.

Calories Per Serving: 40
Fat: 1 g
Cholesterol: 46 mg
Protein: 6 g

Carbohydrates: 0 g
Dietary Fiber: 0 g
Sodium: 45 mg

Jalapeño Shrimp

YIELD: 7 servings (2 each) • *PREPARATION TIME: 15 minutes* • *COOKING TIME: 5 minutes*

Shrimp are sautéed in olive oil, garlic, and jalapeño pepper.

1½ tablespoons light-flavored olive oil
1 clove garlic, minced
½ jalapeño pepper, seeded and thinly sliced

½ pound medium shrimp, shelled and deveined
½ teaspoon black pepper
3 tablespoons water

1. Heat oil in a skillet over medium heat. Sauté garlic and jalapeño for 1 minute.
2. Add shrimp, black pepper, and water. Stir.
3. Cook for 5 minutes or until the shrimp turn a vivid pink.
4. Remove from heat and serve with wooden or plastic party picks.

Calories Per Serving: 53 Carbohydrates: 0 g
Fat: 3 g Dietary Fiber: 0 g
Cholesterol: 48 mg Sodium: 256 mg
Protein: 7 g

❧ *Garlic Shrimp* ❧

YIELD: 24 servings (2 each) • *PREPARATION TIME: 15 minutes plus overnight refrigeration time* • *COOKING TIME: 10 minutes*

Large shrimp are sautéed with onion and garlic and marinated.

½ cup light-flavored olive oil *½ cup white wine vinegar*
3 cloves garlic, minced *½ teaspoon black pepper*
2 onions, minced *1 teaspoon dry mustard*
2 pounds shrimp, cooked, peeled, and
  deveined

1. Heat ¼ cup of the oil in skillet over medium heat. Add garlic and onions. Sauté lightly.
2. Add shrimp and sauté for 5 minutes.
3. Combine remaining ¼ cup oil, vinegar, pepper, and dry mustard in a glass bowl.
4. Add shrimp and onion mixture to bowl, and toss. Chill overnight. Serve in the marinade with wooden or plastic party picks.

Calories Per Serving: 65 Carbohydrates: 1 g
Fat: 3 g Dietary Fiber: 0 g
Cholesterol: 57 g Sodium: 264 mg
Protein: 8 g

❧ *Broiled Shrimp with Barbecue Sauce* ❧

YIELD: 24 servings (1 skewer each) • *PREPARATION TIME: 20 minutes plus*
4 hours refrigeration time • *COOKING TIME: 8 minutes*

Fresh shrimp are marinated in a zesty tomato sauce and then broiled.

8-ounce can low-sodium tomato sauce
½ cup molasses
1 teaspoon dry mustard
¼ teaspoon black pepper
Dash of hot pepper sauce

¼ cup canola oil
⅛ teaspoon dried thyme
2 pounds medium shrimp, shelled and
  deveined

1. Combine tomato sauce, molasses, mustard, pepper, hot pepper sauce, oil, and thyme and mix until well blended.
2. Add shrimp and toss to coat with marinade. Cover and refrigerate for 4 hours. Soak 24 wooden skewers in water for 30 minutes.
3. Preheat broiler. Reserving marinade, remove shrimp from marinade and thread each skewer with 2 shrimp. Place in a shallow baking pan and broil, basting frequently with marinade and turning once, until shrimp are pink, about 4 minutes on each side.

Calories Per Serving: 81
Fat: 3 g
Cholesterol: 57 mg
Protein: 8 g

Carbohydrates: 5 g
Dietary Fiber: 0 g
Sodium: 60 mg

❧ *Pineapple Shrimp* ❧

YIELD: 24 servings (1 skewer each) • *PREPARATION TIME: 15 minutes plus*
2 hours marinating time • *COOKING TIME: 8 minutes*

These Hawaiian-inspired shrimp are marinated in a sauce that combines pineapple juice, soy sauce, honey, and ginger.

2 pounds medium shrimp, shelled and deveined	3 tablespoons honey
1¼ cups pineapple juice	1 tablespoon light-flavored olive oil
⅓ cup light soy sauce	½ teaspoon ground ginger
	1½ tablespoons cornstarch

1. Place shrimp in a glass bowl.
2. Combine 1 cup of the pineapple juice, soy sauce, honey, olive oil, and ginger in a saucepan. Bring to a boil.
3. Dissolve cornstarch into remaining ¼ cup pineapple juice. Stir into boiling sauce. Remove from heat and allow to cool to room temperature.
4. Pour pineapple sauce over shrimp. Place in refrigerator and marinate for 2 hours. Soak 24 wooden skewers in water for 30 minutes.
5. Place 2 shrimp on each skewer and broil for 8 minutes, turning to brown evenly.

Calories Per Serving: 56	Carbohydrates: 5 g
Fat: 1 g	Dietary Fiber: 0 g
Cholesterol: 57 mg	Sodium: 380 mg
Protein: 8 g	

Steamed Shrimp
❧ with Pineapple-Orange Salsa ❧

YIELD: *18 servings (2 each)* • PREPARATION TIME: *25 minutes plus*
2 hours refrigeration time

Dip steamed shrimp in this delicious salsa made with pineapple, oranges, jalapeño pepper, scallions, cilantro, and lime peel.

1 cup canned, water-packed pineapple chunks, drained and chopped	2 tablespoons scallions, finely chopped
2 medium oranges, peeled and chopped	½ teaspoon dried cilantro
1 jalapeño pepper, seeded and finely chopped	1 teaspoon grated lime peel
	36 medium shrimp, cooked, shelled, and deveined

1. Combine pineapple, oranges, jalapeño pepper, scallions, cilantro, and lime peel in a bowl.

2. Cover and chill about 2 hours.
3. Serve salsa in a bowl on a platter surrounded by shrimp. Provide wooden and plastic party picks.

Calories Per Serving: 39	Carbohydrates: 3 g
Fat: 0 g	Dietary Fiber: 1 g
Cholesterol: 3 mg	Sodium: 61 mg
Protein: 5 g	

❧ *Tarragon Shrimp* ✿

YIELD: 24 servings (1 skewer each) ▪ *PREPARATION TIME: 10 minutes plus overnight refrigeration time* ▪ *COOKING TIME: 5 minutes*

Shrimp are marinated in tarragon, bay leaf, dill, cider vinegar, and olive oil, and then broiled.

2 pounds medium shrimp, shelled and deveined
1 cup cider vinegar
1 bay leaf, crumbled
¼ teaspoon black pepper

1 tablespoon dried dill
1 tablespoon dried tarragon
¼ cup light-flavored olive oil plus more for basting

1. Place shrimp in a glass bowl.
2. Combine cider vinegar, bay leaf, black pepper, dill, tarragon, and oil. Pour over shrimp.
3. Place in refrigerator and marinate overnight. Soak 24 wooden skewers in water for 30 minutes.
4. Drain shrimp. Place 2 shrimp on each skewer and brush with olive oil.
5. Broil for 5 minutes, turning to brown evenly, and brushing with more olive oil.

Calories Per Serving: 53	Carbohydrates: 1 g
Fat: 2 g	Dietary Fiber: 0 g
Cholesterol: 57 mg	Sodium: 264 mg
Protein: 8 g	

❧ Mini–Ginger Shrimp ❧

YIELD: 12 servings (1 skewer each) • *PREPARATION TIME: 10 minutes plus 3 hours refrigeration time* • *COOKING TIME: 6 minutes*

Shrimp are marinated in an oriental ginger sauce, broiled, and served on skewers.

1 pound medium shrimp, shelled and deveined
2 tablespoons light soy sauce
2 tablespoons rice vinegar
2 tablespoons light sesame oil

1 tablespoon brown sugar, firmly packed
1 tablespoon finely chopped gingerroot
3 scallions, finely chopped

1. Place shrimp in a glass bowl.
2. Combine soy sauce, rice vinegar, sesame oil, brown sugar, gingerroot, and scallions and pour over shrimp. Place in refrigerator and marinate for 3 hours. Soak 12 wooden skewers in water for 30 minutes.
3. Reserving marinade, place 2 shrimp on each skewer and broil for 5 or 6 minutes, turning to brown evenly and basting with marinade.

Calories Per Serving: 58
Fat: 2 g
Cholesterol: 57 mg
Protein: 8 g

Carbohydrates: 2 g
Dietary Fiber: 0 g
Sodium: 352 mg

❧ Shrimp Delights ❧

YIELD: 12 servings (2 each) • *PREPARATION TIME: 30 minutes* • *COOKING TIME: 12 minutes*

Shrimp, ginger, water chestnuts, scallions, and parsley are blended together, formed into balls, and steamed. Serve with hot mustard.

1 pound medium shrimp, shelled and
   deveined
1 tablespoon grated fresh gingerroot
½ cup canned sliced water chestnuts
2 tablespoons cornstarch

1 tablespoon light soy sauce
1 teaspoon canola or light sesame oil
2 tablespoons chopped scallions
¼ cup chopped fresh parsley or cilantro
1 egg white

1. Combine shrimp, gingerroot, water chestnuts, cornstarch, soy sauce, oil, scallions, parsley, and egg white in a blender or food processor and process until smooth.
2. Form mixture into 1½-inch balls.
3. Lightly oil a heat-proof plate; place balls on prepared plate.
4. Place plate in the top of a steamer over 2 cups of boiling water, cover, and steam for 12 minutes or until firm. Serve with wooden or plastic party picks.

Calories Per Serving: 56
Fat: 1 g
Cholesterol: 58 mg
Protein: 8 g

Carbohydrates: 3 g
Dietary Fiber: 0 g
Sodium: 123 mg

 Shrimp with Dijon Marmalade Dip

YIELD: *18 servings (2 each)* • PREPARATION TIME: *15 minutes*

Steamed shrimp are dunked in a multiflavored dip.

1 cup all-fruit orange marmalade
6 tablespoons prepared horseradish
6 teaspoons Dijon mustard
4 teaspoons lime juice
4 teaspoons dry sherry

¼ teaspoon white pepper
2 teaspoons ground paprika
1½ pounds medium shrimp, cooked,
   shelled, and deveined

1. Place marmalade, horseradish, mustard, lime juice, sherry, pepper, and paprika in a blender or food processor and process for 5 to 7 seconds.
2. Place in a bowl and serve on a platter surrounded by cooked shrimp. Provide wooden or plastic party picks.

Calories Per Serving: 80

Fat: 0 g

Cholesterol: 57 mg

Protein: 8 g

Carbohydrates: 12 g

Dietary Fiber: 0 g

Sodium: 340 mg

DIPS AND SPREADS

VEGETABLE AND FRUIT DIPS

Asparagus Dip • Artichoke Dip • Avocado–Green Pepper Dip •
Beet–Sour Cream Dip • Carrot Dip • Cucumber Dip • Raisin-
Curry Dip • Ricotta Caponata Spread • Baba Ghanoush •
White Wine–Eggplant Caviar • Eggplant-Caper Dip • Harvest
Pumpkin Dip • Spinach-Feta Dip • Empanada Dip • Raw
Zucchini–Caper Dip • Steamed Zucchini Dip • Zucchini-
Cucumber Dip • Tofu Dip • Watercress Dip • Winter
Squash–Sage Dip • Peter Rabbit Dip • Mixed Vegetable–Tomato
Dip • Vegetable Relish • Vegetable-Cheese Ball • Chili-Cheese
Dip • Chunky Guacamole with Mild Green Chile Peppers •
Tomato–Red Onion Dip • Red and Green Onion Dip •
Coriander-Corn Guacamole • Madras Dip • Creamy Fruit-
Yogurt Dip • Pineapple Dip • Plum Dip • Honey-Nut Dip •
Cumin-Curry Dip • Hummus Dip • Chickpea Dip • Kidney
Bean Dip • Broiled Red Pepper–Pinto Dip • Roasted Pepper Dip
• Quick Black Bean Salsa Dip • Black Bean Salsa • Black-Eyed
Pea Dip • Cannellini Bean Dip • Northern Bean and Garlic Dip
• Corn and Bean Salsa • Feta–Ripe Olive Spread • Tomato-
Orange-Jalapeño Dip • Orange-Chocolate Dip

SEAFOOD, POULTRY, EGG, AND CHEESE DIPS

Hot-and-Pungent Crab Dip • Spiced Crabmeat Spread • Tuna-Pepper Dip • Smoked Fish Spread • Smoked Oyster Spread • Crab Dip • Cucumber-Salmon Dip • Lemon–Dijon–Sour Cream Dip with Salmon • Garlic-Dill-Salmon Spread • Salmon Pâté • Smoked Salmon Spread • Salmon Mousse • Curried Shrimp and Chutney Spread • Spinach-Shrimp Dip • Shrimp-Avocado Spread • Clam Spread • Clam-Eggplant Spread • Sardine Spread • Tuna Spread • Turkey Spread • Chicken-Ginger Spread • Almond-Chutney-Chicken Dip • Horseradish-Egg Dip • Scallion-Cheese Dip • Hungarian Cheese Dip • Horseradish-Cheese Dip • Pimento-Cheese Dip • Blue Cheese–Yogurt Dip • Ricotta–Roast Garlic Spread • Salsa-Yogurt Dip

ABOUT DIPS

⚏

Dips can be made ahead and refrigerated in tightly covered, nonaluminum containers. They're ready to be served when the first guests arrive and they will last throughout the party with little more attention than the time it takes to replace an empty bowl with a full one.

The dips in this chapter cover a tremendous range of flavors and textures. Serve them with:

- Bread slices or chunks, including pita bread, French bread, party rye, nonfat melba toast, and whole-grain toast.
- Nonfat breadsticks, crackers, potato chips, corn chips, and pretzels.
- Fresh crisp vegetable sticks, slices, chunks, or florets, and whole baby vegetables served raw. Wash vegetables well, dry them, and chill until serving in damp paper towels inside sealed plastic bags. Good raw vegetable choices include: red, yellow, and green bell peppers; chili peppers; turnips; celery stalks; jicama rounds and sticks; cucumbers; cauliflower and broccoli florets; red or white radishes, whole or cut into sticks or rounds; cherry tomatoes; carrot sticks; romaine or spinach leaves; zucchini and yellow summer squash rounds, sticks, and spears; fennel sticks; scallions; sweet and Vidalia onion rings or strips; canned water chestnuts; snow peas; sugar snap peas; mushroom caps or halves; green beans, pole beans, or wax beans, whole or cut into 3-inch lengths; beets; kohlrabi rounds or sticks; and Belgian endive leaves.
- Blanched vegetables. To blanch, add vegetables to a large pot of boiling water for 20 seconds. Then plunge them into ice water to cool, drain them, and pat them dry. Try blanching: asparagus; green, pole, or wax beans, whole or cut into 3-inch lengths; broccoli florets; brussels sprouts; carrot sticks; cauliflower florets; scallions; kohlrabi rounds or sticks; yellow onion rings or strips; rutabaga sticks; snow peas; and sugar snap peas.

- Marinated or pickled vegetables.
- Fresh fruits such as apple and pear chunks or slices dipped in lemon juice mixed with water; segments of orange, grapefruit, or tangerine; chunks or wedges of pineapple, bananas, cantaloupes, honeydews, nectarines, peaches, mangoes, and papayas; strawberries and large grapes.
- Cooked cubes of chicken and seafood.

Dips can be served in hollowed-out vegetables, unusual glass bowls, soup bowls, or any other imaginative container. The best dip containers are shallow, to accommodate easy dipping. Place your container of dip on a large plate, tray, or cutting board and surround with dippers of your choice.

▪ VEGETABLE AND FRUIT DIPS ▪

✺ *Asparagus Dip* ✺

YIELD: *20 servings (1 tablespoon each)* • PREPARATION TIME: *15 minutes*

Asparagus is pureed with ricotta cheese, vegetables, and spices.

10 ounces steamed fresh asparagus or canned asparagus, drained and chopped
1 cup chopped tomato
¼ cup chopped onion

1 tablespoon lemon juice
2 tablespoons nonfat or reduced-fat ricotta cheese
1 clove garlic, minced

1. Place asparagus, tomato, onion, lemon juice, ricotta cheese, and garlic in a blender or food processor and puree until smooth.

Calories Per Serving: 8
Fat: 0 g
Cholesterol: 0 mg
Protein: 1 g

Carbohydrates: 1 g
Dietary Fiber: 0 g
Sodium: 5 mg

❦ *Artichoke Dip* ❦

YIELD: 32 servings (1 tablespoon each) • *PREPARATION TIME: 20 minutes plus*
45 minutes refrigeration time

Artichoke hearts are combined with herbs, lemon juice, and red pepper.
Serve with nonfat garlic-flavored breadsticks.

*2 cups canned, water-packed artichoke
    hearts, drained and chopped*
3 tablespoons chopped red bell pepper
*4 teaspoons nonfat or reduced-fat may-
    onnaise*
4 teaspoons water

*1½ tablespoons grated nonfat or re-
    duced-fat Parmesan cheese*
1 tablespoon chopped fresh parsley
4 teaspoons lemon juice
1 clove garlic, chopped
½ teaspoon dried basil leaves

1. Place artichokes, red bell pepper, mayonnaise, water, Parmesan cheese,
   parsley, lemon juice, garlic, and basil in a blender or food processor and
   process until smooth. Refrigerate for 45 minutes.

Calories Per Serving: 7
Fat: 0 g
Cholesterol: 0 mg
Protein: 0 g

Carbohydrates: 2 g
Dietary Fiber: 1 g
Sodium: 12 mg

❦ *Avocado–Green Pepper Dip* ❦

YIELD: 48 servings (1 tablespoon each) • *PREPARATION TIME: 20 minutes plus*
2 hours refrigeration time

Avocado and green bell pepper are blended with scallions, lemon juice,
yogurt, tarragon, and pepper in this dip. Serve with nonfat corn chips.

3 scallions, chopped
1 green bell pepper, seeded and
 chopped
2 large ripe avocados, peeled, pitted,
 and quartered
1½ tablespoons lemon juice

½ cup nonfat or reduced-fat plain
 yogurt
½ cup nonfat or reduced-fat mayonnaise
1 teaspoon dried tarragon
¼ teaspoon black pepper

1. Place scallions and green bell pepper in a blender or food processor and mince.
2. Add avocados, lemon juice, yogurt, mayonnaise, tarragon, and black pepper. Process until smooth.
3. Transfer to a serving bowl and cover. Place in refrigerator for 2 hours.

Calories Per Serving: 17
Fat: 1 g
Cholesterol: 0 mg
Protein: 0 g

Carbohydrates: 1 g
Dietary Fiber: 0 g
Sodium: 20 mg

Beet–Sour Cream Dip

YIELD: 32 servings (1 tablespoon each) • PREPARATION TIME: 10 minutes plus
2 hours refrigeration time

Canned beets, red onions, dill, and sour cream are combined in this dip, which makes a colorful and delicious accompaniment for a platter of raw vegetables.

17 ounces canned beets
2 medium red onions, chopped

1 cup nonfat or reduced-fat sour cream
2½ teaspoons dried dill

1. Place beets and red onions in a blender or food processor and process until smooth.
2. Stir in sour cream and dill.
3. Chill for 2 hours.

Calories Per Serving: 18

Carbohydrates: 4 g

Fat: 0 g

Dietary Fiber: 0 g

Cholesterol: 3 mg

Sodium: 49 mg

Protein: 1 g

✎ *Carrot Dip* ✐

YIELD: 36 servings (1 tablespoon each) • *PREPARATION TIME: 15 minutes* •
COOKING TIME: 6 minutes

Serve this attractive dip with red and green pepper strips. It can be made a
day or two ahead of serving.

1½ pounds carrots, cut in large chunks	*¼ teaspoon black pepper*
½ teaspoon ground paprika	*3 tablespoons red wine vinegar*
2 cloves garlic, chopped	*3 tablespoons light-flavored olive oil*
½ teaspoon ground ginger	*10 pitted black olives*
1 tablespoon ground cumin	*¼ cup chopped fresh parsley*

1. Peel carrots and boil until very soft.
2. Drain and place in a blender or food processor with paprika, garlic, ginger, cumin, pepper, vinegar, oil, olives, and parsley. Process until smooth.

Calories Per Serving: 24

Carbohydrates: 2 g

Fat: 2 g

Dietary Fiber: 0 g

Cholesterol: 0 mg

Sodium: 13 mg

Protein: 0 g

✎ *Cucumber Dip* ✐

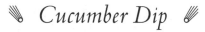

YIELD: 48 servings (1 tablespoon each) • *PREPARATION TIME: 25 minutes plus*
6 hours yogurt-straining time

This Greek-style dip tastes great with sesame breadstick dippers.

1 quart nonfat or reduced-fat plain
  yogurt
2 medium cucumbers, peeled, seeded,
  and shredded

1 teaspoon salt
1 clove garlic, minced
¼ teaspoon black pepper

1. Place 2 cups of the yogurt in a yogurt strainer, or in a cheesecloth-lined colander set over a bowl. Cover and refrigerate for 6 hours. Discard the drained liquid.
2. Place the cucumbers in a colander. Sprinkle with salt and let sit for 15 minutes. Rinse well.
3. Combine strained and unstrained yogurt with cucumbers, garlic, and pepper.

Calories Per Serving: 12
Fat: 0 g
Cholesterol: 0 mg
Protein: 1 g

Carbohydrates: 2 g
Dietary Fiber: 0 g
Sodium: 31 mg

❦ Raisin-Curry Dip ❦

YIELD: 20 servings (1 tablespoon each) • PREPARATION TIME: 25 minutes

Serve this dip with blanched green beans, zucchini sticks, or cooked artichokes.

¼ cup seedless raisins
1 cup nonfat or reduced-fat cottage
  cheese
2 tablespoons cider vinegar

½ small onion, chopped
1 teaspoon chili powder
½ teaspoon curry powder
⅛ teaspoon black pepper

1. Place raisins in a small bowl and cover with hot tap water. Let stand 10 minutes.
2. Place cottage cheese, vinegar, onion, chili powder, curry powder, and pepper in a blender or food processor and process until smooth.
3. Stir in drained raisins. If the dip seems too thick, stir in a teaspoon of water or skim milk at a time until it reaches desired consistency.

Calories Per Serving: 15
Fat: 0 g
Cholesterol: 4 mg
Protein: 1 g

Carbohydrates: 3 g
Dietary Fiber: 0 g
Sodium: 16 mg

Ricotta Caponata Spread

YIELD: 48 servings (1 tablespoon each) • *PREPARATION TIME: 15 minutes* • *COOKING TIME: 10 minutes*

Serve this ricotta-vegetable dip warm with chunks of pumpernickel bread.

¼ cup light-flavored olive oil
1 small eggplant, peeled and diced
2 medium tomatoes, diced
1 small onion, diced
⅛ teaspoon black pepper
2 tablespoons red wine vinegar

1 clove garlic, crushed
1 teaspoon Dijon mustard
¼ cup chopped black olives
1 cup nonfat or reduced-fat ricotta
   cheese

1. Heat the olive oil in a skillet over medium heat. Sauté eggplant for 4 minutes.
2. Add tomatoes, onion, pepper, vinegar, and garlic. Simmer for 5 minutes.
3. Stir in mustard, olives, and ricotta cheese.

Calories Per Serving: 19
Fat: 2 g
Cholesterol: 0 mg
Protein: 1 g

Carbohydrates: 1 g
Dietary Fiber: 0 g
Sodium: 35 mg

Baba Ghanoush

YIELD: 32 servings (1 tablespoon each) • *PREPARATION TIME: 20 minutes* • *COOKING TIME: 50 minutes*

Serve this classic Middle Eastern puree with nonfat sesame crackers.

1 large eggplant
½ cup pine nuts
2 cloves garlic, crushed
¼ cup tahini (sesame seed paste)

¼ cup lemon juice
¼ teaspoon black pepper
¼ cup minced fresh parsley

1. Preheat oven to 400 degrees. Prick the eggplant in several places, place on foil-lined baking sheet, and bake for 40 minutes. Remove eggplant to cool.
2. Reduce oven to 350 degrees. Spread pine nuts on a baking sheet and toast for 4 to 6 minutes.
3. When eggplant is cool, remove pulp and place in a blender or food processor. Process for 2 minutes.
4. Add the garlic, tahini, lemon juice, and black pepper. Process until well blended.
5. Refrigerate until ready to serve. Top dip with toasted nuts and parsley before serving.

Calories Per Serving: 29
Fat: 2 g
Cholesterol: 0 mg
Protein: 1 g

Carbohydrates: 2 g
Dietary Fiber: 0 g
Sodium: 11 mg

❧ White Wine–Eggplant Caviar ❧

YIELD: 32 servings (1 tablespoon each) • *PREPARATION TIME: 25 minutes plus overnight refrigeration time* • *COOKING TIME: 40 minutes*

Garlic and wine provide a wonderful flavor for this mixture of eggplant, onion, bell peppers, and tomatoes. Serve with party-size slices of rye bread.

1 large eggplant
⅓ cup light-flavored olive oil
1 large onion, chopped
1 green bell pepper, chopped
1 large clove garlic, minced

2 fresh or canned, low-sodium tomatoes, peeled and chopped
¼ teaspoon black pepper
¼ cup dry white wine

1. Preheat oven to 400 degrees. Prick eggplant in several places and place on foil-lined baking sheet. Bake for 40 minutes or until soft. Cool, peel, and chop.
2. Heat olive oil in a large skillet over medium heat. Sauté onion and pepper until tender.
3. Add garlic. Sauté for 3 minutes.
4. Add chopped eggplant, tomatoes, black pepper, and wine, and cook until thick.
5. Remove from heat, cover, and refrigerate overnight.

Calories Per Serving: 30
Fat: 2 g
Cholesterol: 0 mg
Protein: 0 g

Carbohydrates: 2 g
Dietary Fiber: 0 g
Sodium: 2 mg

❧ *Eggplant-Caper Dip* ❧

YIELD: 60 servings (1 tablespoon each) • *PREPARATION TIME: 25 minutes plus 24 hours refrigeration time* • *COOKING TIME: 50 minutes*

Capers are the special ingredient in this combination of eggplant, onion, celery, and tomato. Serve with nonfat onion crackers.

¼ cup light-flavored olive oil
1 large eggplant, peeled and cut into
  ¾-inch cubes
1 cup chopped onion
1 cup diced celery

1¼ cups low-sodium tomato puree
1 tablespoon capers, drained
¼ cup cider vinegar
2 tablespoons sugar
¼ teaspoon black pepper

1. Heat olive oil in skillet over medium heat. Add eggplant, and sauté until soft and lightly browned.
2. Remove eggplant with a slotted spoon.
3. Sauté onion and celery until tender.
4. Add tomato puree and simmer, covered, for 15 minutes.
5. Add eggplant, capers, vinegar, sugar, and pepper to skillet. Cover and simmer 20 minutes.
6. Refrigerate for 24 hours before serving.

Calories Per Serving: 8
Fat: 0 g
Cholesterol: 0 mg
Protein: 0 g

Carbohydrates: 2 g
Dietary Fiber: 0 g
Sodium: 2 mg

✎ *Harvest Pumpkin Dip* ✎

YIELD: 28 servings (1 tablespoon each) • *PREPARATION TIME: 15 minutes*

Mashed pumpkin is combined with yogurt, mayonnaise, cilantro, and cumin.
Serve with nonfat tortilla chips.

*1 cup mashed, canned, or fresh-cooked
  pumpkin
½ cup nonfat or reduced-fat plain
  yogurt
¼ cup nonfat or reduced-fat mayonnaise*

*1 tablespoon chopped fresh cilantro or
  parsley
¼ teaspoon ground cumin
⅛ teaspoon ground cayenne pepper*

1. Place pumpkin, yogurt, mayonnaise, cilantro, cumin, and cayenne in
   blender or food processor and process until well combined.

Calories Per Serving: 25
Fat: 0 g
Cholesterol: 3 mg
Protein: 1 g

Carbohydrates: 5 g
Dietary Fiber: 1 g
Sodium: 146 mg

✎ *Spinach-Feta Dip* ✎

YIELD: 32 servings (1 tablespoon each) • *PREPARATION TIME: 20 minutes plus
1½ hours refrigeration time* • *COOKING TIME: 10 minutes*

Feta is a Greek cheese with a rich, tangy flavor. Here a small amount of feta
gives a special taste to a classic spinach dip.

¼ cup light-flavored olive oil
¾ cup finely chopped onion
1 clove garlic, minced
10 ounces frozen chopped spinach,
    cooked, drained, pressed in a colan-
    der to remove excess moisture

1 teaspoon dried dill
⅓ cup crumbled or grated feta cheese
2 tablespoons nonfat or reduced-fat
    plain yogurt
¼ teaspoon black pepper

1. Heat olive oil in a skillet over medium heat. Sauté onions and garlic until tender.
2. Add spinach and dill to skillet. Stir and heat for 2 minutes.
3. Transfer spinach mixture to a bowl with a slotted spoon, pressing out any excess moisture.
4. Stir feta cheese, yogurt, and pepper into spinach mixture. Chill for 1½ hours.

Calories Per Serving: 27
Fat: 2 g
Cholesterol: 2 mg
Protein: 1 g

Carbohydrates: 1 g
Dietary Fiber: 0 g
Sodium: 38 mg

❧ *Empanada Dip* ❧

YIELD: 40 servings (1 tablespoon each) • *PREPARATION TIME: 15 minutes*

Chile pepper, ground turkey, onion, tomatoes, raisins, and garlic are combined in this flavorful dip. Serve with nonfat tortilla chips.

¼ cup low-sodium, nonfat or reduced-
    fat chicken broth
½ pound low-fat ground turkey breast
1 small onion, chopped
1 clove garlic, minced

2 tomatoes, chopped
6 ounces low-sodium tomato paste
1 jalapeño pepper, seeded and finely
    chopped
¼ cup chopped raisins

1. In a medium skillet, heat chicken broth, then cook ground turkey and onion until turkey is browned. Drain.
2. Stir in garlic, tomatoes, tomato paste, jalapeño pepper, and raisins. Cook over low heat for about 10 minutes.

Calories Per Serving: 17
Fat: 0 g
Cholesterol: 5 mg
Protein: 2 g

Carbohydrates: 3 g
Dietary Fiber: 0 g
Sodium: 20 mg

❦ *Raw Zucchini–Caper Dip* ❦

YIELD: 60 servings (1 tablespoon each) • *PREPARATION TIME: 20 minutes*

Zucchini is combined with Dijon mustard, parsley, tarragon, and capers. Serve with corn chips, toasted pita wedges, or French bread.

1½ pounds zucchini, grated
1 tablespoon Dijon mustard
1 tablespoon chopped fresh parsley

1 tablespoon capers, drained and
chopped
¼ teaspoon dried tarragon

1. Squeeze the zucchini between paper towels to remove some of the moisture.
2. Combine zucchini, mustard, parsley, capers, and tarragon.

Calories Per Serving: 5
Fat: 0 g
Cholesterol: 0 mg
Protein: 0 g

Carbohydrates: 1 g
Dietary Fiber: 0 g
Sodium: 24 mg

❦ *Steamed Zucchini Dip* ❦

YIELD: 32 servings (1 tablespoon each) • *PREPARATION TIME: 20 minutes plus*
1 hour refrigeration time • *COOKING TIME: 5 minutes*

Steamed zucchini is mixed with onion, garlic, paprika, cream cheese, basil, Worcestershire sauce, and lemon juice.

2 cups diced zucchini
2 tablespoons chopped onion
1 clove garlic, minced
⅛ teaspoon ground paprika
⅛ teaspoon black pepper

½ teaspoon dried basil
3 ounces nonfat or reduced-fat cream cheese, softened
1 teaspoon Worcestershire sauce
2 tablespoons lemon juice

1. Place zucchini in a steamer basket over boiling water and steam for 5 minutes. Cool.
2. Combine zucchini, onion, garlic, paprika, pepper, basil, cream cheese, Worcestershire sauce, and lemon juice.
3. Chill for 1 hour before serving.

Calories Per Serving: 5
Fat: 0 g
Cholesterol: 0 mg
Protein: 1 g

Carbohydrates: 1 g
Dietary Fiber: 0 g
Sodium: 21 mg

⚘ *Zucchini-Cucumber Dip* ⚘

YIELD: *48 servings (1 tablespoon each)* • PREPARATION TIME: *20 minutes plus 2 hours refrigeration time*

This dip is made with grated zucchini, cucumber, caraway seeds, and yogurt.

1 cup nonfat or reduced-fat plain yogurt
¼ teaspoon black pepper
1 teaspoon caraway seeds

1 medium cucumber, peeled, seeded, and grated
2 medium zucchini, grated

1. Combine yogurt, pepper, caraway seeds, cucumber, and zucchini.
2. Cover and chill for 2 hours.

Calories Per Serving: 5
Fat: 0 g
Cholesterol: 0 mg
Protein: 0 g

Carbohydrates: 1 g
Dietary Fiber: 0 g
Sodium: 4 mg

❧ *Tofu Dip* ❧

YIELD: 32 servings (1 tablespoon each) • *PREPARATION TIME: 20 minutes plus 1 hour refrigeration time*

Tofu is combined with garlic, ginger, soy sauce, sesame oil, rice vinegar, water chestnuts, and scallions.

2 cloves garlic, minced
1 tablespoon minced fresh gingerroot
¼ cup light soy sauce
2 tablespoons light sesame or canola oil
1 tablespoon rice vinegar

10 ounces firm tofu
6 ounces canned water chestnuts, finely chopped
3 tablespoons finely chopped scallions

1. Place garlic, gingerroot, soy sauce, oil, rice vinegar, and tofu in a blender or food processor and process until smooth.
2. Stir in water chestnuts and scallions.
3. Cover and chill for 1 hour.

Calories Per Serving: 17
Fat: 1 g
Cholesterol: 0 mg
Protein: 1 g

Carbohydrates: 1 g
Dietary Fiber: 0 g
Sodium: 73 mg

❧ *Watercress Dip* ❧

YIELD: 20 servings (1 tablespoon each) • *PREPARATION TIME: 15 minutes plus overnight refrigeration time*

This zesty dip is made with watercress, cream cheese, scallions, and yogurt. Serve it with crudités and nonfat crackers.

6 ounces nonfat or reduced-fat cream cheese, softened
1 bunch watercress, stemmed, washed, dried, and finely chopped

¼ cup finely chopped scallions
2 tablespoons nonfat or reduced-fat plain yogurt

1. Combine cream cheese, watercress, scallions, and yogurt with a large spoon until well blended.
2. Cover and place in refrigerator overnight.

Calories Per Serving: 10
Fat: 0 g
Cholesterol: 2 mg
Protein: 2 g

Carbohydrates: 1 g
Dietary Fiber: 0 g
Sodium: 61 mg

Winter Squash–Sage Dip

YIELD: 64 servings (1 tablespoon each) ∙ *PREPARATION TIME: 25 minutes* ∙
COOKING TIME: 25 minutes

Winter squash is simmered with onion, carrot, celery, tomatoes, parsley, garlic, and sage and served as a dip for nonfat corn chips or toasted pita chunks.

2 tablespoons light-flavored olive or canola oil
1½ pounds winter squash such as banana, butternut, or hubbard, peeled and cut into ½-inch cubes
1 onion, chopped
1 carrot, scrubbed and shredded

2 celery stalks, finely chopped
2 tomatoes, chopped
2 tablespoons chopped fresh parsley
2 cloves garlic, minced
1 tablespoon red wine vinegar
¼ teaspoon black pepper
½ teaspoon dried sage

1. Heat olive oil in a skillet over medium heat. Sauté squash, onion, and carrot for 3 minutes.
2. Add celery, tomatoes, parsley, garlic, vinegar, pepper, and sage. Cover and simmer for 15 minutes. Serve warm.

Calories Per Serving: 10
Fat: 0 g
Cholesterol: 0 mg
Protein: 0 g

Carbohydrates: 2 g
Dietary Fiber: 0 g
Sodium: 2 mg

❦ *Peter Rabbit Dip* ❦

YIELD: 60 servings (1 tablespoon each) • *PREPARATION TIME: 25 minutes*

This chunky dip includes radishes, green pepper, carrots, celery, and scallions. Serve with crisp, thin breadsticks for dipping.

1 cup nonfat or reduced-fat cream cheese, softened
1 cup nonfat or reduced-fat sour cream
1 cup chopped radishes
½ cup chopped carrots

½ cup chopped scallions
½ cup chopped green bell pepper
½ cup chopped celery
¼ teaspoon black pepper
Dash of hot pepper sauce

1. Combine cream cheese and sour cream.
2. Stir in radishes, carrots, scallions, green pepper, celery, black pepper, and hot pepper sauce.

Calories Per Serving: 37
Fat: 0 g
Cholesterol: 5 mg
Protein: 4 g

Carbohydrates: 5 g
Dietary Fiber: 0 g
Sodium: 121 mg

❦ *Mixed Vegetable–Tomato Dip* ❦

YIELD: 60 servings (1 tablespoon each) • *PREPARATION TIME: 20 minutes plus 1½ hours refrigeration time* • *COOKING TIME: 25 minutes*

Serve this chilled vegetable dip with nonfat multigrain melba toast rounds.

¼ cup light-flavored olive oil
2 medium onions, finely chopped
1 green bell pepper, seeded and finely chopped
1 eggplant, peeled and finely chopped

2 medium tomatoes, peeled, chopped, and drained
¼ teaspoon black pepper
1 teaspoon sugar
1 teaspoon white wine vinegar

1. Heat olive oil in a skillet over medium heat. Sauté onions for 2 or 3 minutes.
2. Add green pepper and eggplant. Sauté for 3 minutes.
3. Add tomatoes, black pepper, sugar, and vinegar. Simmer for 15 to 20 minutes.
4. Refrigerate for 1½ hours before serving.

Calories Per Serving: 21   Carbohydrates: 3 g
Fat: 1 g   Dietary Fiber: 1 g
Cholesterol: 0 mg   Sodium: 4 mg
Protein: 0 g

❧ *Vegetable Relish* ❧

YIELD: 8 servings (½ cup each) • *PREPARATION TIME: 25 minutes plus overnight standing time*

This works wonderfully as a dip for steamed shrimp or as a sauce for fresh oyster appetizers. It can be stored in the refrigerator for up to 3 days.

1 cup minced green bell pepper   *2 tablespoons mustard seeds*
½ cup minced red bell pepper   *2 tablespoons brown sugar, firmly*
4 cups minced green cabbage   *packed*
1 cup minced celery   *½ cup cider vinegar*

1. Combine the green and red bell peppers, cabbage, and celery.
2. Combine the mustard seeds, brown sugar, and vinegar in a nonaluminum saucepan and bring to a boil.
3. Pour the vinegar mixture over the vegetable mixture and stir.
4. Let the mixture stand overnight. Drain and serve.

Calories Per Serving: 40   Carbohydrates: 8 g
Fat: 1 g   Dietary Fiber: 2 g
Cholesterol: 0 mg   Sodium: 23 mg
Protein: 2 g

❧ *Vegetable-Cheese Ball* ✤

YIELD: 12 servings (2 tablespoons each) • *PREPARATION TIME: 25 minutes plus 1 hour refrigeration time*

Serve this combination of carrots, green pepper, pineapple, cream cheese, and sunflower seeds with whole-grain crackers.

¼ cup finely chopped green bell pepper
¼ cup shredded carrot
8 ounces nonfat or reduced-fat cream cheese, softened

8 ounces canned, juice-packed crushed pineapple, drained
½ cup dry-roasted sunflower seeds, unsalted

1. Combine green pepper, carrot, cream cheese, and pineapple. Cover and refrigerate for 1 hour.
2. Spread sunflower seeds out onto a sheet of wax paper. Shape mixture into a ball. Roll ball in sunflower seeds.

Calories Per Serving: 62
Fat: 3 g
Cholesterol: 3 mg
Protein: 5 g

Carbohydrates: 4 g
Dietary Fiber: 0 g
Sodium: 168 mg

❧ *Chili-Cheese Dip* ✤

YIELD: 48 servings (1 tablespoon each) • *PREPARATION TIME: 15 minutes*

Serve this fiery cheese dip with nonfat tortilla chips, corn chips, or crisp crackers. You can find the canned tomatoes with chiles in the international foods section of your supermarket.

2 cups nonfat or reduced-fat, large-curd cottage cheese
½ cup canned tomatoes flavored with green chiles

3 tablespoons seeded and chopped jalapeño peppers
1 avocado, cut in small chunks

1. Combine cottage cheese, tomatoes with chiles, jalapeño peppers, and avocado. Chill until ready to serve.

Calories Per Serving: 45
Fat: 2 g
Cholesterol: 2 mg
Protein: 3 g

Carbohydrates: 3 g
Dietary Fiber: 0 g
Sodium: 436 mg

Chunky Guacamole
with Mild Green Chile Peppers

YIELD: 32 servings (1 tablespoon each) • PREPARATION TIME: 15 minutes plus 2 hours refrigeration time

This is a chunky guacamole that is mixed with a fork instead of being blended. Serve it with seafood or vegetable dippers.

2 large ripe avocados, peeled and pitted
2 tablespoons lime juice
1 tablespoon minced onion
1 clove garlic, minced
¼ teaspoon white pepper
⅛ teaspoon ground cumin

⅛ teaspoon chili powder
1 medium tomato, chopped and drained
⅓ cup minced, drained, canned mild green chili peppers

1. Mash avocados with lime juice using a fork.
2. Stir in onion, garlic, white pepper, cumin, and chili powder.
3. Stir in tomato and chili peppers.
4. Transfer to a bowl and cover tightly with plastic wrap. Place in refrigerator for 2 hours.

Calories Per Serving: 21
Fat: 2 g
Cholesterol: 0 mg
Protein: 0 g

Carbohydrates: 1 g
Dietary Fiber: 1 g
Sodium: 2 mg

❧ *Tomato–Red Onion Dip* ❧

YIELD: 32 servings (1 tablespoon each) • *PREPARATION TIME: 20 minutes*

This dip is lower in fat than most guacamoles and is flavored with lime juice, garlic, and jalapeño pepper. If you don't plan to serve this dip as soon as you make it, to prevent discoloration stick the avocado pit into the guacamole, then cover tightly with plastic wrap and refrigerate.

1 small ripe avocado, peeled and pitted
2 tablespoons nonfat or reduced-fat
  plain yogurt
2 medium tomatoes, peeled, seeded,
  and chopped
½ cup chopped fresh parsley

½ red onion, finely chopped
4 teaspoons lime juice
1 clove garlic, minced
½ jalapeño pepper, seeded and finely
  chopped

1. Place avocado in a large bowl and mash until smooth.
2. Add yogurt, tomatoes, parsley, red onion, lime juice, garlic, and jalapeño pepper.

Calories Per Serving: 14
Fat: 1 g
Cholesterol: 0 mg
Protein: 0 g

Carbohydrates: 1 g
Dietary Fiber: 0 g
Sodium: 3 mg

❧ *Red and Green Onion Dip* ❧

YIELD: 32 servings (1 tablespoon each) • *PREPARATION TIME: 15 minutes plus
1 hour refrigeration time* • *COOKING TIME: 5 minutes*

This easy dip features cottage cheese, red onion, scallions, garlic, and chili powder. Serve with raw vegetables.

¼ cup water or 1 tablespoon canola oil
1 cup minced red onion
1 tablespoon sugar
1 tablespoon red wine vinegar
1½ cups nonfat or reduced-fat cottage cheese

¼ cup nonfat or reduced-fat mayonnaise
1 teaspoon hot pepper sauce
1 clove garlic, minced
¼ teaspoon chili powder
2 scallions, minced

1. Heat water or canola oil in a small skillet over medium heat. Add onion, reduce heat slightly, and sauté for 5 minutes.
2. Combine sugar, vinegar, and 2 tablespoons water. Add to skillet and simmer onions for 2 minutes. Spoon onions and liquid into a bowl and allow to cool.
3. Place cottage cheese, mayonnaise, hot sauce, garlic, and chili powder in a blender and process until smooth.
4. Add cottage cheese mixture and scallions to onion mixture and stir well. Refrigerate 1 hour before serving.

Calories Per Serving: 13
Fat: 0 g
Cholesterol: 4 mg
Protein: 1 g

Carbohydrates: 2 g
Dietary Fiber: 0 g
Sodium: 15 mg

❧ Coriander-Corn Guacamole ❧

YIELD: 60 servings (1 tablespoon each) • *PREPARATION TIME: 30 minutes*

Corn and jalapeños are special additions to this guacamole. Serve with nonfat corn chips.

1½ cups canned corn
3 large ripe avocados, peeled and diced
1 tablespoon dried coriander
3 cloves garlic, minced
½ cup diced tomato

6 tablespoons minced red onion
3 jalapeño peppers, seeded and minced
3 tablespoons lime juice
3 tablespoons light-flavored olive oil
¼ teaspoon black pepper

1. Combine corn, avocados, coriander, garlic, tomato, red onion, jalapeño peppers, lime juice, olive oil, and black pepper. Slightly mash the ingredients to create a chunky texture.

Calories Per Serving: 29
Fat: 2 g
Cholesterol: 0 mg
Protein: 0 g
Carbohydrates: 2 g
Dietary Fiber: 1 g
Sodium: 22 mg

Madras Dip

Yield: 16 servings (1 tablespoon each) ▪ Preparation Time: 10 minutes plus overnight refrigeration time

Serve this fiery, curry-flavored dip with chunks of pineapple, mango, and papaya.

¼ teaspoon ground cayenne pepper
1 tablespoon curry powder
¾ cup nonfat or reduced-fat sour cream
3 tablespoons nonfat or reduced-fat mayonnaise
2 cloves garlic, minced
¼ teaspoon Worcestershire sauce

1. Combine cayenne pepper, curry powder, sour cream, mayonnaise, garlic, and Worcestershire sauce in a bowl.
2. Cover and place in refrigerator overnight.

Calories Per Serving: 17
Fat: 0 g
Cholesterol: 4 mg
Protein: 1 g
Carbohydrates: 3 g
Dietary Fiber: 0 g
Sodium: 11 mg

Creamy Fruit-Yogurt Dip

Yield: 10 servings (2 tablespoons each) ▪ Preparation Time: 10 minutes plus 2 hours refrigeration time

Serve this dip with a tray of fresh fruit.

8 ounces nonfat or reduced-fat strawberry or other fruit-flavored yogurt
3 ounces nonfat or reduced-fat cream
cheese, softened

1 tablespoon powdered sugar
¼ teaspoon vanilla extract

1. Place yogurt, cream cheese, sugar, and vanilla in a blender or food processor and blend until smooth.
2. Chill for 2 hours.

Calories Per Serving: 36
Fat: 0 g
Cholesterol: 2 mg
Protein: 2 g

Carbohydrates: 6 g
Dietary Fiber: 0 g
Sodium: 74 mg

❧ *Pineapple Dip* ❧

YIELD: 48 servings (1 tablespoon each) • *PREPARATION TIME: 10 minutes plus
6 hours yogurt-draining time*

Yogurt cheese, cream cheese, and drained crushed pineapple are combined
with honey and grated fresh gingerroot. Serve with fruit dippers.

2 cups nonfat or reduced-fat plain
yogurt
1 cup nonfat or reduced-fat cream
cheese

1 cup drained, crushed pineapple
2 tablespoons honey
2 teaspoons grated fresh gingerroot

1. Place yogurt in a yogurt strainer, or in a cheesecloth-lined colander set
over a bowl. Cover and refrigerate for 6 hours. Discard the drained liquid.
2. Combine yogurt cheese, cream cheese, pineapple, honey, and gingerroot
in a blender or food processor and process until well blended.

Calories Per Serving: 14
Fat: 0 g
Cholesterol: 1 mg
Protein: 2 g

Carbohydrates: 2 g
Dietary Fiber: 0 g
Sodium: 40 mg

❧ Plum Dip ❧

YIELD: 24 servings (1 tablespoon each) • *PREPARATION TIME: 15 minutes* •
COOKING TIME: 5 minutes

Serve this tangy plum dip with skewered chicken bites.

1⅓ cups all-fruit plum jam	½ teaspoon light soy sauce
¼ cup orange juice	¼ teaspoon grated lemon peel
2 tablespoons red wine vinegar	⅛ teaspoon ground cardamom
½ teaspoon dry mustard	

1. Combine plum jam, orange juice, vinegar, dry mustard, soy sauce, lemon peel, and cardamom in a small saucepan.
2. Cook over low heat, stirring until the dip is smooth. Serve warm.

Calories Per Serving: 23	Carbohydrates: 6 g
Fat: 0 g	Dietary Fiber: 0 g
Cholesterol: 0 mg	Sodium: 19 mg
Protein: 0 g	

❧ Honey-Nut Dip ❧

YIELD: 24 servings (1 tablespoon each) • *PREPARATION TIME: 5 minutes*

Serve this honey-almond dip with a bowl of cantaloupe and honeydew melon balls skewered on party picks.

1⅓ cups nonfat or reduced-fat plain yogurt	6 tablespoons chopped toasted almonds
	5 tablespoons honey

1. Combine yogurt, almonds, and honey in a serving bowl.

Calories Per Serving: 32	Carbohydrates: 5 g
Fat: 1 g	Dietary Fiber: 0 g
Cholesterol: 0 mg	Sodium: 10 mg
Protein: 1 g	

❧ *Cumin-Curry Dip* ❧

YIELD: 32 servings (1 tablespoon each) • *PREPARATION TIME: 15 minutes plus 1 hour refrigeration time*

Serve this dip with apple slices and pear chunks.

2 cups nonfat or reduced-fat plain yogurt
2 teaspoons curry powder

1 teaspoon lemon juice
1 teaspoon ground cumin
¼ teaspoon black pepper

1. Combine yogurt, curry, lemon juice, cumin, and pepper in a small bowl. Mix well and chill for 1 hour.

Calories Per Serving: 8
Fat: 0 g
Cholesterol: 0 mg
Protein: 1 g

Carbohydrates: 1 g
Dietary Fiber: 0 g
Sodium: 10 mg

❧ *Hummus Dip* ❧

YIELD: 48 servings (1 tablespoon each) • *PREPARATION TIME: 10 minutes*

Serve this with warmed pita bread chunks and a platter of sweet pepper strips, carrot sticks, radishes, and slivered large olives.

15½ ounces canned or home-cooked chickpeas, rinsed and drained
1 clove garlic, minced
¼ cup tahini (sesame seed paste)

⅓ cup lemon juice
¼ teaspoon ground cumin
⅛ teaspoon ground cayenne pepper

1. Mash chickpeas in a large bowl.
2. Combine with garlic, tahini, lemon juice, ground cumin, and cayenne. Or for a smoother dip, place mixture in a blender or food processor and puree.

Calories Per Serving: 27
Fat: 1 g
Cholesterol: 1 mg
Protein: 1 g

Carbohydrates: 3 g
Dietary Fiber: 1 g
Sodium: 32 mg

≷ *Chickpea Dip* ≷

YIELD: 40 servings (1 tablespoon each) · *PREPARATION TIME: 15 minutes plus overnight refrigeration time*

Chickpeas are combined with red wine vinegar, olive oil, scallions, garlic, and black pepper. Serve with nonfat sesame bread sticks.

2 tablespoons red wine vinegar
¼ cup light-flavored olive oil
⅔ cup nonfat or reduced-fat, low-sodium chicken broth
¼ cup minced scallions
2 cloves garlic, minced

½ teaspoon black pepper
2 cups canned or home-cooked chickpeas, rinsed and drained
¼ cup chopped fresh parsley
1 tablespoon chopped black olives

1. Whisk together vinegar, oil, chicken broth, scallions, garlic, and black pepper.
2. Pour over chickpeas in a glass bowl and cover. Place in refrigerator overnight.
3. Place chickpea mixture in a blender or food processor and blend until smooth.
4. Transfer to a serving bowl. Garnish with parsley and olives.

Calories Per Serving: 39
Fat: 2 g
Cholesterol: 1 mg
Protein: 1 g

Carbohydrates: 3 g
Dietary Fiber: 1 g
Sodium: 49 mg

✎ *Kidney Bean Dip* ✎

YIELD: 32 servings (1 tablespoon each) ▪ *PREPARATION TIME: 15 minutes plus overnight refrigeration time*

Red kidney beans are blended with onion, garlic, oregano, olive oil, and pepper to make this tangy dip. Serve with nonfat tortilla chips.

2 tablespoons minced onion
1 clove garlic, minced
2 cups canned or home-cooked red
   kidney beans, rinsed and drained

½ teaspoon dried oregano
2 teaspoons light-flavored olive oil
¼ teaspoon black pepper
2 tablespoons water

1. Place onion, garlic, beans, oregano, oil, black pepper, and water in a blender or food processor and puree.
2. Cover and place in refrigerator overnight. Stir, and serve at room temperature.

Calories Per Serving: 17
Fat: 0 g
Cholesterol: 0 mg
Protein: 1 g

Carbohydrates: 3 g
Dietary Fiber: 1 g
Sodium: 1 mg

✎ *Broiled Red Pepper–Pinto Dip* ✎

YIELD: 40 servings (1 tablespoon each) ▪ *PREPARATION TIME: 15 minutes* ▪ *COOKING TIME: 10 minutes*

Broiled red pepper chunks are chopped and added to a combination of onion, pinto beans, and basil.

2 medium red bell peppers, seeded,
   halved, and cut into chunks
2 tablespoons light-flavored olive oil
1 cup chopped onions

2 cups canned or home-cooked pinto
   beans, rinsed and drained
½ teaspoon dried basil

1. Preheat broiler. Coat red pepper chunks with 1 tablespoon olive oil and place them on a broiler pan about 4 inches from the heat. Broil on one side for about 3 minutes or until browned. Then turn and broil on the other side until browned. Remove from oven and set aside to cool.
2. Heat remaining tablespoon oil in a skillet over medium heat, add onions, and sauté for 4 minutes.
3. Add beans and basil. Simmer over low heat for 6 minutes.
4. Partially mash beans.
5. Chop cooled red pepper chunks and stir into beans. Serve warm.

Calories Per Serving: 19   Carbohydrates: 2 g
Fat: 1 g   Dietary Fiber: 0 g
Cholesterol: 0 mg   Sodium: 50 mg
Protein: 1 g

⚜ *Roasted Pepper Dip* ⚜

YIELD: *24 servings (1 tablespoon each)* • PREPARATION TIME: *25 minutes* •
COOKING TIME: *10 minutes*

Roasted red or green peppers give this dip a subtle, smoky flavor. Serve with raw vegetables.

3 large red or green bell peppers,   *2 tablespoons chopped fresh parsley*
* halved and seeded*   *¼ teaspoon black pepper*
1 small clove garlic, minced   *½ teaspoon lemon juice*
½ cup nonfat or reduced-fat sour cream

1. Preheat broiler. Place peppers, skin side up, on a foil-lined baking sheet, flattening them with your palm. Broil for 10 minutes or until blackened.
2. Place peppers in ice water for 5 minutes. Drain, and remove skins.
3. Place garlic, roasted peppers, sour cream, parsley, black pepper, and lemon juice in a blender or food processor and process until smooth.

Calories Per Serving: 38   Carbohydrates: 7 g
Fat: 0 g   Dietary Fiber: 1 g
Cholesterol: 3 mg   Sodium: 19 mg
Protein: 2 g

❧ *Quick Black Bean Salsa Dip* ❧

YIELD: 48 servings (1 tablespoon each) • *PREPARATION TIME: 10 minutes*

This superquick dip is made with canned black beans, chiles, and prepared salsa. Serve it with nonfat tortilla or corn chips.

15 ounces canned black beans, rinsed and drained

4 ounces canned chopped green chiles

1 cup chopped fresh or canned, low-sodium tomatoes

1 cup prepared salsa

1 tablespoon chopped fresh cilantro or parsley

½ teaspoon ground cumin

1. Combine beans, chiles, tomatoes, salsa, cilantro, and cumin.

Calories Per Serving: 21
Fat: 0 g
Cholesterol: 0 mg
Protein: 1 g

Carbohydrates: 4 g
Dietary Fiber: 0 g
Sodium: 235 mg

❧ *Black Bean Salsa* ❧

YIELD: 48 servings (1 tablespoon each) • *PREPARATION TIME: 20 minutes plus 1 hour refrigeration time*

Serve this combination of black beans, vegetables, herbs, and spices with nonfat cheese-flavored tortilla chips.

2 cups canned or home-cooked black beans, rinsed and drained

⅓ cup diced green bell pepper

¼ cup finely chopped red onion

¼ cup unpeeled and diced cucumber

¼ cup diced celery

1 jalapeño pepper, seeded and minced

2 tablespoons light-flavored olive oil

1 small tomato, chopped

2 tablespoons red wine vinegar

1 tablespoon lemon juice

½ teaspoon dried thyme

½ teaspoon ground cumin

½ teaspoon chili powder

¼ teaspoon black pepper

1 clove garlic, minced

1. Combine black beans, green pepper, red onion, cucumber, celery, jalapeño, oil, tomato, vinegar, lemon juice, thyme, cumin, chili powder, black pepper, and garlic in a bowl and stir well.
2. Cover and chill for 1 hour.

Calories Per Serving: 17   Carbohydrates: 2 g
Fat: 1 g   Dietary Fiber: 0 g
Cholesterol: 0 mg   Sodium: 10 mg
Protein: 1 g

❧ *Black-Eyed Pea Dip* ☙

YIELD: 16 servings (1 tablespoon each) • *PREPARATION TIME: 15 minutes plus overnight refrigeration time*

Black-eyed peas, garlic, red onion, chopped sun-dried tomatoes, black olives, and chili powder unite to make this unique dip.

1 clove garlic, minced
2 teaspoons red onion, minced
2 teaspoons chopped, oil-packed sun-dried tomatoes, drained
1 cup canned or home-cooked black-eyed peas, rinsed and drained

2 teaspoons light-flavored olive oil
¼ teaspoon black pepper
¼ teaspoon chili powder
2 tablespoons water
3 tablespoons chopped black olives

1. Place garlic, onion, sun-dried tomatoes, black-eyed peas, olive oil, black pepper, chili powder, and water in a blender or food processor and puree. Add water if needed to give mixture a good dipping consistency.
2. Transfer to a bowl. Stir in olives and place in refrigerator overnight. Stir and serve at room temperature.

Calories Per Serving: 35   Carbohydrates: 5 g
Fat: 1 g   Dietary Fiber: 0 g
Cholesterol: 0 mg   Sodium: 55 mg
Protein: 1 g

❧ *Cannellini Bean Dip* ❧

YIELD: *24 servings (1 tablespoon each)* • PREPARATION TIME: *20 minutes plus*
overnight refrigeration time

This smooth and delicious cannellini bean dip with hints of lemon, garlic, parsley, and almond is great served with blanched fresh green beans and asparagus stalks.

1 clove garlic, minced
2 tablespoons minced red onion
¼ cup chopped fresh parsley
1½ cups canned or home-cooked cannellini beans, rinsed and drained
2 tablespoons light-flavored olive oil

1 tablespoon lemon juice
¼ cup skim or 1% milk
¼ teaspoon white pepper
2 tablespoons water
½ cup toasted, chopped almonds

1. Place garlic, onion, parsley, beans, olive oil, lemon juice, milk, pepper, and water in a blender or food processor. Puree, adding water if needed to create a good dipping consistency.
2. Transfer dip to bowl. Stir in almonds and cover. Refrigerate overnight. Bring to room temperature and stir before serving.

Calories Per Serving: 47
Fat: 3 g
Cholesterol: 0 mg
Protein: 2 g

Carbohydrates: 4 g
Dietary Fiber: 0 g
Sodium: 3 mg

❧ *Northern Bean and Garlic Dip* ❧

YIELD: *48 servings (1 tablespoon each)* • PREPARATION TIME: *30 minutes* •
COOKING TIME: *15 minutes*

Roasted garlic gives this bean dip a special pungency. Serve with chunks of toasted whole-grain bread.

12 unpeeled garlic cloves

32 ounces canned or home-cooked
Great Northern beans, rinsed and
drained

¼ cup lemon juice

1 tablespoon light-flavored olive oil

1 tablespoon chopped fresh parsley

¼ teaspoon black pepper

¼ cup minced scallions

¼ cup minced green bell pepper

1. Preheat oven to 400 degrees. Place the garlic cloves on a baking sheet and bake for 15 minutes or until soft.
2. Cool, peel, and trim ends of garlic cloves.
3. Place half the beans, the lemon juice, oil, and roasted garlic in a blender or food processor and puree.
4. Combine pureed beans with the remaining whole beans, parsley, black pepper, scallions, and green pepper.

Calories Per Serving: 89
Fat: 1 g
Cholesterol: 0 mg
Protein: 5 g

Carbohydrates: 15 g
Dietary Fiber: 0 g
Sodium: 3 mg

◈ Corn and Bean Salsa ◈

YIELD: 60 servings (1 tablespoon each) • PREPARATION TIME: 20 minutes •
COOKING TIME: 8 minutes

Serve this corn and bean salsa with nonfat, white corn tortilla chips.

3 tablespoons light-flavored olive oil

1¼ cups fresh or canned corn kernels,
drained

30 ounces canned or home-cooked
Great Northern beans, rinsed and
drained

1 cup chopped green bell pepper

¾ cup chopped red onion

2 tablespoons lime juice

3 large cloves garlic, minced

1 large jalapeño pepper, seeded and
minced

½ teaspoon dried oregano

1 tablespoon chili powder

½ teaspoon ground cumin

1. Heat 1 tablespoon of the oil in a large skillet over high heat. Add corn and sauté until brown, about 3 minutes. Pour corn into a large bowl.
2. Place the remaining 2 tablespoons oil in skillet, stir in beans, green bell pepper, onion, lime juice, garlic, jalapeño, oregano, chili powder, and cumin. Cook for 5 minutes.
3. Add to corn, mix well, and serve warm.

Calories Per Serving: 38
Fat: 1 g
Cholesterol: 0 mg
Protein: 2 g

Carbohydrates: 6 g
Dietary Fiber: 1 g
Sodium: 10 mg

❧ *Feta–Ripe Olive Spread* ❧

YIELD: 24 servings (1 tablespoon each) • *PREPARATION TIME: 20 minutes plus 2 hours refrigeration time*

This spread has all the flavors of a terrific Greek salad. Serve with nonfat sesame crackers.

½ pound feta cheese, drained and crumbled
1 small cucumber, peeled, seeded, and chopped
1 teaspoon dried dill

3 tablespoons chopped black olives
2 tablespoons chopped scallions
¼ teaspoon black pepper
2 tablespoons nonfat or reduced-fat plain yogurt

1. Place feta cheese, cucumber, dill, olives, scallions, black pepper, and yogurt in a bowl and stir to blend.
2. Cover and chill for 2 hours before serving.

Calories Per Serving: 28
Fat: 2 g
Cholesterol: 8 mg
Protein: 2 g

Carbohydrates: 1 g
Dietary Fiber: 0 g
Sodium: 113 mg

❧ *Tomato-Orange-Jalapeño Dip* ⑃

YIELD: *32 servings (1 tablespoon each)* • PREPARATION TIME: *20 minutes plus*
1 hour refrigeration time

Serve this flavorful dip with nonfat corn chips and raw vegetables.

2 scallions, chopped
¼ cup chopped red onion
1 tablespoon dried cilantro
2 jalapeño peppers, seeded and minced
½ teaspoon sugar

Grated peel of one orange
2 cups fresh or canned, low-sodium
  chopped tomatoes, juice reserved
¼ teaspoon hot pepper sauce

1. Combine scallions, onion, cilantro, jalapeños, sugar, orange peel, tomatoes, and hot pepper sauce.
2. Place in refrigerator to marinate for 1 hour before serving.

Calories Per Serving: 5
Fat: 0 g
Cholesterol: 0 mg
Protein: 0 g

Carbohydrates: 1 g
Dietary Fiber: 0 g
Sodium: 28 mg

❧ *Orange-Chocolate Dip* ⑃

YIELD: *24 servings (1 tablespoon each)* • PREPARATION TIME: *10 minutes*

Serve cubes of nonfat pound cake or angel food cake on party picks with this sweet dip.

¾ cup nonfat or reduced-fat plain
  yogurt

¾ cup chocolate syrup
2 tablespoons orange juice

1. Combine yogurt, chocolate syrup, and orange juice in a serving bowl.

Calories Per Serving: 27

Fat: 0 g

Cholesterol: 0 mg

Protein: 1 g

Carbohydrates: 7 g

Dietary Fiber: 0 g

Sodium: 20 mg

SEAFOOD, POULTRY,
• EGG, AND CHEESE DIPS •

Hot-and-Pungent Crab Dip

YIELD: 32 servings (1 tablespoon each) • *PREPARATION TIME: 10 minutes* • *COOKING TIME: 10 minutes*

Crabmeat is mixed with cream cheese, wine, onion, parsley, Dijon mustard, and cayenne pepper in this spicy dip. Serve it with an assortment of raw vegetables.

1 teaspoon ground cayenne pepper

1 teaspoon Dijon mustard

8 ounces nonfat or reduced-fat cream cheese, softened

¼ cup dry white wine

¼ cup minced onion

¼ cup chopped fresh parsley

½ pound cooked crabmeat, drained and flaked

1. Combine cayenne, mustard, cream cheese, white wine, onion, and parsley in a saucepan. Simmer over low heat until thoroughly heated.
2. Stir in the crabmeat. Either serve at once, or store in the refrigerator for up to 2 days.

Calories Per Serving: 16

Fat: 0 g

Cholesterol: 7 mg

Protein: 1 g

Carbohydrates: 2 g

Dietary Fiber: 0 g

Sodium: 26 mg

❧ Spiced Crabmeat Spread ❧

YIELD: 30 servings (2 tablespoons each) • *PREPARATION TIME: 15 minutes plus 3 hours refrigeration time*

Crabmeat, spices, cream cheese, and sour cream are molded and chilled before serving. Serve with raw zucchini and cucumber medallions.

16 ounces nonfat or reduced-fat cream cheese, softened
2 tablespoons nonfat or reduced-fat sour cream
½ teaspoon ground paprika
½ teaspoon ground cayenne pepper
¼ teaspoon minced garlic
¼ teaspoon dried thyme
1 cup cooked crabmeat, drained
¼ cup finely chopped green bell pepper

1. Combine cream cheese, sour cream, paprika, cayenne pepper, garlic, and thyme.
2. Stir in crabmeat and green pepper.
3. Line a deep 1½-pint bowl with plastic wrap. Press mixture into bowl. Cover and chill for 3 hours or until firm.
4. Carefully turn bowl over onto serving plate. Remove plastic wrap.

Calories Per Serving: 23
Fat: 0 g
Cholesterol: 7 mg
Protein: 4 g

Carbohydrates: 1 g
Dietary Fiber: 0 g
Sodium: 120 mg

❧ Tuna-Pepper Dip ❧

YIELD: 40 servings (1 tablespoon each) • *PREPARATION TIME: 20 minutes*

Serve this wonderful combination of white albacore tuna and canned jalapeño peppers with pita wedges or nonfat potato chips.

14 ounces canned, water-packed, white albacore tuna, drained
6 ounces canned jalapeño peppers, coarsely chopped, liquid reserved
½ cup nonfat or reduced-fat mayonnaise
¼ cup chopped fresh cilantro or parsley

1. Combine tuna with peppers and their liquid.
2. Combine tuna-pepper mixture with mayonnaise.
3. Place in a serving bowl and sprinkle with chopped cilantro or parsley.

Calories Per Serving: 46
Fat: 1 g
Cholesterol: 11 mg
Protein: 7 g

Carbohydrates: 2 g
Dietary Fiber: 0 g
Sodium: 251 mg

⚜ *Smoked Fish Spread* ⚜

YIELD: 20 servings (1 tablespoon each) • *PREPARATION TIME: 10 minutes*

Serve this delicious smoked fish spread with thinly sliced pumpernickel.

1 pound smoked fish fillets, skinned
2 tablespoons lemon juice
1 tablespoon chopped fresh parsley

1 to 2 scallions, coarsely chopped
¼ teaspoon white pepper

1. Mash the fish with a fork.
2. Combine fish, lemon juice, parsley, scallions, and white pepper.
3. Chill until ready to serve.

Calories Per Serving: 31
Fat: 0 g
Cholesterol: 26 mg
Protein: 6 g

Carbohydrates: 0 g
Dietary Fiber: 0 g
Sodium: 290 mg

⚜ *Smoked Oyster Spread* ⚜

YIELD: 16 servings (1 tablespoon each) • *PREPARATION TIME: 15 minutes*

Canned smoked oysters are combined with scallions, garlic, soy sauce, lemon juice, and cream cheese. Serve on garlic crackers accompanied by bite-size pieces of red and green peppers.

8 ounces nonfat or reduced-fat cream
  cheese, softened
7 ounces canned smoked oysters,
  drained

2 tablespoons chopped scallions
1 clove garlic, minced
1 tablespoon light soy sauce
2 tablespoons lemon juice

1. Place cream cheese, oysters, scallions, garlic, soy sauce, and lemon juice in a blender or food processor. Process until well blended.

Calories Per Serving: 13 g
Fat: 0 g
Cholesterol: 5 mg
Protein: 2 g

Carbohydrates: 1 g
Dietary Fiber: 0 g
Sodium: 74 mg

❧ *Crab Dip* ❧

YIELD: 54 servings (1 tablespoon each) • *PREPARATION TIME: 15 minutes plus 1 hour refrigeration time*

This dip features cheddar cheese and horseradish. Serve in a bowl surrounded by a variety of nonfat crackers and breadsticks.

½ cup nonfat or reduced-fat sour cream
2 tablespoons nonfat or reduced-fat
  mayonnaise
1 tablespoon skim or 1% milk
1 tablespoon prepared horseradish
½ teaspoon dry mustard
¼ teaspoon hot pepper sauce

8 ounces nonfat or reduced-fat cream
  cheese, softened
½ pound cooked crabmeat, drained and
  flaked
1 cup grated nonfat or reduced-fat
  cheddar cheese
¼ teaspoon ground paprika

1. Place sour cream, mayonnaise, milk, horseradish, dry mustard, hot sauce, and cream cheese in a blender or food processor and process until smooth.
2. Transfer to a serving bowl. Stir in crabmeat and cheddar cheese. Sprinkle with paprika.
3. Cover and refrigerate for 1 hour.

Calories Per Serving: 16
Fat: 0 g
Cholesterol: 6 mg
Protein: 3 g

Carbohydrates: 1 g
Dietary Fiber: 0 g
Sodium: 92 mg

✿ *Cucumber-Salmon Dip* ✿

YIELD: 40 servings (1 tablespoon each) • *PREPARATION TIME: 15 minutes*

Serve this lemon- and dill-flavored salmon-cucumber dip with nonfat ridged potato chips.

1 large cucumber, coarsely grated and
   drained
1 cup nonfat or reduced-fat sour cream
½ cup nonfat or reduced-fat mayonnaise

¼ teaspoon black pepper
2 teaspoons dried dill
1 tablespoon lemon juice
7½ ounces canned salmon, drained and
   flaked

1. Combine cucumber, sour cream, mayonnaise, pepper, dill, lemon juice, and salmon.
2. Refrigerate until served.

Calories Per Serving: 83
Fat: 2 g
Cholesterol: 10 mg
Protein: 6 g

Carbohydrates: 8 g
Dietary Fiber: 0 g
Sodium: 120 mg

✿ *Lemon–Dijon–Sour Cream Dip with Salmon* ✿

YIELD: 28 servings (1 tablespoon each) • *PREPARATION TIME: 15 minutes*

This dip combines salmon, sour cream, lemon juice, Dijon mustard, and herbs. Serve with broccoli florets and carrot sticks.

1 cup nonfat or reduced-fat sour cream
1 clove garlic, minced
1 teaspoon Dijon mustard
½ teaspoon dried tarragon
1 tablespoon minced fresh parsley

1 teaspoon lemon juice
1 hard-boiled egg white, finely chopped
7½ ounces canned salmon, drained and
　flaked

1. Combine sour cream, garlic, mustard, tarragon, parsley, lemon juice, egg white, and salmon. Chill until served.

Calories Per Serving: 23
Fat: 1 g
Cholesterol: 6 mg
Protein: 2 g

Carbohydrates: 2 g
Dietary Fiber: 0 g
Sodium: 55 mg

❧ Garlic-Dill-Salmon Spread ❧

YIELD: 32 servings (1 tablespoon each) • *PREPARATION TIME: 20 minutes*

Serve this salmon spread, which is flavored with garlic, dill, and sherry, with nonfat rye crackers and celery sticks.

6 ounces nonfat or reduced-fat cream
　cheese, softened
2 cloves garlic, minced
2 tablespoons dry sherry

¼ teaspoon black pepper
½ teaspoon dried dill
7½ ounces canned salmon, drained and
　flaked

1. Combine cream cheese, garlic, sherry, pepper, and dill.
2. Add salmon and mix until well blended.

Calories Per Serving: 74
Fat: 3 g
Cholesterol: 11 mg
Protein: 9 g

Carbohydrates: 2 g
Dietary Fiber: 0 g
Sodium: 270 mg

❧ *Salmon Pâté* ❧

*YIELD: 40 servings (1 tablespoon each) • PREPARATION TIME: 15 minutes plus
2 hours refrigeration time*

Serve this salmon spread chilled, with rye crackers.

*7½ ounces canned salmon, skin and
bones removed*
*⅓ cup nonfat or reduced-fat cottage
cheese*
*½ cup canned, water-packed artichoke
hearts, drained*

⅓ cup prepared salsa
½ cup chopped celery
3 tablespoons chopped red bell pepper
1 clove garlic, minced
1 tablespoon chopped onion
½ teaspoon dried dill

1. Place salmon, cottage cheese, artichoke hearts, salsa, celery, red pepper, garlic, onion, and dill in a blender or food processor and process until smooth.
2. Transfer to a bowl and chill for 2 hours.

Calories Per Serving: 12
Fat: 0 g
Cholesterol: 4 mg
Protein: 2 g

Carbohydrates: 1 g
Dietary Fiber: 0 g
Sodium: 58 mg

❧ *Smoked Salmon Spread* ❧

YIELD: 32 servings (1 tablespoon each) • PREPARATION TIME: 15 minutes

Serve this luscious spread on rye crackers topped with sprigs of fresh parsley or dill.

2 cups nonfat or reduced-fat sour cream
4 ounces smoked salmon, minced
2 tablespoons scallions or chives

1 teaspoon lemon juice
1 teaspoon Dijon mustard

1. Combine sour cream, salmon, scallions, lemon juice, and mustard and mix well.

Calories Per Serving: 21

Carbohydrates: 3 g

Fat: 0 g

Dietary Fiber: 0 g

Cholesterol: 6 mg

Sodium: 45 mg

Protein: 2 g

❧ *Salmon Mousse* ❧

YIELD: 12 servings (¼ cup each) • *PREPARATION TIME: 25 minutes plus 4 hours refrigeration time*

Serve this lemon-accented salmon mousse with nonfat sesame crackers.

1 package plain gelatin
2 tablespoons lemon juice
1 onion, sliced
½ cup boiling water
¼ teaspoon ground paprika

1 teaspoon chopped fresh parsley
16 ounces canned salmon, drained
1 cup nonfat or reduced-fat plain
* yogurt*

1. Put the gelatin, lemon juice, onion, and boiling water into blender or food processor. Blend for 40 seconds.
2. Add the paprika, parsley, salmon, and yogurt and blend 30 seconds.
3. Pour the mixture into a mold and chill until firm, about 4 hours.
4. Wrap a hot towel around the bottom of the mold to loosen the gelatin. Hold a serving platter facedown on top of mold and carefully turn over the platter and mold.

Calories Per Serving: 79

Carbohydrates: 3 g

Fat: 2 g

Dietary Fiber: 0 g

Cholesterol: 15 mg

Sodium: 202 mg

Protein: 12 g

❧ *Curried Shrimp and Chutney Spread* ❧

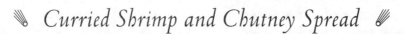

YIELD: 48 servings (1 tablespoon each) • *PREPARATION TIME: 10 minutes*

Serve this curried shrimp spread with thinly sliced toasted French bread and celery sticks. *Chutney* comes from the Hindi word *chatni*.

8 ounces nonfat or reduced-fat cream
  cheese, softened
1 tablespoon curry powder
1 clove garlic, minced
¼ cup chopped mango chutney

1 cup finely chopped cooked shrimp
1 cup chopped unsalted peanuts
½ cup nonfat or reduced-fat sour cream
3 tablespoons skim or 1% milk

1. Combine cream cheese, curry powder, garlic, chutney, shrimp, peanuts, sour cream, and milk.

Calories Per Serving: 34
Fat: 2 g
Cholesterol: 9 mg
Protein: 3 g

Carbohydrates: 2 g
Dietary Fiber: 0 g
Sodium: 69 mg

⚘ *Spinach-Shrimp Dip* ⚘

YIELD: 40 servings (1 tablespoon each) • *PREPARATION TIME: 15 minutes plus 1 hour refrigeration time*

Cooked spinach is mixed with shrimp, lemon juice, scallions, garlic, spices, and yogurt. Serve with carrot and celery dippers.

2 cloves garlic, minced
2 scallions, chopped
1 10-ounce package frozen chopped
  spinach, cooked and well drained
2 cups nonfat or reduced-fat plain yogurt

1½ teaspoons lemon juice
¼ teaspoon white pepper
¼ teaspoon ground paprika
⅛ teaspoon ground cayenne pepper
⅔ cup minced cooked shrimp

1. Place garlic, scallions, and spinach in a blender or food processor and chop finely.
2. Add yogurt, lemon juice, white pepper, paprika, and cayenne and process until smooth.
3. Transfer to a bowl and cover. Refrigerate for 1 hour.
4. Stir shrimp into dip immediately before serving.

Calories Per Serving: 12
Fat: 0 g
Cholesterol: 7 mg
Protein: 2 g

Carbohydrates: 1 g
Dietary Fiber: 0 g
Sodium: 46 mg

❧ *Shrimp-Avocado Spread* ✎

YIELD: 32 servings (1 tablespoon each) • *PREPARATION TIME: 20 minutes plus overnight refrigeration time*

Serve this mixture of shrimp, avocado, and egg whites with rye crackers.

2 hard-boiled egg whites, chopped
1 large ripe avocado, chopped
½ pound cooked shrimp, shelled, de-
  veined, and finely chopped

2 scallions, finely chopped
1 tablespoon lemon juice
¼ teaspoon dried tarragon
Hot pepper sauce to taste

1. Combine chopped eggs, chopped avocado, shrimp, scallions, lemon juice, tarragon, and hot pepper sauce.
2. Refrigerate overnight.

Calories Per Serving: 17
Fat: 1 g
Cholesterol: 11 mg
Protein: 2 g

Carbohydrates: 0 g
Dietary Fiber: 0 g
Sodium: 54 mg

❧ *Clam Spread* ✎

YIELD: 40 servings (1 tablespoon each) • *PREPARATION TIME: 10 minutes plus 1 hour refrigeration time*

In this rich-tasting but fat-free spread, minced clams are combined with scallion, garlic, dill, sour cream, mayonnaise, and cream cheese. Serve with fat-free crackers or flat bread.

1 tablespoon minced scallion
1 clove garlic, minced
½ teaspoon dried dill
2 tablespoons nonfat or reduced-fat
  mayonnaise

8 ounces nonfat or reduced-fat cream
  cheese, softened
½ cup nonfat or reduced-fat sour cream
7 ounces canned minced clams, drained
Paprika

1. Combine scallion, garlic, dill, mayonnaise, cream cheese, and sour cream in a bowl.
2. Stir in clams.
3. Cover tightly and place in refrigerator for 1 hour. Sprinkle with paprika before serving.

Calories Per Serving: 4
Fat: 0 g
Cholesterol: 1 mg
Protein: 0 g

Carbohydrates: 1 g
Dietary Fiber: 0 g
Sodium: 16 mg

◊ *Clam-Eggplant Spread* ◊

YIELD: 24 servings (1 tablespoon each) • *PREPARATION TIME: 45 minutes* •
COOKING TIME: 45 minutes

Serve this unique combination of minced clams and baked eggplant with toasted pita rounds.

1 medium eggplant
7½ ounces canned minced clams,
drained, 1 tablespoon liquid reserved
¼ cup chopped fresh parsley

2 cloves garlic, chopped
½ teaspoon black pepper
2 tablespoons chopped red bell pepper

1. Preheat oven to 400 degrees. Prick the skin of the eggplant in several places and put it on a foil-lined baking sheet. Bake for 45 minutes.
2. Cool eggplant; scoop out pulp and chop.
3. Place the chopped eggplant in a strainer over a bowl to drain for 20 minutes.
4. Combine the eggplant, clams, reserved clam juice, parsley, garlic, black pepper, and red pepper.
5. Refrigerate until ready to serve.

Calories Per Serving: 13
Fat: 0 g
Cholesterol: 4 mg
Protein: 2 g

Carbohydrates: 1 g
Dietary Fiber: 0 g
Sodium: 8 mg

❧ *Sardine Spread* ✒

YIELD: 16 servings (1 tablespoon each) • *PREPARATION TIME: 10 minutes plus 1 hour refrigeration time*

This simple sardine spread can be served on slices of toasted baguette or crackers.

3¾ ounces canned, boneless sardines packed in olive oil, drained
1 teaspoon Dijon mustard

¼ teaspoon Worcestershire sauce
Juice of 1 lemon

1. Mash together sardines, mustard, Worcestershire sauce, and lemon juice.
2. Cover bowl tightly and place in refrigerator for 1 hour.

Calories Per Serving: 17
Fat: 1 g
Cholesterol: 10 mg
Protein: 2 g

Carbohydrates: 0 g
Dietary Fiber: 0 g
Sodium: 49 mg

❧ *Tuna Spread* ✒

YIELD: 16 servings (2 tablespoons each) • *PREPARATION TIME: 20 minutes*

Canned tuna is combined with cottage cheese and mayonnaise in this simple creamy spread, ideal on party-size slices of sourdough toast.

6½ ounces canned, water-packed, white albacore tuna, drained
2 tablespoons nonfat or reduced-fat mayonnaise

1 cup nonfat or reduced-fat small-curd cottage cheese

1. Place tuna, mayonnaise, and cottage cheese in a blender or food processor. Process until smooth. Chill until ready to serve.

Calories Per Serving: 27
Fat: 0 g
Cholesterol: 10 mg
Protein: 5 g

Carbohydrates: 1 g
Dietary Fiber: 0 g
Sodium: 64 mg

🌿 *Turkey Spread* 🌿

YIELD: 20 servings (1 tablespoon each) • *PREPARATION TIME: 15 minutes plus 2½ hours refrigeration time* • *COOKING TIME: 5 minutes*

Ground turkey is sautéed with onion, relish, yogurt, paprika, nutmeg, and pepper. Serve this spread as a substitute for high-fat pâtés.

¼ cup low-sodium, nonfat or reduced-
   fat chicken broth
½ pound low-fat ground turkey breast
1 small onion, chopped
2 tablespoons sweet pickle relish

2 tablespoons nonfat or reduced-fat
   plain yogurt
¼ teaspoon ground paprika
⅛ teaspoon ground nutmeg
⅛ teaspoon black pepper

1. Heat the chicken broth in a nonstick skillet and brown the turkey over medium heat for 5 minutes or until cooked.
2. Place turkey in a food processor or blender; add onion, relish, yogurt, paprika, nutmeg, and pepper. Blend for 15 seconds. Transfer to a bowl, cover, and refrigerate for 2½ hours.

Calories Per Serving: 14
Fat: 0 g
Cholesterol: 2 mg
Protein: 1 g

Carbohydrates: 3 g
Dietary Fiber: 0 g
Sodium: 35 mg

🌿 *Chicken-Ginger Spread* 🌿

YIELD: 32 servings (1 tablespoon each) • *PREPARATION TIME: 20 minutes*

This spread features a medley of tastes, including crystallized ginger. Serve with nonfat sesame crackers.

1 cup finely chopped cooked chicken
    breast
½ cup nonfat or reduced-fat mayon-
    naise
1 tablespoon minced crystallized ginger

2 teaspoons light soy sauce
1 teaspoon curry powder
1 tablespoon minced scallion
8½ ounces water chestnuts, drained
    and chopped

1. Combine chicken, mayonnaise, ginger, soy sauce, curry powder, scallion, and water chestnuts and mix well.

Calories Per Serving: 15
Fat: 0 g
Cholesterol: 3 mg
Protein: 1 g

Carbohydrates: 2 g
Dietary Fiber: 0 g
Sodium: 15 mg

❧ Almond-Chutney-Chicken Dip ❧

YIELD: 24 servings (2 tablespoons each) • PREPARATION TIME: 10 minutes •
COOKING TIME: 8 minutes

This tangy dip combines toasted almonds, chicken, cream cheese, curry powder, and chutney. Toasting the almonds intensifies their flavor and adds crunch. Serve with crisp nonfat crackers or toast triangles.

¾ cup sliced almonds
1 cup finely chopped cooked chicken
    breast
8 ounces nonfat or reduced-fat cream
    cheese, softened

2 tablespoons nonfat or reduced-fat
    mayonnaise
1 tablespoon curry powder
1 clove garlic, minced
1 tablespoon chopped chutney

1. Preheat oven to 300 degrees. Spread almonds on baking sheet and bake for 8 minutes, or until toasted.
2. Combine toasted almonds, chicken, cream cheese, mayonnaise, curry powder, garlic, and chutney.
3. Serve at room temperature.

Calories Per Serving: 44
Fat: 2 g
Cholesterol: 5 mg
Protein: 4 g

Carbohydrates: 3 g
Dietary Fiber: 1 g
Sodium: 56 mg

❦ *Horseradish-Egg Dip* ❦

YIELD: 24 servings (1 tablespoon each) • *PREPARATION TIME: 15 minutes*

This hard-boiled egg, Dijon mustard, and horseradish dip is delicious with nonfat melba toast.

¼ cup nonfat or reduced-fat mayonnaise
3 ounces nonfat or reduced-fat cream
   cheese, softened
1 tablespoon skim or 1% milk
1 teaspoon Dijon mustard

⅛ teaspoon black pepper
¼ teaspoon prepared horseradish
1 teaspoon chopped scallion
6 hard-boiled egg whites, finely
   chopped

1. Combine mayonnaise, cream cheese, and skim milk. Mix until smooth.
2. Stir in mustard, pepper, horseradish, scallion, and eggs.

Calories Per Serving: 17
Fat: 0 g
Cholesterol: 0 mg
Protein: 2 g

Carbohydrates: 1 g
Dietary Fiber: 0 g
Sodium: 91 mg

❦ *Scallion-Cheese Dip* ❦

YIELD: 54 servings (1 tablespoon each) • *PREPARATION TIME: 10 minutes*

This instant dip has a bouquet of unexpected flavors.

3 cups nonfat or reduced-fat cottage
   cheese
3 tablespoons grated nonfat or reduced-
   fat Parmesan cheese
2 tablespoons white wine vinegar

1 tablespoon prepared horseradish
1 tablespoon sweet-pickle juice
½ teaspoon sugar
⅔ cup chopped scallions

1. Place cottage cheese, Parmesan cheese, vinegar, horseradish, pickle juice, and sugar in a blender or food processor and process until smooth.
2. Transfer to a serving bowl and stir in scallions.

Calories Per Serving: 11
Fat: 0 g
Cholesterol: 5 mg
Protein: 1 g

Carbohydrates: 1 g
Dietary Fiber: 0 g
Sodium: 29 mg

❧ *Hungarian Cheese Dip* ❧

YIELD: 16 servings (1 tablespoon each) • *PREPARATION TIME: 15 minutes plus 1 hour refrigeration time*

This classic dip includes cottage cheese, sour cream, caraway seeds, onion, Dijon mustard, capers, paprika, and scallion. Serve with bite-size pieces of crisp fresh vegetables.

½ cup nonfat or reduced-fat cottage cheese
½ cup nonfat or reduced-fat sour cream
1 tablespoon caraway seeds
2 teaspoons minced onion

2 teaspoons Dijon mustard
2 teaspoons capers, drained and chopped
1 teaspoon ground paprika
1 teaspoon chopped scallion

1. Whisk cottage cheese and sour cream together until smooth. Add caraway seeds, onion, mustard, capers, paprika, and scallion.
2. Cover and place in refrigerator for 1 hour.

Calories Per Serving: 16
Fat: 0 g
Cholesterol: 5 mg
Protein: 1 g

Carbohydrates: 2 g
Dietary Fiber: 0 g
Sodium: 32 mg

❧ *Horseradish-Cheese Dip* ❧

YIELD: 28 servings (1 tablespoon each) • *PREPARATION TIME: 10 minutes*

Serve this simple dip with a platter of fresh, raw vegetables.

2 cups nonfat or reduced-fat cottage
   cheese
1 teaspoon ground paprika
1 tablespoon prepared horseradish

1 clove garlic, minced
1 teaspoon dried dill
¼ teaspoon dry mustard

1. Place cottage cheese, paprika, horseradish, garlic, dill, and dry mustard in a blender or food processor. Process until nearly smooth.

Calories Per Serving: 12
Fat: 0 g
Cholesterol: 6 mg
Protein: 27 g

Carbohydrates: 1 g
Dietary Fiber: 0 g
Sodium: 28 mg

❧ *Pimento-Cheese Dip* ❧

YIELD: *24 servings (1 tablespoon each)* • PREPARATION TIME: *10 minutes*

Pimento is another name for a large, red, heart-shaped sweet pepper. Serve this orange-colored dip with nonfat corn chips and raw vegetables.

7 ounces canned pimentos, drained
8 ounces nonfat or reduced-fat cream
   cheese, softened

½ teaspoon hot pepper sauce

1. Combine pimento, cream cheese, and hot pepper sauce. Blend thoroughly.

Calories Per Serving: 12
Fat: 0 g
Cholesterol: 2 mg
Protein: 2 g

Carbohydrates: 1 g
Dietary Fiber: 0 g
Sodium: 70 mg

❧ Blue Cheese–Yogurt Dip ❧

YIELD: 36 servings (1 tablespoon each) • PREPARATION TIME: 10 minutes

By combining blue cheese with yogurt, this dip offers the zesty flavor without the calories of many traditional blue cheese dips. Serve with carrot sticks and broccoli florets.

*2 cups nonfat or reduced-fat plain
  yogurt
4 ounces blue cheese, crumbled*

*1 teaspoon Worcestershire sauce
1 tablespoon minced scallions
⅛ teaspoon black pepper*

1. Combine yogurt, blue cheese, Worcestershire sauce, scallions, and pepper and blend well.

Calories Per Serving: 17
Fat: 1 g
Cholesterol: 3 mg
Protein: 1 g

Carbohydrates: 1 g
Dietary Fiber: 0 g
Sodium: 54 mg

❧ Ricotta–Roast Garlic Spread ❧

*YIELD: 22 servings (1 tablespoon each) • PREPARATION TIME: 20 minutes •
COOKING TIME: 1 hour*

Let the garlic for this dip roast while you're making final preparations for your party.

*1 large head garlic
1 cup nonfat or reduced-fat ricotta
  cheese*

¼ teaspoon black pepper

1. Preheat oven to 375 degrees. Wrap garlic in aluminum foil and roast for 1 hour.
2. Remove the garlic and cool until cool enough to handle.
3. Separate the garlic into cloves. Trim ends and peel cloves. Place the garlic, ricotta cheese, and pepper in a blender or food processor and puree.

Calories Per Serving: 10

Carbohydrates: 1 g

Fat: 0 g

Dietary Fiber: 0 g

Cholesterol: 1 mg

Sodium: 19 mg

Protein: 2 g

✎ *Salsa-Yogurt Dip* ✎

YIELD: 32 servings (1 tablespoon each) • *PREPARATION TIME: 5 minutes*

Salsa and yogurt are combined in this instant dip.

1 cup salsa

1 cup nonfat or reduced-fat plain yogurt or sour cream

1. Stir salsa into yogurt or sour cream.
2. Chill until ready to serve.

Calories Per Serving: 5

Carbohydrates: 1 g

Fat: 0 g

Dietary Fiber: 0 g

Cholesterol: 0 mg

Sodium: 61 mg

Protein: 0 g

GRILLED APPETIZERS

Chicken Yakitori · Cherry-Chicken Kabobs · Grilled Clams
with Horseradish · Barbecued Shrimp and Red Peppers · Grilled
Chicken and Peppers · Grilled Marinated Eggplant ·
Grilled Chicken Wings with Garlic-Parsley Sauce · Barbecued
Chicken Wings · Chicken-Scallion Skewers · Vegetables on
Skewers · Oriental Veggie Kabobs · Tiny Grilled Turkey Bites ·
Mango Clams · Scallop Kabobs · Scallop Brochettes · Grilled
Shrimp · Salmon Skewers · Mussels Grilled in Wine Sauce

GRILLING
APPETIZERS

∷

Since appetizers are small portions, they can dry out very rapidly over high heat. Keep the barbecue fire low and place the grill 5 to 8 inches from the flame or coals. Small bamboo sticks or skewers 4 to 6 inches long are ideal for many grilled appetizers. The skewers won't char or burn if you soak them in water for 30 minutes before threading. Leave a little space between skewered items, particularly meat, fish, and poultry, so that they cook through.

❦ *Chicken Yakitori* ❦

YIELD: 16 servings (1 skewer each) • *PREPARATION TIME: 15 minutes plus 1 hour refrigeration time* • *COOKING TIME: 10 minutes*

Chicken chunks are marinated in soy sauce, sherry, brown sugar, and ginger, and then grilled.

4 boneless chicken breast halves, skinned and cut into ¾-inch chunks
6 scallions, cut into ¾-inch lengths
½ cup light soy sauce
½ cup dry sherry
2 tablespoons brown sugar, firmly packed
½ teaspoon ground ginger

1. Alternate chicken pieces and scallion pieces on each of 16 wooden skewers that have been soaked in water for 30 minutes. Place skewers in a shallow baking dish.
2. Combine soy sauce, sherry, brown sugar, and ginger. Pour over skewered chicken. Place in refrigerator to marinate for 1 hour, turning several times.

3. Reserve the marinade for basting. Place skewers on grill and grill for 10 minutes, basting several times.

Calories Per Serving: 93

Fat: 2 g

Cholesterol: 37 mg

Protein: 14 g

Carbohydrates: 3 g

Dietary Fiber: 0 g

Sodium: 297 mg

❧ *Cherry-Chicken Kabobs* ❧

YIELD: 16 servings (1 each) • PREPARATION TIME: 15 minutes plus 1 hour refrigeration time • COOKING TIME: 10 minutes

Bing cherries and mushrooms are skewered and broiled with marinated chicken chunks.

4 boneless chicken halves, skinned and cut into ¾-inch chunks

1 #2 can pitted Bing cherries, ½ cup syrup reserved

¼ cup dry red wine

¼ cup lemon juice

2 tablespoons light-flavored olive oil

3 tablespoons finely chopped scallions

½ teaspoon black pepper

1 teaspoon dry mustard

½ teaspoon ground nutmeg

32 small fresh mushrooms, cleaned and stemmed

1. Place chicken in glass bowl.
2. Combine cherry syrup, red wine, lemon juice, olive oil, scallions, black pepper, dry mustard, and nutmeg and pour over chicken.
3. Place in refrigerator and marinate for 1 hour. Meanwhile, soak 16 wooden skewers in water for 30 minutes.
4. Thread skewers, alternating chicken chunks with cherries and mushrooms. Reserve marinade.
5. Grill for 10 minutes, turning and basting frequently with marinade.

Calories Per Serving: 104

Fat: 3 g

Cholesterol: 37 mg

Protein: 14 g

Carbohydrates: 4 g

Dietary Fiber: 0 g

Sodium: 35 mg

❧ *Grilled Clams with Horseradish* ❧

YIELD: 12 servings (2 each) • *PREPARATION TIME: 10 minutes* •
COOKING TIME: 3 minutes

Simple grilled clams are served with horseradish, parsley, and lemon wedges.

24 small clams in shells, scrubbed
½ cup grated fresh or prepared horse-
  radish

2 teaspoons chopped fresh parsley
12 lemon wedges

1. Place clams on a grill rack over hot coals; cook 10 minutes or until shells open.
2. Combine horseradish and parsley.
3. Serve clams with horseradish mixture and lemon wedges. Provide plates and cocktail forks.

Calories Per Serving: 51
Fat: 1 g
Cholesterol: 18 mg
Protein: 7 g

Carbohydrates: 5 g
Dietary Fiber: 0 g
Sodium: 31 mg

❧ *Barbecued Shrimp and Red Peppers* ❧

YIELD: 8 servings (1 skewer each) • *PREPARATION TIME: 25 minutes plus*
1 hour refrigeration time • *COOKING TIME: 6 minutes*

Large fresh shrimp are marinated in lemon–wine–soy sauce and then grilled.

¼ cup light soy sauce
¼ cup lemon juice
2 cloves garlic, minced
¼ teaspoon black pepper
¼ cup dry white wine

4 teaspoons grated fresh gingerroot
1 tablespoon light-flavored olive oil
8 large uncooked shrimp, shelled and
  deveined but with tails left on
16 1-inch squares red bell pepper

1. Combine soy sauce, lemon juice, garlic, black pepper, wine, gingerroot, and oil.

2. Add shrimp; cover and refrigerate at least 1 hour. Meanwhile, soak 8 wooden skewers in water for 30 minutes.
3. Place 1 shrimp and 2 red pepper pieces on each skewer. Reserve marinade.
4. Brush with reserved marinade. Place on a moderately hot grill.
5. Cook for 2 to 3 minutes. Turn, brush with marinade, and cook for 2 to 3 additional minutes, or until done.

Calories Per Serving: 51
Fat: 2 g
Cholesterol: 42 mg
Protein: 6 g

Carbohydrates: 2 g
Dietary Fiber: 0 g
Sodium: 510 mg

❧ *Grilled Chicken and Peppers* ❧

YIELD: 24 servings (1 skewer each) • *PREPARATION TIME: 25 minutes plus 4 hours refrigeration time* • *COOKING TIME: 6 minutes*

Chicken cubes and peppers are marinated in a sherry-flavored sauce and grilled.

2 tablespoons light-flavored olive oil
1½ tablespoons light soy sauce
2 tablespoons rice vinegar
¼ cup dry sherry

½ cup chopped fresh parsley
1¼ pounds chicken cutlets
3 green bell peppers, seeded and cut into ¾-inch cubes

DIPPING SAUCE

½ cup dry sherry
2 tablespoons brown sugar, firmly packed

2 tablespoons light soy sauce
1½ tablespoons rice vinegar
2 scallions, chopped

1. For the skewers, combine the oil, soy sauce, vinegar, ¼ cup sherry, and parsley in a mixing bowl. Add the chicken and marinate at least 4 hours. Meanwhile, soak 24 wooden skewers in water for 30 minutes.
2. Arrange the chicken and the bell pepper pieces alternately on the skewers. Reserve marinade.
3. For the dipping sauce, combine sherry, brown sugar, soy sauce, rice vinegar, and scallions in a saucepan and simmer for 20 minutes.

4. Cook chicken skewers over hot charcoal for 4 to 5 minutes; baste with reserved marinade, turning once. Serve hot with dipping sauce.

Calories Per Serving: 71   Carbohydrates: 2 g
Fat: 3 g   Dietary Fiber: 0 g
Cholesterol: 21 mg   Sodium: 96 mg
Protein: 8 g

❧ *Grilled Marinated Eggplant* ❧

YIELD: *20 servings (1 each)* • PREPARATION TIME: *20 minutes plus overnight refrigeration time* • COOKING TIME: *20 minutes*

Eggplant slices are briefly baked, lightly grilled, and marinated overnight.

2 medium eggplants   *½ cup red wine vinegar*
½ cup dry white wine   *3 cloves garlic, chopped*
½ cup light-flavored olive oil   *¼ teaspoon black pepper*

1. Preheat oven to 450 degrees. Slice off tops and bottoms of eggplants. Slice into ¾-inch slices and arrange in a single layer on a baking sheet. Bake for 10 minutes.
2. Cook eggplant on a hot grill until grill marks begin to show on each side of eggplant.
3. Arrange eggplant in a glass baking dish.
4. Combine white wine, olive oil, red wine vinegar, garlic, and pepper.
5. Pour marinade over eggplant and refrigerate overnight. Serve slices cold.

Calories Per Serving: 37   Carbohydrates: 2 g
Fat: 3 g   Dietary Fiber: 0 g
Cholesterol: 0 mg   Sodium: 1 mg
Protein: 1 g

Grilled Chicken Wings
◊ with Garlic-Parsley Sauce ◊

YIELD: *20 servings (2 pieces each)* • PREPARATION TIME: *20 minutes* •
COOKING TIME: *5 minutes*

Grilled chicken wings are served with a sauce spiced with garlic, parsley, and
hot pepper sauce.

3 cloves garlic, chopped
¾ cup lemon juice
1 tablespoon light-flavored olive oil
⅛ teaspoon hot pepper sauce

¼ teaspoon black pepper
20 chicken wings, skinned, cut into 2
*   pieces, tips trimmed and discarded*
3 tablespoons chopped fresh parsley

1. Combine garlic, lemon juice, olive oil, hot pepper sauce, and black pepper.
2. Place wing sections on medium-hot grill. Grill, basting and turning several times, until golden brown (approximately 5 minutes).
3. Place wings on a platter. Sprinkle parsley over wings and serve hot.

Calories Per Serving: 53
Fat: 2 g
Cholesterol: 18 mg
Protein: 6 g

Carbohydrates: 1 g
Dietary Fiber: 0 g
Sodium: 20 mg

◊ Barbecued Chicken Wings ◊

YIELD: *16 servings (1 each)* • PREPARATION TIME: *15 minutes plus 24 hours*
refrigeration time • COOKING TIME: *20 minutes*

Chicken wings are marinated overnight in a richly flavored sauce and
grilled.

1 tablespoon light-flavored olive oil
¼ cup chopped onions

½ cup water
¼ cup red wine vinegar

1 tablespoon plus ¾ teaspoon
  Worcestershire sauce
¼ cup lemon juice
2 tablespoons brown sugar, firmly
  packed

1 cup low-sodium catsup
1½ teaspoons ground paprika
¼ teaspoon black pepper
16 chicken wings, skinned, tips
  trimmed and discarded

1. Heat oil in a skillet over medium heat. Sauté the onions 5 minutes, or until soft.
2. Add water, vinegar, Worcestershire sauce, lemon juice, sugar, catsup, paprika, and pepper. Bring to a simmer and cook for 20 minutes.
3. Remove from heat and cool completely.
4. Put the chicken wings and cooled sauce in a glass bowl. Cover and marinate in the refrigerator for 24 hours.
5. Grill the chicken over hot charcoal for about 20 minutes, basting often with marinade.

Calories Per Serving: 78
Fat: 3 g
Cholesterol: 18 mg
Protein: 7 g

Carbohydrates: 5 g
Dietary Fiber: 0 g
Sodium: 121 mg

❧ *Chicken-Scallion Skewers* ❧

YIELD: 12 servings (2 each) • *PREPARATION TIME: 30 minutes plus 6 hours refrigeration time* • *COOKING TIME: 8 minutes*

Strips of chicken breast and scallions are marinated and grilled.

2 boneless, skinless chicken breasts, cut
  into approximately 48 strips
16 scallions, cut into 2-inch pieces
¼ cup light soy sauce
3 cloves garlic, minced

1½ tablespoons minced fresh gingerroot
1 tablespoon honey
1 tablespoon toasted sesame seeds
½ teaspoon canola or light sesame oil
⅛ teaspoon black pepper

1. Soak 24 wooden skewers in water for 30 minutes. Place 2 pieces of chicken and 2 pieces of scallion on each skewer.
2. Lay the skewers in a baking dish.
3. Combine the soy sauce, garlic, gingerroot, honey, sesame seeds, oil, and black pepper. Pour half the marinade over the chicken.
4. Cover and marinate in the refrigerator for 6 hours, turning occasionally.
5. Brush the chicken with the reserved marinade and grill approximately 4 minutes on each side.

Calories Per Serving: 29   Carbohydrates: 3 g
Fat: 1 g   Dietary Fiber: 0 g
Cholesterol: 9 mg   Sodium: 219 mg
Protein: 4 g

Vegetables on Skewers

Yield: 16 servings (1 each) • *Preparation Time: 20 minutes plus 2 hours refrigeration time* • *Cooking Time: 10 minutes*

An array of vegetables are marinated in the refrigerator and then grilled.

16 ounces canned, water-packed arti-
choke hearts, drained
16 small white onions, peeled
16 cherry tomatoes
2 green bell peppers, cut into 1-inch
squares

16 mushroom caps
2 tablespoons light-flavored olive oil
⅓ cup cider vinegar
⅛ teaspoon black pepper
1 clove garlic, split

1. Place artichoke hearts, onions, tomatoes, peppers, and mushroom caps in a large bowl.
2. Combine oil, vinegar, black pepper, and garlic. Pour over vegetables.
3. Cover and refrigerate for 2 hours. Toss several times. Meanwhile, soak 16 wooden skewers in water for 30 minutes.
4. Drain vegetables, reserving marinade.
5. Thread each skewer with a mushroom cap, artichoke heart, green pepper square, tomato, and an onion.

6. Grill for 10 minutes or until thoroughly heated. Turn and baste with the marinade several times.

Calories Per Serving: 53
Fat: 2 g
Cholesterol: 0 mg
Protein: 2 g

Carbohydrates: 9 g
Dietary Fiber: 3 g
Sodium: 25 mg

❧ *Oriental Veggie Kabobs* ❧

YIELD: 12 servings (1 each) • *PREPARATION TIME: 25 minutes* •
COOKING TIME: 15 minutes

Sweet bell peppers, onions, and zucchini are brushed with a ginger-garlic sauce and grilled.

2 tablespoons canola or light sesame oil
2 cloves garlic, minced
1½ teaspoons fresh gingerroot, minced
¼ teaspoon ground cayenne pepper
2 tablespoons light soy sauce
2 tablespoons water
1 tablespoon rice vinegar

2 red bell peppers, cut into 1-inch pieces
2 yellow bell peppers, cut into 1-inch pieces
4 zucchini, cut into 1-inch pieces
4 onions, peeled and cut into quarters

1. Heat oil in a saucepan over medium heat. Add garlic, gingerroot, and cayenne. Stir-fry for 1 minute.
2. Stir in soy sauce, water, and vinegar. Bring to a boil. Set aside.
3. Arrange vegetables on 12 wooden skewers that have been soaked in water for 30 minutes, alternating red peppers, yellow peppers, zucchini, and onions. Brush with sauce.
4. Place on oiled grill above hot coals.
5. Cook for 4 minutes, turn, brush again with the sauce, and cook for 4 more minutes or until zucchini is tender-crisp.

Calories Per Serving: 59
Fat: 3 g
Cholesterol: 0 mg
Protein: 2 g

Carbohydrates: 8 g
Dietary Fiber: 2 g
Sodium: 93 mg

🖋 *Tiny Grilled Turkey Bites* 🖋

YIELD: *16 servings (2 each)* • PREPARATION TIME: *25 minutes* •
COOKING TIME: *4 minutes*

Ground turkey is combined with herbs, formed into tiny sausages, and grilled.

1¼ pounds low-fat ground turkey breast, crumbled	*½ teaspoon dried marjoram*
3 scallions, minced	*1 egg white, slightly beaten*
¾ teaspoon dried sage	*¼ cup minced fresh parsley*
	¼ teaspoon white pepper

1. Combine turkey with scallions, sage, marjoram, egg white, parsley, and pepper.
2. Shape turkey mixture into 2-inch-long sausages. Place sausages on oiled grill over hot coals. Cook for about 2 minutes or until they begin to brown. Turn and cook for 2 minutes on the other side.
3. Serve hot with wooden party picks.

Calories Per Serving: 33	Carbohydrates: 5 g
Fat: 0 g	Dietary Fiber: 0 g
Cholesterol: 5 mg	Sodium: 71 mg
Protein: 3 g	

🖋 *Mango Clams* 🖋

YIELD: *12 servings (2 each)* • PREPARATION TIME: *20 minutes* •
COOKING TIME: *10 minutes*

Clams are grilled and served with a fresh mango topping.

½ cup chopped fresh ripe mango	*1 tablespoon lime juice*
½ cup diced fresh tomato	*24 small clams in shells, scrubbed*
1 tablespoon minced onion	

1. Combine mango, tomato, onion, and lime juice in a bowl. Chill until clams are ready.
2. Place clams on a grill rack over hot coals. Grill for 10 minutes or until shells open. Discard any unopened clams.
3. Serve with a spoonful of mango topping on each clam.

Calories Per Serving: 77

Fat: 1 g

Cholesterol: 29 mg

Protein: 11 g

Carbohydrates: 5 g

Dietary Fiber: 0 g

Sodium: 64 mg

❧ *Scallop Kabobs* ❧

YIELD: 8 servings (2 each) • *PREPARATION TIME: 20 minutes plus 30 minutes refrigeration time* • *COOKING TIME: 8 minutes*

Sea scallops are grilled with green pepper, red pepper, yellow squash, and zucchini.

1 tablespoon lemon juice

2 teaspoons light-flavored olive oil

⅛ teaspoon black pepper

1 clove garlic, minced

32 large sea scallops, cut in half

16 1-inch pieces red bell pepper

8 ½-inch slices yellow summer squash, cut in half

16 1-inch pieces green bell pepper

8 ½-inch slices zucchini, cut in half

1. Combine lemon juice, olive oil, pepper, and garlic. Pour over sea scallops in a glass bowl. Cover and marinate in refrigerator for 30 minutes. Meanwhile, soak 16 wooden skewers in water for 30 minutes.
2. Remove scallops, reserving marinade.
3. Thread each skewer with a half-scallop, a piece of red pepper, a half-scallop, a piece of yellow squash, a half-scallop, a piece of green pepper, a half-scallop, and a piece of zucchini.
4. Grill over medium-hot coals, cooking for 4 minutes on each side, or until scallops are done. Baste frequently with reserved marinade.

Calories Per Serving: 74
Fat: 2 g
Cholesterol: 19 mg
Protein: 10 g

Carbohydrates: 4 g
Dietary Fiber: 1 g
Sodium: 93 mg

🌿 *Scallop Brochettes* 🌿

YIELD: 10 servings (2 each) • *PREPARATION TIME: 15 minutes* •
COOKING TIME: 10 minutes

Scallops, cherry tomatoes, artichokes, and mushrooms are grilled on skewers.

40 small scallops
20 medium mushrooms
20 cherry tomatoes
20 canned water-packed artichoke
    hearts
20 pitted black olives (optional)

3 tablespoons light-flavored olive oil
2 tablespoons lime juice
2 tablespoons minced fresh parsley
¼ teaspoon white pepper
¼ teaspoon dried oregano

1. Thread 2 scallops, 1 mushroom, 1 cherry tomato, 1 artichoke heart, and 1 olive, if using, on each of 20 wooden skewers that have been soaked in water for 30 minutes.
2. Combine olive oil, lime juice, parsley, white pepper, and oregano.
3. Brush skewered scallops and vegetables with olive oil mixture and grill for about 10 minutes, turning several times and brushing with oil mixture. Serve immediately.

Calories Per Serving: 98
Fat: 3 g
Cholesterol: 26 mg
Protein: 14 g

Carbohydrates: 4 g
Dietary Fiber: 1 g
Sodium: 128 mg

🌿 *Grilled Shrimp* 🌿

YIELD: 30 servings (2 each) • *PREPARATION TIME: 30 minutes plus overnight
refrigeration time* • *COOKING TIME: 4 minutes*

Medium shrimp are shelled and deveined, then marinated overnight in a mixture of beer, dry mustard, parsley, and scallions.

2 cups regular or nonalcoholic beer
2 tablespoons chopped scallions
1 tablespoon chopped fresh parsley
2 teaspoons dry mustard

⅛ teaspoon garlic powder
½ teaspoon black pepper
2 pounds uncooked medium shrimp,
shelled and deveined

1. Combine beer, scallions, parsley, mustard, garlic powder, and black pepper in a large bowl.
2. Add shrimp to bowl and refrigerate overnight, stirring several times.
3. Drain shrimp and reserve marinade.
4. Grill shrimp about 2 minutes on each side, basting with marinade.
5. Serve at once with wooden party picks.

Calories Per Serving: 32
Fat: 0 g
Cholesterol: 45 mg
Protein: 6 g

Carbohydrates: 1 g
Dietary Fiber: 0 g
Sodium: 212 mg

❧ *Salmon Skewers* ❧

YIELD: 16 servings (1 each) • *PREPARATION TIME: 15 minutes* •
COOKING TIME: 6 minutes

Cubes of salmon fillet are skewered with pineapple chunks and grilled.

1 pound salmon fillet, cut into ¾-inch
cubes
2 cups canned, water-packed pineapple
chunks, drained
1 tablespoon light-flavored olive oil

5 tablespoons orange or pineapple juice
½ teaspoon ground cinnamon
¼ teaspoon ground nutmeg
2 tablespoons brown sugar, firmly
packed

1. Soak 16 wooden skewers in water for 30 minutes. Thread skewers with alternating pieces of salmon and pineapple chunks.
2. Combine olive oil, juice, cinnamon, nutmeg, and brown sugar.
3. Brush skewered salmon and pineapple with olive oil mixture.
4. Grill skewers over hot coals on a grill for 3 minutes. Turn skewers over. Grill for 3 minutes more. The salmon is done when it flakes easily when tested with a fork.

Calories Per Serving: 78

Fat: 3 g

Cholesterol: 20 mg

Protein: 7 g

Carbohydrates: 5 g

Dietary Fiber: 0 g

Sodium: 17 mg

❦ Mussels Grilled in Wine Sauce ❦

YIELD: 12 servings (1 packet each) • *PREPARATION TIME: 20 minutes* •
COOKING TIME: 6 minutes

Guests love these surprise packets that are cooked on the grill and filled with
mussels in a wine-garlic sauce. Serve with chunks of French bread.

*4 dozen small mussels, scrubbed and
debearded*
½ cup dry white wine

1 medium onion, minced
3 cloves garlic, minced
1 teaspoon dried thyme

1. Tear 12 12-inch-long sheets of heavy-duty aluminum foil.
2. Place 4 mussels in the center of each sheet of foil.
3. Gather up sides of foil around mussels but do not seal.
4. Sprinkle each package of mussels with wine, onion, garlic, and thyme.
   Twist the top of each package securely.
5. Place foil packets on hot coals and cook for 3 minutes. Turn package and
   cook for 3 minutes more. Stop cooking as soon as mussels are open.
   Discard any unopened mussels.
6. Serve each guest a packet of mussels with small plates and cocktail forks.

Calories Per Serving: 143

Fat: 3 g

Cholesterol: 42 mg

Protein: 18 g

Carbohydrates: 7 g

Dietary Fiber: 0 g

Sodium: 434 mg

CHIPS, SNACKS, AND SWEETS

Tortilla Chips • Garlic Bagel Chips • Broiled Lemon–Sesame Bagel Thins • Sesame Pita Chips • French Parmesan Toasts • Root-Veggie Chips • Idaho Potato Chips • Sweet-Potato Chips • Wonton Chips • Sesame Wonton Snacks • Mexicali Wontons • Curried Wontons • Parmesan Wontons • Parmesan Bread Sticks • Sesame–Wheat Thins • Tomato-Cheese Biscuits • Hacienda Popcorn • Popcorn Italia • Peanut Butter Popcorn • Cinnamon–Maple Popcorn • Honey-Spice Popcorn • Herbed Popcorn • Spicy Crunch Mix • Popcorn Crunch • Spiced Chickpeas • Olives with Onions and Herbs • Tiny Walnut Wonton Turnovers • Raisin Brown Bread Minimuffins • Tiny Corn Muffins • Berry Bites • Angel Food–Walnut Ice Cream Treats • Walnut-Meringue Treats

❦ Tortilla Chips ❦

YIELD: 4 servings (12 each) • *PREPARATION TIME: 5 minutes* •
COOKING TIME: 3 minutes

These easy-to-fix chips are low in fat and ideal for snacking and dipping.

6 corn tortillas　　　　　　　　　　*Ground cumin*
Olive oil cooking spray

1. Preheat oven to 400 degrees. Cut tortillas into 8 triangles each. Place in a single layer on a baking sheet.
2. Coat tortilla pieces lightly with olive oil spray and sprinkle with cumin.
3. Bake in the top part of the oven for 3 minutes. Cool and serve.

Calories Per Serving: 102　　　　　Carbohydrates: 19 g
Fat: 2 g　　　　　　　　　　　　　Dietary Fiber: 2 g
Cholesterol: 0 mg　　　　　　　　Sodium: 80 mg
Protein: 3 g

❦ Garlic Bagel Chips ❦

YIELD: 8 servings (4 each) • *PREPARATION TIME: 10 minutes* •
COOKING TIME: 10 minutes

Use plain, rye, or pumpernickel bagels for these crunchy chips. Serve with cheese-based dips.

4 bagels sliced crosswise into ⅛-inch　　*Olive oil cooking spray*
*　slices*　　　　　　　　　　　　　　　*Garlic powder*

1. Preheat oven to 300 degrees. Arrange bagel slices in a single layer on a baking sheet and spray with olive oil cooking spray.
2. Sprinkle with garlic powder and bake for 10 minutes or until lightly browned.

Calories Per Serving: 82

Carbohydrates: 15 g

Fat: 1 g

Dietary Fiber: 1 g

Cholesterol: 0 mg

Sodium: 99 mg

Protein: 3 g

✎ *Broiled Lemon-Sesame Bagel Thins* ✎

YIELD: 5 servings (5 each) • *PREPARATION TIME: 15 minutes* •
COOKING TIME: 6 minutes

Try these flavored bagels with yogurt-based dips and other dips with a Mediterranean flavor.

5 sesame bagels

6 cloves garlic, minced

⅓ cup light-flavored olive oil

2 tablespoons lemon juice

1. Preheat broiler. Slice bagels crosswise into fifths.
2. Heat oil in a skillet over medium heat. Add garlic and sauté until tender. Stir in lemon juice.
3. Brush side of each bagel slice with olive oil mixture.
4. Toast bagels on one side for 1 minute or until lightly browned. Turn and broil the other side. Serve warm.

Calories Per Serving: 67

Carbohydrates: 13 g

Fat: 1 g

Dietary Fiber: 0 g

Cholesterol: 0 mg

Sodium: 79 mg

Protein: 2 g

✎ *Sesame Pita Chips* ✎

YIELD: 6 servings (8 each) • *PREPARATION TIME: 10 minutes* •
COOKING TIME: 8 minutes

Serve these chips with eggplant and chickpea dips.

3 pita breads   Sesame seeds
Olive oil cooking spray

1. Preheat oven to 375 degrees. Split 3 pita breads to make 6 large rounds. Cut each round into 8 wedges. Place in a single layer on a baking sheet.
2. Coat with olive oil spray. Sprinkle with sesame seeds.
3. Bake in the top part of the oven for 7 minutes or until crisp.

Calories Per Serving: 70   Carbohydrates: 11 g
Fat: 2 g   Dietary Fiber: 1 g
Cholesterol: 0 mg   Sodium: 108 mg
Protein: 3 g

❧ *French Parmesan Toasts* ❧

YIELD: *10 servings (1 each)* • PREPARATION TIME: *10 minutes* •
COOKING TIME: *15 minutes*

Serve these Parmesan toasts with salsa or bean dips.

3 teaspoons light-flavored olive oil   2 teaspoons dried oregano
2 tablespoons hot water   2 cloves garlic, minced
3 tablespoons nonfat or reduced-fat   1 loaf French bread, cut into 10 slices
   Parmesan cheese

1. Preheat oven to 350 degrees. Whisk together oil, water, Parmesan, oregano, and garlic.
2. Brush both sides of each bread slice with the garlic mixture.
3. Reassemble the loaf and wrap tightly in a piece of foil.
4. Bake for 15 minutes.

Calories Per Serving: 126   Carbohydrates: 20 g
Fat: 3 g   Dietary Fiber: 0 g
Cholesterol: 1 mg   Sodium: 263 mg
Protein: 4 g

❧ *Root-Veggie Chips* ❧

YIELD: 8 servings (4 each) ▪ PREPARATION TIME: 15 minutes ▪
COOKING TIME: 30 minutes

Turnips and parsnips are baked to make these crisp snacks.

4 ounces turnips   *Olive oil cooking spray*
4 ounces parsnips

1. Preheat oven to 300 degrees. Cut turnips and parsnips into ¼-inch slices.
2. Place in a single layer on a baking sheet. Lightly mist with olive oil spray.
3. Bake for 30 minutes or until crisp and lightly browned.

Calories Per Serving: 29   Carbohydrates: 7 g
Fat: 0 g   Dietary Fiber: 2 g
Cholesterol: 0 mg   Sodium: 11 mg
Protein: 1 g

❧ *Idaho Potato Chips* ❧

YIELD: 8 servings (4 each) ▪ PREPARATION TIME: 15 minutes ▪
COOKING TIME: 40 to 50 minutes

Idaho potatoes are sliced and baked until crisp and brown and may be sprinkled with herbs and grated cheese.

8 ounces Idaho potatoes, scrubbed

1. Preheat oven to 300 degrees. Cut potatoes into thin slices.
2. Place in a single layer on a baking sheet. Bake until crisp and lightly browned, between 40 and 50 minutes. Serve at once.

Calories Per Serving: 26   Carbohydrates: 6 g
Fat: 0 g   Dietary Fiber: 1 g
Cholesterol: 0 mg   Sodium: 1 mg
Protein: 1 g

❧ *Sweet-Potato Chips* ❧

YIELD: 8 servings (¼ cup each) ▪ *PREPARATION TIME: 15 minutes* ▪
COOKING TIME: 40 to 50 minutes

Baked sweet potato chips are a healthy, crispy snack and also make excellent dippers.

8 ounces sweet potatoes, scrubbed

1. Preheat oven to 300 degrees. Cut potatoes into thin slices.
2. Place in a single layer on a baking sheet. Bake until crisp and lightly browned, between 40 and 50 minutes. Serve at once.

Calories Per Serving: 16   Carbohydrates: 4 g
Fat: 0 g   Dietary Fiber: 1 g
Cholesterol: 0 mg   Sodium: 6 mg
Protein: 0 g

❧ *Wonton Chips* ❧

YIELD: 12 servings (4 chips each) ▪ *PREPARATION TIME: 15 minutes* ▪
COOKING TIME: 5 minutes

Wonton skins are baked into crispy, golden brown chips that can be enjoyed on their own or served with dips that have an oriental flavor.

Olive oil cooking spray
24 square wonton wrappers, stacked
and cut in half diagonally

1. Preheat oven to 400 degrees. Coat baking sheet with olive oil spray.
2. Arrange wonton halves on baking sheet so that their edges aren't touching. Coat the tops of each of the 48 wonton triangles with olive oil spray.
3. Bake for 5 minutes or until wontons are lightly browned.

Calories Per Serving: 66

Fat: 3 g

Cholesterol: 2 mg

Protein: 2 g

Carbohydrates: 9 g

Dietary Fiber: 0 g

Sodium: 92 mg

❧ *Sesame Wonton Snacks* ❧

YIELD: 24 servings (2 each) • *PREPARATION TIME: 10 minutes* • *COOKING TIME: 7 minutes*

Wonton skins are baked with soy sauce, sesame seeds, and light sesame oil.

2 tablespoons light soy sauce
1 tablespoon light sesame or canola oil

24 wonton wrappers, stacked and cut in half diagonally
2 tablespoons sesame seeds

1. Preheat oven to 375. Combine soy sauce and oil.
2. Arrange wonton halves on a foil-lined baking sheet so that their edges are not touching.
3. Brush with soy-oil mixture. Sprinkle with sesame seeds.
4. Bake for 7 minutes. Cool on a wire rack.

Calories Per Serving: 33

Fat: 1 g

Cholesterol: 1 mg

Protein: 1 g

Carbohydrates: 5 g

Dietary Fiber: 0 g

Sodium: 92 mg

❧ *Mexicali Wontons* ❧

YIELD: 24 servings (2 each) • *PREPARATION TIME: 10 minutes* • *COOKING TIME: 7 minutes*

Wontons are baked with olive oil and chili powder.

24 wonton wrappers, stacked and cut in half diagonally

¼ cup light-flavored olive oil
Chili powder

1. Preheat oven to 375 degrees. Arrange wonton halves on a foil-lined baking sheet so that their edges are not touching.
2. Brush wontons with olive oil and sprinkle with chili powder.
3. Bake for 7 minutes. Cool on a wire rack.

Calories Per Serving: 43
Fat: 2 g
Cholesterol: 1 mg
Protein: 1 g

Carbohydrates: 5 g
Dietary Fiber: 0 g
Sodium: 47 mg

❧ *Curried Wontons* ❧

YIELD: 24 servings (2 each) • *PREPARATION TIME: 10 minutes* •
COOKING TIME: 7 minutes

Wontons are baked with olive oil and curry powder.

*24 wonton wrappers, stacked and cut
in half diagonally*

*¼ cup light-flavored olive oil
Curry powder*

1. Preheat oven to 375 degrees. Arrange wonton halves on a foil-lined baking sheet so that their edges are not touching.
2. Brush wontons with olive oil and sprinkle with curry powder.
3. Bake for 7 minutes. Cool on a wire rack.

Calories Per Serving: 43
Fat: 2 g
Cholesterol: 1 mg
Protein: 1 g

Carbohydrates: 5 g
Dietary Fiber: 0 g
Sodium: 46 mg

❧ *Parmesan Wontons* ❧

YIELD: 24 servings (2 each) • *PREPARATION TIME: 10 minutes* •
COOKING TIME: 7 minutes

Wontons are baked with olive oil and Parmesan cheese.

24 wonton wrappers, stacked and cut
  in half diagonally
¼ cup light-flavored olive oil

¼ cup grated nonfat or reduced-fat
  Parmesan cheese

1. Preheat oven to 375 degrees. Arrange wonton halves on a foil-lined baking sheet so that their edges are not touching.
2. Brush wontons with olive oil and sprinkle with Parmesan cheese.
3. Bake for 7 minutes. Cool on a wire rack.

Calories Per Serving: 48
Fat: 3 g
Cholesterol: 2 mg
Protein: 1 g

Carbohydrates: 5 g
Dietary Fiber: 0 g
Sodium: 65 mg

❦ *Parmesan Bread Sticks* ❦

YIELD: 10 servings (4 each) • *PREPARATION TIME: 20 minutes* •
COOKING TIME: 25 minutes

You can quickly and easily make fresh bread sticks to serve with dips or spreads using frozen bread dough. Substitute sesame seeds, garlic powder, dill, or other favorite herbs and spices for the topping.

1 pound frozen bread dough, defrosted
Chili powder

½ cup grated nonfat or reduced-fat
  Parmesan cheese

1. Preheat oven to 350 degrees. Use 1 tablespoon of dough per stick, and roll dough with hands into 8-inch sticks. Dip each stick in water. Sprinkle with chili powder and roll in Parmesan cheese.
2. Place sticks on an ungreased cookie sheet. Bake for 25 minutes.

Calories Per Serving: 12
Fat: 0 g
Cholesterol: 4 mg
Protein: 2 g

Carbohydrates: 2 g
Dietary Fiber: 0 g
Sodium: 37 mg

✒ *Sesame-Wheat Thins* ✒

YIELD: 25 servings (3 each) • *PREPARATION TIME: 25 minutes* •
COOKING TIME: 18 minutes

If you want to avoid serving crackers that are loaded with saturated or polyunsaturated fat with your dips, try making these simple wheat thins with canola oil.

1 cup whole wheat flour	*½ teaspoon salt*
1 cup unbleached, all-purpose flour	*¼ cup canola oil*
¼ cup sesame seeds	*½ cup water*

1. Preheat oven to 350 degrees. Combine whole wheat flour and all-purpose flour, sesame seeds, and salt.
2. Make a well in center of mixture; pour oil and water into well. Stir until blended.
3. Shape dough into a ball; roll out ⅛ inch thick on a lightly floured board. Cut into 2-inch-by-1-inch strips.
4. Arrange on an ungreased baking sheet and bake 15 to 20 minutes until golden brown.

Calories Per Serving: 62	Carbohydrates: 8 g
Fat: 3 g	Dietary Fiber: 1 g
Cholesterol: 0 mg	Sodium: 43 mg
Protein: 1 g	

✒ *Tomato-Cheese Biscuits* ✒

YIELD: 8 servings (2 each) • *PREPARATION TIME: 20 minutes* •
COOKING TIME: 15 minutes

Low-fat biscuits are made special by the addition of tomato juice, basil, and cheddar cheese.

2 cups unbleached, all-purpose flour
2 teaspoons baking powder
¼ teaspoon baking soda
½ teaspoon salt
½ cup grated nonfat or reduced-fat
  cheddar cheese

⅓ cup canola oil
⅔ cup low-sodium tomato juice
½ teaspoon dried basil

1. Preheat oven to 475 degrees. Sift together the flour, baking powder, soda, and salt into a mixing bowl.
2. Stir cheese into flour mixture.
3. Add oil, tomato juice, and basil to flour mixture and stir with a fork until dough is well mixed.
4. Place dough on a lightly floured board and knead about 10 times.
5. Roll out to ½-inch thickness on a lightly floured board and cut into rounds with a 2-inch biscuit cutter.
6. Place on an ungreased baking sheet and bake for 15 minutes or until golden.

Calories Per Serving: 211
Fat: 1 g
Cholesterol: 0 mg
Protein: 5 g

Carbohydrates: 26 g
Dietary Fiber: 1 g
Sodium: 294 mg

⚜ *Hacienda Popcorn* ⚜

YIELD: 16 servings (½ cup each) • *PREPARATION TIME: 10 minutes* •
COOKING TIME: 5 minutes

Air-popped popcorn is mixed with Mexican spices and Parmesan cheese.

8 cups air-popped popcorn
1 tablespoon canola oil
½ teaspoon chili powder
½ teaspoon dried cumin

⅛ teaspoon ground cayenne pepper
¼ cup grated nonfat or reduced-fat
  Parmesan cheese

1. Place the popcorn in a bowl while hot.
2. Heat the oil in a skillet; add the chili powder, cumin, and cayenne pepper. Stir for 1 minute.
3. Pour the oil mixture over the popcorn. Toss with Parmesan cheese and serve.

Calories Per Serving: 32
Fat: 1 g
Cholesterol: 1 mg
Protein: 1 g

Carbohydrates: 5 g
Dietary Fiber: 0 g
Sodium: 12 mg

Popcorn Italia

YIELD: 16 servings (½ cup each) • *PREPARATION TIME: 10 minutes* • *COOKING TIME: 5 minutes*

Air-popped popcorn is tossed with Italian herbs and Parmesan cheese.

8 cups air-popped popcorn
2 tablespoons light-flavored olive oil
1 teaspoon dried oregano

½ teaspoon dried thyme
¼ cup grated nonfat or reduced-fat Parmesan cheese

1. Place the popcorn in a large bowl while hot.
2. Heat the oil; add the oregano and thyme and stir for 1 minute.
3. Pour the oil mixture over the popcorn. Toss with Parmesan cheese and serve.

Calories Per Serving: 39
Fat: 2 g
Cholesterol: 1 mg
Protein: 1 g

Carbohydrates: 5 g
Dietary Fiber: 0 g
Sodium: 11 mg

✎ *Peanut Butter Popcorn* ✎

YIELD: 16 servings (½ cup each) • *PREPARATION TIME: 10 minutes* •
COOKING TIME: 5 minutes

Popcorn and raisins are tossed with peanut butter and honey.

8 cups air-popped popcorn
2 cups seedless raisins
½ cup reduced-fat peanut butter
  substitute

¼ cup honey

1. Place the hot popcorn in a bowl and stir in the raisins.
2. Gently heat the peanut butter and honey together in a small saucepan.
3. Pour the heated peanut butter–honey mixture over the popcorn, toss, and
   serve.

Calories Per Serving: 116
Fat: 1 g
Cholesterol: 0 mg
Protein: 2 g

Carbohydrates: 25 g
Dietary Fiber: 1 g
Sodium: 65 mg

✎ *Cinnamon-Maple Popcorn* ✎

YIELD: 16 servings (½ cup each) • *PREPARATION TIME: 10 minutes* •
COOKING TIME: 15 minutes

Maple syrup and cinnamon are baked with popcorn.

8 cups air-popped popcorn
2 tablespoons canola oil

6 tablespoons maple syrup
1 teaspoon ground cinnamon

1. Preheat oven to 250 degrees. Place popcorn in a large baking pan.
2. Heat oil in a skillet and stir in maple syrup and cinnamon.
3. Stir maple syrup mixture into popcorn in baking pan.
4. Bake for 15 minutes.

Calories Per Serving: 60
Fat: 3 g
Cholesterol: 0 mg
Protein: 1 g

Carbohydrates: 9 g
Dietary Fiber: 0 g
Sodium: 1 mg

☙ *Honey-Spice Popcorn* ☙

YIELD: 16 servings (½ cup each) • *PREPARATION TIME: 10 minutes* •
COOKING TIME: 15 minutes

Honey, cloves, nutmeg, and cinnamon are baked with popcorn and almonds.

8 cups air-popped popcorn
¼ cup canola oil
¼ cup honey

¼ teaspoon ground cloves
¼ teaspoon ground nutmeg
¼ teaspoon ground cinnamon

1. Preheat oven to 250 degrees. Place popcorn in a large baking pan.
2. Heat oil in a skillet and stir in honey, cloves, nutmeg, and cinnamon.
3. Stir honey mixture into popped corn in baking pan.
4. Bake for 15 minutes.

Calories Per Serving: 49
Fat: 3 g
Cholesterol: 0 mg
Protein: 0 g

Carbohydrates: 5 g
Dietary Fiber: 0 g
Sodium: 0 mg

☙ *Herbed Popcorn* ☙

YIELD: 16 servings (½ cup each) • *PREPARATION TIME: 10 minutes*

Air-popped popcorn is tossed with scallions and basil.

8 cups air-popped popcorn
¼ cup minced scallion tops

1 tablespoon canola oil
1 teaspoon dried basil

1. Place hot popcorn in a large bowl and toss with scallions.
2. Heat oil in a skillet and stir in basil.
3. Pour oil over popcorn and toss well.

Calories Per Serving: 28
Fat: 1 g
Cholesterol: 0 mg
Protein: 1 g

Carbohydrates: 4 g
Dietary Fiber: 0 g
Sodium: 0 mg

❦ *Spicy Crunch Mix* ❦

YIELD: 20 servings (½ cup each) • PREPARATION TIME: 15 minutes •
COOKING TIME: 20 minutes

Popcorn, pretzels, and cereal squares are combined with raisins, walnuts, and a variety of spices.

3 tablespoons canola oil
2 teaspoons Worcestershire sauce
2 teaspoons light soy sauce
½ teaspoon dry mustard
½ teaspoon ground ginger
½ teaspoon minced garlic
⅛ teaspoon hot pepper sauce

4 cups air-popped popcorn
2 cups unsalted thin pretzel sticks
2 cups nonfat wheat or corn cereal squares
2 cups seedless raisins
¾ cup chopped apricots
¼ cup walnut pieces

1. Preheat oven to 350 degrees. Combine oil, Worcestershire sauce, soy sauce, mustard, ginger, garlic, and hot pepper sauce.
2. In a separate bowl, combine popcorn, pretzels, cereal squares, raisins, apricots, and walnuts.
3. Combine oil mixture with popcorn mixture and toss well.
4. Spread in a shallow baking pan. Bake for 10 minutes, stirring several times. Turn oven off.
5. Let mix stand in oven 10 minutes. Remove and cool.

Calories Per Serving: 118
Fat: 3 g
Cholesterol: 0 mg
Protein: 2 g

Carbohydrates: 22 g
Dietary Fiber: 1 g
Sodium: 128 mg

❧ *Popcorn Crunch* ❧

YIELD: 14 servings (½ cup each) • *PREPARATION TIME: 10 minutes*

Serve this combination of popcorn, whole-grain cereal, peanuts, and raisins as a healthy, great-tasting snack.

5 cups air-popped popcorn	*¼ cup unsalted dry-roasted peanuts*
1 cup unsweetened whole-grain cereal	*½ cup seedless raisins*

1. Place the popcorn, cereal, peanuts, and raisins in a large bowl and toss well.

Calories Per Serving: 51	Carbohydrates: 9 g
Fat: 1 g	Dietary Fiber: 1 g
Cholesterol: 0 mg	Sodium: 21 mg
Protein: 1 g	

❧ *Spiced Chickpeas* ❧

YIELD: 18 servings (2 tablespoons each) • *PREPARATION TIME: 10 minutes* •
COOKING TIME: 8 minutes

Serve this unusual snack as an extra taste treat with a curried dip and vegetables.

2 tablespoons sugar	*⅛ teaspoon ground cayenne pepper*
½ teaspoon ground cumin	*2 cups canned or home-cooked chick-*
½ teaspoon chili powder	*peas, rinsed and drained*
½ teaspoon ground paprika	*2 teaspoons canola oil*
¼ teaspoon ground coriander	

1. Combine the sugar, cumin, chili powder, paprika, coriander, and cayenne pepper. Add the chickpeas and toss.
2. Heat the oil in a skillet over medium heat, add the chickpea mixture, and cook, shaking the pan frequently, about 8 minutes or until the chickpeas become crispy.

3. Transfer the chickpeas to a wire rack covered with paper towels to cool.

Calories Per Serving: 67
Fat: 3 g
Cholesterol: 2 mg
Protein: 2 g

Carbohydrates: 8 g
Dietary Fiber: 2 g
Sodium: 90 mg

✏ *Olives with Onions and Herbs* ✏

YIELD: 60 servings (2 each) • *PREPARATION TIME: 15 minutes plus overnight refrigeration time*

Green olives, onion, and celery are marinated in olive oil, vinegar, chili powder, basil, and oregano.

3½ cups pitted green olives
1 small onion, finely chopped
1 stalk celery, finely chopped
¼ cup light-flavored olive oil

¼ cup white wine vinegar
⅛ teaspoon chili powder
1 tablespoon dried basil
1½ teaspoons dried oregano

1. Combine olives, onion, celery, olive oil, vinegar, chili powder, basil, and oregano in a glass bowl. Toss well.
2. Cover and refrigerate overnight.

Calories Per Serving: 19
Fat: 2 g
Cholesterol: 0 mg
Protein: 0 g

Carbohydrates: 0 g
Dietary Fiber: 0 g
Sodium: 207 mg

✏ *Tiny Walnut Wonton Turnovers* ✏

YIELD: 16 servings (1 each) • *PREPARATION TIME: 25 minutes* • *COOKING TIME: 15 minutes*

Wonton wrappers are filled with walnuts, honey, and lemon peel.

½ *cup finely chopped walnuts*
2 *tablespoons honey*
¼ *teaspoon grated lemon peel*
16 *square wonton wrappers*

2 *egg whites, lightly beaten*
3 *tablespoons canola oil*
2 *tablespoons powdered sugar*

1. Combine walnuts, honey, and lemon peel.
2. Place a teaspoon of filling in the middle of each wonton wrapper.
3. Brush egg white around edges of wrapper. Fold over and press to seal.
4. Heat oil in a skillet over medium heat. Cook wontons in oil until they are lightly browned. Drain on paper towels and dust with powdered sugar.

Calories Per Serving: 67
Fat: 3 g
Cholesterol: 1 mg
Protein: 2 g

Carbohydrates: 8 g
Dietary Fiber: 0 g
Sodium: 53 mg

◿ *Raisin Brown Bread Minimuffins* ◿

YIELD: 18 servings (2 each) • PREPARATION TIME: 20 minutes •
COOKING TIME: 12 to 14 minutes

These tasty muffins are a combination of whole wheat flour, brown sugar, pumpkin pie spice, buttermilk, and raisins. Serve with pumpkin or apple butter.

Olive oil cooking spray
2 *cups whole wheat flour*
⅔ *cup unbleached, all-purpose flour*
⅔ *cup brown sugar, firmly packed*

2 *teaspoons baking soda*
1 *teaspoon pumpkin pie spice*
2 *cups nonfat buttermilk*
¾ *cup raisins*

1. Preheat oven to 350 degrees. Lightly coat 36 miniature muffin cups with olive oil cooking spray.
2. Combine whole wheat flour, all-purpose flour, brown sugar, baking soda, and pumpkin pie spice.
3. Stir buttermilk into flour mixture until dry ingredients are just moistened. Stir in raisins.
4. Pour into muffin cups.

5. Bake for 12 to 14 minutes or until a wooden pick inserted in the center comes out clean.

Calories Per Serving: 115
Fat: 0 g
Cholesterol: 0 mg
Protein: 3 g

Carbohydrates: 26 g
Dietary Fiber: 2 g
Sodium: 150 mg

❧ *Tiny Corn Muffins* ❧

YIELD: 18 servings (2 each) • PREPARATION TIME: 20 minutes •
COOKING TIME: 12 to 15 minutes

Jalapeño peppers spice up these tiny cornmeal muffins.

Olive oil cooking spray
1½ cups cornmeal
½ cup unbleached, all-purpose flour
1 tablespoon sugar
2 teaspoons baking powder

½ teaspoon baking soda
⅛ teaspoon salt (optional)
1 cup nonfat or reduced-fat sour cream
4 egg whites, lightly beaten
2 teaspoons minced jalapeño peppers

1. Preheat oven to 350 degrees. Lightly coat 36 miniature muffin cups with olive oil cooking spray.
2. Combine cornmeal, flour, sugar, baking powder, baking soda, and salt, if using, in a bowl.
3. Combine sour cream, egg whites, and peppers in a second bowl.
4. Stir sour cream mixture into flour mixture until ingredients are just moistened. Pour into muffin cups.
5. Bake for 12 to 15 minutes or until a wooden pick inserted in the center comes out clean.

Calories Per Serving: 77
Fat: 0 g
Cholesterol: 4 mg
Protein: 3 g

Carbohydrates: 15 g
Dietary Fiber: 1 g
Sodium: 102 mg

❧ *Berry Bites* ❧

YIELD: 36 servings (1 each) • *PREPARATION TIME: 20 minutes* •
COOKING TIME: 15 minutes

Fresh strawberry or blueberry minimuffins are a perfect choice to serve with coffee or tea, or as an offering on a buffet of appetizers.

Olive oil cooking spray
2 cups unbleached all-purpose flour
½ cup sugar
1 tablespoon baking powder
¼ teaspoon salt

¾ cup skim or 1% milk
⅓ cup canola oil
2 egg whites, lightly beaten
1 cup chopped fresh strawberries or blueberries

1. Preheat oven to 375 degrees. Spray 36 minimuffin cups with olive oil cooking spray.
2. Combine flour, sugar, baking powder, and salt in a bowl.
3. Combine milk, oil, and egg whites in a second bowl.
4. Add wet ingredients to dry ingredients and stir until dry ingredients are just moistened.
5. Fold in berries.
6. Spoon 1 rounded tablespoonful of batter into each minimuffin cup.
7. Bake for 13 to 15 minutes or until lightly golden around the edges.
8. Cool for 5 minutes and remove from pan.

Calories Per Serving: 58
Fat: 2 g
Cholesterol: 0 mg
Protein: 1 g

Carbohydrates: 9 g
Dietary Fiber: 0 g
Sodium: 7 mg

❧ *Angel Food–Walnut Ice Cream Treats*

YIELD: 8 servings (1 each) • *PREPARATION TIME: 25 minutes* •
COOKING TIME: 10 minutes

Serve these frozen treats as a minidessert with an appetizer buffet.

2 cups miniature marshmallows
¼ cup skim milk
6 ounces angel food cake
1 pint nonfat or reduced-fat chocolate
* yogurt or tofu frozen dessert*

½ cup walnuts, chopped
2 teaspoons unsweetened cocoa
* powder*

1. Combine marshmallows and milk in a small pot and simmer over very low heat, stirring constantly. When marshmallows are partially dissolved, remove from heat; set aside to cool. Stir several times while cooling.
2. Cut cake into 16 slices.
3. When marshmallow mixture has cooled, soften frozen yogurt slightly and stir in a bowl with nuts.
4. Swirl marshmallow mixture into frozen yogurt.
5. Spread about ¼ cup of the yogurt/marshmallow mixture on a slice of cake. Top yogurt with another cake slice.
6. Dust each sandwich with cocoa powder and wrap in foil or plastic wrap. Place sandwiches in a freezer bag, seal, and store until ready to serve.

Calories Per Serving: 192
Fat: 3 g
Cholesterol: 1 mg
Protein: 8 g

Carbohydrates: 35 g
Dietary Fiber: 0 g
Sodium: 118 mg

❧ *Walnut-Meringue Treats* ❧

YIELD: 18 servings (2 cookies each) • *PREPARATION TIME: 20 minutes* •
COOKING TIME: 25 minutes

These meringue cookies with walnuts make a special sweet addition to a selection of appetizers.

2 egg whites
⅛ teaspoon salt
⅛ teaspoon cream of tartar

1 teaspoon vanilla extract
¾ cup sugar
6 ounces finely chopped walnuts

1. Preheat oven to 300 degrees. Beat egg whites, salt, cream of tartar, and vanilla until soft peaks form.
2. Continue beating while adding sugar, a tablespoon at a time, until stiff peaks form.
3. Fold in walnuts.
4. Drop a tablespoonful of batter for each cookie on cookie sheets covered with brown paper. Bake for 25 minutes.

Calories Per Serving: 92
Fat: 2 g
Cholesterol: 0 mg
Protein: 1 g

Carbohydrates: 21 g
Dietary Fiber: 2 g
Sodium: 3 mg

MICROWAVE APPETIZERS

Hot Spinach-Carrot Dip · Eggplant-Dijon Dip · Sesame-Eggplant Dip · Chile-Cheese Dip · Southwestern Chile Dip · Mushroom Spread · Parmesan Pita Chips · Pita Chips · Bagel Bites · Little Tortillas · Mushrooms with Sun-Dried Tomatoes · Parmesan Mushrooms · Sardine Mushrooms · Anchovy Mushrooms · Sausage-Pizza Mushroom Caps · Mushroom–Pita Pizza Snacks · Minipizzas · Chili Bean Cups · Minimeatballs with Yogurt Sauce · Meatballs with Tangy Apricot Sauce · Basic Shrimp · Ginger-Honey Chicken Wings · Apple Chunks with Peanut Sauce · Snow Peas with Sesame-Soy Dipping Sauce · Salmon-Stuffed Snow Peas · Zucchini Strips · Yellow Summer Squash with Greek Tomato Sauce · Squash Nachos · Carrots with Red Pepper Sauce · Cauliflower with Mustard and Parsley · Yogurt-Scallion–Stuffed Potatoes · Potatoes with Tomato-Jalapeño Topping

❦ *Hot Spinach-Carrot Dip* ❦

YIELD: 32 servings (1 tablespoon each) ▪ *PREPARATION TIME: 15 minutes* ▪
COOKING TIME: 5 minutes

You can make this classic spinach dip the quick and easy way in your microwave.

9 ounces frozen spinach, thawed,
   drained, and chopped
½ cup shredded carrot
½ red bell pepper, chopped

½ teaspoon dried dill
8 ounces nonfat or reduced-fat cream
   cheese, softened
½ cup nonfat or reduced-fat sour cream

1. Combine spinach, carrot, bell pepper, dill, cream cheese, and sour cream in a 1-quart microwave-safe casserole. Cover with microwave-safe plastic wrap.
2. Microwave on HIGH for 5 minutes, stirring several times.

Calories Per Serving: 15
Fat: 0 g
Cholesterol: 2 mg
Protein: 2 g

Carbohydrates: 2 g
Dietary Fiber: 0 g
Sodium: 60 mg

❦ *Eggplant-Dijon Dip* ❦

YIELD: 24 servings (1 tablespoon each) ▪ *PREPARATION TIME: 20 minutes plus
2 hours refrigeration time* ▪ *COOKING TIME: 10 minutes*

Eggplant, mustard, basil, parsley, yogurt, garlic, and sun-dried tomatoes are combined in this dip.

1 medium eggplant, peeled and diced
2 tablespoons water
1 teaspoon Dijon mustard
1 teaspoon dried basil
2 tablespoons chopped fresh parsley
2 tablespoons nonfat or reduced-fat
   plain yogurt

1 clove garlic, chopped
2 tablespoons oil-packed sun-dried
   tomatoes, drained and patted dry
1/8 teaspoon black pepper
1 tablespoon light-flavored olive oil

1. Place eggplant in a 2-quart microwave-safe dish. Stir in water. Cover with wax paper and microwave on 100% HIGH for 5 minutes. Stir and microwave 4 minutes more or until eggplant is fork-tender.
2. Drain eggplant thoroughly, then place in a food processor or blender. Add mustard, basil, parsley, yogurt, garlic, sun-dried tomatoes, pepper, and olive oil. Process until almost smooth.
3. Cover and refrigerate at least 2 hours.

Calories Per Serving: 14
Fat: 1 g
Cholesterol: 0 mg
Protein: 0 g

Carbohydrates: 2 g
Dietary Fiber: 1 g
Sodium: 8 mg

Sesame-Eggplant Dip

YIELD: 24 servings (1 tablespoon each) • PREPARATION TIME: 20 minutes •
COOKING TIME: 15 minutes

This dip is made with eggplant, soy sauce, garlic, sesame oil, rice vinegar, and sesame seeds.

1 medium eggplant, peeled and cubed
1 tablespoon light soy sauce
1 clove garlic, minced

1 tablespoon canola or light sesame oil
2 tablespoons rice vinegar
1/4 cup toasted sesame seeds

1. Place eggplant, soy sauce, garlic, oil, and rice vinegar in a 2-quart microwave-safe bowl. Cover with vented plastic wrap.
2. Microwave on 100% HIGH for 15 minutes or until eggplant is quite soft.
3. Transfer eggplant mixture to a blender or food processor and process until smooth.

4. Stir in sesame seeds. Chill until ready to serve.

Calories Per Serving: 18   Carbohydrates: 2 g
Fat: 1 g   Dietary Fiber: 1 g
Cholesterol: 0 mg   Sodium: 23 mg
Protein: 0 g

❧ *Chile-Cheese Dip* ✍

YIELD: 40 servings (1 tablespoon each) • *PREPARATION TIME: 15 minutes* •
COOKING TIME: 14 minutes

Chiles, tomatoes, onion, and cheese are combined and microwaved to create
this dip. Serve with nonfat blue corn chips.

1 medium onion, finely chopped   *⅛ teaspoon hot pepper sauce*
4 ounces canned green chiles, drained   *6 ounces nonfat or reduced-fat cream*
* and chopped*   * cheese, cut into ½-inch cubes*
1 cup fresh or canned low-sodium   *½ cup shredded nonfat or reduced-fat*
* tomatoes, chopped*   * cheddar cheese*
⅛ teaspoon black pepper

1. Place onion and 2 tablespoons water in a microwave-safe casserole dish.
   Cover with wax paper. Microwave on 100% HIGH for 3 minutes.
2. Add chiles, tomatoes, black pepper, and hot pepper sauce. Microwave on
   50% MEDIUM for 4 minutes. Stir. Microwave 2 additional minutes.
3. Stir in half of the cream cheese and half of the cheddar cheese. Cover and
   microwave on 50% MEDIUM for 2 minutes.
4. Stir in rest of both cheeses. Microwave on 50% MEDIUM for 3 minutes.
   Serve hot.

Calories Per Serving: 12   Carbohydrates: 1 g
Fat: 0 g   Dietary Fiber: 0 g
Cholesterol: 1 mg   Sodium: 66 mg
Protein: 2 g

❦ *Southwestern Chile Dip* ❦

YIELD: 32 servings (1 tablespoon each) • *PREPARATION TIME: 15 minutes* •
COOKING TIME: 13 minutes

This chile-flavored dip is easy to prepare in the microwave. Keep the cheese warm enough for dipping by popping it back into the microwave for a couple of minutes.

1 tablespoon canola oil
1 medium onion, chopped
1 cup canned low-sodium tomatoes,
   juice reserved
4 ounces canned, chopped chiles

1 jalapeño pepper, peeled and
   chopped
¾ pound nonfat or reduced-fat mild
   cheddar cheese, cut into ½-inch cubes

1. Combine the oil and the onion in a microwave-safe casserole dish. Cook on 100% HIGH for 3 minutes or until onion is tender.
2. Stir in the tomatoes, chiles, and jalapeño pepper. Cook, uncovered, on 100% HIGH for 4 minutes, stirring once.
3. Stir in the cheese. Cook on 50% MEDIUM for 6 minutes, or until cheese is melted, stirring twice.

Calories Per Serving: 23
Fat: 0 g
Cholesterol: 0 mg
Protein: 3 g

Carbohydrates: 2 g
Dietary Fiber: 0 g
Sodium: 223 mg

❦ *Mushroom Spread* ❦

YIELD: 16 servings (1 tablespoon each) • *PREPARATION TIME: 30 minutes plus
2 hours refrigeration time* • *COOKING TIME: 7 minutes*

Mushrooms are combined with scallions, yogurt, sherry, nutmeg, and walnuts.

2 tablespoons light-flavored olive oil
¼ cup thinly sliced scallions

2 tablespoons unbleached all-purpose
   flour

2 tablespoons nonfat or reduced-fat
   plain yogurt
8 ounces fresh mushrooms, minced
2 tablespoons dry sherry

¼ teaspoon black pepper
¼ teaspoon grated nutmeg
¼ cup finely chopped walnuts

1. Combine oil and scallions in a microwave-safe 1-quart container. Cook on 100% HIGH for 2 minutes. Stir in flour to make a paste.
2. Stir in yogurt, mushrooms, sherry, pepper, and nutmeg.
3. Cook on 100% HIGH for 2 minutes. Stir. Cook for 3 more minutes.
4. Stir in walnuts.
5. Pack the mixture into a serving dish and chill for 2 hours.

Calories Per Serving: 34
Fat: 3 g
Cholesterol: 0 mg
Protein: 1 g

Carbohydrates: 2 g
Dietary Fiber: 0 g
Sodium: 2 mg

≫ *Parmesan Pita Chips* ⧹

YIELD: *20 servings (2 each)* • PREPARATION TIME: *15 minutes* •
COOKING TIME: *4 minutes*

Pita breads are brushed with olive oil and garlic, and then sprinkled with oregano and Parmesan cheese.

2 cloves garlic, minced
½ cup light-flavored olive oil
5 small pita breads

1 teaspoon dried oregano
¼ cup grated nonfat or reduced-fat
   Parmesan cheese

1. Combine garlic and olive oil in a small container.
2. Split each pita bread into 2 rounds. Cut each pita round into quarters.
3. Brush insides of chips with olive oil–garlic mixture.
4. Sprinkle chips with oregano and Parmesan cheese.
5. Place the chips on 4 paper plates, 8 to a plate.

6. Place 2 paper plates with chips in the microwave and cook uncovered on 100% HIGH for 2 minutes or until cheese is slightly melted. Repeat with the other batch of chips.

Calories Per Serving: 66
Fat: 3 g
Cholesterol: 0 mg
Protein: 1 g

Carbohydrates: 8 g
Dietary Fiber: 0 g
Sodium: 81 mg

◊ *Pita Chips* ◊

YIELD: 12 servings (6 each) • *PREPARATION TIME: 10 minutes* • *COOKING TIME: 10 minutes*

These crispy pita chips can be substituted for crackers.

3 whole wheat pita breads

1. Split each pita into two rounds. Cut each round in half, and each half into 6 wedges.
2. Place a paper towel on a plate and arrange 12 pieces of the pita in a circle. Microwave on 100% HIGH for 30 seconds or until crisp. Remove to cool and repeat process with remaining pita sections.

Calories Per Serving: 43
Fat: 0 g
Cholesterol: 0 mg
Protein: 2 g

Carbohydrates: 9 g
Dietary Fiber: 0 g
Sodium: 85 mg

◊ *Bagel Bites* ◊

YIELD: 24 servings (2 each) • *PREPARATION TIME: 5 minutes* • *COOKING TIME: 10 minutes*

Bagels are thinly sliced, brushed with olive oil, and microwaved.

4 bagels   *¼ cup light-flavored olive oil*

1. Using a bread knife, cut the bagels horizontally into 12 slices ⅛ inch thick. Brush both sides with olive oil. Arrange on a microwave roasting rack.
2. Microwave on 50% MEDIUM for 5 minutes. Turn and microwave for 5 minutes more or until both sides are crisp.

Calories Per Serving: 47   Carbohydrates: 5 g
Fat: 3 g   Dietary Fiber: 0 g
Cholesterol: 0 mg   Sodium: 53 mg
Protein: 3 g

❧ *Little Tortillas* ❧

YIELD: 16 servings (1 each) • *PREPARATION TIME: 25 minutes plus 3 minutes standing time* • *COOKING TIME: 10 minutes*

Soft flour tortillas are filled with a microwaved mixture of ground turkey, apple, tomatoes, jalapeño peppers, garlic, raisins, and spices.

1 pound low-fat ground turkey breast   *¼ cup chopped raisins*
1 large apple, peeled and grated   *½ teaspoon dried oregano*
2 large tomatoes, chopped and drained   *¼ teaspoon ground cumin*
2 jalapeño peppers, seeded and minced   *¼ teaspoon ground cinnamon*
2 cloves garlic, minced   *16 small soft flour tortillas*

1. Combine the turkey, apple, tomatoes, jalapeños, garlic, raisins, oregano, cumin, and cinnamon in a bowl.
2. Transfer half the mixture to a glass pie plate and cover with vented plastic wrap. Microwave on 100% HIGH for 4 minutes and stir. Microwave for 4 more minutes on HIGH and stir again. Microwave for 2 minutes more on HIGH or until the turkey is cooked and the mixture has thickened. Let stand for 3 minutes.
3. Repeat step 2 with remainder of turkey mixture.
4. While the second half of mixture is cooking, begin to fill tortillas. Spoon ¼ cup of the mixture into the center of a small tortilla. Fold in the sides

and roll. Set seam side down on serving dish. Serve with plates and cocktail forks.

Calories Per Serving: 122

Fat: 2 g

Cholesterol: 4 mg

Protein: 4 g

Carbohydrates: 24 g

Dietary Fiber: 2 g

Sodium: 147 mg

✹ *Mushrooms with Sun-Dried Tomatoes* ✹

YIELD: 9 servings (2 each) • *PREPARATION TIME: 20 minutes* •
COOKING TIME: 3 minutes

Mushroom caps are stuffed with a mixture of sun-dried tomatoes and goat cheese.

18 medium mushrooms, stems removed and chopped

1 tablespoon finely chopped black olives

2 tablespoons oil-packed sun-dried tomatoes, drained, patted dry, and finely chopped

2 tablespoons goat cheese

⅛ teaspoon black pepper

½ teaspoon dried basil

1 tablespoon chopped scallions

1. Combine chopped mushroom stems, olives, sun-dried tomatoes, goat cheese, pepper, basil, and scallions. Spoon into mushroom caps.
2. Arrange mushrooms in a circle on a round microwave-safe dish.
3. Cover with wax paper and microwave on HIGH for 2 minutes. Reverse mushrooms on inside of dish with those on outside of dish and microwave on HIGH for an additional minute or until heated through.

Calories Per Serving: 27

Fat: 1 g

Cholesterol: 3 mg

Protein: 1 g

Carbohydrates: 4 g

Dietary Fiber: 1 g

Sodium: 47 mg

✎ *Parmesan Mushrooms* ✎

YIELD: 18 servings (2 each) ▪ *PREPARATION TIME: 25 minutes* ▪
COOKING TIME: 10 minutes

Mushroom caps are stuffed with a Parmesan cheese filling.

36 medium fresh mushrooms, stems removed and finely chopped
¼ cup grated nonfat or reduced-fat Parmesan cheese
¼ cup bread crumbs

¼ cup finely chopped onion
½ teaspoon dried oregano
⅛ teaspoon black pepper
1 clove garlic, minced

1. Combine mushroom stems, Parmesan cheese, bread crumbs, onion, oregano, black pepper, and garlic.
2. Press mixture into mushroom caps.
3. Place half of the stuffed mushroom caps in a microwave-safe dish, with the larger mushrooms toward the outside, and cover with wax paper.
4. Microwave on 100% HIGH for 5 minutes or until heated through. Repeat with remaining mushroom caps.

Calories Per Serving: 16
Fat: 0 g
Cholesterol: 1 mg
Protein: 1 g

Carbohydrates: 3 g
Dietary Fiber: 0 g
Sodium: 24 mg

✎ *Sardine Mushrooms* ✎

YIELD: 10 servings (2 each) ▪ *PREPARATION TIME: 15 minutes* ▪
COOKING TIME: 5 minutes

Large mushroom caps are stuffed with a mixture of sardines and fresh bread crumbs.

1 can oil-packed sardines, drained and patted dry

½ cup fresh bread crumbs
20 large fresh mushroom caps

1. Mash sardines and combine with bread crumbs.
2. Fill mushroom caps with sardine mixture.
3. Place 10 mushroom caps on a glass pie pan. Cover with vented plastic wrap.
4. Microwave on 100% HIGH for 2½ minutes.
5. Repeat step 4 with the remaining 10 mushrooms. Serve warm.

Calories Per Serving: 38
Fat: 1 g
Cholesterol: 12 mg
Protein: 3 g

Carbohydrates: 5 g
Dietary Fiber: 0 g
Sodium: 74 mg

❧ *Anchovy Mushrooms* ✎

YIELD: 10 servings (1 each) • *PREPARATION TIME: 15 minutes* •
COOKING TIME: 2½ minutes

This two-ingredient appetizer is simple and delicious.

10 large fresh mushroom caps   *10 anchovy fillets*

1. Roll anchovy fillets and place one in each mushroom cap.
2. Place mushroom caps in a glass pie pan. Cover with vented plastic wrap.
3. Microwave on 100% HIGH for 2½ minutes.

Calories Per Serving: 14
Fat: 0 g
Cholesterol: 3 mg
Protein: 2 g

Carbohydrates: 1 g
Dietary Fiber: 0 g
Sodium: 148 mg

❧ *Sausage-Pizza Mushroom Caps* ✎

YIELD: 10 servings (1 each) • *PREPARATION TIME: 20 minutes* •
COOKING TIME: 3 minutes

Large mushroom caps are stuffed with a mixture of turkey sausage, cheese, and tomato puree.

10 large fresh mushrooms, stems removed and chopped
¼ pound low-fat turkey sausage

½ cup nonfat or reduced-fat mozzarella cheese
¼ cup canned, low-sodium tomato puree

1. Combine chopped mushroom stems, sausage, mozzarella, and tomato puree.
2. Fill mushroom caps with mixture.
3. Place mushroom caps on a large glass pie pan.
4. Cover with vented microwave-safe plastic wrap.
5. Microwave on 100% HIGH for 3 minutes or until sausage is cooked.

Calories Per Serving: 46
Fat: 2 g
Cholesterol: 12 mg
Protein: 6 g

Carbohydrates: 2 g
Dietary Fiber: 0 g
Sodium: 171 mg

⚜ *Mushroom–Pita Pizza Snacks* ⚜

YIELD: 16 servings (2 each) • *PREPARATION TIME: 20 minutes* •
COOKING TIME: 12 minutes

Fresh mushrooms, tomato sauce, and mozzarella cheese are the toppings on these pita snacks.

1 cup canned low-sodium tomato sauce
4 6-inch pita breads, split
1 teaspoon dried oregano

4 ounces grated nonfat or reduced-fat mozzarella cheese
¼ pound fresh mushrooms, sliced

1. Spread 2 tablespoons tomato sauce on each pita round, leaving ½ inch around the edge uncovered. Sprinkle with oregano and cheese. Arrange mushrooms on top of tomato sauce.
2. Place 4 pita rounds on a paper plate and place in a microwave. Cook, uncovered, on 50% MEDIUM for 3 minutes, rotate on plate, and cook for 2 additional minutes or until cheese is melted.
3. Repeat with the remaining 4 pita halves. Cut pitas in quarters and serve.

Calories Per Serving: 59
Fat: 0 g
Cholesterol: 1 mg
Protein: 4 g

Carbohydrates: 10 g
Dietary Fiber: 0 g
Sodium: 135 mg

❧ *Minipizzas* ❧

YIELD: 8 servings (1 each) • *PREPARATION TIME: 20 minutes* •
COOKING TIME: 10 minutes

Toasted English muffin halves are topped with an array of bell pepper slivers, scallions, cheese, and jalapeño.

1 small red, green, or yellow bell pepper, seeded and thinly sliced
2 scallions, thinly sliced
2 cups shredded nonfat or reduced-fat
  mozzarella or Swiss cheese

4 English muffins, split and toasted
1 jalapeño pepper, seeded and thinly
  sliced

1. Evenly divide the peppers, scallions, and cheese on top of the muffin halves. Top with slices of jalapeño.
2. Place a paper towel on a microwave-safe glass plate. Place 4 pizzas on top of the paper towel. Microwave on 50% MEDIUM for 5 minutes or until cheese has melted. Repeat with other 4 pizzas.

Calories Per Serving: 129
Fat: 3 g
Cholesterol: 6 mg
Protein: 14 g

Carbohydrates: 18 g
Dietary Fiber: 1 g
Sodium: 366 mg

❧ *Chili Bean Cups* ❧

YIELD: 20 servings (1 each) • *PREPARATION TIME: 15 minutes* •
COOKING TIME: 6 minutes microwave plus 8 minutes conventional oven for toast cups

Black beans with onion and chili powder are served in whole wheat toast cups.

20 3-inch rounds cut from thin-sliced
   whole wheat bread
⅓ cup minced onion
⅓ cup minced red bell pepper
2 cloves garlic, minced
2 tablespoons light-flavored olive oil
½ teaspoon dried oregano

1 tablespoon chili powder
1 cup home-cooked or canned black
   beans, rinsed and drained
1½ teaspoons red wine vinegar
⅛ teaspoon black pepper
⅓ cup nonfat or reduced-fat plain
   yogurt

1. Preheat oven to 400 degrees. Press a bread round into each of 20 1½-inch lightly oiled muffin cups. Bake for 8 minutes or until the edges are lightly browned. Cool on a wire rack.
2. Combine onion, red pepper, garlic, oil, oregano, and chili powder in a microwave-safe bowl. Microwave on 100% HIGH for 3 minutes.
3. Stir in black beans, red wine vinegar, and pepper. Microwave on 100% HIGH for 3 minutes, stirring once. Remove from microwave and allow to reach room temperature.
4. Spoon black bean mixture into toast cups and top with a dab of yogurt.

Calories Per Serving: 69
Fat: 2 g
Cholesterol: 0 mg
Protein: 3 g

Carbohydrates: 13 g
Dietary Fiber: 3 g
Sodium: 97 mg

❧ *Minimeatballs with Yogurt Sauce* ❧

YIELD: 20 servings (2 each) • *PREPARATION TIME: 25 minutes* •
COOKING TIME: 9 minutes

Tiny meatballs are made of ground turkey, onion, bread crumbs, garlic, oregano, and lemon juice.

1 pound low-fat ground turkey breast
2 egg whites, beaten
¼ cup finely chopped onion
2 tablespoons finely ground bread
   crumbs
1 clove garlic, minced

1 teaspoon dried oregano
3 tablespoons lemon juice
2 cups nonfat or reduced-fat plain
   yogurt
½ cup chopped fresh parsley
½ teaspoon ground cumin

1. Combine turkey, egg whites, onion, bread crumbs, garlic, oregano, and 1 tablespoon of the lemon juice.
2. Shape the turkey mixture into 40 tiny meatballs.
3. Place a third of the meatballs around the rim of a large microwave-safe plate and cover with vented plastic wrap. Microwave on 100% HIGH for 3 minutes or until done. Transfer meatballs to a covered dish.
4. Repeat step 3 with remaining meatballs in two batches.
5. Combine yogurt, the remaining 2 tablespoons of the lemon juice, parsley, and cumin.
6. Serve yogurt sauce in a bowl surrounded by meatballs. Provide wooden or plastic party picks.

Calories Per Serving: 39
Fat: 0 g
Cholesterol: 4 mg
Protein: 3 g

Carbohydrates: 6 g
Dietary Fiber: 0 g
Sodium: 72 mg

❧ *Meatballs with Tangy Apricot Sauce* ❧

YIELD: 10 servings (2 each) • *PREPARATION TIME: 20 minutes* •
COOKING TIME: 8 minutes

Turkey meatballs are microwaved and served with a sweet-and-sour dipping sauce.

1 pound low-fat ground turkey breast
2 egg whites, beaten
1 medium onion, finely chopped
2 tablespoons chopped fresh parsley
¼ cup fine dry bread crumbs

¼ teaspoon black pepper
1 cup all-fruit apricot jam
1 tablespoon light soy sauce
1 tablespoon rice vinegar
1 tablespoon lemon juice

1. Combine turkey, egg whites, onion, parsley, bread crumbs, and black pepper in a large bowl.
2. Shape 20 1½-inch meatballs from the turkey mixture.
3. Arrange meatballs in a circle around the outside rim of a large flat microwave-safe plate, cover with vented plastic wrap, and cook on 100%

HIGH for 4 minutes. Turn meatballs over and continue cooking on 100% HIGH for 4 more minutes or until done. Drain. Set aside in a covered dish.

4. Combine jam, soy sauce, vinegar, and lemon juice in a 2-cup container.
5. Microwave on 100% HIGH for 2 to 3 minutes or until boiling. Stir and transfer to a bowl. Serve surrounded by meatballs. Provide wooden or plastic party picks.

Calories Per Serving: 142
Fat: 1 g
Cholesterol: 6 mg
Protein: 5 g

Carbohydrates: 31 g
Dietary Fiber: 0 g
Sodium: 176 mg

Basic Shrimp

YIELD: 10 servings (2 each) • *PREPARATION TIME: 20 minutes* •
COOKING TIME: 3 minutes

Serve shrimp prepared in your microwave with one of the dips in the Dips and Spreads chapter, or with a prepared seafood cocktail sauce or salsa.

20 large shrimp, shelled and deveined

1. Place shrimp in a single layer in a microwave-safe 10-inch glass pie plate. Cover with vented microwave-safe plastic wrap.
2. Microwave on 100% HIGH for 1 minute.
3. Switch the shrimp on the outer edges of the plate with those near the center of the plate.
4. Re-cover and microwave on 100% HIGH for 1 minute.
5. Let stand (covered) for 1 minute. Uncover and rinse with cold water to stop the cooking process.

Calories Per Serving: 55
Fat: 0 g
Cholesterol: 102 mg
Protein: 14 g

Carbohydrates: 0 g
Dietary Fiber: 0 g
Sodium: 474 mg

✺ *Ginger-Honey Chicken Wings* ✺

YIELD: 8 servings (2 pieces each) • *PREPARATION TIME: 15 minutes plus*
2 hours refrigeration time • *COOKING TIME: 10 minutes*

Chicken wings prepared in your microwave are coated with sesame seeds.

2 tablespoons light soy sauce
1 tablespoon honey
1 tablespoon red wine vinegar
1 teaspoon minced fresh gingerroot
1 tablespoon canola oil

1 clove garlic, minced
⅛ teaspoon hot pepper sauce
8 chicken wings, skinned, tips trimmed
  and discarded, cut into 2 pieces
2 tablespoons sesame seeds

1. Combine the soy sauce, honey, vinegar, gingerroot, oil, garlic, and hot pepper sauce.
2. Add the wings to the marinade. Refrigerate for 2 hours, turning two or three times.
3. Drain the marinade and reserve. Place the wings around the outer rim of a 10-inch microwave-safe platter.
4. Sprinkle with 1 tablespoon of the sesame seeds.
5. Cook, uncovered, on 100% HIGH for 5 minutes.
6. Turn the wings and brush with the reserved marinade; sprinkle with the remaining tablespoon of sesame seeds. Cook, uncovered, on 100% HIGH for 5 minutes or until chicken is done.
7. Cool for 5 minutes and serve.

Calories Per Serving: 132
Fat: 3 g
Cholesterol: 32 mg
Protein: 11 g

Carbohydrates: 2 g
Dietary Fiber: 0 g
Sodium: 120 mg

❦ *Apple Chunks with Peanut Sauce* ❦

YIELD: *18 servings (2 each)* • PREPARATION TIME: *15 minutes* •
COOKING TIME: *6 minutes*

Chunks of apple are served with an Indonesian peanut sauce.

*6 apples, peeled, cored, and cut into 6
    chunks each*
¼ cup lemon juice
1 tablespoon light-flavored olive oil
1 clove garlic, minced
1 medium onion, finely chopped
⅔ cup water

*½ cup reduced-fat peanut butter substi-
    tute*
3 tablespoons light soy sauce
*2 tablespoons brown sugar, firmly
    packed*
2 tablespoons low-sodium catsup
¼ teaspoon ground cayenne pepper

1. Toss apple chunks with 3 tablespoons of the lemon juice to prevent discoloration.
2. Place oil, garlic, and onion in a 4-cup microwave-safe container. Cook on
   100% HIGH for 3 minutes or until onion is tender. Stir in the water.
3. Cook on 100% HIGH for 3 minutes or until water boils.
4. Stir in peanut butter, soy sauce, brown sugar, catsup, cayenne pepper, and
   the remaining 1 tablespoon lemon juice.
5. Transfer sauce to serving bowl and surround with apple chunks.

Calories Per Serving: 208
Fat: 3 g
Cholesterol: 0 mg
Protein: 3 g

Carbohydrates: 46 g
Dietary Fiber: 10 g
Sodium: 229 mg

❦ *Snow Peas with Sesame-Soy Dipping Sauce* ❦

YIELD: *8 servings (3 each)* • PREPARATION TIME: *10 minutes* •
COOKING TIME: *3½ minutes*

This appetizer is inspired by the French name for snow peas, *mange-tout,*
which means "eat it all."

1 pound snow peas, ends trimmed
¾ cup nonfat or reduced-fat, low-sodium chicken broth

1 tablespoon light soy sauce
½ teaspoon light sesame oil

1. Place snow peas in a glass pie plate. Cover with vented plastic wrap and microwave at 100% HIGH for 3 minutes. Let stand for 1 minute.
2. Combine chicken broth, soy sauce, and sesame oil in a microwave-safe container. Cover with vented plastic wrap and microwave at 100% HIGH for 30 seconds.
3. Arrange peas on a platter around the dipping sauce.

Calories Per Serving: 35
Fat: 1 g
Cholesterol: 0 mg
Protein: 2 g

Carbohydrates: 5 g
Dietary Fiber: 1 g
Sodium: 103 mg

✎ *Salmon-Stuffed Snow Peas* ✎

YIELD: 12 servings (2 each) • *PREPARATION TIME: 25 minutes plus 1 hour refrigeration time*

Snow peas are stuffed with a mixture of smoked salmon and whipped cream cheese.

24 snow peas, ends trimmed
1 tablespoon water
4 ounces nonfat or reduced-fat whipped cream cheese

2 ounces smoked salmon, cut into tiny slivers

1. Place snow peas on a glass pie plate. Sprinkle with water. Cover with vented plastic wrap and cook on 100% HIGH for 1 minute. Cool.
2. Split each snow pea pod open with a sharp knife.
3. Spread cream cheese on the inside of each pod.
4. Place several slivers of salmon on top of the cream cheese. Close the pods and chill for 1 hour.

Calories Per Serving: 26

Carbohydrates: 2 g

Fat: 0 g

Dietary Fiber: 1 g

Cholesterol: 3 mg

Sodium: 105 mg

Protein: 4 g

❧ *Zucchini Strips* ❧

YIELD: 24 servings (1 each) • *PREPARATION TIME: 10 minutes* •
COOKING TIME: 4 minutes

Zucchini is dipped in a Parmesan–bread crumb mixture and microwaved.

*3 medium zucchini, ends trimmed,
each cut into 2 3-inch-thick sections*
*½ cup grated nonfat or reduced-fat
Parmesan cheese*

½ cup dry bread crumbs
¼ teaspoon black pepper
⅓ cup light-flavored olive oil

1. Cut each zucchini segment into 4 slices lengthwise.
2. Combine cheese, bread crumbs, and pepper in a bowl.
3. Dip each zucchini slice in olive oil, and then in Parmesan–bread crumb
   mixture. Arrange in one layer on a microwave-safe dish.
4. Microwave on 100% HIGH for 5 minutes or until just tender.

Calories Per Servings: 43

Carbohydrates: 3 g

Fat: 3 g

Dietary Fiber: 0 g

Cholesterol: 2 mg

Sodium: 35 mg

Protein: 1 g

Yellow Summer Squash
❧ *with Greek Tomato Sauce* ❧

YIELD: 12 servings (2 each) • *PREPARATION TIME: 20 minutes plus
10 minutes standing time* • *COOKING TIME: 15 minutes*

Summer squash is microwaved and served with a microwaved tomato dipping sauce.

3 medium yellow summer squash, trimmed and cut into ¼-inch slices	1 tablespoon light-flavored olive oil
12 seeded and chopped plum tomatoes	1 teaspoon lemon juice
2 cloves garlic, minced	1 teaspoon dried dill
2 chopped scallions	⅛ teaspoon ground cinnamon

1. Place ⅓ of the squash slices in a 2-quart microwave-safe casserole and cover with vented plastic wrap. Microwave on 100% HIGH for 1 minute. Stir. Microwave on HIGH for 2 more minutes or until squash is just tender. Transfer to serving platter.
2. Repeat step 1 with remaining squash slices in two more batches.
3. Place tomatoes, garlic, scallions, olive oil, lemon juice, dill, and cinnamon in a blender or food processor and process until just blended.
4. Transfer the sauce to a glass pie plate and microwave, uncovered, on 100% HIGH for 3 minutes. Stir and microwave on HIGH for 3 more minutes.
5. Let sauce stand for 10 minutes. Then transfer to serving bowl and place in center of platter of squash.

Calories Per Serving: 25	Carbohydrates: 3 g
Fat: 1 g	Dietary Fiber: 1 g
Cholesterol: 0 mg	Sodium: 5 mg
Protein: 1 g	

❧ Squash Nachos ❧

YIELD: 24 servings (2 each)   •   PREPARATION TIME: 20 minutes   •
COOKING TIME: 8 minutes

Sliced zucchini and yellow squash are microwaved with chopped tomatoes, scallions, parsley, and Swiss cheese.

2 medium zucchini, cut into ¼-inch rounds	¼ cup chopped scallions
2 yellow summer squash, cut into ¼-inch rounds	1 tablespoon chopped fresh parsley
	⅛ teaspoon black pepper
1 medium tomato, chopped	1 cup shredded nonfat or reduced-fat Swiss cheese

1. In a round microwave-safe dish, alternate rounds of zucchini and yellow squash. Cover with wax paper. Microwave on 100% HIGH for 3 minutes.
2. Sprinkle tomato, scallions, parsley, pepper, and cheese over squash. Microwave on 75% MEDIUM-HIGH until cheese melts.

Calories Per Serving: 15
Fat: 0 g
Cholesterol: 0 mg
Protein: 2 g

Carbohydrates: 2 g
Dietary Fiber: 0 g
Sodium: 117 mg

◖ *Carrots with Red Pepper Sauce* ◗

YIELD: 20 servings (2 each) • *PREPARATION TIME: 25 minutes plus 8 minutes standing time* • *COOKING TIME: 16 minutes*

Microwaved carrot chunks are served with an aromatic sauce made with red peppers and rosemary.

10 carrots, scrubbed and cut into 2-inch chunks
¼ cup nonfat or reduced-fat, low-sodium chicken broth
3 tablespoons minced scallions

2 cloves garlic, chopped
1 teaspoon dried rosemary
2 large red bell peppers, seeded and chopped
¼ cup skim or 1% milk

1. Place half of the carrots in a 1-quart casserole with 2 tablespoons of water. Cover with plastic wrap. Microwave on 100% HIGH for 3 minutes. Stir. Microwave on HIGH for 3 more minutes. Let stand, covered, for 3 minutes.
2. Repeat step 1 with the remaining carrots.
3. Combine the chicken broth, scallions, garlic, rosemary, and bell peppers in a glass pie plate. Cover with vented plastic wrap. Microwave on 100% HIGH for 2 minutes. Stir. Microwave on HIGH for 2 more minutes or until peppers are tender. Let stand for 2 minutes.
4. Transfer pepper mixture to a blender or processor and puree until smooth, adding the milk while the machine is running.
5. Transfer pepper sauce to a bowl and place in the center of a platter surrounded by carrot chunks. Provide wooden or plastic party picks.

Calories Per Serving: 20   Carbohydrates: 5 g
Fat: 0 g   Dietary Fiber: 1 g
Cholesterol: 0 mg   Sodium: 19 mg
Protein: 1 g

❧ *Cauliflower with Mustard and Parsley* ❧

*YIELD: 16 servings (¼ cup each) • PREPARATION TIME: 15 minutes plus
2 minutes standing time • COOKING TIME: 10 minutes*

Cauliflower florets are microwaved and served with a mustard dipping sauce.

4 cups cauliflower florets   4 teaspoons Dijon mustard
½ cup nonfat or reduced-fat, low-   ¼ cup orange juice
  sodium chicken broth   2 tablespoons chopped fresh parsley
4 teaspoons light-flavored olive oil

1. Place half of the cauliflower florets in a 1½-quart casserole dish with ¼ cup broth. Cover with plastic wrap. Cook on 100% HIGH for 3 minutes. Stir, and cook on 100% HIGH for 2 more minutes. Let stand, covered, for 2 minutes.
2. Repeat step 1 with remaining cauliflower florets.
3. Combine oil, mustard, orange juice, and parsley.
4. Serve sauce in a bowl surrounded by cauliflower florets. Provide wooden or plastic party picks.

Calories Per Serving: 20   Carbohydrates: 2 g
Fat: 1 g   Dietary Fiber: 0 g
Cholesterol: 0 mg   Sodium: 44 mg
Protein: 1 g

✎ *Yogurt-Scallion–Stuffed Potatoes* ✎

YIELD: *12 servings (2 each)* • PREPARATION TIME: *15 minutes plus 5 minutes standing time* • COOKING TIME: *20 minutes*

New potatoes are microwaved, scooped out, and filled with herb–yogurt sauce.

12 small new potatoes
1½ cups nonfat or reduced-fat plain
  yogurt or sour cream

1 tablespoon chopped scallion
2 tablespoons chopped fresh parsley

1. Pierce the potatoes with a fork and place them in a ring on a paper towel in the microwave.
2. Cook on 100% HIGH for 13 minutes. Turn the potatoes and cook for 7 additional minutes. Let stand for 5 minutes.
3. Cut the potatoes in half. Trim bottoms slightly so potatoes will not tip. Scoop out about a teaspoon of potato from each half.
4. Combine the yogurt with scallions and parsley.
5. Fill hollows of potatoes with yogurt mixture.

Calories Per Serving: 96
Fat: 0 g
Cholesterol: 1 mg
Protein: 4 g

Carbohydrates: 21 g
Dietary Fiber: 2 g
Sodium: 30 mg

✎ *Potatoes with Tomato-Jalapeño Topping* ✎

YIELD: *12 servings (3 each)* • PREPARATION TIME: *20 minutes* •
COOKING TIME: *9 minutes*

Potato slices are microwaved and then topped with a spicy tomato and cheese combination.

3 medium potatoes, thinly sliced
2 tomatoes, diced
½ small onion, finely chopped
3 tablespoons finely chopped green bell
  pepper

1 jalapeño pepper, seeded and minced
½ teaspoon chili powder
⅔ cup nonfat or reduced-fat grated
  cheese

1. Place potatoes in a glass pie plate and sprinkle with water. Cover with vented plastic wrap and microwave on 100% HIGH for 6 minutes.
2. Combine tomatoes, onion, green pepper, jalapeño pepper, and chili powder.
3. Spoon tomato mixture on top of potatoes.
4. Sprinkle with cheese.
5. Cover with vented plastic wrap and microwave on 50% MEDIUM for 3 minutes.

Calories Per Serving: 78
Fat: 0 g
Cholesterol: 0 mg
Protein: 3 g

Carbohydrates: 16 g
Dietary Fiber: 2 g
Sodium: 174 mg

INDEX

⬛⬛

ABOUT THE AUTHOR

SARAH SCHLESINGER began researching and writing about healthful cooking in response to her husband's ongoing battle against coronary-artery disease. She is the author of *500 Fat-Free Recipes* and *500 Low-Fat Fruit and Vegetable Recipes,* and is the coauthor of *The Low-Cholesterol Oat Plan* and *The Low-Cholesterol Olive Oil Cookbook.* She also coauthored *The Pointe Book,* which focuses on health issues for dancers. Ms. Schlesinger is Associate Chair of the Graduate Musical Theatre Writing Program at New York University's Tisch School of the Arts. She lives in New York City and in Lewes, Delaware.